MAJOR TAYLOR

MAJOR TAYLOR

The Inspiring Story of a Black Cyclist and the Men Who Helped Him Achieve Worldwide Fame

CONRAD KERBER
AND
TERRY KERBER

FOREWORD BY GREG LeMOND

Skyhorse Publishing

Skyhorse Publishing books may be purchased in bulk at special discounts for sales promotion, corporate gifts, fund-raising, or educational purposes. Special editions can also be created to specifications. For details, contact the Special Sales Department, Skyhorse Publishing, 307 West 36th Street, 11th Floor, New York, NY 10018 or info@skyhorsepublishing.com.

Skyhorse® and Skyhorse Publishing® are registered trademarks of Skyhorse Publishing, Inc.®, a Delaware corporation.

Visit our website at www.skyhorsepublishing.com.

10 9 8 7 6 5 4

Every effort has been made to trace copyright holders. If any unintended omissions have been made, the authors would be pleased to add appropriate acknowledgments in future printings.

Library of Congress Cataloging-in-Publication Data is available on file.

ISBN: 978-1-51070-416-9

Printed in the United States of America

"Cycle tracks will abound in Utopia."

—H. G. Wells

CONTENTS

FOREWORD

BY GREG LEMOND

Major Taylor's extraordinary story of triumph over adversity is near and dear to my heart. In order to reach the pinnacle of their chosen sport, all professional athletes have to endure countless setbacks and unforeseen hardships. It is, in fact, their singular capacity to endure such hardships that often separates them from their competitors. And it is when they reach their lowest ebb, with thoughts of giving up racing in their heads, that they inevitably seek inspiration from those pioneering souls who suffered and endured before them.

For me, that nadir presented itself while hunting with relatives shortly after becoming the only American to win the Tour de France. It was the spring of 1987; I was just twenty-six years old, a two-time World Champion, seemingly on my way to a string of consecutive Tour wins. It was as if I was on top of the world. But while camouflaging behind spring foliage near the foothills of the Sierra Nevadas that spring morning, scouring the bushy landscape for turkeys, the world as I knew it twisted upside down.

There was the startling sound of shotgun fire from behind me, the sulfurous odor of spent shells, the sight of scattering birds, and the piercing pain of sixty pellets lodging in my heart lining, liver, back, arms, and legs. I slipped into a surreal state of shock, largely detached from the world around me. As if from out of nowhere, the twirling blades of a helicopter soon swooped down from the sky. Within minutes, I lay recumbent in a hospital bed, a few breaths away from bleeding to death.

Instead of looking forward to the July day when I could defend my yellow jersey, I spent the next two years hobbling in and out of hospitals, fretting over my physical and mental health. I was concerned about my contract and my ability to pursue my life's passion. I convalesced, searching for answers and inspiration.

Eighty-three years earlier, a similar cloud hung over Taylor's seven-bedroom home in Worcester, Massachusetts. In 1904, during a match race in front of yet another packed house at a bike track in Australia, Taylor was knocked unconscious by the wheels of an envious rival. He spent the next two years away from the sport he loved. He slid into a state of depression, struggling to overcome nearly a decade of racial abuse, both physical and emotional.

Though we captivated the racing world with our attempted comebacks, both of us were left with divergent scars. I still have numerous lead pellets embedded in my heart lining, arms, and legs, which act as a constant reminder of how precious life is and how close I was to an early, shocking death. Taylor's racial scars, like the sins of our nation's past, could never be removed. His entire life story, deftly recited in all its drama by authors Conrad Kerber and Terry Kerber, is the stuff of legends, especially his courageous fight to become sprint champion of America and then world champion, and his highly publicized match race against French Triple-Crown winner Edmond Jaquelin. But it was his comeback that has inspired me the most over the years, as well as the honest and ethical way he lived his life.

There are so many lessons in the pages of this epic story, but perhaps none are nobler than Taylor's transcendent ability to forgive those who tormented him on and off bike tracks. That is why I was honored to speak at the unveiling of the Major Taylor statue at the Worcester Public Library, to stand in the very city that sheltered him from the racial storms a century before. I am equally honored to write the foreword to this engrossing book, written by two gifted writers and passionate cycling fans who just happen to live near my suburban Twin Cities' home. As the sport of bike racing and our nation attempt to transition to a new and refreshing era of transparency, we would all be well-served to seek wisdom and guidance from the lessons left behind by this remarkable sportsman.

PROLOGUE

In 1907, amid a time of unspeakable racial cruelty, the world's most popular athlete was not pitcher Cy Young or Christy Mathewson. It wasn't shortstop Honus Wagner, center fielder Ty Cobb, nor was he a baseball player. During a period of frequent lynchings, the world's most popular athlete wasn't even white. He was an oft-persecuted, black bicycle racer named Marshall W. "Major" Taylor.

At the height of the Jim Crow era, Taylor became an inspirational idol in America, Europe, and Australia, experiencing adoration so profound that it transcended race. Long before Jackie Robinson, people of all colors passed under Major Taylor billboards, exchanged Taylor trading cards, cooled themselves with Taylor accordion fans, and wore buttons bearing his likeness. When he competed, his admirers swarmed local streets, spilled out of "Major Taylor Carnival" trains, flooded the cafés, and waited for him in the rain outside packed hotels. His face stared out from newspaper pages on four continents. His appearances shattered attendance records at nearly every bike track and drew the largest throng ever to see a sporting event. At a time when the population was less than one quarter its current size, more than fifty thousand people watched him race, a crowd on par with today's baseball games. Countless thousands paid just to watch his workouts, while thousands of others gathered at train stations to greet him and his elegant wife.

But his immense fame, achieved in what was one of the nation's most popular sports, came against incredible odds. He was repeatedly kicked out of restaurants and hotels, forced to sleep in horse stables, and terrorized out of cities by threats of violence. On the more than one hundred bike tracks called velodromes, he endured incessant racism, including being shoved headfirst into track rails. On a sweltering New England day in 1897, a rival nearly choked him to death, a violent incident *The New York Times* called among the most talked-about events that year.

Along his turbulent path that began as a penniless horsetender from bucolic Indiana, Taylor received help from the most unlikely of men, all of whom happened to be white. When hotel and restaurant operators refused him food and lodging, forcing him to race hungry, a benevolent racer-turned-trainer named Birdie Munger took Taylor under his wing and into his home. One of Taylor's managers was famed Broadway producer William Brady, a feisty Irishman who had brawled with Virgil Earp in cow-town boxing rings. He stood up for Taylor when track owners tried to bar him from competing. While winning more than one thousand bike races himself, Arthur Zimmerman, America's first superstar, mentored Taylor even though others called him a useless little "pickanninny." In the mid-1890s during a devastating depression, the extraordinary kindness these men bestowed helped elevate Taylor from rags to riches.

But for Taylor and his helpers, it was merely the start of a fourteen-year journey filled with suffering and jubilation. From 1896 to 1910, Taylor emerged as one of history's most remarkable sportsmen. Endowed with blazing speed and indomitable bravery, he traveled more than two hundred thousand grueling miles by rail and ship, started two-mile handicap races as far back as three hundred yards, and set numerous world speed records. His danger-filled struggle for equality on American tracks eventually drove him overseas where he became the most heavily advertised man in Europe, was talked about as often as presidents of countries, and captured more attention than some of the world's wealthiest citizens. His dramatic match races with French Triple Crown winner Edmond Jacquelin, which attracted barons, dukes, and paupers from nearly every nation in Europe, were widely remembered a quarter-century later. And in 1907 after a fall instigated by an envious rival—a severe injury that led to a mental breakdown—the much-maligned black man attempted a comeback many thought impossible.

But it wasn't just athletic prowess that attracted people to him. Carrying the Scriptures with him always, this deeply religious man turned down enormous sums of money because he refused to race on Sunday. Thousands were captivated by his eloquent, peaceful delivery of messages about faith and kindness, and his mystical capacity to forgive those who persecuted him.

During his ride from anonymity to superstardom, the gentle black man and the few white men who helped him starred in an epic story for the ages.

It began with two boys on bicycles, riding free.

PART I

Chapter 1

THE WAR BETWEEN WHEELMEN AND HORSEMEN

Marshall Taylor felt a powerful force tugging at him—a force not unlike that of a sheet of steel to a giant magnet. In the spring of 1891, he was thirteen, tired of rural life, and even more tired of being at the whims of slow, sometimes unruly horses. He was a restless and ambitious boy, and if later photos were any indication, he was tautly muscled yet thin as a rail. He had frizzy hair and smooth, charcoal-colored skin that would later be described as polished ebony. The most successful jockeys at the time were African Americans—winning twelve of the first twenty-two Kentucky Derbies—and with his short, wiry frame, Taylor too had the makings of an ideal jockey. His father, Gilbert, a noble, white-haired Civil War veteran, taught his son all he knew about tending horses on their rustic Indianapolis farm. But even at a young age, Marshall had other aspirations. He was country born and bred, but rural life stifled him. He desperately wanted to expand his horizons. On a warm day that spring, he would get his chance.

Despite his family's penury, his childhood seems to have been a decent one. Born November 26, 1878, Marshall was the most ambitious member of the staid but proud Taylor family. His mother, Saphronia, raised eight genial, jaunty children while his father, Gilbert, worked long, hard days as coachman for a wealthy Indianapolis railroad family named Southards. Marshall helped out with the horses, trimming their hooves, hunching over an anvil to forge their shoes, mucking their stalls, feeding them oats, carrots, and water, exercising them, then washing, grooming, and brushing their manes and tails. Intensely competitive, young Marshall probably competed with his siblings over who could tend to the horses quickest, hoping to fall into his father's good graces. It was a rugged existence for man and beast. "All we had was just what we needed," he would later say, "and only such comforts as farm life affords."

But Gilbert and Saphronia still found time to smother their children with affection, instill a strong work ethic, and weave the word of God into their lives—words that would guide Marshall's judgments and channel his energies throughout his life. In the Taylor home, a well-worn Bible was surely always open, a piano played, James Bland songs sung, Civil War stories spun.

One of three boys and five girls, Marshall may have been the only one with itchy feet. His brother William was said to be athletic, but he seems to have been more content with farm life. Seeing Marshall's restlessness, his parents must have known he wouldn't stay in the countryside for long.

Marshall's first taste of the broader world came sometime around the age of eight. During his duties as a coachman, his father began taking him to the Southards' quarters on the outskirts of Indianapolis. There, young Marshall was introduced to Daniel, the Southards' eight-year-old son. The young boys, oblivious to their color differences, soon became best friends. Eventually he was employed as Daniel's playmate and companion, was provided with clothing, and was given access to a playroom filled to the rafters with every toy imaginable. But Marshall preferred whiling his time away in the great outdoors, playing on the grassy fields of the Southard estate or in their family workshop where he could tinker with machinery. Each day, a private tutor stopped by the Southards' Victorian home to instill a rudimentary education into the two boys. Back on the family farm, Taylor's siblings, educated by a man named Milton Lewis, continued to toil away. This difference surely caused family friction.

Taylor played with young Daniel, licking him in impromptu roller-skating, running, and tennis matches. He also handled the farriery needs of his father's horses and waited for something exciting to come along. It came when Daniel and several of Daniel's friends wearing euphoric smiles returned to his sprawling estate atop strange, two-wheeled contraptions. Reportedly all of Daniel's friends, except penniless Marshall, had expensive new machines some were calling "wheels." Seeing the forlorn expression on Marshall's face when they rolled in each day, Daniel talked his parents into buying one for him.

For centuries, man had been concocting outlandish devices in the futile attempt to replace the horse as the primary means of personal locomotion. Most of these early "bone-shakers," "hobby horses," and "velocipedes" were ponderous, impractical, and a serious threat to one's manhood. But in the 1860s, a handful of men with nothing better to do dreamed up the first semiworkable models and shoved them on the market. The peculiar men who bought those first versions often blew half a year's wages on these absurd steel skeletons known as high-wheelers. Many of them would repent their decision. Initially, the public and the press didn't know what to think of them. Thus the machines—and the odd individuals who first rode them— were rebuked and disparaged, especially by horsemen.

Their loathing was not without merit. So exciting at first glance, those "high-wheelers" with their giant front wheels, tiny rear wheels, and solid rubber tires, were in reality a public nuisance, and scared the wits out of veteran draymen, teamsters, dogs, and midsummer strollers. Irate local lawmakers— many with extensive ties to the livery industry—responded with laws ranging from the absurd to the draconian. In the early 1880s, an Ohio legislator was among the first to weigh in, proposing punitive legislation after his prized horses had twice been "frightened" by a high-wheelsman. Jersey City ordered that if the driver of a buggy or wagon raised his hand at the approach of a cyclist, this signal constituted a warning that the horse was getting skittish. The gesture repeated was a direct command for the invading cyclist to pull over, dismount immediately, then quietly tiptoe around the sacred beast. Not to be outdone, the Illinois legislature floated a bill compelling cyclists to dismount anytime they came within one hundred yards of teams of horses.

Many cities mandated that bikes be saddled with bells, gongs, whistles, sirens, and kerosene or carbide lanterns. And if all those gadgets didn't slow a rider down, the six-mile-per-hour speed limit imposed in some towns did. Some legislators simply couldn't take all the complaints from horsemen. In several urban centers, including Boston, Massachusetts, and Hartford, Connecticut, they went so far as to ban wheelmen from riding their bicycles on public streets or in parks, effectively outlawing all bicycles from those cities. To add further insult, pedestrians—also no friends of the wheelmen— joined with the teamsters and horsemen to pass laws dictating where bicycles could be used and at what speed.

According to one early report, there was a brief but "obligingly friendly" détente between the horsemen and this new breed of "wheelmen." But as more and more cyclists took to the streets, horsemen responded the best ways they could think of: by spreading glass, scrap metal, and tacks to keep the intruders off "their" roads. When they were in a really diabolical mood, horsemen took the law into their own hands, gleefully pointing their horses at the nearest cyclists and purposely running them down. The wheelmen retaliated, carrying small pistols from which they squirted diluted ammonia on overly aggressive horsemen or barking dogs. These first instances of road rage triggered a war between the wheelmen and horsemen that would span decades. "For some reason the equine mind has a distinct aversion to motion whose secret it does not understand," hollered a sympathetic *Brooklyn Eagle* reporter.

Bewildered politicians agonized over just how to classify bicycles and bicyclists. "He is not a pedestrian and cannot be catalogued as a horse," said one lawmaker, "and consequently he is ordinarily at war with commissioners, superintendents, and policemen." In nearly every instance, the omnipotent League of American Wheelmen (LAW), soon to be "the most powerful athletic group in the world," rumbled into town, fighting the mighty horsemen tooth and nail, paving the way for people like young Marshall Taylor to ride freely.

Finally, riding those first high-wheelers was a precarious endeavor. Without multiple gears, climbing even the most innocuous hills required Herculean efforts. With crude brakes or no brakes at all, descending those hills became a bloodcurdling adventure. And with the front wheel much larger than the rear, these tipsy, top-heavy machines required exceptional handling skills, an unusual desire for risk, and a high threshold for pain. Countless times, battered men stumbled into hospitals dirty and bloody, hands over their broken noses, after taking a "header." But for some people, living in an era before practical helmets, a mere broken nose was the least of their concerns. In fact, until the safety bicycle came along, riding high-wheelers turned into such a bloodbath some newspapers created special obituary sections titled "Death by Wheel." "Get a bicycle," Mark Twain recommended after his eighth lesson on a high-wheeler, "you will not regret it, if you live."

Whatever type of bicycle Daniel Southard gave his friend Taylor, he could not have had any inkling where it would eventually lead him. In the short term, it would become the instrument of his freedom from the drudgery of rural life, a life for which he would later proclaim he detested. In the long run, it would mean a great deal more.

After his private daily tutoring, dressed in Sears & Roebuck denim overalls, Taylor surveyed the Southards' vast estate from the leather saddle of his sparkling new wheels. There, his legs spinning out of time, face radiating an endorphic glow, Taylor, like many children at the time, probably first dreamed of being a professional bike racer. Whenever he found time, he'd square off with Daniel and his friends in ad hoc races, fulfilling his need for risk, danger, and speed—things he lacked at home. On the bicycle, Taylor found a welcome diversion from his family's staid lifestyle. When he wasn't whipping his friends in mock races, he practiced trick riding for hours on end, imagining a large crowd watching him pedal with his hands, his bare feet pointing to the sky. Dashing across the undulating countryside, his thoughts were being forged by the bicycle. Until the day he died, he would remember those early days speeding under the broad Indianapolis skies.

Where horsemen saw a colossal irritant, Taylor saw potential. He strapped makeshift panniers on his bike, then talked a local newspaper into giving him a job as a delivery boy at five dollars a week. Loaded down with bundles of papers, he scampered around the outskirts of town, zipping by angry horsemen, putting on base riding miles that would put him in good stead later. In the evening, off in the distance, he could see the glow of brush arc lamps flickering in the bustling industrial city of Indianapolis.

The same powerful force that had tugged at young Marshall had driven him to the Southard estate. There, he developed a love affair with the bicycle, mingled with whites as if there was no difference between them, and experienced the privileged lifestyle of the wealthy. Both his father—who had chosen him over his other children—and the Southards—who entrusted him with their son—must have seen something special in young Taylor.

Perhaps it was because he was a quick learner and intensely inquisitive. Or maybe it was his curious combination of coyness and assertiveness. Most notably, even at an early age, he had a way about him, something intangible.

But on a gloomy afternoon, sometime in the waning days of the 1880s, this happy scene came to an abrupt halt. The Southards sold their sprawling estate, packed their bags, and headed west to Chicago. Suddenly, teenaged Taylor had lost his best friend. What's more, he was forced to move back to his parents' modest farm where a never-ending stream of tedious barn duties awaited. "I dropped from the happy life of a 'millionaire kid,'" he wrote in his 1928 autobiography, "to that of a common errand boy, all within a few weeks."

Marshall Taylor was saved by a problem with his bike. He had become mechanically inclined from all the tinkering in the Southards' workshop, but in the spring of 1891, his bicycle needed a repair he couldn't fix on his own. With his broken-down bike dangling out the back of his wagon, he and his horse strayed into Indianapolis and the beginning of a new life. It was quite a sight for the impressionable thirteen-year-old to see. On either side of North Pennsylvania Street, extending as far as the eye could see, was "bicycle row," a stretch of bicycle manufacturers, wholesalers, and retail bike shops. Amid a beehive of activity, his horse by chance paused in front of the Hay & Willits Bike Shop. Inside, owner Tom Hay, twisting a strip of jerky in his mouth, peered out the window at the reedy black boy dismounting his well-traveled horse. Taylor rolled his bike inside and gawked wide-eyed at a new model beckoning him from the front window.

After his repairs were completed, Taylor spontaneously mounted his bike and began performing stunts right in the middle of the bike shop. Mr. Hay stood dumbfounded as this unknown black boy rolled around his shop, flawlessly performing one daredevil trick after another. Curious, Hay asked where he learned to ride like that. Quick to answer, Taylor told him he was self-taught, a pioneer of sorts. Having never seen anything like it before, Hay cleared his shop floor and asked Taylor to carry on. Countless hours spent riding with Daniel Southard paid off; Hay was blown away.

Word of Taylor's unique talent quickly spread to nearby businesses. As inquisitive people began gathering inside, Hay had a brainstorm. He shooed Taylor and his antics out to the street, a marketing strategy that drew such a large assembly, the police had to gallop onto the scene to move the stalled traffic. Anyone attracting that kind of publicity in a highly competitive industry deserved a reward. Hay offered the boy a job paying six dollars a week, a buck more than his paper route. Taylor hesitated, muttering something about first needing his mother's approval. Ever the businessman, Hay upped the ante, adding the Holy Grail—that shiny new bike in the window. Taylor was sold hook, line, and sinker. "My eyes nearly popped out of my head," he remembered later. He immediately raced home and appealed to his mother. Saphronia, knowing she couldn't possibly contain such an ambitious boy in the confines of their small farm, hastily okayed the new job offer.

Taylor got busy sweeping and dusting Hay's shop in the morning, then donning a colorful military uniform with bright buttons and a military cap to put on a streetside exhibition in the afternoon. Curious crowds continued to congregate. On a scorching summer day, one legend has it, someone saw him in his military outfit outside Hay & Willits and first uttered the word "Major." This nickname would eventually echo around the world and stick with him until death.

Taylor was, by all accounts, a productive worker. But he had one notable weakness. Shop owner Hay, chief sponsor of a popular ten-mile road race, left the future winner's gold medal glistening in his store window. "I spent more time fondling that medal than I did wielding the duster," Taylor admitted. One afternoon when his boss wasn't looking, he pulled the medal down from the windowsill and pinned it on his lapel. He drew up in front of a mirror, stared at himself, and then strutted around proud as a peacock.

When the day for Hay's ten-mile race arrived—an event that attracted the better local amateurs—Taylor camped out at the starting line to see the riders off. Hay spotted Taylor and, for the benefit of a few good laughs, insisted that he enter the race. Only thirteen, Taylor refused, kicking, screaming, and crying. "I know *you can't* go the full distance," Hay whispered in his ear, "but just ride up the road a little way, it will please the crowd . . ."

Taylor's competitive ears perked up, as they would for the next few decades whenever he heard the words *you can't*. This, and the fifteen-minute handicap (in other words, a head start) he received because of his age, convinced him to start his first official bicycle race. Thousands of fans lined the side of the road as the riders pushed off, dust drifting up and darkening their faces. Taylor sped through a corridor of noise, listening as the "friendly" crowd egged him on. When the more experienced riders began closing on him toward the end of the race, Hay rode up alongside the boy, dangling the gold medal in front of his eyes. Physically he was drained to the bottom, but the sight of the medal spurred him on. "It gave me a fresh start," he remembered, "and I felt as though I had only just begun the race."

Within sight of the finish line, Walter Marmon lunged for the finish line. Still in front of the pack, Taylor gritted his teeth, crossing the line just seconds ahead of a speeding Marmon. Taylor collapsed in a heap on the side of the road, only to be revived by the sight of the crowd and the medal about to be pinned on his chest.

The fact that he had been given a fifteen-minute head start didn't quell his excitement. Somehow, he found the strength to ride home where he laughed and cried in his mother's arms, his gold medal glinting in the Indiana sun.

Emboldened by his win, Taylor continued poking around the racing scene. By the summer of 1892, he had saved enough from his meager earnings to leave home and compete in a track meet. He booked a train west and hopped off in Peoria, Illinois, a racing mecca at the time. It was a memorable experience. Reporters were crawling all over the place, jotting down enough notes to fill columns for several days before and after the multiday event. Following his impressive third-place finish in the under-sixteen category, Taylor lingered around the track waiting to watch the headliner event. He sat spellbound as national stars—men like Windle, Van Sicklen, Lumsen, and Spooner—competed before a large and boisterous crowd. They were riding safety bikes sporting the latest and most significant invention called pneumatic tires. Those ungainly high-wheelers with rock-hard tires had gone the way of the hobby horse and boneshakers. With these exciting inventions, a galaxy of known stars, and large paying crowds, bike racing was well on its way to becoming America's most heavily attended sport.

Sitting alone in the grandstand that summer day, viewing the world with childlike wonder, Major Taylor knew he wanted to be part of it.

In the spring of 1893, Taylor drifted into a larger, more established Indianapolis bike shop called H. T. Hearsey's, owned by Harry Hearsey. By then the bicycle craze had shifted into a higher gear. Seemingly everyone was either already riding or desperately waiting to learn how to ride. Supply followed demand; sleek new riding schools began webbing the land from coast to coast. In New York, the Vanderbilts and Goulds honed their skills at the prestigious Michaux Club. As wheelmen moved up the social ladder, horsemen and the insular world they had spawned were slowly being replaced by the whirling eddy of bicycle spokes. Saddle-makers and harness-makers either went out of business or began making bicycle saddles. Horse riding academies were converted into bicycle schools, forcing riding masters to begin life again in other occupations. Modernity, spearheaded by the bicycle, was penetrating the suburbs, cities, and countryside. Guests at William K. Vanderbilt's Newport mansion began requesting bicycles; before they had always thrown their legs over a horse. John D. Rockefeller was also well prepared, stocking his vast estate with thirty-eight bicycles for visiting friends.

Bike shops geared up for the historic conversion; the most successful ones had staff dedicated to teaching people how to ride. With his history of trick riding and showing well in a few competitions, Taylor was able to talk his way into a job as head trainer at Hearsey's shop. He gave free lessons to the locals, making the conversion from horseman to wheelman easier for customers. Despite his color, customers apparently took well to his teaching and showed their patronage by buying new bicycles in vast quantities. The lessons and subsequent riding adventures even brought families closer together. "Why, I feel as if I had never known my mother," beamed one twelve-year-old girl, "until we came here for lessons."

It seems natural for Taylor to have found his way into Hearsey's high-end shop. All the famous local riders—and on occasion national "cracks"—lingered there for hours conversing in the jargon of cyclists: soft arguments over gear ratios, wheel size, frame material, and components. Taylor especially enjoyed hearing tales of their racing exploits, stories that often grew in animation over time.

From inside his riding school room, Major Taylor could look out at a city slowly being overrun by the instrument of his passion. The year 1893 was the first year Americans bought more bicycles than horses, a fact affirmed every time he peered at the streets below his school's window. All around Indy and in nearly every city and village in the country, people were viewing the world through new lenses. Railcars were refitted to carry bicycles. Newspapers were snowed under with bicycle-related ads and commentary detailing every aspect of the sport and recreation. Families sat around their fireplaces listening to their Regina music boxes churn out *Bicycle Built for Two*, *The Cycle Man*, and *The March of the Bloomers*. Preachers spoke of bicycles during sermons, doctors during exams, barbers during haircuts. They influenced what people wore, enhanced the nation's roadways, and improved map-making.

Politicians ran on platforms of "being friendly to wheelmen." One-third of all patents issued that year were bicycle related. Those who could not afford them simply employed a little American ingenuity. "Will swap my wife," read one classified ad, "28 years old and trim looking, for any two-wheeled bicycle." The bicycle phenomenon, exulted the *New York Tribune*, is "one of much larger importance than all the victories and defeats of Napoleon."

The notion that a steel mechanical device should enjoy the same rights as God's creatures was still hard for some people to grasp. Over time, committed horsemen would put up the good fight, continually lobbying against the advance of wheelmen. But theirs was a fading world, a world in which their once-mighty powers would continually erode until the automobile came along to feed on whatever carcasses remained. This erosion brought about some unusual consequences for an animal that had perhaps been taken for granted before the bicycle. "It is pleasant to read in our livery trade," wrote one horseman, "that people who own good horses are treating them better than they use to."

In the coming years, significant opportunities would materialize for ambitious men in what was becoming one of the fastest growing industries in history. But few of these men were, or would be, black. In the racially charged milieu of 1890s America, if Major Taylor wished to stake *his* claim in the industry, he would need help. Without black role models, this young pioneer would have to align himself with strong, benevolent white men who didn't care about the color of a man's skin.

Sometime that summer, in the crucible of Hearsey's Bike Shop and the busy streets of Indianapolis, two such men would find him.

Chapter 2

ZIMMIE AND THE BIRDMAN

Louis Munger's racing career was rolling backward with all the might of an onrushing tsunami. In the summer of 1893 he was thirty, and in the youth-obsessed world of bike racing his strong but aging legs had all but spent themselves on the nation's tracks. He was a stylish man, firmly muscled, with a full crop of hair rarely allowed to creep out of place. At times, he sported a Napoleonic mustache, giving him a more worldly appeal.

Born in Iowa in 1863 and raised in Detroit, Michigan, Munger was a tall, good-looking bachelor whose humor and charm seldom left him wanting for attention from those around him. He had a pronounced bird-like nose, giving rise to his nickname "Birdie." He moved with a gentle swagger, a kinetic pantomime of silent confidence that some people could mistake for cockiness. No one seemed to know why, but when he spoke, he often raised his voice to a thunderous level; perhaps a serious accident involving his bicycle and a horse cart had caused partial hearing loss for which he compensated by speaking with a deep, penetrating voice. Regardless of the reason, people could hear him coming. His voice, quipped one acquaintance, "was a cross between the noises made by a cornet five miles away, two cats over a clothes line, and a man churning mush with a feather duster."

Known in racing circles as "The Western Flyer," Munger was a well-traveled man. Before arriving in Indianapolis, he lived on the road of the racing circuit, sleeping in long-ago motels, hostelries, or homes of admiring fans. Other times, the train or train station served as his home, and his bicycle was his best friend as the circuit looped almost nonstop from Detroit to Illinois to Kentucky, then up and down the East Coast. His past had the yesteryear feel of tire tracks on dusty country roads. The exact times and places of his early days are unrecorded, but there were always racing bikes, dirt or wooden ovals, and that familiar clatter of passenger trains rolling over windblown rails.

While Taylor had been befriending young Daniel on the grassy knolls near the Southards' estate, Munger set a few records on the road, receiving medals that he clung to like the child he'd yet to have. Despite the records he set in those early days, he remained a middling rider on the track, never to become among the nation's elite. But the perfectionist in him left him wanting more. Since his early years, he'd had tunnel vision, viewing the world from eight feet up, perched high atop the leather saddle of a high-wheeler. So it seemed natural for him to eventually climb down and slip into the business end of the bicycle world.

Arriving in Indianapolis from Chicago in the early 1890s—"he left after his voice," joked a reporter—Munger brought with him his medals, big dreams, and vivid memories of the speed and pageantry of the early days of bike racing. Hoping to regain his youthful form, he entered local competitions, but his racing career continued eroding there. So Munger quickly staked his business claim, parlaying his race winnings into a prosperous firm called the Munger Cycle Manufacturing Company. He made good use of his racing notoriety as well as his newfound manufacturing and marketing skills, creating an ultralight safety racing bicycle ingeniously called "The Munger." Though of little importance to the average person for whom casual biking was becoming an obsession, Munger's eponymous bikes would prove to be popular among the racing fraternity. Perhaps if he had sought the favor of the common rider and concentrated on wider rims or broader seats, his company may have joined the ranks of Schwinn and Co. But Munger was unable to shake the infectious racing bug, so his products followed his passion.

First a racer, then a manufacturer, Munger had dedicated himself so enthusiastically to bicycles it was as if he was deficient without them—an affliction not uncommon at the time. "Munger," wrote one cycling historian, "lived, ate, talked, slept, and breathed bicycles."

When he wasn't on the road peddling his racing bike to dealers nation-wide, Munger would stroll into various shops along Indy's bicycle row to mingle with other wheelmen. Though his bittersweet legend preceded him, he was a big enough star to become a hero in the eyes of many who gathered there. On a day in 1893, he stumbled into H. T. Hearsey's Bike Shop. With his winning percentage dropping to a woeful level, perhaps he was already thinking about training or managing aspiring young riders.

He couldn't help but stare at him. Munger was roaming Harry Hearsey's Bike Shop, probably trying to smooth-talk old Harry into placing another order for his racing models, when a reedy black kid strutted around the training room with a riding talent and composure that belied his youth. Customers looked on inquisitively. Each time Munger returned to the shop, the same smooth black face, the same underfed look piqued his curiosity. When he had time, Munger watched the youngster's surprisingly seamless interaction with both black and white customers. There's something about this kid, he thought. If Munger had already been thinking about race managing or finding a rider to lead a future cycling team for his company, he could not have stumbled upon a more unlikely prospect than little Taylor.

Practically speaking, Taylor was everything that an 1890s race manager would have run away from. Unlike road racers, short-distance track racers often carry extra brawn for the requisite fast-twitch explosiveness, especially in their meaty thighs and sturdy upper bodies. Physically, Taylor was still a runty speck of a kid, with spindle-shanked legs and round, protuberant knees—seemingly a lesson in frailty. His upper body was a poignant continuation of his lower—short, slight, toothpick arms, flairless back, and puny shoulders no wider than his waist. When he showed up at bike tracks, trainers surely thought he was lost, pointing him to the horse track where all the like-sized black jockeys converged at the time. Given his diminutive size, one wouldn't think Taylor would ever possess the leg or lung power to blow out a candle, much less compete with international sprint giants. Sure, he could grow into it, but neither his circumstances nor his bloodlines seemed to suggest future greatness.

Without prosperous parents or any real money of his own to help defray extensive travel and equipment costs, Taylor would be a risky investment. And to top it all off, he was black. At that moment in American history, few managers would have had any interest in someone like Major Taylor other than as a servant or a low-paid manual laborer. No "darkey," one race reporter wrote, had ever amounted "to a pinch of snuff in the racing game." Major Taylor and all his worldly ambitions would have been viewed by virtually everyone as a hopeless cause, especially those who were calling him a little "pickaninny," a highly offensive term that was then used to describe throwaway black kids.

Everyone, that is, except Louis D. "Birdie" Munger. If Taylor possessed unseen attributes ripe for elite track racing, Louis Munger had the mind of a prophet, saint, or both.

On a day in 1893, he and Taylor came face-to-face. The two stood on opposite ends of the racing spectrum. Munger was a refuge from the vanishing world of high-wheelsmen who had been squeezed out; Taylor was a boy hoping to blaze trails on the new safety bikes, moving bravely forward with the eager, naïve eyes of youth. Munger was trying to pave the nation's tracks with the tread of his new racing machine; Taylor was dreaming of the day when he could ride on those same tracks atop such a bike. Munger had the wisdom and the machine; Taylor had the determination and, perhaps with endless schooling, the engine.

From skills honed over a decade of viewing other riders, Munger had developed a knack for finding hidden talents and rare qualities in people. Spending as much time at Hearsey's shop soaking up the local flavor as he did his own company, Munger was impressed with the vibrant, young Taylor as he gave lessons in the store's custom riding school. He first noticed his inherent skills with a bicycle that despite its dominance at Hearsey's was still an awkward new possession for folks. He was also impressed with Taylor's work habits and inquisitiveness; the boy constantly drilled him with questions on bike racing tactics and the latest trends in racing bikes.

The two slowly formed an unlikely friendship away from Hearsey's. Taylor followed Munger to races, begging him to let him try out his latest racing bike. Munger eventually obliged, and the two wheelmen rode together on Indy's hilly scapes lined with oak trees, enjoying the competition as much as the companionship. While younger riders were often too aggressive, blowing through their physical reserves like jackrabbits early in a ride, Munger conveyed a calming presence. He taught Taylor that the strongest man can lose to the most cunning. He instructed Taylor how to conserve his energy and control his emotions while feeding off his opponents' aggressiveness. Taylor had a tendency to obey the bike's mechanical imperatives, its instinctive quest for perpetual motion. Using the all-important technique of drafting behind rivals to cut down on wind resistance—a technique that can save 30 percent of a cyclist's energy—Munger taught Taylor to restrain himself early on and then unleash his fastest sprint at the finish.

When on the tracks, Munger taught Taylor to weigh the unique angles, surfaces, speeds, and propensities of each individual one. He would have told him to build dossiers on his competitors—slow starter, fast closer, hugs the pole, loves the rail—and track the subtleties of each race like wind direction and the best spot to begin his sprint. He schooled in him the import of proper eating habits, and most importantly, to stay away from alcohol, drugs, cigarettes, and cigars—all used in mass quantities at the time. Always a willing student, Taylor didn't just listen; he heard.

Sharing years of invaluable insight into the secrets of racing, Munger was amazed at the relentless pace Taylor kept on their rides, sometimes even challenging his more experienced form. Initial thoughts of becoming a manager-trainer began to percolate. And as Taylor's endurance and pace improved after nearly every outing, it appeared as if the young lad speeding alongside him might be a good, albeit trouble-bound pupil. But Munger wasn't above having considerable fun at Taylor's expense. On one occasion, he and a few riding buddies got him to bleach his pitch-black hair inside a velodrome locker room. "We will bleach you and make you white," joked Munger. To great laughter, Taylor's black head was then nudged out onto the track sporting a sticky, tangled head of platinum blondish-red hair. "Its effect was ludicrous," joked Charles Sinsabaugh, a preeminent race reporter and the man who named Chicago's baseball team the Cubs.

Hundreds of wheelmen had passed through Hearsey's Bike Shop and fixed their gaze on Taylor's pint-sized black body, but no one had seen the possibilities that Munger saw. One had to look beyond the small frame, the black skin, and deep into his psyche. Clearly, a fire burned there. That's why, after spending time with Taylor training and tinkering in his workshop, he offered to hire Taylor away from Hearsey's. Munger's "famous" bachelor's apartment above his warehouse, which was used to entertain countless wheelmen and women, was a disaster—business books, periodicals, and clothing were strewn everywhere. Munger, who employed ninety workers inside a three-story building half the size of a football field, needed a porter, cook, and all-around handyman. Excited about the possibilities, Taylor signed on, agreeing to do various jobs around Munger's apartment and factory, including, in those days before widespread telephone use, delivering messages.

Under Munger, a regimented pattern developed. They would wake early, work long, hard days, train until dark, and hit the sack early. Like many teenagers at the time, Taylor probably rolled his bicycle inside at night, washed the wheels, polished the spokes, and fell asleep with its shiny exterior at his feet. With almost a canine loyalty, Taylor committed himself to his sundry new responsibilities as he had all others. "He was as faithful and conscientious about the servile duties of those days," a reporter later wrote, "as he is in his training today."

While Taylor was impressed with Birdie's knowledge and race stories, what really endeared him to Munger was the patient and kindly intimacy of his friendship—and that he did not care about the color of a man's skin. "Mr. Munger became closer and closer attached to me as time went on," he remembered. "Had I been his own son, he could not have acted more kindly toward me." The sentiment was mutual. "Munger," recalled a reporter, "took to Taylor as a duck takes to water."

On a sweltering August day, Munger gave Taylor his most momentous assignment. The Zig Zag cycling club led by Harry Hearsay, Tom Hay, and Bert Willits had organized an important local race with national significance. They had invited some of the best riders in the country. Munger handed over the name of an acquaintance who had committed to the race and directed Taylor to pick him up at the train station and escort him for the weekend. His hands trembling with emotion, Taylor instantly recognized the name.

At the train station in the warm Indianapolis summer of 1893, Major Taylor first laid eyes on Arthur Augustus Zimmerman. He was quite a sight for the young boy. Everything about Zimmerman exuded kindness, warmth, and success. Draped over his nearly six-foot-tall frame was a gabardine jacket tailored to his broad chest and shoulders, a crisply laid tie, and a silk pocket square. His Swiss watch was made of real gold, and he sported genuine green snakeskin shoes. As was the style, diamonds glinted from his tie, badge, and as many fingers as taste would allow.

A ladies' favorite, Arthur had a hard chin, sagacious eyes, midlength blond hair parted a lick off center, and occasionally a restrained handlebar moustache. In his body language, Zimmie, as his friends called him, spoke with a stutter. He walked with a surprisingly slow and shambling gait. Yet when stationary, he stood straight up military style, no doubt stemming from his days as a military school cadet.

As a general rule, Zimmerman wouldn't speak in front of large crowds—at a banquet in his honor, he once famously strayed into the hotel saloon for a cocktail, leaving British dignitaries scrambling onstage. But alone with close friends or admiring fans, he was chatty and spoke with a pleasant South Jersey drawl that blended with his jovial disposition. Unlike many athletes of his era, he was an intellectual; before his racing days, he considered going the way of academia—immersing himself in writing and law school. Yet much to the chagrin of his rivals, he delayed his education, only to become an author later. In the summer of '93 he was twenty-four, rich, jovial, and chock full of life. He also was the greatest rider the sport had ever seen, and one of the world's most popular athletes. "We are in favor of Zimmerman for president of the United States," gloated one reporter. "He would get it if he would only start."

On June 11, 1869, in the rapidly growing industrial region of Camden, New Jersey, Arthur was born to Theodore and Anna Zimmerman. After moving to Asbury Park, his parents used their rambunctious boy's athleticism as a good excuse to boot him out of the house and into military school. There, his natural talents and long legs found him winning running meets. In an era when medals were awarded for the long jump, high jump, and hop, skip, and jump, Zimmerman medaled in all three. Unlike Taylor, who took to two wheels at a very young age, Zimmerman would not discover cycling until he was seventeen years old. But the attraction was instant. "I liked it so well," he said, "that I jumped into the game with all the spirit that was in me."

The elite racing world that Zimmerman plunged into was a colorful one. This was racing in its purest form: raw, unrefined, quick, and often flat-out dangerous. And people could not get enough of it. In cities and burgs up one coast and down the other, hundreds, then thousands, then tens of thousands fought their way into packed bleachers. They spilled onto the infield and cheered their favorites, often at nose-to-nose finishes.

The sport grew so rapidly, entrepreneurs were unable to build new tracks fast enough, leaving cycling fans temporarily bumping elbows with horse racing fans as they raced around horse tracks before the daily equine matches. But once bike racing crowds began to rival those for horse racing, entrepreneurs jumped into action. Thousands of small ovals built specifically for bike racing sprang up in villages nationwide. Dozens of modern tracks, called velodromes, were erected in larger towns, usually equipped with press boxes, smooth wooden or concrete tracks, concessions stands, training and massage rooms. A third type of track combined the two, with a dirt horse track on the outside and a concrete or wooden bicycle track on the inside.

While technically considered amateurs before 1893, stars like Zimmerman won hordes of gifts that, when cashed in, may have exceeded earnings of any other athletes, save a few prizefighters and matadors. According to the *New York Times*, Zimmie's haul for 1892 included twenty-nine bicycles, several horses and carriages, half a dozen pianos, household furniture of all descriptions, and enough silver plates, medals, and jewelry to stock a jewelry store. All this was augmented by his earnings as the main sponsor of Raleigh bikes, a stack of Raleigh stock shares received at ground floor prices, and royalties from Zimmie shoes, Zimmie toe clips, and Zimmie clothing. In 1893, the first year of America's massive economic downturn and when other sports were reeling, his earnings were estimated to be well over $10,000.

The sporting world had never seen anyone quite like Arthur Zimmerman. From the first day he roared around a track, he proved to be a dominating figure, winning fourteen hundred races by the time he retired. He was a spectacular sight for all to see with his muscular body hovering over his bike, his hands grasping the bars, his eyes leveled on the finish line, and his legs spinning like pistons. His form was stealthy, a paragon of balance, agility, and prepotency. "It was as if the man was mounted on rails," wrote Victor Breyer, a noted cycling journalist, "so complete is the absence of wobbling and the semblance of effort."

The press followed his every move. Photographers snapped and sketch artists drew pictures of a calm, cool-looking Zimmerman passing a field of riders in various degrees of agony, their faces and bodies twisting and contorting under the strain. "He at present runs a chance of being pictured more extensively and in more varied styles," wrote one editor during the '92 election campaign, "than either of the presidential candidates."

Because he trained fewer hours than many of his rivals, Zimmerman was labeled lazy by some sportswriters. In reality he was among the first to employ a more scientific, interval training approach while his rivals, haunted by a fear of losing their jobs, marched through the same rigid daily routine of riding for long hours at the same pace. Unhindered by tradition, superstitions, or old wives' tales, Zimmerman rode fewer hours but varied his distance and speed. He trained on the road and track, used "Professor Roberts's dumb-bell drills" for increased explosive power, played basketball and hand-ball, and ran during the offseason. "Perhaps I can stand a little more than my share of rest," he said coyly when someone questioned him about his brisk workouts. But he was not, nor did he like being called, indolent, as one newspaper that made such a claim found out. "I'll go down and clean out that office," he threatened, "if they don't set me right in the matter."

After successfully conquering America, Zimmie shipped overseas with similar effect. In England, where oversized Zimmerman posters were displayed in numerous locations, there was talk of a riders' "strike" because of his dominance. "His path," complained one scribe, "was littered with the defeat of England's best men." In a nation with a rich tradition of athlete prowess, his supremacy caused such a stir that one Brit actually called for a public hearing on the matter. "What happened to our eccentric riders?" she demanded to know. "Why doesn't she ask Zimmerman?" retorted a London columnist.

In an era when fouling and rough play happened fairly often, Zimmerman prided himself on good, clean riding, becoming a perfect role model for an aspiring young rider like Taylor.

Along with his phenomenal racing success came equally remarkable folktales: how he outpaced a speeding train or passed a greyhound at full stride. One story had him defeating the great racehorse Salvator in a man-versus-horse match race, with Zimmerman, of course, riding on an older and slower high-wheel bicycle. The rumor stuck and made for spicy conversation until someone discovered Salvator wasn't even alive at the time of the alleged race.

To racing fans, especially young boys who played with toy models of his likeness, Arthur Zimmerman was a godlike figure. He was for the sport of bike racing what James Corbett was for boxing, Salvator was for horse racing, and Cy Young would become for baseball.

From the outset, Arthur Zimmerman was several tire treads ahead of Birdie Munger and all other wheelmen. With the benefit of more than seven decades watching hundreds of bike racers from all over the world, French journalist Victor Breyer summed up Zimmerman's talents thus: "He was simply the greatest pedaler of all time."

When Taylor arrived at Union Station, he had no difficulty distinguishing Zimmerman from the large group of cyclists, some of whom had come from as far away as South Africa. There was a crush of fans, journalists, and race organizers enveloping him, clamoring for his autograph or a prized interview. Taylor slithered through the crowd while a large brass band filled the air. He slipped past Zimmie's porter, trainer, manager, and biographer, who had been recording his every feat down to the finest detail. Taylor recognized the affable smile, the fine clothes, and the glittering jewelry from the many pictures that filled the newspapers. Unaware of Zimmerman's attitude toward blacks, Taylor was excited and fearful as he neared the celebrated white man. He peered nervously up at his towering figure. Their eyes met. Taylor mentioned that Munger had sent him to escort him back to his home. Zimmerman, who despite his fame was surprisingly approachable, extended his white hand. With a warm smile on his face, he shook Taylor's small, black hand, instantly putting him at ease.

The slow carriage ride back to Munger's home would be the most inspirational experience of Taylor's early life. After returning from Europe with "a trunk full of gold and silver," and then winning the World Championships in Chicago earlier that month, Zimmerman had returned to his New Jersey home to one of the most intense hero's welcomes ever seen. More than five thousand people had greeted him, tossed him on their shoulders, then carried him into town. Nearly every home, business, and government building in the Manasquan borough, and later in Asbury Park, flew American flags with a giant "Z" attached. Large blue streamers with national colors in graceful folds adorned every cornice. The parade route, which had been heavily advertised weeks before his arrival, was lit up with Chinese lanterns, Roman candles, and Greek fires. The air crackled with the endless thunder of cannon fire. Later in the evening, Parkers Hall was taxed beyond capacity. Thousand more spilled out onto South Street, never to make it inside. Young boys had shimmied up the columns of the building's portico, fighting for a glimpse of Zimmerman through the windows. "The town is yours," proclaimed the mayor.

And here was Taylor, a fourteen-year-old obscure black boy from rural Indianapolis, already with bike racing aspirations, alone with a man who was the daily cynosure of thousands of eyes. If he was nervous, Zimmerman quickly put him at ease, smothering him in wide smiles and warm gestures. "I was always the friend of the struggling amateur," he told a reporter, "and many times have gone out of my way, at a loss of time and money, to assist a brother rider in poor luck."

In stark contrast to the constant drone of racing sycophants following Zimmie everywhere he went, Taylor was evidently a welcome change. To Taylor, Zimmie was a welcome surprise. Instead of treating him like a servant as most blacks were at the time, and instead of talking about himself the whole trip, Zimmerman showed interest in learning about Taylor. He spent much of the time inquiring about the gold medal that Taylor had won in the ten-mile race in Indianapolis. "He was surprised when I told him of that feat," Taylor recalled, "and even more so when I told him of many other boys' races since winning that gold medal."

When they arrived at Munger's home later that evening, dinner was served. At Zimmerman's insistence, Taylor joined in. The three of them ate a large dinner, then sat around talking about bike racing into the night. Taylor must have been mesmerized as Zimmerman shared story after story of his racing exploits at cities nationwide. His ears must have perked up when Zimmerman poured over his experiences overseas, meeting princes and dukes in exotic faraway cities, where he was hailed by "crowds greater than would turn out to greet the king." He beamed about meeting, learning from, and competing against the greatest cyclists in the world. He described the fervor of the crowds, the masses clamoring for his autograph, the extensive coverage in the press, and the beautiful scenery and history of the countries he had visited.

Before bedding down for the evening, Munger—sipping an ice-cold glass of egg lemonade—looked Zimmerman in the eye and made a bold prophecy. "I am going to make a champion out of that boy some day," he said unreservedly. "I have told Major Taylor that if he refrains from using liquor and cigarettes, and continues to live a clean life, I will make him the fastest bicycle rider in the world." Having been through the trials and tribulations that go with being an elite athlete, Zimmerman reminded Munger and Taylor that they had a long, difficult road ahead. He then turned to Taylor and uttered words that would forever remain seared in his head. "Mr. Munger is an excellent advisor," he said in a sincere tone, "and if he tells me that you have the makings of a champion in you, I feel sure you will scale the heights some day."

On August 23, 1893—the night before the race that brought Zimmerman into town—the streets of Indianapolis were lit up with elaborate events. The largest parade of its kind ever given was put on by the Zig Zag Club, and the streets were lined with thousands of people. All the usual horse and pedestrian traffic came to a halt to make way for elegant carriages and five hundred cyclists, seven blocks deep. There were lanterns and bunting and bright-colored paper in abundance. The streets over which they passed, noted the *Indianapolis Sun*, "looked as though peopled with harlequins of some other time and place." Regally dressed, Taylor's former employers Harry Hearsey and Tom Hay caused a royal stir, rolling down the parade route in an elegant four-horse tally-ho, winding up their horns and making the course ring with their imitation of the Zig Zag yell. ·

Taylor looked on bewitched, his eyes glittering in the bright lights as his heroes, Munger, Zimmerman, and other crack cyclists circled by him several times. Awards were handed out for best decorated rider-bicycle combinations. Known for his eccentric costumes, Birdie Munger had gone all out, flitting through the streets sporting a white duck frock suit, an immense buzz-saw hat, and a conspicuous paper monocle. A writer for the *Indianapolis Sentinel* clearly wasn't too impressed with his getup. "It was the most ridiculous exhibition of them all," he wrote.

As the riders prepared to earn their share of the $5,000 purse the following day, Taylor met another cycling hero named Willie Windle. Windle had been the Sprint Champion of America for several years before Zimmerman came along and stole his thunder. "While on my way out to the track on an errand," Taylor gushed, "I found myself sitting alongside one of the biggest champions of the day, Willie Windle, of Millbury, Massachusetts. I was the proudest boy in the world as it became noised about that I had shaken the hand of the two outstanding greats."

For a young black boy living in 1890s America and poking around in local bike races, Zimmerman and Windle formed towering athletic figures. But it was their genial personalities and kindness—qualities that transcended their athleticism—that Taylor cherished most. "I was especially impressed with the friendliness of the two of them, especially toward me, a colored boy. In my youthful mind the thought flashed that men can be champions and still be broad-minded in strange contrast to the young would-be champions that I had met in and about Indianapolis. There was no race prejudice in the makeup of Zimmerman and Windle; they were too big for that."

The Indianapolis Military Band greeted the large crowd as people streamed into the state fairgrounds for the one-mile open. Taylor watched with a keen eye as trick riders warmed up the crowd, bringing back memories of his days on the Southards' estate. As always, the press doted on

Zimmerman. "He is closely watched by a hundred critics as if he were a derby favorite," someone wrote. When one reporter punched through the crowd and asked him for his opinion of the track, Zimmie gazed out at the oval, his angular body leaning over his bicycle. "I think I will set a world record today, boys," he sang out, cocksure.

With Munger, Zimmerman, and Windle all lined up alongside a large field of riders, it must have been difficult for Taylor to decide who to root for. He wouldn't have much time to decide. Zimmerman "shot by the grandstand like a stone from a catapult," leaving the rest of the field gasping in his wake. And, as he had prophesized, he had set a new record. "They might as well have chased a locomotive," wrote one reporter, "so far as there was any chance of catching him." Windle drifted back to fourth place. Further confirming his best days were behind him, Munger's homely legs waddled in near the back and out of the money.

At a post-race soiree held at Tomlinson Hall, corncob pipes with Zig Zag ribbons were smoked, and champagne glasses were clinked. Men and women danced while the swift fingers of two black pianists arched over the long ivory keys of their Steinways—all ignoring the thunderstorm brewing outside. A crowd hovered over Zimmerman as he accepted a diamond-studded gold cup and then quickly got off the stage before anyone asked him to speak. Taylor surely squeezed his eyes shut, visualizing himself accepting those medals in front of a rapturous crowd.

Following the festivities, with the rail station overwhelmed by departing racegoers and eventually shuttered down from the storm, Munger likely escorted Zimmerman back to his home for one last night before he shipped overseas. To the sound of raindrops pinging off the carriage top, his new bicycle nestled by his side, Taylor could fall fast asleep, the indelible images of the past few days still burning in his head.

In the summer of 1893, Munger, Zimmerman, and Taylor found solidarity in their worldly dreams, tolerant minds, and common obsession with bike racing. But impossibly hard times would dawn with an unprecedented economic depression, government-sanctioned race segregation laws, and unspeakable racial cruelty. During these times young Taylor would need strong allies and enduring inspiration. Above the frames, spokes, and wheels of the Munger Cycle Manufacturing Company, he had found just that in the unusual partnership that had formed among them.

Chapter 3

ALL THAT REMAINED OF A BLACK DESPERADO

On July 7, 1893, fifty miles south of Taylor's hometown state of Indiana near the Western Kentucky town of Bardwell, a husband and wife finished their breakfast while browsing an advertisement that invited locals to an event in town. Excited about attending, they told their coachman to prepare the horse and carriage for the ride into town.

When they arrived in Bardwell around ten o'clock that morning, a long line of horses, carriages, and bicycles already filled both sides of the street in the small, normally sedate town. Numerous trains coming from the north continued to drop off spectators throughout the morning. Near Cairo, Illinois, the steamboat *The Three States*, having been hastily chartered, steamed south down the Mississippi River with another five hundred people onboard. By ten-thirty the carriages had backed up to the city limits and the clamor from the throng rose. By eleven o'clock well over one thousand people hovered outside the local rail station waiting for a special train to arrive. When the train finally sighed into town, the local sheriff struggled to hold back the animated crowd. Once the railcar door flung open, a bound and handcuffed black man stumbled out of the train and into the onrushing crowd. In concert with the crowd, the couple began calling for a burning. Just then, the black man spoke, momentarily silencing the crowd.

"My name is C. J. Miller, of Springfield Illinois . . . I am here among you, a stranger; am looked on by you as the most brutal man that ever stood on God's green earth. I am standing here, an innocent man, among men excited, and who do not propose to let the law take its course. I have committed no crime . . . I am not guilty."

Working his way up to the front of the crowd, the husband yelled for someone to prepare the fire pit. His wife joined in, followed by their two children. Soon the entire orgy of spectators, joining in the chant, lunged at Miller, trying to separate him from the deputies. Of the more than one thousand men, women, and children in the crowd, only two were reluctant to drop the gauntlet on Miller just yet. One was the sheriff. The other was the father of two girls who were recently slain.

On a clammy afternoon two days before the heavily advertised event, sisters Mary and Ruby Ray, ages twelve and sixteen, had gone with their dog to pick berries near their family's farm north of Bardwell. When the family dog returned home alone and in an agitated state, the girl's mother became alarmed. A search of the area by police and neighbors discovered Mary and Ruby lying near each other, their throats slashed with a razor.

People with their bloodhounds came from miles to help find the "hell-fiend" responsible for the slaying. The trail went cold until the next morning when a report arrived from Bird's Point, near Sikeston, Missouri. Officials there believed a young black man they had arrested for freeriding on a freight train might be the Bardwell murderer. When the abducted girls' father and the county sheriff went to interrogate the man, they were disconcerted to discover that he was very dark, not mulatto, as witnesses had described. The sheriff then made the ill-fated decision to bring Miller, whose guilt seemed improbable, back to Bardwell where the bloodthirsty mob stood waiting.

Meanwhile back at the rail station, the crowd had nearly overtaken the deputies when John Ray, the father of the slain girls, arrived. At first Ray, who appeared uneasy about disappointing the people who had traveled so far, tried to delay their calls for "justice." But after seeing the intensity of the crowd, he changed tactics. "This is the man who killed my daughters," he told them, "but let us keep quiet and at the proper time burn him." He went on to say that the authorities would take Miller to jail, and promised the teaming crowd that they would complete their investigation by three o'clock that afternoon. As the police nervously telegraphed Springfield to corroborate Miller's alibi, trains continued dropping people off outside their station.

When the appointed hour arrived and no verdict had been rendered, the crowd became unruly, demanding that they stick with the 3:00 deadline. At 3:30, Ray emerged. Clearly trying to balance his own misgivings with the inevitability of violence, he announced that he was still not convinced Miller was the culprit who had murdered his daughters. Therefore, he reasoned, a burning would be inappropriate. His next words did not, however, disappoint some of the people there. "Under the circumstance," he continued, "a hanging would be acceptable."

The mob would not be denied. They rushed forward and seized Miller, stripping the clothes from his body and placing a heavy log chain around his neck. He was dragged through the streets to a crude platform of old barrel staves and other kindling. With one end of the chain around his neck and the other attached to a telegraph pole, he was raised several feet from the ground and let to fall. Though the first fall broke his neck, his body was repeatedly raised and lowered while the crowd peppered him with gunfire. Miller's corpse hung high above the street for two hours and was repeatedly photographed by the newsmen who placed the ads to draw the large crowd. Miller's toes and fingers were cut off, then his riddled corpse was lowered onto the waiting pyre and set ablaze.

Another couple, unaware of the event, trotted into town the next day. Noticing a miasma of particles floating in the air and settling in the trees, they asked a local man what it was and where it came from. "They were all that remained of a notorious character who lived by crime," they were told, "a black desperado who had murdered two white girls."

No one ever produced evidence definitively placing Miller at the scene of the crime or even in the state of Kentucky on the day of the murders. The murdered girls' father—the only one who seemed troubled by what had occurred—tried to have the case reopened after he found evidence that the guilty person was a white man living in Missouri. No crowd large or small was interested and the case was never officially reopened. "In Kentucky this Christmas," read one editorial later that year, "the favorite decoration of trees is strangled Negroes."

During the latter third of the 1800s, graphic stories like C. J. Miller's were as common in the South as falling snow in the North. It was, by some accounts, among the harshest era for blacks in America. Writing in the 1890s, Ida Wells, one of the first antilynching advocates (whose letters Major Taylor would keep in his scrapbook), estimated that ten thousand negroes had been killed at the hands of whites since 1865. Author Dorothy Sterling, who had combed through thousands of documents and oral histories, cited twenty thousand as the number killed by the Ku Klux Klan over just a four-year period. In the 1890s, the back-to-Africa leader Bishop Henry McNeal Turner, eschewing numerical estimates, noted that enough black people had been lynched in America that the victims would "reach a mile high if laid one upon the other."

Raised in the relative serenity of the Southard estate, Major Taylor's adolescent eyes had been largely unexposed to the extreme racism taking place just miles from the Indiana borders. But there was no escaping its hideous grip entirely. Occasionally, he and Daniel had wandered into the local YMCA to play and exercise. But because blacks were not allowed to join the Y, Taylor was forced to watch from the gallery while his white friends played down below. Disgusted, Daniel had appealed to his parents who enjoyed a position of prominence in the community. Their appeals had fallen on deaf ears. "It was there," Taylor remembered, "that I was first introduced to that dreadful monster prejudice, which became my bitterest foe from that very same day . . ."

In states like Indiana, exclusionary policies like those at the Y replaced lynching as a means of control. Blacks were often separated on trains, trolleys, restaurants, and restrooms. Miscegenation was illegal until the 1960s and schools remained segregated until 1949. Indiana also gave rise to a breed of "regulators" called the White Caps. Influenced by the original Ku Klux Klan, these White Cappers wore masks and bed sheets to intimidate, and disciplined their subjects with castration or painful floggings. They meted out punishment without trial against alleged adulterers, drunkards, petty thieves, or any others they so decided. They justified their acts by comparing them to something even worse. "Why kill out the race by lynching," asked the *Herald & Advertise*, "when subordinancy through fear of the lash will stop it all?" Supreme Court Justice Simeon E. Baldwin promoted legalizing floggings and castration as a "humanitarian policy" that would save lives and spare society the shame of lynching.

Apart from the physical horror of lynchings, castrations, and floggings, perhaps the greatest legacy arising from the period was the sheer degradation of the human spirit. The steady weakening of one's confidence and assertiveness and the vast outlay of time and energy spent thwarting the forces of iniquity happened at the expense of personal advancement. As innocuous as nonviolent racial policies may have appeared, it was their compounded effect over days, months, and years that caused all but the strongest people to succumb. Blacks were effectively put in their place and asked to heal. "How my poor little heart would ache," Taylor wrote of the incident at the Y, "to think that I was denied the opportunity to exercise and develop my muscles in the same manner as they, and for really no reason that I was responsible for."

The economic depression that began in 1893 further exacerbated the plight of blacks. Its tragedy enveloped the entire country. Competition for jobs and even basics like food became fierce. Desperate whites often took their anger out on blacks. A black man who was sexually, physically, intellectually, or economically threatening became a sacrificial scapegoat.

Successful athletes became especially vulnerable. Black jockeys who had long dominated horse racing were already feeling the pressure. They would soon be pushed overseas or out of the sport altogether, never to return. On the equine backstretch, it was all about owner and horse. The black men piloting the winning thoroughbreds in one Kentucky Derby after another were often viewed as diminutive extensions of the animals they rode. Major League Baseball gave up on its fleeting toleration of blacks and wouldn't revisit the issue until the Jackie Robinson era a half-century later.

In the halls of the League of American Wheelmen—bike racing's governing body—influential forces were already gathering, hoping to prevent African American infiltration into "their" sport. Down in Louisville, a particularly militant man named Colonel Watts tried etching exclusionary language into racings bylaws. It would have disallowed blacks from racing on Kentucky tracks and, if he got his way, national ones as well. After failing to get a majority vote against blacks in '92 and '93, Watts, who was running for mayor with a slogan of "no discrimination against wheelmen," returned in 1894 with a grand new scheme. At the league's annual convention held on his home turf—usually festive affairs attracting large delegations from all over the country—instead of selling the virtues of his beautiful city to visiting dignitaries or addressing pressing financial matters, he used his pulpit to further his racial aims.

To sway his visitors, he had concocted a fantastical plan. With the aid of a case of Kentucky Wild Turkey Whiskey, Watts had bribed a rather myopic leader of a local black cycling club into signing a letter stating that his club no longer wanted to be part of the league. Some hoodwinked delegates felt relieved; if blacks didn't want to be a part of the League of American Wheelmen, they would feel less remorse voting against them. A few Northeastern states, sensing mischief by the Southern leader, objected. But in a secret vote, inserting the words "whites only" gained 127 votes against 54, only to be blocked by the Massachusetts delegation.

Soon afterward, a heated debate spilled out into the nation's newspapers, sometimes alongside articles or advertisements of a lynching. A civil war of words continued between Northern and Southern states. But since few elite black cyclists were pounding down their doors, many delegates took the same tack that national politicians used when faced with issues they didn't want to address: wait for the problem to come to them and when it does, shift it into the hands of individual states to handle.

As 1894 melded into 1895, the issue remained open, controversial, and ambiguous. In New York, the lords of American racing crossed their fingers, hoping no talented black rider would come along and press the issue.

June 30, 1895, dawned cloudy and muggy. Major Taylor secreted himself behind a stand of oak trees, staring nervously at a field of riders as they prepared for a road race. A wealthy realtor, railroad magnate, and cycling enthusiast named George Catterson was sponsoring the annual seventy-five-mile race from Indianapolis to Matthews, Indiana. Though short-distance track racing was his forte, Taylor was attracted to the significant prizes and high-caliber competition slated for the distance event. Catterson was familiar with Taylor and wanted him to compete in the race, but Taylor had already been taking heat from some locals for having the cheek to compete against whites. Foretelling racial tension, Catterson—probably with Munger's blessing—decided to keep Taylor's entry secret. Had the other riders known, Catterson reasoned, few if any would have competed.

Seventy-five miles northeast in the finishing town of Matthews, Indiana, a solid wall of rain had formed and was driving right for Indianapolis. At the starting line, the first few droplets began falling. Thousands of racing fans holding umbrellas choked off Massachusetts Avenue, peering up at the ominous skies and questioning whether they could get the race in.

Shortly after the crack of the pistol with the field in full flight, Taylor emerged from behind the tree line. He mounted a bike he had borrowed from

Munger and began plowing a lonely furrow through the back of the field. He raced up to the peloton (in racing parlance, peloton means main pack of riders) and began feeding off their vacuum. His stealth tactic only worked for so long. When his white rivals finally spotted his dark form stealing in behind them, a steady barrage of racial epithets, attempts to knock him down, and threats of violence followed. Taylor was stuck in a cloud of angry riders, draping over him like a parka. He soldiered on, enduring the same brand of threats that would dog him for the next fifteen years. The intimidation grew nastier as the peloton wended down a serpentine patch of road, thinly inhabited. On one side of the road were weeping willows, on the other, a cemetery. "The thought ran through my mind," Taylor later recalled, "that this would make an ideal spot for my competitors to carry out their dire threats."

At the halfway point, Taylor had finally had enough. Fearing for his safety, he rose out of his saddle and mashed on his pedals, trying to separate himself from the pack. Suddenly the dark, threatening skies opened in a fury, dumping buckets of rain on the riders and the unpaved clay roads below. Before long, the earth beneath them softened, coagulated, and turned into mud pie. When they neared the town of Muncie, three-quarters of the way in, the sludge was flinging up into the riders' eyes, drenching their uniforms, and clinging to their tires, spokes, and rims. Taylor, sloshing along in the slop, took the lead. Riders tried desperately to shepherd in behind him, but one by one they began peeling off, succumbing to fatigue, saturation, or mechanical failure. Taylor began thriving on the elements as though the mud was flowing up in a lyrical slow motion. Like a spray of gold dust, it was transfiguring him from a gentle young boy into a streaking cheetah.

Somewhere near the outskirts of Matthews, Taylor craned his neck back, waiting for his rivals to counterattack. No one was there. At the finish, with prizes in hand, promoter Catterson looked on as a solitary figure pedaling for the line materialized from under the dark skies, his body soaked through and through. It was Taylor, the only rider to even finish the race.

It was just a local race on an inclement afternoon, but those who braved the rainstorm that day witnessed the embryonic stages of an athlete with an indomitable will to win and an unusual capacity to either ignore all obstacles or to feed off them. Despite the pouring rain, they saw an intense fire burning in him.

Waterlogged and rubber-legged, Taylor quickly tucked the first-place prize into his pocket—a deed to a lot in the center of Matthews—sped home, and gave it to his stunned mother. Saphronia was proud of his ambition to race and the free lot was nice, but the danger of riding among those white folks made her cautious. "She made me promise I would never ride a road race of that length again," he remembered.

He never would.

The effects from Jim Crow—the name of the infamous laws that symbolized lynching and race separation in America—still live with us today. In one form or another, the Jim Crow era was responsible for keeping blacks and whites apart and often hostile toward one another from the 1830s to the 1960s. In line with the segregationist mentality of the time and the hostility directed toward them, black cyclists, like black ballplayers, talked of forming a separate league similar to the League of American Wheelmen. Names were bandied about—The Colored Men's Protective Association, the Afro-American Racing Union, and the Afro-American Cyclists, to name a few. They would never become as well organized or have the caliber of riders as the League of American Wheelmen, but they did provide a safe sanctuary where blacks could compete against one another.

After enduring the enmity of his white rivals during the Indianapolis-Matthews race, Taylor decided to join the See-Saw Cycling Club, a local organization consisting of one hundred black men. On July 4, 1895, less than a week after the Matthews race, the all-black club sponsored a ten-mile road race. The winner was to receive a personal trainer and an all-expenses-paid trip to the Black National Championships in Chicago. Taylor was already considered among the best overall local riders, so winning the ten-mile race in Indianapolis against a field of thirty-three local black men came fairly easy to him.

A few weeks later, Taylor's free train ride clattered northwest to Chicago where the competition would prove to be more formidable. In 1895, there were few places in America more bike crazy than the Windy City. On any given day, there was almost always a bike race, bike parade, or bike show of some type clogging up the streets. New bike tracks were being erected in alarming numbers, making it a place and a time of bliss for dedicated wheelmen. Legions of riders rode in testosterone-laden wolf packs by day, then gathered in dense, loud cliques by night, committing to games of ten cent poker and rounds of ale at one of the myriad local cycling clubs. When Taylor arrived, the best black riders from all over the country were already there, surrounded by thousands of cheering black men and women, most of them hovering around one man.

Not long afterward, Taylor first saw the massive physique of Henry F. Stewart. Dubbed the "St. Louis Flyer," Stewart, who had been racing since 1887, was the undisputed king of black bike racing. Everywhere he went, blacks idolized him. With broad shoulders, tree-trunk thighs, and only somewhat smaller tree-trunk arms, his imposing figure could have passed as a bodybuilder's. Some even described him as a "brick shit-house." Unlike Zimmerman, Stewart appeared to be somewhat of a misanthrope who had little time for aspiring young riders. He had more of a boxer's mentality, using intimidation tactics against his rivals to scare them half out of their wits before races even began. And it usually worked.

But with patient schooling, Munger had trained Taylor well. Rarely the strongest rider in his day, Munger had to rely on cunning and superior strategy to win races. He transferred his vast pool of knowledge, teaching Taylor to feed off his rivals' aggressiveness when they were strong and prey on their weaknesses when they weren't. As the heavy race favorite, Stewart started from scratch (the scratchman starts from the rearmost position). Because of his recent victories, Taylor was also placed on scratch. Regrettably, someone introduced Taylor to Stewart. Twelve years his senior, Stewart, cocky and high on himself, stared Taylor's reedy body up and down with his cold, resolute eyes. He smirked and then stalked off. Taylor, a few months shy of seventeen, winced nervously. "It was the first time in my life that I had experienced such a reaction," he said of the meeting. Stewart's next move converted Taylor's disposition from fright to one of anger. He walked over to the racing officials and, within earshot of Taylor, suggested they move Taylor to the limit (or front) position. "He looks as though he's going to need it," Stewart bellowed for all to hear.

At the starting line, Stewart peeled off his bright purple bathrobe—a common garment worn by cyclists before a race at the time—exposing his muscular frame and further intimidating his weary rivals. Given his prerace antics, Stewart had no choice but to affirm his supremacy by leading the pack. Aggressively, he did just that, setting a gut-wrenching pace right from the start—the kind of pace better suited to two miles, not ten. Taylor slowly moved up through the pack, positioning himself right behind Stewart, whose large body formed a perfect wedge from the blowing wind. It was well into the race before Stewart finally realized, much to his surprise, that he wasn't going to shake Taylor from his rear wheel easily. But by then it was too late; he had wrung himself to exhaustion while Taylor had been husbanding his energy. He could only watch as the young upstart from Indianapolis stormed by him at a blistering pace right before the finish line. Taylor crossed it ten lengths ahead, the new Colored Champion of America. His accomplishment went virtually unnoticed by the nation's press.

After defeating Stewart during that summer of 1895, Taylor kept finding the winner's circle, including at three blacks-only events in Kentucky.

At Munger's behest, he also began coaching other would-be cyclists. During his era, nearly every high school and college featured cycling as a centerpiece of its athletic curriculum. In search of valuable publicity, manufacturers tripped over one another in their zeal to infiltrate schools with their products. Their strategy was elementary: help youths get a few wins under their belts while simultaneously thrilling them so much with their shiny new models that they would charge home, bat their eyes at their parents, and leave them no choice but to clean out their bank accounts.

Munger had two secret weapons. He assembled a superlight custom bicycle and sent Taylor, who was becoming known around town, to various high schools to train their students. Munger added further sizzle by offering a free Birdie Special bicycle with a silver emblem featuring an owl on the front—thus the name Birdie—for any student who could defeat Taylor in a race. It was a strong incentive. As a percentage of the average person's annual income—about 30 percent—custom bicycles were exceedingly expensive at the time. Being intimately aware of Taylor's fledgling speed, however, Munger probably wasn't too concerned about any run on his bank account.

The high schools were singular places for a black man to be, but the nascent young stars apparently took well to Taylor's tutelage. He espoused the virtues of Munger bicycles, trained the kids well, and listened gaily as they tried every kind of bribery they could think of to get their hooks on a free custom bike. Surely Munger dropped by on occasion, so he could peer out over the track rail and laugh as the high schoolers tried in vain to catch Taylor. Throughout the training process, Taylor's own form continued to blossom.

As summer waned, Taylor's name had been appearing in local papers more often than certain people in certain entrenched circles cared to see. Most of the attention had centered on his road-racing victories, but as time rolled on it became obvious to him, and to Munger, that his greatest strength was in the faster, more explosive sport of track racing. So Taylor began haunting Indianapolis racetracks during his spare time, trying to talk his way into races, once again testing the racial divide.

The timing of his partial conversion was good and bad. Cities were overwhelmed with road races, and enough horsemen had voiced their contempt that some cities began regulating their frequency. Unfortunately for Taylor, there were no blacks-only racetracks to speak of. His development was effectively in the hands of track owners and local riders, virtually all of them white. Some days he was able to use the track for training purposes while on others he met stiff resistance.

Occasionally, he would test his speed against proven local white riders. Because of his color, he couldn't compete head to head against them, so he would wait until they had finished, then quickly rip around the track, often unofficially besting their times. These were bold moves that few if any blacks dared try at the time. But for Taylor, it was just the beginning of a lifetime filled with nonconformity and the fearless rejection of stale traditions. These incidents would prove to be seminal moments for Taylor and Munger. While living in the cloistered environment of the Southard home or toiling in Hearsey's shop, he had experienced little of "that dreaded monster prejudice." But now that he emerged into the broader world and had shown promise in the nation's fastest growing sport, he found himself entering a new life dynamic. Faced with angry riders, some track owners began barring him from their tracks. His world was getting squeezed—an agonizing reality for a young man whose life's passion was bike racing.

Less ambitious men may have quit right then and there, retreating to the relative safety of factory life or the simplicity of farm life. But Major Taylor was wired differently. "Down in my heart," he noted, "I felt that if I could get an *even break*, I could make good as a sprinter on the bicycle tracks of the country." But for a black man living in 1890s America, getting an *even break* came as often as snowfall in summer.

The vibrant colors of summer gave way to the variegated hues of autumn. Because of his racing successes, Taylor gained confidence daily.

He was also becoming more inconspicuous at Munger's factory and home. When Taylor was nowhere to be found one morning, Munger threw a leg over his bicycle and set out in search of his protégé. He rolled through an

Indianapolis that, like other cities, was scarred by the depression. He finally halted at one of the worst of the local tracks—nothing but a rundown old horse track, probably one of the only tracks that Taylor hadn't been kicked off of yet. Sure enough, there was Taylor, zigging and zagging around the oval at breakneck speed. With the track nearly deserted, Munger leaned his bike against the grandstand, gnawed on a strip of buffalo jerky, and watched Taylor uncoil.

Sensing that Taylor had good legs that day, he instructed him to ride an unpaced mile flat out. Taylor nodded. Bending over the track rail, Munger reached into his pocket and fished out his stopwatch. Like a flat rock skimming across a glassy pond, Taylor skipped around the track, his small, jockey-like frame showing remarkable power and grace, all things moving forward. As Taylor crossed the mile marker, beads of sweat rolling down his forehead, Munger snapped his thumb down on his stopwatch and then looked up. His face was a picture of sheer joy. *Taylor had spun off an unpaced mile in 2:09.* The record was 2:07. This blackbird could fly! "I can ride a wheel almost as fast as some of the cracks," he would tell Munger, the words bounding out his mouth.

Adrenaline coursing through his veins, Birdie Munger was fully conscious of the fact. A veteran racetracker, he knew two seconds to be an eternity in short-distance track racing, but considering Taylor's age, Munger believed he was looking in the eyes of greatness. It was obvious, he told himself, that Taylor had to be driven to the next level. But two questions loomed large for him: where, and against what odds?

On the backstretch, secrets were hard to keep. Locally, at least, word of young Taylor's precocity spread through the bike-racing grapevine. Indianapolis reporters had chronicled his results; under their breath, local wheelmen whispered his name during training rides and at meets. On occasion, they were whispers of awe and wonderment at how someone his age and of such slight build could achieve that kind of speed. But more often than not, they were sardonic and degrading. When Taylor was a horse tender, porter, and bike-shop duster, locals had paid less attention to him. Then, like his brethren, he was residing in his proper place of subservience, that place where man lingers in a steady state of habitual invisibility.

Now, the Indianapolis air had suddenly become cold, inhospitable, and outwardly hostile. And not just toward him. For the crime of trying to help get an African American out from under the shadow of obscurity and insignificance, Munger also took heat, even among his business partners and friends.

Restless and uneasy, Munger began seeking greener grass, further prosperity, and greater freedom for himself and his young friend. He ambled up to a large map of America that hung from his factory wall. He looked at its open frontier, the vast Pacific to the West, the mighty Atlantic to the East, and everything in between. He marveled at its sheer breath and its seemingly endless possibilities. He surely debated, meditated, and brooded before finally jamming a pin in the center of Massachusetts. With little to lose except closeness to his family, Taylor nodded his head. They rounded up their belongings, bought red-eye train tickets for the East, and braced themselves for the great unknown.

On a fall day in 1895, Munger walked through his Indianapolis factory for the last time. A cadre of friends and associates came to see him off. They gathered around in silent attention, tipping back a round of beers and staring quizzically at him. One of them broke the silence, asking why he was leaving a good thing behind—Indianapolis was the third largest manufacturer of bicycles—to partner up "with that little darkey." Munger stood up, leveled his back, and raised his head defiantly. "Someday," he declared with an edge to his foghorn voice, "he will return to this city as Champion Bicycle Rider of America." Given the sheer number of cyclists vying to be champion of America—virtually all of them white—it was a proclamation astounding for its boldness. His friends shook their heads, turned their backs, and walked away.

At Indy's Union Station, Taylor hugged his parents, then loaded his belongings—nothing more than a bag full of tattered clothes, a well-traveled bicycle, and a copy of the Scriptures. Evening fell. Gilbert and Saphronia, who couldn't bear the idea of parting with him, tried concealing their trepidation as they said their good-byes and handed him over to Munger, his surrogate father. As the train ground forward, Taylor peered out the window and watched his mother's dark face blurring in the distance. Frightened and empty, Saphronia watched her son steam headlong into the cruel Jim Crow era flat broke amid a wrenching depression. He was not yet seventeen, but his childhood had just ended.

Chapter 4

PRISONERS IN A GOLDEN CAGE

On a Wednesday morning in July 1896, a downhearted young man drifted into a store in Lima, Ohio, to shop for shoes. After sifting through the infant rack, he picked out two of the nicest pairs of shoes he could find, then brought them to the sales counter. Because he had but a few cents to his name, he asked the salesclerk if she would hold on to them until that afternoon when he would return with the money. Before leaving, he pulled out a picture of his two babies and his wife and showed them to the clerk. "I'm going to win one of the races," he said in a concerned tone. Glancing at the attractive, young family curled up together in a loving pose, the salesclerk kindly obliged.

The man, "Poor Joe" Griebler, a quiet rider who had recently turned professional, walked out of the store and headed to the Lima racetrack. Standing at the starting line of a half-mile race with twelve other riders that afternoon, some observers thought Griebler looked and spoke nervously. Out of the gate, the riders bunched together in close formation until the final turn when Griebler suddenly broke from the pack. He dropped his head lower to his bike, then oddly raced toward the outside lane at a "frightful speed." As he charged farther toward the crowd in his all-red silks, racegoers noticed his face had a crazed, almost demonic look to it. When it became obvious he would soon run out of track but had not yet slowed down, they sensed something was wrong. They were right. Griebler catapulted up the track's four-foot embankment and soared over racegoers' heads, missing them by inches.

Behind them, they heard a loud *splat*.

The helmet-less Griebler had hit a post, cracking his skull.

With one of his ears ripped off, chin smashed in, and one eye loosed from his head, he lay prostrate on the ground, blood running out of his nose, ear, and mouth. Not knowing any better, a few people picked him up and carried him under the shade of a weeping willow tree, probably further injuring his neck and pressing a fractured bone farther into his brain. While the races continued unabated, a few general practitioners who were at the race stood vigil over him, but were of little help. Before dying twenty minutes later, Griebler eked out his last words. "Soft pillow-shoes," he muttered, his one good eye flickering in and out. "I'm awfully sick."

Afterward, there was talk of setting up a fund for his wife, Delia, three-year-old son, Walter William, and eight-month-old daughter, Pearl. The idea seemed to resonate with the young riders who could better relate to Griebler's plight but had little money to contribute. Fred Longhead, one of the few successful riders who seemed shaken, went to the store and bought both pairs of shoes from a tearful salesclerk. He sent the tiny shoes and a touching letter back to Griebler's inconsolable widow in Granite Falls, Minnesota, along with "Poor Joe" in a coffin.

Walter Sanger, one of the experienced riders in the race who had seen such desperation before, told authorities that Griebler "passed him with his face set and riding like a wild man." When the rest of the wheelmen learned of his bizarre death, few seemed shocked. Their seeming indifference had roots in experience. At the time, there was much discussion among doctors and laypersons about the supposed harmful effects of bike riding. One doctor claimed that such irrational riding was caused by vertigo, dizziness, or ruptured blood vessels. Another claimed that cycling caused "irritation and congestion," which led to chronic disease and insanity. Yet another contended that cycling caused thirst, which inevitably led to beer drinking, which triggered kidney stones. Together, they fashioned terrifying names for these maladies like "bicycle heart," "bicycle eye," "bicycle walk," "bicycle face," and "bicycle twitch."

There was never one definitive diagnosis for Griebler's tragic death. But for veterans like Sanger, Munger, and Zimmerman, it further symbolized what they had seen or experienced over the years. The life of a professional bicycle racer could be downright brutal. With all the un-air-conditioned train and sea travel, the countless hours training in intense summer heat or cold spring rains, the tremendous nutritional needs, and the high monetary cost of meeting those needs, few sports were more physically and mentally demanding than professional bike racing. In those days before effective helmets, nearly every seasoned racer suffered physical injuries. During his career Taylor himself would witness, or know of, more than a dozen riders who died of racing injuries. He would see many more knocked out of racing with debilitating injuries or for more mysterious reasons.

In Griebler's case, there were two likely causes. One was long gaps in and incomplete knowledge of nutrition; Griebler was a penniless new pro rider who had trained relentlessly for years without a full understanding of the nutritional demands of such a lifestyle. As a result, he probably yo-yoed between energy gluts and shortages. Second, given the era and several witnesses who said he had "glassy eyes," drugs likely played a role. Griebler had heard stories of the fame and fortune of riders like Arthur Zimmerman. In his need to provide for his family during those depression years, he had likely punished his body and mind beyond its capacity to cope. He had ridden in the star's shadow and had eventually been crushed under the wheels of his evasive greatness. As bike racers would often say, Griebler had "cracked."

In the days of horse and train travel and before readily available supplements, bike racers often had large gaps in their daily food and beverage needs, resulting in nitrogen imbalances. Water quality also varied drastically from one town to the next, often causing gastrointestinal problems. With little real data with which to work, the first nutritionists basically just winged it. Their first utterance in the late 1880s was for *fewer* fruit and vegetables. Their ignorance is understandable. Few knew about vitamins and enzymes until the 1910s, and vitamin-enriched foods didn't hit grocery shelves until the 1920s. No one had even broken down the carbohydrates, proteins, or fats in foods until the federal government's first director of agriculture began tabulating those figures in the late 1880s. When he did, few people listened to his call for increased fruits and vegetables, preferring instead to mock his findings as "lacking significance."

Even if they had heeded his call, without widespread refrigeration in homes, athletes would have found it difficult to do so regularly. Moreover, most Americans were not yet familiar with the benefit of eating more frequent but lighter meals—an approach that stabilizes nitrogen balance resulting in fewer energy spikes and increased endurance, both crucial for athletes. So people ate infrequently and when they did, it was often in marathon feeding sessions involving fat-rich meals. The era rightfully became known as the "groaning tables" period. In line with this ritual popularized during the Gilded Age, people associated corpulence with "success and well-being." Fittingly, a book named *How to be Plump* flew off the shelves. Dyspepsia and other digestive problems were so common in the 1880s and 1890s that a handful of men became exceedingly wealthy peddling their supposed cures.

Eaten mainly by the middle and upper classes, fresh fruit was considered exotic and expensive. And because 50 to 60 percent of the average person's wages was spent on food, the lower class, and even some middle-class families, often went without these important nutritional staples. During the severe economic downturn of the 1890s, many athletes had to cut back on essentials.

If a rider could afford and manage a proper diet, he would have found it at least as difficult to avoid harmful drugs. When Birdie Munger forecast a bright future for Taylor, he was careful to insert a disclaimer: He must abstain from drugs and alcohol. As a veteran racer, Munger had good reason for adding that clause. Their era was described as a "dope fiend's paradise." Opium was for sale legally at low prices throughout the century. Morphine came into common use during and after the Civil War. And heroin was marketed toward the end of the century as a "safer" substitute for morphine. These opiates and countless pharmaceutical preparations containing them were as freely accessible as aspirin is today. Grocery stores, general stores, and drugstores sold opiates over the counter or by mail without a prescription.

To avoid any stigma attached to being a street "druggie," riders could easily buy any of six hundred "legitimate" medicines laced with opiates— magic potions like Ayer's Cherry Pectoral, Mrs. Winslow's Soothing Syrup, Darby's Carminative, Godfrey's Cordial, McMunn's Elixir of Opium, and Dover's Powder. Opium also found its way into alcohol in the form of a highly addictive concoction called laudanum, or wine of opium, which was popular because it was cheaper than gin or wine and produced a vicious initial kick. Some of these products were marketed as teething syrups for young children, some as soothing syrups, and others for diarrhea, dyspepsia, and dysentery. Cocaine, because of its easy abundance, was also used by cyclists, racehorses, and prizefighters—the most popular cocaine mixtures were called "Physic" and "Eagle Soup," or "fly like an eagle"—as was strychnine and trimethylene. All of these products were addictive and their long-term effects not yet fully understood.

Despite the drugs' addictiveness, this term was seldom used. Addicts continued their daily routines instead of being treated or institutionalized. Riders kept riding, children stayed in school, and workers worked. Newsmen largely kept their editorial mouths shut, giving the epidemic, as some called it, scant attention; they had been strong-armed by manufacturers into signing a "code of silence" forbidding them from writing about the addictiveness of their products. They had their rationale: their biggest advertisers were the cycling industry and the patent medicine men. In the 1890s, sixteen thousand newspapers carried ads for Halls Catarrh Cure alone. And the face of their national ad was a popular professional cyclist named Tom Cooper, "the prettiest rider in the business." The prevalence of the drug habit, warned one reformer in his lonely speech before Congress, "is now startling the whole civilized and uncivilized world."

The exact scope of drug use in the professional peloton was murky, but not because it was uncommon. Considering the strain of the profession— "you have to be a masochist to suffer so much," recalled one wheelman—the problem was surely at least as significant with riders as with the population in general. A caricature in one paper left some clues. It depicted a sweaty, half-crazed cyclist—his body looking skeletal and malnourished—a $1,300 prize dangling in front of his eyes and a deep, dark hole dug in the track ahead, as if waiting for him to fall into the abyss.

Cyclists took opiates and cocaine for the immediate "rush" or, more often than not, as a form of escapism. Since medicinal ingredients were not required to be listed in most states, sometimes users didn't even know they were taking them. In the mid-'90s, racing officials became suspicious when, out of the blue, an elite rider named Jimmy Michaels collapsed on the track. Michaels picked himself up, stared airily into space, remounted, then tore around the track. He was clipping along at a surprisingly fast pace—that is, until someone told him he was going in the wrong direction. Apparently his coach Choppy Warburton—whose riders almost always won and nearly as often died young—had a secret he kept from his rider. Hidden in his shirt pocket, Warburton held a tiny bottle housing his secret formula—probably laudanum or cocaine-cola, "the drink that relieves exhaustion."

Whatever it was, the ICU, bike racing's international governing body, didn't particularly care for it. Figuring he needed a little rehabbing of his own, they eventually suspended Warburton for life, making him perhaps the first casualty in cycling's long war on drugs.

All these factors—when combined with brutal travel schedules and demands from managers, fans, and sponsors—could make riders weak, emaciated, restless, delusional, neurotic, peevish, and apathetic. They resulted in injuries, or in Griebler's case, death.

Certainly, the resulting injuries could be extensive. Reggie McNamara, a well-known six-day racer, clearly deserved his status as a wheelsman legend and the nickname "Iron Man." During his career, in addition to almost daily scrapes and bruises, he crashed fifteen-hundred times, broke his collarbone twenty-seven times, his jaw twice, and his skull once. He also had a hard time hanging on to his teeth. At more than one race, he crashed violently, passed out, eventually woke up, plucked several of his teeth out of the track's wooden slats, handed them to his trainer-dentist, then returned to riding. McNamara knew he was cut out for the rough-and-tumble world of bike racing at an early age. After his finger had been bitten by a snake when he was nine, his brother suggested that they cut it off just in case it had been poisoned. "All right," he deadpanned, as if someone just asked him if he wanted his fingernails clipped, "chop it off." And off it went! "Now you won't die," his ten-year-old brother blurted right before receiving the thrashing of his life from their parents.

While McNamara somehow rode on, others were not so fortunate. Before a sold-out crowd at the Cleveland Track, a rider named Harry Hovan became a human projectile, flying over the track rail before coming to a flesh-tearing halt. When they finally plucked his hapless form from the crowd, he had a broken leg, a broken jaw, four cracked ribs, a fractured wrist, a broken arm, and a concussion. "Other than that," remarked one hardened rider, "he was just fine."

Being a hardened tough guy like McNamara and Hovan was a byproduct of the era and the vocation, and professional cyclists took this ethos seriously. The first crude helmets—nothing more than pillbox-peaked cloth caps or colorized pith helmets—emanated from the hellish facial blood-lettings inherent during the high-wheel period. These helmets were better than nothing, but usually accomplished little more than to soak up whatever blood resulted after one of those infamous high-wheelers took a "header."

Helmets improved little once the "safety" bike arrived—leather rings around riders' foreheads and thick, woolen pads that crossed the top of their heads—yet few cyclists dared to be seen wearing one. After all, the public viewed cyclists in the same vein as matadors. A rider didn't dare show signs of weakness or dearth of bravado for fear of his rivals swooping in for the kill. When one rider was asked about helmets, he responded as any strapping matador would. "Only the clumsy get themselves killed," he boasted. Soon after, he did just that, cracking his helmet-less skull on a concrete track. He would not be the only one. Forty-seven cyclists were killed on bicycle tracks in the early decades of the sport.

Since the first bicycle race took place two years after the first Kentucky Derby, wheelmen borrowed some of the same tactics, language, and even the same tracks as horsemen. And like horse racing, due to the high speeds involved, the sport of bike-track racing was dangerous enough without the riders making it even more so. But some did just that. Elbowing is evident in old photos that show riders dipping their heads toward their handlebars, trying to avoid another elbow blow to their faces or bodies.

In races involving multiple riders, the borrowed horseracing tactic of "pocketing" was often employed to "smoke out" the race favorite. An example of this scheme would find the race favorite trapped behind one rider while a second man rode up on the outside and pinned him in a box. For further effect, a third man would ride up from the back tightening the pocket all the more. A fourth man would then come streaking from the back, slipping by the boxed group and in for the money. While perhaps unfair, this tactic was not then illegal. When race favorites began adjusting to the tactics, the offending jockeys would occasionally pay a third-class rider—usually someone who had no chance of winning—to "dump" the competition. As the number one target of these tactics during his career, Taylor had to be vastly superior to his competitors to overcome them.

Some of the most horrific spills were the mass pileups. During one six-day race at the Mutual Street Indoor Arena in Toronto, Reggie McNamara and Charlie Winter were in the final sprint for the finish. The two men were in the lead riding side by side when suddenly their handlebars jammed, meshing them together like two deer locking horns. As though they were piloting what looked like a sideways bicycle built for two, they veered together toward the rail, then sailed in unison up the steep bank and over the fence, sending them to the hospital with serious wounds. But the real horror took place behind them. In their wake, their accident triggered an avalanche of carnage, with bodies and twisted steel strewn all over the track. In tending to the riders, track doctors disposed of two hundred yards of adhesive tape, ten gallons of witch hazel, five gallons of olive oil, and three dozen bottles of iodine and petrogen.

Perhaps the most bizarre pileup came at an indoor race before a packed house in Montreal. While a full field of riders circled the track at top speed, the lights in the arena suddenly went out. For the first time all day, the crowd went completely silent. The only noise permeating the smoky auditorium was first the Doppler drone of the racers' tires, followed by the clanging of metal on metal, wooden fences snapping, bones breaking, and the distinctive echo of men discharging their agony through a series of earsplitting profanities. After gathering their senses, people noticed something unusual about the black out. It had lasted exactly one minute. The lights had flickered on sixty seconds later, revealing thousands of horrified fans as well as a mangled pile of wheels, frames, and broken bodies. The only man left intact was Peter Van Kempen, a rider who somehow found his way to the top rail, which he clung to for dear life. It turns out it was Thomas Edison Day. And in those days before widespread electricity and communications, instead of honoring this invention by flying a flag or scheduling a national holiday, unbeknownst to racing officials, the power was shut off in the city for exactly one minute.

Extreme soreness resulting from overtraining or malnutrition was also a problem. Riders trained for hours every day and usually hurt all over. They habitually had sore necks, knees, hamstrings, rumps, calves, and backs stemming from spills or from riding in a fixed position for long periods. The most painful injuries came from road or track rash—injuries that often knocked them out for days, weeks, or even months. Most riders were battle-hardened men who could easily get over minor scrapes and bruises. "Sometimes," wrote the *Washington Post*, "riders appeared on the track, done up in bandages almost from head to foot."

Nearly every rider left chunks of their hide ensconced in tracks throughout the country. Or, large chunks of the track wound up inside the rider. Flying along at a race in Providence, Rhode Island, a rider named Dan Pisceone was slammed into the boards on the outside railing. While his rim and frame fell to the ground twisting like a pretzel, Pisceone skidded face down on the track, leaving a long, lurid trail of blood behind. One of the wooden slats on the track had loosened and lodged in his abdomen. When he failed to get up, his horrified trainer ran to him, then proceeded to turn over a dead man.

Wherever there were accidents, there were doctors—or those who hung out a shingle to that effect. One man affectionately referred to as "Spills" prowled around the tracks during major races, always ready to comfort a fallen rider. Whenever a racer who looked seriously injured asked if he should go to the hospital, Spills assured the rider he would take good care of him. His methods were decidedly unorthodox, but somehow he kept riders going while orthopedic surgeons would have had them bedside, all trussed up with casts, pulleys, and weights. "Get 'em back on the bikes as quick as you can," Spills often said. "That stops congestion and swelling." Race managers loved him as well. "He'd kid 'em into thinking they aren't hurt, tired or highly strung," raved one manager. "Keep 'em working."

Bike racers were a very tough breed in those days—they had to be. "If you didn't ride," remembered one former rider, "you didn't eat." And there was no such thing as an injured reserve list. Bad strains and fractures of the wrist, collar bone, and ribs were quickly assuaged with yards of tape, laxatives, liver pills, a bottle of Payne's celery tonic, a few quick prayers, and for some, a side of whiskey. Then it was back in the saddle. In fact, the only time "Iron Man" McNamara left his bike was when a "regular" doctor taped his shoulder the "right" way. "If Fred [Spills] had done it," he told a reporter, "I'd been back riding in thirty minutes instead of the six months recommended by the doctor."

Since meaningful insurance was nonexistent at the time, riders either paid for their medical care out of their own pockets or received financial help from sympathetic cycling fans, including famous celebrities. In the 1890s, it was men like Diamond Jim Brady, his actress girlfriend Lillian Russell, and Broadway producer William Brady. In later years, it was two of bike racing's most avid fans, Bing Crosby and Ernest Hemingway. Both men traveled extensively throughout the United States and Europe to see the races. Crosby enjoyed the races so much he often picked up the hospital tab for injured riders, hoping to see them back on the track as soon as possible.

Hemingway helped out as well. He was known to linger all night in his box at the races with his wife Hadley passed out on his lap. "I'll never forget the time I set up operations in a box at the finish line of the six-day bike races to work on the proofs of *A Farewell to Arms*. There was good, inexpensive champagne," he wrote, "and when I got hungry, they sent over Crab Mexicaine from Prunier. I had rewritten the ending thirty-nine times in manuscript and now I worked it over thirty times in proof, trying to get it right. There [at the racetrack], I finally got it right."

In their never-ending quest for more speed, riders occasionally employed pacers to block the wind in front of them. At first the pacers rode tandem bikes, or bicycles built for two. When their speed no longer sufficed, they moved up to quads, sextuplets, even octuplets. Six to eight men on one long, unwieldy bike dashing along at more than forty miles per hour bred the potential for serious carnage. A pace rider on one of these machines had to be strong and absolutely fearless. At one race in Cleveland, a sextuplet clipped along at a record-breaking pace when the front tire buckled under the strain of nearly a half-ton of riders. Choosing the lesser of several evils, the riders simply "abandoned ship," all six of them catapulting into a complicated pile of humanity that even Spills couldn't cure.

When the hell-for-leather pace set by octuplets no longer satisfied America's appetite for speed, a new contraption called the motorcycle entered the scene in the late 1890s. Early motorpace riding (bicycle racers riding behind a speeding motorcycle) was not for the faint of heart. Charles Walthour set twenty-six motorpace world records, but only after enduring twenty-eight fractures of his right collarbone, eighteen of the left, thirty-two broken ribs, and sixty stitches to his face and head. Bike racing, concluded the *Washington Post*, "is the most dangerous sport in the entire catalogue . . . by the side of it, football appears a game fit for juveniles only."

Walthour's brushes with serious injury, even death, had no bounds. Once, according to his family, he was given up for dead after a spill in Paris and abruptly whisked off to the county morgue. There, a man wearing black sepulchral clothing and a shiny silver cross hovered over his remains while reading from the Scriptures. Whatever he said, Walthour apparently didn't care for it. He opened his eyes, got up off the slat, walked out of his premature eulogy, and went on to live another thirty-three years.

George Leander, Walthour's good friend and rival, wasn't so fortunate. In 1903, while zinging along behind motorpace at ninety kilometers per hour, an inexplicable encounter between bicycle and motorcycle occurred. To this day, no one knows exactly how Leander's long frame wound up airborne, hovering some sixteen feet above the track. What is known is that his body belly flopped on the top of the steep wooden track and teetered there for thousands of horrified fans to see before finally rolling back to the center of the track, lifeless. His decidedly dead body wound up in the same morgue where his good friend had decided not to die.

The fate of Harry Elkes and Will Stinson, friends of dead Leander and almost-dead Walthour, capped off the particularly gruesome motorpace year of 1903. At the Charles River Track in Boston, a motorpace driver named E. A. Gateley slowed to pace Stinson while Elkes sped ahead. Tragically Elkes, whose doctor told him "he will someday drop from his wheel a corpse," blew a tire. He then fell off his bike right in front of the motorcycle, causing all hell to break loose on top of him. In addition to bicycle and motorcycle parts strewn everywhere, a horror-stricken crowd of ten thousand people saw Stinson wind up on top of the heap, Gateley in the middle, Elkes on the bottom. From the scrum's apex came a noisy trio of crashing bodies and screaming men. By the time it was all sorted out, Elkes, by then a friend of Taylor's, was hauled to the morgue, his head crushed. The motorpace driver was stammering around the track with an amputated foot. And Stinson lay in a hospital bed suffering from internal injuries and loss of an eye—all while the remaining races continued unabated. Miraculously, from what some believed was his deathbed, Stinson was somehow able to push out a few words. "I want to ride again," said the cycling matador, his remaining eye twitching uncontrollably, "tonight."

Through it all, riders kept riding and people kept attending races—"it is the danger in the sport that makes it thrilling," wrote the *Washington Post*, "and it's the thrilling feature that makes it attractive." In the '90s, thousands would join the pro ranks looking for fame and fortune. And for good reason: the financial rewards for elite riders were substantial. But many riders, clinging to the hope that they would someday be the next Zimmerman, struggled just to meet expenses or afford their next meals. The bigger the sport became, the more it was necessary for a racer to have a good handler and a well-designed program of individual training. But this did not come cheaply. A personal trainer cost between eighteen and thirty dollars a week, plus his expenses and a share of any winnings. Then there was the extensive train travel, cost of hotels, and the huge nutritional intake needed by the riders. And if a racer was a real "flash," he had to factor in the cost of a valet.

But few were so fortunate. Some of the low-level riders took to sleeping on cots at the track or train stations to save on hotel costs. For most riders, this day-to-day grind formed a brutal, hardscrabble existence. In the end, only a small fraction of them became affluent, a few lived well, and the rest—the bulk of the men like "Poor Joe" Griebler—were flat broke. "Let us be content to applaud these few cycle stars," wrote *Bearings*, "because there exist a large number of ciphers who have a hard time to keep body and soul together."

This itinerant way of life strained personal relationships, forcing most riders, including Munger and Zimmerman, to be bachelors, marry later in life, or scatter their passions from one city to the next. For those few riders who had them, it could also be hell on their families. In their private moments together before his tragic racing death, Joseph Griebler shared his darkest fears with his young wife, Delia. But he didn't have to say too much to convince her of the hazards and hardships of his chosen profession. "Poor Joe," touted as another "promising" future Zimmerman, had been away from home and injured enough times to make her dread the next race—or the telegram telling her of another injury.

She may in fact have been the only one who knew of the grim eye injury he had received during a pileup; had he told League officials, he may have had his racing license stripped from him. His doctor had told him he needed to see an eye specialist or face losing all sight in his bum eye. But without meaningful insurance and no money, he continued competing while his eye went uncared for—"going after a few more dollars for the kids," he would often say.

Before boarding a train from Minneapolis to Lima, Ohio, days before that fatal July day, he had just recovered from another injury that had sidelined him for months, bringing him near bankruptcy. He seemed to be too proud to tell anyone of his circumstances besides Delia, the love of his life and the pretty woman whose pictures he showed to everybody he met. "He was doubtless thinking of how the prize money would gladden the hearts of the little ones at home," wrote one reporter after his death.

During his life, Delia was seized with fear, thinking of the moment she and her two infants would be left alone with nothing but memories of his short life and a future wrought with emptiness and poverty. "Well," he had strangely augured as he hugged and kissed her for the last time, "I expect that you will see me brought back dead before two weeks are gone."

At the moment doctors stood sentinel over Joe's dying body under that stand of weeping willow trees and hearing his last grieving words—"I'm awfully sick"—Delia was visiting family and friends in the backyard of a home in Granite Falls. She was rolling a ball to Walter William with one arm, holding Pearl in her other arm, when Joe's mother, who had just buried another son in a similar tragedy, handed her the telegram: *Joe Griebler is dead, killed in a race in Lima, Ohio. You notify his wife.*

None of Joe's extraordinary premonitions could have adequately prepared her for that frightful message. His coffin soon arrived, along with the two tiny pair of shoes that he had carefully picked out—probably his only material possessions that passed on through the years. While her kids continued to play on in the lazy summer sun, oblivious to it all, Delia stood there speechless, rivulets of sweat and tears dripping down her face. Described as being on the brink of collapse and possibly suicidal, Delia likely heard Joe's recent words ring in her head. "If I don't get killed before the season closes," he had confided, "I am going to quit."

Sometime in the early 1900s, a man took his daily ride around the grounds of his school, the Munich University in Germany, atop a fat-tired bicycle. As the sun dropped below the horizon, he reached down and flipped on the headlamp. On those regular evening rides, he began observing a few important things that would eventually change the world. One was that the bobbing beam cast from his headlamp always traveled at the same speed whether he was cruising at a quick pace or coasting to a stop. A theory—that light from a moving source has the same speed as light from a stationary source—was born on those rides. The man, perhaps the greatest genius who ever lived, was Albert Einstein; his discovery, Einstein's theory of relativity, laid the foundation for an explosion of scientific theory.

As significant and well-known as that discovery was to the world, Einstein's other discoveries were as important to him personally as any of his later inventions. There were two items that he—and more than one billion people since—noticed about the bicycle while riding. The first was how it made him feel—the sensations of youth, how freely discovery came to him, the intoxicating adrenaline rush.

Einstein's second discovery was that, despite its apparent simplicity, the bicycle itself was nothing short of a scientific, mechanical, and technological wonder. In the nearly two hundred years since the first crude velocipede was wheeled out of an anonymous shed somewhere in Europe, man had yet to duplicate its efficiency. "The machine appears uncomplicated but the theories governing its motion are nightmarish," explained bicycle physicist Chester Kyle. "Some things can't be easily defined by physics and mathematics. The interactions of the body, mind, muscles, terrain, gravity, air, and bicycle are so complex that they defy exact mathematical solutions. The feel and handling of a bike borders on art," Kyle continued. "Like the violin, it's been largely designed by touch, inspiration, and experimentation." The bicycle is indeed a remarkable feet of engineering. It can carry ten times its own weight and uses energy more efficiently than a soaring eagle. Yet a six-year-old child can master its mechanics.

In those early years, even hardened pros with thousands of miles on their machines still harbored fresh memories of their first childhood rides down their neighborhood roads. Before the bicycle, children experienced similar emotions when they were first hoisted atop the family horse. But the horse had a mind of its own and a large stomach to feed. The bicycle was under their control, free from the bucking, kicking, and neighing they had become accustomed to. Despite the many machines professional cyclists burned out over their careers, fond memories of each one clung to them like old friends throughout their lives. "No sport," remembered one pro rider, "has a greater connection between man and machine than bike racing."

Major Taylor, Arthur Zimmerman, and Birdie Munger had become bewitched by the world of bike track racing, a sport that could chew men up and spit them out. When man and bicycle whirled over the finish line with thousands cheering him on, his mind and body became overwhelmed with a sense of liberation and supreme personal empowerment. "Hearing that bell on the last lap," explained one rider, "is a lot like being on some powerful drug . . ."

Riders who struggled to describe the emotions in their own words deferred to those of Arthur Conan Doyle, author of the Sherlock Holmes' stories. "When the spirits are low," he wrote at the bottom of the '90s depression, "when the day appears dark, when work becomes monotonous, when hope hardly seems worth having, just mount a bicycle and go out for a spin down the road, *without thought on anything but the ride you are taking.*"

On an August day in 1890, a crowd had filled the new horsetrack at Monmouth Park in New Jersey. People peered down in awe as a regal chestnut named Salvator blazed down the track. At the tape, timekeepers glanced at their watches. As with bike-track racing, slashing a horse-racing record by one second raises eyebrows. Salvator had destroyed not only the American record but also the world record by four full seconds, finishing the mile in 1:35.5.*

At a different track, a few years after Salvator's record, another man would throw his legs over his steed and charge out of the gate, breaking Salvator's record. Only this time he would be piloting a steel steed. Decades worth of technological advances and improved conditioning would finally resolve the issue of speed in favor of the bicycle over the horse.

For a few decades before and after the turn of the century, bike racers were the men of the hour. The eyes of the nation's press and sporting public were fixed on them. Gracefully riding high atop their saddles, with their lungs wide open and hearts thumping, Taylor, Zimmerman, and the rest of the peloton sped full steam ahead. Their magical moment was upon them. They were Arthur Doyle's men, *"without thought on anything but the ride they were taking."*

---

* Salvator's one-mile record stood for more than twenty-eight years before it was finally eclipsed by another horse named Roamer. Much like bike-racing records, it is difficult to compare the records of horses from different eras because of the varying track conditions. Salvator's record—and the wheelman's—were achieved on a straight track, which some historians believe is faster than an oval.

Chapter 5

UTOPIA

If a man manufactured bicycles in 1895, had blindfolds placed over his eyes, and was spun in circles until disoriented, an unexplainable energy field would have tossed him on a train, then dropped him off somewhere in New England. If a black man was employed by a bicycle manufacturer in 1895, had grandiose dreams of racing bicycles as a professional, and was searching for a safer place to live, that energy field would have placed him on the same train.

The gravitational pull that drove Birdie Munger and Major Taylor to Worcester, Massachusetts, that year had already attracted more than two hundred bike manufacturers to the greater New England region. From these industrial masses came every conceivable type and size of bike maker. On one end of the spectrum stood the Irish and European emigrants recently disgorged from the steerage section of myriad ships, working in small groups from cramped work sheds, copies of Horatio Alger's book by their sides.

The opposite end of the spectrum produced giants like the Pope Manufacturing Company, the largest employer in all of New England. Its founder, Colonel Albert A. Pope, was a colossal figure, with a Burl Ives beard, a bone-crushing handshake, and an insatiable appetite for good food, great wine, and even greater women. Following his exemplar service as a captain in the Civil War, Pope took such a liking to the title of colonel, he went ahead and promoted himself. Having witnessed all the blood, guts, and dead-horse stench one man could possibly endure, Pope had decided he never wanted to see or smell despair again. But when he moved to Boston in 1876, it was during an unsightly equine epizootic, "giving the air," recalled one historian, "a rich equine flavor." Soon to become the man most responsible for the decline of the horse, he evidently didn't much like the stench and set out to do something about it.

Only a few short years after barnstorming into Boston, Colonel Pope became the undisputed king of the bicycle world. When he wasn't lavishly entertaining at his fifty-acre Cohasset estate on Boston's South Shore, he shuttled via private railcar between his plush four-fireplace Hartford penthouse office and his even plusher Boston office. From the assembly lines of his six-story factory buildings snaking over endless city blocks, more than one million "Columbia" bicycles—some six hundred a day—would roll onto the streets.

Known as a pioneer in labor relations, Pope had 3,800 sales agents positioned all over the world. And his machines were found everywhere; after President McKinley's assassination in 1901, Teddy Roosevelt—the first president to ride in an automobile—was escorted in a *Pope* automobile, flanked by argus-eyed secret servicemen on *Pope* bicycles.

Pope, a high school dropout, virtually owned the press. He glossed the pages of nearly every paper in America with glitzy ads, hauled in their best scribes via private railcar for tours of his elaborate headquarters, and then dazzled them with his latest models, finest food, and best wine.

He was also the father of the League of American Wheelmen and the 1880 "good roads movement," the lobby group that began paving America from coast to coast decades before the widespread use of automobiles. From his cavernous factory interior, the first assembly lines were employed. During his reported visits, Henry Ford would have seen the first use of electric welding, cold-drawn steel, case-hardening, pneumatic tires, brakes, refined ball bearings, and hollow metal rims. Ford must have taken mental notes as the Columbia bicycles, made up of eight hundred separate parts, were inspected five hundred times by twenty-four quality control inspectors. "If the Carnegies and Rockefellers were the captains of industry," wrote Pope's biographer Stephan Goddard, "Pope would rank as second lieutenant."

Between the small underfunded emigrant shops and the mammoth Pope Manufacturing Company stood the Worcester Cycle Manufacturing Company, run by Birdie Munger and his bear-faced partner, Charles Boyd.

With his recognizable name and experience in the business world, Munger found raising capital easier than most, and he and his partner did just that. They bought loads of expensive machinery, leased seven acres of prime Worcester land from the largest trust in the country, and lined it with spacious factory buildings. There they churned out six models of bicycles with names like The Boyd and the $100 Lady Worcester.

They added another factory in Middletown, Connecticut, where the sleek $125 Birdie Specials were built. Following Pope's lead, they placed large ads in several papers aggressively touting The Mechanical Wonders of the World, and even opened a "general office" on prestigious 45 Wall Street. "These models bear out all that was promised of them," raved a *New York Times* reporter.

Munger's plants were a beehive of activity as the demand for bicycles, especially women's models, at times exceeded supply. Hundreds of blue-shirted craftsmen standing in knee-length stockings toiled amid a riot of belts, pulleys, whirring wheels, and grinding machines. In separate rooms were men who specialized in forging, brazing, buffing, polishing, nickel plating, and case hardening. Demand for bicycles was so high, manufacturers like Pope, and probably Munger, had to make extensive use of outsiders. Watch factories made cyclometers, knit-kneading factories made spokes, and rubber hose factories made tires.

With all the activity, Munger had no problem keeping Taylor busy. He had him working as a machinist, accompanying him to bicycle trade shows, and shuffling between Worcester and Middletown as messenger of important company documents. In his duties as a machinist, Taylor was said to be twice as productive as many of his peers, earning him the nickname "Speed Boy." As a messenger of valuable documents and possible handler of company money, he had also gained his employer's confidence.

But inside those factory walls where the entrails of myriad bicycles were splayed out around him, Taylor's mind occasionally drifted as it had in Indianapolis. The itchy feet he'd had since his youth still radiated from him, gnawing at him, making him feel like a caged lion. It is hard to imagine Major Taylor, given the talent he had already shown, plugging away in a noisy factory, grinding down metal tubes and assembling parts, and not believe that valuable time was being frittered away.

For a short time, he lived with Munger and Munger's new wife, Harriet, at a Bay State house, probably eating hearty home-cooked meals. At some point, he moved out on his own, sharing a tiny flat at 13 Parker Street with a friend named Ben Walker. Whenever he had a spare moment, he'd pore over his options; there was always the grease and the sweat and the dollar-a-day manual labor inherent in building bicycles. And then there was the challenge, the potential riches, and the notoriety of racing them. On its surface, it seems like it would have been a simple decision. But he was a black man living away from his family in a strange city. And as much as he wanted to race, the fearful memories of the treatment he'd received in Indianapolis had never left his mind. He had already been scarred, and at times, he would say later, he even considered quitting racing. Furthermore, he was no longer in the midsized pond that was Indianapolis. He was living in the East, seat of racing's influential governing body and home to most of the nation's top riders. The competition would be much stiffer than anything he had ever experienced.

Shortly after the doors at the Worcester Cycle Manufacturing Company flung open, the firm received a valuable publicity boost. From his office on Wall and Broad, Munger sat down to a cup of coffee, gazing out at the financial district as the Dow reached 45 and Colonel Pope's stock, recently at $5, rose to $75. He nearly spilled his coffee as he read a letter crossing the wire from Deming, New Mexico. A rider named A. B. Simons had set world records for the one-quarter and one-third mile sprint while riding his Birdie Special. Like winning a stage of the Tour de France today, setting world records was good for business in the 1890s. Simons was elated. "The Birdie Special is the fastest wheel made," he beamed through a cross-country wire. Simons's records, proclaimed the *New York Times*, "set people talking about the Birdie Special, the wheel on which the record was made."

Surely Munger slipped Simons's memo into Taylor's envious hands. And Taylor surely read it and began dreaming big dreams again. He immediately joined the Albion Cycling Club, an all-black local racing team, and started training at every opportunity. He had some honing to do. He had turned seventeen in November 1895, but his body had yet to fill out beyond its slight, jockey-like stature; his skin and muscles still had the soft, pillowy look of youth. From years of bike riding, Taylor had developed decent leg muscles, but his lesser-used upper body lacked girth. In long-distance endurance races, not wanting extra weight of any kind, cyclists often had muscular imbalances. But Taylor's real interest was in short-distance track racing, a sport in which brute force is essential and a heavier all-around build is warranted. Knowing this, Taylor had tried developing his muscles at the Indianapolis YMCA, but had been thwarted by its rules against blacks.

So after noticing a YMCA in Worcester, he and Munger decided to test the racial waters one autumn day shortly after arriving in town. At the time, only one percent of the town's population of 100,000 was African American, and neither he nor Munger knew exactly what to expect.

Because he had already pondered giving up racing, the day they walked into the Worcester Y may have been among the most important in Taylor's life as well as in the hierarchy of African American sports history. When they entered, they were greeted by a gracious man named Edward Wilder, the Y's athletic director. Wilder sat them down and listened as they spelled out Taylor's wants and needs. Paying no attention to Taylor's color, Wilder then devised an intensive training routine consisting of light dumbbells, Indian clubs—two ten-pound wooden baseball bat–like objects used for strength training—and the use of a Whitley exerciser, a pulley and cable device he could use at the Y, on the road, and at home. Wilder also introduced him to deep-breathing exercises, probably something akin to modern yoga—a routine Taylor would use during his career.

From that day forward, partially for his sport and partially perhaps as a form of affirming payback for Wilder's compassion, Taylor followed his instruction to the letter, taking great pride in his physique and overall appearance. It would become the physical foundation from which he would build his incredible power and stamina in the years to come. The absence of racial tension at the Y, the freedom to finally develop like his rivals, and the extraordinary sensation of social equality meant the world to him. "I was pleased beyond expression," he later gushed. It was such an emotional event he remembered it vividly when he sat down to write his memoirs three decades later. "I wish to pay my respects at this time to Mr. Edward W. Wilder . . ." he wrote. "I am firmly convinced that I shortly would have dropped riding . . . were it not for the cordial manner in which the people [Wilder and others in Worcester] received me." That a stranger would spend time with, and care about, a reedy little black kid who had just arrived in town inspired and motivated him. It was time, he and Munger believed, to feed off his motivation, to stick his toe into the local amateur scene.

A spring sun hovered in the Massachusetts sky as Taylor strolled out of the Worcester YMCA early in 1896. At Wilder's and Munger's urging, he had trained diligently throughout the winter, including during his travels between factories and trade shows. Munger had watched with keen interest as his protégé morphed from a thin-as-a-rake sixteen-year-old, into a slightly less thin-as-a-rake seventeen-and-a-half-year-old. With the biggest local amateur event of the season, the *Worcester Telegram* Race, scheduled for May, Munger, surely aware of the publicity value in a good showing, laid out a stiff riding program to supplement Wilder's routine.

Reconnoitering the race route—a strategy well ahead of its time—Taylor repeatedly rode every inch of the route for weeks in advance. Munger also took him to the now-famous George Street hill climb for hard-core training. While not a lengthy hill, George Street is a veritable goat path that tilts upward at a lung-piercing incline of nearly 20 percent, making it excellent training grounds. Today, even with twenty-speed carbon fiber bikes, thinner tires, and a well-surfaced road, it's a horrendous ascent. But in 1896, riding up its unpaved outer banks on a single-speed track bicycle was a quad-busting, heart-pounding affair. For years, hubristic locals had gathered at its imposing base with every intention of making it to the peak, only to wind up in oxygen debt halfway up its precipice.

When word spread that the black kid from Indianapolis was about to try his luck on the harrowing climb, a crowd gathered on both sides of the street, eager to watch the inevitable suffering and eventual capitulation. Probably snickering into the collar of his light spring coat, Munger held his watch as Taylor tore up the brutal climb with comparative ease. Taylor then amazed the locals by repeating his conquest seemingly at will. The hill apparently became part of his treacherous all-around training routine and to this day, locals challenge themselves at the annual Major Taylor George Street climb. "Everyone who knew him," remembered elder Worcester resident Francis Jesse Owens, "knew he was about the only guy who put a bike up the George Street hill and he did that before they blacktopped it."

After months of intensive conditioning, Munger, with Wilder's help, believed Taylor was ready to test the local racing scene. Having seen the silver *Telegram* trophy shining through the window of a local business, Taylor agreed. Collectively, all they could do was hope that the vote against a whites-only racing world by the Massachusetts delegates a few years earlier suggested a more racially open society.

The ten-mile *Worcester Telegram* race held on May 9, 1896, was for Taylor the greatest example yet of the wild popularity bike racing enjoyed in

America. Though it was just an amateur race with no national significance, it was the biggest local race of the season and fans showed up in droves. In the days leading up to it, operators at the Kyle & Woodbury telephone service heard talk of almost nothing but the race. On race day, the trolley car management team was completely overwhelmed. All day long, their cars were loaded down to the gunwales, every inch jammed with bodies hanging over the sides. Overanxious fans jumped out of windows—or climbed over the motormen's shoulders—and tumbled onto streets, some forgetting to pay.

Block after block of horse carriages lined both sides of the street, competing for space with thousands of bicycles and the crush of people. One unfortunate reporter, given the thankless job of counting bicycles, finally gave up after reaching 4,200. High-society gents rolled into town in their elegant Brougham or Ivory Surrey carriages, arguing over gear ratios, the best racing models, and who they believed to be the best rider. After thoughtful technical analysis, they tracked down the nearest bookmaker and placed their money on the most logical rider. Their wives, according to one reporter, had a simpler and perhaps more accurate means of picking the winner—"The rider with the prettiest colors," of course.

By race time, the town's business district was a virtual ghost town. All told, fifty thousand people—more than had ever turned out for a daytime event in Worcester's long history—lined the race route. "Everybody was there," wrote one scribe, "except the men in the accident ward of the county hospital." Eighty riders competing on ten different teams threw off their sweaters at the start.

Taylor was there, standing inconspicuously alongside his Albion teammates. A ring of reporters stood around looking indifferently at him and his team of black riders. They jotted down a few notes about him, unknowingly the first of hundreds they would write in coming years, and walked away. Perched in the trees above him, Taylor saw flocks of boys and girls as thick as birds. One of Taylor's heroes, Willie Windle, whom he had met in Indianapolis as an impressionable fourteen-year-old, came to watch the race.

After several unsuccessful attempts, the starter squeezed the gun and the riders piled on the course. Because of the tight thicket of riders, Taylor, according to one report, was repeatedly bashed by another rider. Though he was on a weaker team with a few out-of-condition riders, Taylor stayed with the leaders, seesawing back and forth between second and sixth place.

Once he and the rest of the peloton had pushed out of sight, the crowd hovered around a gold-trimmed race bulletin board that was updated every few minutes—or as fast as the phone operators could take down notes. Those who were unable to attend the race jammed phone lines with one subject on their mind. "Any news from the race?" "Who's winning the race?" "Who won?" "How did the clubs show in the race?" Toward the end, Taylor's teammates faded. One rider, believed to be hopped up on drugs, fell three times. Taylor was able to stay with most front-runners, but ahead of him, a rider named James Casey of the well-trained Vernon team had built an insurmountable lead. Lacking a strong team to pace him, Taylor rallied in vain to catch Casey, his grit carrying him to a respectable sixth place.

Though he hadn't won, it was an important day for Taylor and Munger. While the newsmen with their front-page coverage couldn't get enough of the bike race, they were surprisingly silent on the other race—the usually volatile issue of blacks competing opposite whites. In their coverage, which included a few mentions of Taylor, the word "black" hardly came up. New England, with its abolitionist history, was proving to be more than just a haven for bicycle manufacturing. For the time being at least, Taylor had found his personal utopia. "I was in Worcester only a very short time," he later beamed, "before I realized that there was no such race prejudice existing among the bicycle riders there as I had experienced in Indianapolis. When I realized I would have a fair chance to compete against them in races, I took on a new lease of life."

Taylor spread his new life-lease around the Eastern amateur racing scene. From Worcester, he trained to New Jersey to compete in the popular twenty-five-mile Irvington-Millburn race, or Derby of the East. It was a gamble on his part; the race had a history of racial strife. In the preceding years, a black rider named Simmons had been tossed in and out of the race like a hot potato. The race organizers had fought bitterly among themselves and with local cycling teams over whether to allow Simmons, or any blacks, into their decade-old event. Endless meetings in front of packed houses were held, but they had difficulty reaching a consensus. Some men got fired over the flack, several threatened to leave, and others actually left.

Taylor somehow snuck in among the 153 white riders without incident. Escaping his notice among the crowd of twenty thousand, the Great Arthur Zimmerman attended, watching Taylor's progression with keen interest. Fortunately, Taylor had lively legs that day. He found himself in a vicious head-to-head dual with Monte Scott, the race leader, and one of the best amateur road racers in the East. Everything went well until the last half mile when someone materialized, seemingly from nowhere, with a large pail of ice water. He dumped it in Taylor's face. Temporarily startled, Taylor lost Scott's wheel and his wide draft, finishing twenty-third. With his focus shifting to track racing, it would be one of the last road races in which Taylor competed.

His amateur days rolled on. At a one-mile open track meet in New Haven, Connecticut, Taylor took first place and a shiny gold watch, which he promptly gave to Munger in appreciation, he said, "for some of the many kindnesses he had extended to me." In Meridian, Connecticut, he took second place, earning a beautiful dinner set, which he packaged and sent to his mother for her birthday.

Shortly after the Connecticut races, Munger and Taylor received an invitation to a special event in Indianapolis. They wasted no time packing their bags. The former high-wheel racer and his black protégé were coming back, and they had something to prove.

The train carrying Major Taylor and Birdie Munger clattered into Indianapolis in August of 1896. George Catterson, the real estate mogul who had sponsored the muddy Indianapolis-Matthews road race that Taylor had won, had recently opened a velodrome called the Capital City Racetrack. The fifteen thousand–person track, erected on Catterson's land near today's Indianapolis 500, was large and modern enough to attract big names. At its grand opening a professional rider named Walter Sanger had set the one-mile track record, charging around the surprisingly slow track in 2:19 2/5. Sanger wasn't in the same league as American heavyweight Eddie Bald, soon to be named 1896 American sprint champion, or Tom Cooper, Bald's chief rival, but he was a seasoned pro.

Munger knew Taylor had improved rapidly, placing top ten in nearly every one of his amateur races, but he wasn't sure if he was ready to go up against a professional. He was dying to find out. Unfortunately, either because of Taylor's color or his amateur status, Munger wouldn't get to see Taylor compete against Sanger, the doyen of the peloton. But Catterson, a kindly man who had been friendly to Taylor in years past, did allow him to use the track for an unofficial race against time. After the treatment he'd received in Indianapolis, including being barred from some of their tracks, Taylor wanted to show his hometown fans how much he had progressed.

He would get his chance.

A curious crowd arrived to see if the native lad could come anywhere near the speed of Sanger, the wily veteran. It would take them just 2:11 to find out. Munger stood on the track apron watching Taylor's body flatten out, his pace building, his Birdie Special humming over the track. Munger, and several other clockers, held a watch by his side, the seconds ticking off in his hand. At the half-mile marker, Munger knew something special was happening. Taylor was on a tear! In over a decade spent around countless cyclists, Munger had never seen a seventeen-year-old display that kind of speed on a slow track. Not in an open race, not in an exhibition.

Taylor kept steamrolling ahead, quicker and quicker, flying over huge swaths of track. Taylor careened around the oval for the third and final lap before ripping into the homestretch. There was a remarkable grace to his form, not unlike a manta ray slicing through the ocean floor. When the teenager, still three months shy of eighteen, passed under the one-mile marker, Munger looked down at his hand in disbelief. At the slow Capital City track, Taylor had worked a mile in 2:11!

It was an unofficial record on a new track, but he had trounced Sanger's mark by eight-plus seconds. The crowd couldn't fathom what they were seeing.

This extraordinary performance was no fluke. Later that evening, buoyed by his success and the animated crowd, Taylor made a run at the one-fifth-mile track record. Flanked by a few pacesetting friends, he powered around the track with everything he had left. At the finish line, the timekeepers clicked their watches and looked up in stunned silence again: he had lowered the record by two-fifths of a second.

On hearing the news from the race announcer, the crowd let out a roar. The white riders milling about in the locker room made a beeline for the track to see what all the commotion was about. Just then, Taylor walked past an earful of racial slurs and outright threats of violence if he dare show his black face at the track again. Though he hadn't even raced opposite a white rider, they also cussed out race director Catterson for allowing a black man on the track.

Old wounds had been reopened, but Taylor had his track records, though unofficial. He clopped off to Indy's Union Station, reliving memories of his youth and anguishing over the harsh realities of his coming adulthood. With mixed emotions, he and Munger boarded a red-eye train pointed toward Worcester. In a move of curious prescience, Taylor placed another newspaper article describing his achievements in his growing scrapbook, as though he knew where his life was headed. Stretching out in his wide berth, Munger could peer over at his protégé and smile.

But back at Munger's factory headquarters, the bicycling industry was beginning to shake at its core. In the coming days, he and his promising black prodigy would have tough decisions to make.

The bicycle manufacturing world tilted on its axis in 1896, less than a year after Munger had opened his New England factories. At Colonel Pope's "fireproof" Boston headquarters one chilly day, William Ashton, Pope's head janitor, walked over to a fifth-story windowsill and saw smoke rising. Six stories beneath him, down in the bowels of the basement, wood crates near the boiler had somehow ignited. For the next few hours, a fiery chain reaction took place, treating Bostonians to a spectacular pyrotechnic display the likes of which they hadn't seen since the Great Fire of '72. What began as a tiny spark became a flame, percolated, rolled up through the woodpile, morphed, took a right turn out of the boiler room, licked at the backs of retreating mechanics, then jetted straight for the stairwell.

Startled, janitor Ashton stormed past bloomer-clad Back Bay ladies taking lessons in the fifth-floor riding academy, then began a death-defying descent down the steps, smoke piercing his lungs. The blaze continued up the elevator wells and stairwells, ripped through the pine-wood ceiling of the first few floors, taking out 1,700 bicycles and 20,000 pieces of machinery in its destructive wake. Thirty-five terrified employees working overtime scattered in all directions, some smashing windows, others stampeding toward stairs in hopes of beating the inferno to the exits, their bloomers crackling down the steps. In the hallway, a black-suited elevator conductor stood doggedly at his post like a loyal captain on a sinking ship.

Then, on the fourth floor, the inexorable force of angry red flames met the highly flammable tire room filled with five thousand tires as well as the grease-filled ball bearing room. The advancing flame won. In the middle of it all, an electric power plant sang out a booming chorus heard throughout Boston. Meanwhile, thousands of lights popped under the heat, shooting beams of light like lightning bolts in all directions. Outside, walls of snarling flames melted the elaborate terra-cotta trimming and, because no one had turned off the power, a thicket of downed power lines danced on the sodden streets, zapping onlookers below.

Within a half hour, the one-alarm fire became two, three, four, and then a full-scale, citywide general alarm. Nearly every fireman in town circled the place, hooking up hoses, setting up ladders, and dousing the building in water, one fireman snapping his leg in the confusion. Like sweating bodies trying to cool themselves, hotel buildings across the street began smoking from the scorching heat. Panicked guests scalded their hands when they touched their windows.

Meanwhile, Ashton clawed his way to the second floor before succumbing to smoke inhalation. Somehow, he slid into the second-floor sanctum of Pope's personal secretary, R. W. Winkley, where the two of them, half delirious, were helped down a ladder by Boston's finest.

The mammoth conflagration shuddered along in an unbridled push toward total annihilation. It crackled up to the fifth and final floor, taking out the riding academy and all freshly used bicycles, their rubber tires and leather saddles vaporized, steel wheels still gyrating in eerie suspense. Finally, it made a beeline for Pope's sacred penthouse suite filled with reams of Civil War memorabilia, priceless oil paintings, and a vast library of *Wheelmen* and various other cycling periodicals. Like the Great Fire of London, it hovered there, lapping and licking its blistering, one-thousand-degree flames at decades of colorful volumes of American literature and rare artifacts.

At 11:30 p.m., the all-out siren finally sounded. Miraculously, no one died in the fire—it could have been a mini-holocaust. In the weeks before the fire, as many as six thousand people a day had attended banner exhibitions inside its doors—but within eight hours the massive "fireproof" factory was no more. POPE BICYCLE BUILDING IN RUINS, headlined the next morning's *Boston Post*.

The colonel, who was in Manhattan designing a nationwide swath of bicycle ads, received a pithy telegram from his round-faced, playboy son: Burned to the Ground. Wire Instructions. Only partially insured and fully angry, Pope sped home. Arriving in Boston, the bicycle giant stood under the smoldering hulk of his former headquarters, picking through the skeletal remains—scorched bicycles with icicles dangling from them, charred machinery, unrecognizable furnishings. Losing his precious, fortune-building bicycles was bad enough, but losing his Civil War memorabilia clearly irked the bicycle magnate.

His anger had actually surfaced a few months before, but the fire really heated him up. Many of the small manufacturers and some midsized firms had been hawking bikes at prices that didn't fit into his business model, and he didn't much like it. "Colonel Pope," warned one reporter, "is tired of the small dealers and makers." He had talked a handful of them into folding their firms into his, but many refused.

However, after the fire, all bets seemed to be off. Knowing he wielded enough power to move markets, Pope issued a dictum that would achieve just that. Much like the auto industry in the early 1900s, he and his larger manufacturing friends like A. G. Spaulding and A. H. Overman began slashing prices from $100 down to $75. Their competition-pruning strategy sent shock waves throughout the industry. And it worked. Almost overnight, scores of small, lightly funded shops, which had survived by offering bikes cheaper than his Columbias, went out of business. A few midsized firms survived.

Others shivered in their expensive factory offices.

Thirty-eight miles to the west, in Worcester, Birdie Munger must have read the news and blanched. Niche models like his Birdie Special could command higher prices, but the big sellers like the family-oriented Boyd and the Lady Worcester could not. Before long, he placed the first of several pay-cut notices on his factory bulletin board. Hundreds of employees were suddenly faced with a wrenching dilemma. They could accept a pay cut—an unappealing alternative considering many were earning only a dollar a day to begin with. They could take their noble bike-making skills and try rapping on other employers' doors in the depths of America's financial crisis. Or they could train like mad six or seven days a week, muddle through the amateur leagues, qualify for a professional racing license, and throw in their hats with thousands of starry-eyed wannabe Zimmermans.

If he hadn't already, surely Taylor began reading the tea leaves when those first notices arrived. In the fall of 1896, he turned eighteen. As a young man living far away from his family, he had taken comfort inside his good friend's factory walls. But he must have feared giants like Pope pushing midsized bike makers like Munger's over the brink, leaving him out on the streets or back at the dreaded farm.

If not a machinist, he could always be a racer. But unlike the hundreds of bike-builders-turned-racers about to join more than a thousand existing pros, Taylor, if he chose that route, faced an added challenge that would pale in comparison to all others. He was, after all, black, while almost all of them were white. This fact became an even greater defiance when the

U.S. Supreme Court codified race segregation with the landmark *Plessey v. Ferguson* case that same year. From a race relations standpoint, with the nebulous new doctrine of "separate but equal," the nation, according to many, was regressing.

In this increasingly hostile environment, there was no guarantee Taylor would be granted a professional license, no matter how prodigious his talents appeared to be. Even if he were able to turn pro, would he be guaranteed access to every track, including those in important Southern states? The odds could not have been more against him in the difficult days that lay ahead.

As evening neared one fall day in 1896, Taylor could peer out his factory window and watch flaky, black soot rise from the chimney stacks. He felt a sense of unease in the metallic whir of Munger's factory floors. So did the hundreds of blue-shirted workers engaging in their specialties—wheel assembly, framing, enameling, and brazing. Outside, the public lamplighter, all dressed in black, raised a long pole to the streetlights, igniting them with the spark generated from the pole's tip.

Somewhere along the line, perhaps from Munger's many contacts in the industry, Taylor was given the names and numbers of a few men who could, they believed, help him turn professional. Taylor sauntered into Munger's office, walked by the pay-cut notices hanging on the wall, and picked up a phone, an old rectangular oak box with a crank handle on the side. He rotated the handle one full turn. At Kyle & Woodbury's central office, a switchboard operator would have picked up the line and asked to whom he wished to be connected. He told her. She scanned the list of subscribers tacked up on the wall, probably let out a hearty laugh, and then dialed. The phone rang somewhere in New York, startling, among others, a wiry, high-strung man speed-puffing a cigar in his office suite. He picked the phone up. Taylor's voice crackled over the noisy line . . .

Some historians believe that the 1890s produced the greatest number of truly eccentric characters. In addition to Colonel Albert A. Pope, there was also Diamond Jim Brady, the colossal railroad baron, and, of course, the stern-faced Carnegies, Rockefellers, and Morgans. But on the other end of Taylor's phone line sat perhaps the greatest character of them all—someone working his name into the zeitgeist of 1890s America. His name was William A. Brady, a man the likes of which this country may never see again.

Chapter 6

THE FIGHTING
SHOWMAN FROM
THE WEST

William A. Brady was the E. F. Hutton of the 1890s: When he spoke, people leaned forward and listened. And they usually did exactly what he asked. With his persuasive oratory skills, Brady could sail through a room full of prominent businessmen, flicking the ashes from his cigar, and if he wished, have them dumping their entire fortunes into snake oil. People seemed to sway willingly to his commands. But it wasn't so much what he said that attracted people to him; it was how he said it. His booming voice filled the room while an air of confidence radiated around him. Though he was a scrawny, 130-pound man of average height, people paid heed to the strength of his words.

Only thirty-three years old in 1896, Brady could already look back at a life filled with remarkable adventures. A flamboyant, inflammable Celt with a bottomless capacity for liquor, Brady would have felt smothered in today's more politically correct environment. He was a classic 1890s man, unfettered and recalcitrant. He lived large, said exactly what was on his mind, was obsessed with gambling, and could care less about money so long as he had piles of it.

Decades before he was lured by the glamour and bright lights of Broadway—and all the cash—Brady's childhood was, itself, like an old-time melodrama. Born in San Francisco to a mother named O'Keefe and a father named Brady, perhaps trouble was inevitable. On an afternoon in 1869, his quick-tongued father—who emigrated from Dublin to find gold—was released from Alcatraz prison just in time to get into more trouble. His first act as a free man was to kidnap six-year-old William from his ex-wife, then stuff him on the first boat headed for New York. Once there, young William found himself living atop a dingy bowery saloon and joining an Irish gang that habitually shut down city blocks while clashing with the natives. "We fought all the time on the bowery," he wrote in one of his autobiographies, "not only rough-and-tumble impromptu brawls, but formal stand-up matches too, with seconds and water buckets and regular rules—the old, grueling, London Prize Ring rules in my time."

His was a jagged upbringing, which would shape and define him in adulthood. "Plenty of times I sat hungry and shivering in an unheated room, waiting for Father to come home with bad news and crying myself to sleep when he didn't."

Life became even rougher when his combative father was found on the street, the life mysteriously squeezed out of him. Grief-stricken, teenaged Brady was eventually booted out of his shabby room in the heart of New York's East Side, and then began "rustling whatever cash was rustleable." He took on odd jobs waiting tables, delivering newspapers, stoking fires, and shining shoes. His first introduction to sports came when, for thirty cents, he delivered updates of the six-day races at the first Madison Square Garden to local newspapers. "I never met the late Horatio Alger Jr.," he later wrote, "but he would have liked to meet me. I was no such high-flown prig as his newsboy's heroes—I'd have shied a brick at one in real life—but if anybody ever went through the whole mill of the traditional how-to-get-along-on-the-cold-streets-of-a-great-city racket, I was that somebody."

Before his decade-long involvement with bike racing and boxing, he satisfied his first love by haunting local theaters. Shabbily dressed and usually flat broke, he would scrunch up on the edge of the hard gallery bench, while fifty feet below, the heroes of the day—Tony Hart, Edwin Booth, and Nat Goodwin—captivated crowds.

In the bright lexicon of his youth, Brady's restlessness often landed him in trouble. After being kicked out of town for mouthing off outside theaters in the finer districts of New York, he booked a train west, got off in his hometown of San Francisco with no money but large dreams. "I felt the West owed me and I was scheduled to own it." Upon arrival, he became a peanut butcher, selling everything from reading material to groceries, hardware, tobacco, and candy on trains.

But starting a brawl with a traveling Chinamen assured his career as a peanut butcher was not long for this world. So the ex–peanut butcher took to haunting theaters around San Francisco, eventually sweet-talking his way into contract plays. He played everything from soldier to sailor, stage door Johnny, medieval swashbuckler, and Indians of every tribe—"including some," he said, "that never existed outside a hack dramatist imagination." Clearly, the pay for the future bike race promoter was barely enough to cover the basics. "If you couldn't starve well on occasion" he often said, "you didn't belong in the old-time theatre."

Stiffed by one too many managers, Brady decided to take a stab at managing himself. Around the time Major Taylor roamed the Southards' estate with his first bicycle, Brady got his first big break. He paid fifteen cents for a copy of Dion Boucicault's famous melodrama *After Dark*, which had played to standing room crowds for thirteen straight weeks. Success bred cockiness: "It gave me a swelled head that wouldn't have gone through a man-hole without shoving."

But his early managerial success was fleeting. One night he noticed a distinguished gentleman sitting in the crowd with a wide grin on his face. Following the show, the man complimented him on the fine performance, then asked him how the play had been doing. Shortly after Brady had finished boasting about the show's financial success, the man introduced himself as none other than Boucicault—*the owner of the story*. When Boucicault threatened legal action, Brady handed him a paltry $1,100 for the rights to the play. At first glance, it seemed like a steal considering the daily sellouts. But it was, he said, "the worst pup I was ever sold in the course of a highly checkered career."

So Brady took the act east, only to be greeted with an injunction. The injunction was initiated by a sophisticated gentleman named Augustin Daly. Daly claimed that Boucicault had plagiarized his play *Under the Gaslight*. Unfortunately, Daly did not like Brady. "I was an upstart pigmy, a barnstorming sharpshooter, trying to crash New York with a pirated manuscript." Thirteen years and thousands of dollars in legal costs later, the U.S. Supreme

Court ruled in a famous precedent-setting case that Daly was indeed the rightful owner. But in a strange twist of fate, it was discovered that Daly's copyright for *Under the Gaslight* had since expired, leaving Brady sole owner "lock, stock, and barrel." Brady would go on to make a fortune on the play, which he would use to finance sports promotions.

Since play managing was getting him in trouble, he began seeking other opportunities. Sometime in 1891, around the time of Taylor's first race, he ran into an old friend he'd met in San Francisco during his peanut butcher days. The man had grown tremendously since he last saw him. Brady sized him up, scanning his brawny arms, sweeping back muscles, and lady-killer good looks. A light bulb went off in his promotional mind: *I'm going to get this man in the ring.*

His old friend was "Gentleman" Jim Corbett, a man Taylor would soon meet. Since boxing was illegal in most states and frowned on in others, Brady offered him $150 a week to box in private clubs and in bootlegged bouts on barges. Corbett rose through the ranks rapidly, prompting Brady to try pitting him against the world champion, Jim Sullivan. Knowing that nearly every fighter and promoter in the world was after Sullivan, Brady tried every promotional trick he could think of to get Sullivan's attention. In the end, he simply outbid everyone else; after approaching wealthy horseman Phil Dwyer, co-founder of the Dwyer Stakes horse race, they were able to foot boxing's largest purse ever.

The nation had rarely seen a more natural promotional wizard. Brady papered New Orleans periodicals with huge ads. He littered the main railway lines with screeching lithograph posters announcing in huge letters that James J. Corbett, champion of the world, would appear at Madison Square Garden the week after the fight.

His aggressive promotion paid off, though, as a raucous sellout crowd wedged into the Olympic A. C. in New Orleans in 1892 to see the fight of the century. Brady's zeal for life was on full display as he pranced up and down during the entire fight, screaming his lungs out and throwing wild jabs into the smoke-filled air. Corbett cut Sullivan to ribbons, netting Brady another fortune. On his first try, Brady's keen eye for spotting talent had uncovered a world champion.

Around the time Major Taylor landed a job at Hearsey's Bike Shop, Brady and Corbett clattered into Butte, Kalamazoo, Tombstone, Ashtabula, and other Wild West towns. On one occasion, their train drifted onto the open continuity of Arizona's San Bernardino region for another brawl in another dark, smoky saloon. While Corbett was pummeling another young man in the ring, Brady kept an eye out for "deadheads." Behind him, he heard a rasping voice from somewhere in the shadows—"the kind of voice," he claimed "a rattlesnake would have if it could talk."

"Corbett," the man hollered, "lay another hand on that boy and I'm telling you now that you'll never live to tell about it."

Brady swung around and saw a man he'd met during his peanut butcher days with his hands in each pocket. It was the notorious Virgil Earp, Wyatt Earp's brother. Brady pinned Earp's arms to his side while Corbett ran out of the building. "I don't know what kind of begging, pleading, cajoling nonsense I poured into his ears," he remembered, "but it worked." With Earp lying prostrate on the ground, "I abandoned my loving embrace of Mr. Earp," wrote Brady, who then quickly followed Corbett out the door. The two men bailed out of Arizona minus the $300 prize money, but sparing the life of a world champion.

Brady combined his two vocations and wrote *Gentleman Jack*, a hugely successful play starring Corbett. They were besieged by frantic "feminine theatergoers" everywhere they went. "They got in our hair, they clogged our mail, they made themselves the worst nuisance possible—and we took it like men, and we liked it . . ." First *After Dark*, then Corbett, Brady was rolling in money and living lavishly. He began dressing in the most expensive suits money could buy, wore loads of diamonds, rarely left home without a brown felt hat, and was always seen puffing on an expensive Cuban cigar.

His interest in pugilism waning, Brady looked elsewhere for excitement and profit. After a failed bid to buy the St. Louis Cardinals baseball team (called Browns at the time), he promoted exotic contests like cake-walking, tug-of-war, kangaroo fighting, and lion shows. Most of them had a short shelf life. The lion show came to a screaming halt one eventful evening when part of the trainer's hindquarters disappeared following a losing battle with the beast. The kangaroo fighting also died an early death when his human sparring partner—who took over for Corbett who was deathly afraid of the animal—quit after the animal floored him.

Brady's first love was the theater, but the economic depression hit some of the flossier theaters hard. They were not alone. Complaints came from hatters, booksellers, jewelers, and shoemakers. The worst hit were horse dealers and tobacco manufacturers—horse dealers were going out of business daily and cigar consumption was declining at a rate of a million a month. Theatrical managers searched for the root cause of their misfortune. Like other businessmen, they sensed something beyond the troubled economy was out there wrecking their businesses. After careful analysis, they finally had an answer. The cause of their hard times, the *New York Evening Post* decreed, "was not the tariffs, not the currency, not the uncertainty of the McKinley financial position, but the *bicycle*."

William Brady was never one to ignore profitable and exciting new trends. With his air of inevitability and a steady stream of cash from his plays, he began searching for something fast-paced and, to match his colorful past, something with an element of danger. While delivering updates on six-day races to newspapers in the early days of racing, he fell wildly and incurably in love with bike racing. He decided to get involved with race promoting and later managing.

But as much as he loved the sport, he was unimpressed with the condition of many of the tracks and set out to do something about it. During his days on the boxing circuit, the fighting man had met Pat Powers, president of baseball's minor leagues, and James Kennedy, a wealthy, rotund boxing promoter, newspaperman, and avid racing fan. The three men had kindred spirits: all were great orators, prodigious spotters of talent, and natural leaders. "None of these men," wrote the *Minneapolis Journal*, "were known to purchase a dead horse or bet on a shell game." They were also control freaks who were as good as friends as they were as enemies. During the day, they were known to fight like cats and dogs, occasionally suing one another just to make sure the other was paying attention. In the evening, they'd swill champagne together, flirt with showgirls, and puff on Cuban cigars like best friends.

Shortly after meeting, they formed a business partnership called the American Cycle Racing Association. Then, as was their nature, they set out to control some of racing's top tracks. Through much of the second half of the 1890s and early 1900s, they controlled Madison Square Garden, home of the wildly popular six-day races, the immense bicycle conventions, and the annual horse show. They also controlled the Mechanics Pavilion in Brady's hometown of San Francisco, the popular Coliseum in Chicago, Willow Grove Park Racetrack in Philadelphia, Charles Park Track in Boston, a track in Rochester, New York, and Manhattan Beach Track in Manhattan, site of many of track racing's greatest showdowns.

With this tight control over several major tracks, the triumvirate wielded such considerable power it was sometimes unclear who was in charge of racing—them or the potent League of American Wheelmen. Despite occasional clashes with racing's governing body, their New York–based organization helped make bike racing among the most modern sports in America. By pooling their capital and promotional skills, they increased the number and the comfort of seats at several tracks, outfitting some with as many as twenty-five thousand seats. They installed modern press boxes, race scoreboards, dark rooms for cameramen, more comfortable dressing rooms, massage salons, and billiard rooms. They hired entertaining race announcers and added more and friendlier concessionaires. They improved tracks by laying fresh concrete or steeply banked, bowling-alley-smooth wood surfaces, vastly improving racers' speeds.

Using his promotional skills, Brady introduced an important element to the sport: *women*. Before it was proper for women to attend boxing matches, he designed ads specifically tailored to their unique interest. He coaxed sportswriters into penning articles that were less male-centric in tone. In so doing, he took boxing out of the alley and into the "royal suite." Women who formerly had no interest in sports began dressing up as men so they could sneak into matches without incident. Brady brought these pioneering promotional methods into his partnership with Powers and Kennedy, much to the delight of male race patrons.

Unlike baseball, football, and basketball, the sport that emerged from their era was, with a few minor exceptions, largely the same as it is today: people on one-speed bicycles with no brakes tearing around a steeply banked track, first one to the tape wins.

Their influence was such that if a biker was having trouble turning pro and wanted to race on the best tracks, he—say, a talent like Major Taylor— would likely have appealed to them. On a fall day in 1896, in their second-floor office inside Madison Square Garden, Brady, Powers, and Kennedy heard the phone ring. On the other end of the line came a crackly but lyrical young voice. It was Taylor, asking if he could "engage" in a major race they were sponsoring at Madison Square Garden, one of the indoor tracks under their control. Since it was a professional race, Taylor also needed their help securing a professional license. With the writing already on Munger's factory walls, Major Taylor's livelihood—indeed his very future—was riding on their answer.

There was a long, agonizing pause on the line while Kennedy and Powers weighed the harmful effects of a black man in the professional peloton. Powers, a beady-eyed, portly, cigar-chomping man whose language and disposition were more forceful than eloquent, had experience in racial matters. As baseball's International League president, he had presided over an era that played under a "gentlemen's agreement." This was a silent agreement among teams to bar nonwhite players—a bar which stood until the days of Jackie Robinson in 1947.

If this was Taylor's future, his prospects were looking bleak. "They [Powers and Kennedy] contended that the presence of this little Negro would not be right at the race," wrote French journalist Robert Coquelle. "It would stir the whole of New York." After careful deliberation, they were ready to send him away, "that is," Coquelle continued, "to shine the Fifth Avenue gentlemen's shoes." Taylor appeared to have reached the end of a road that had begun as a restless eight-year-old on Southard's given bike.

Taylor's prospects changed when the commanding voice of the fighting Irishman entered the conversation. From his days living atop a cold bowery saloon, William Brady had also felt the sting of racism. At the time the Irish, like blacks, were ridiculed for their skin and their distinctive dialect, and were often told by employers that "no Irish need apply." They were dubbed "drug-abusing monkeys" and "white Negroes." In 1867 American cartoonist Thomas Nast drew "The Day We Celebrate," which was a cartoon depicting the Irish on St. Patrick's Day as violent, drunken apes. And, in 1899, *Harper's Weekly* featured a drawing of three men's heads in profile: Irish, Anglo-Teutonic, and Negro, in order to illustrate the similarity between the Irish and the Negro (and, the supposed superiority of the Anglo-Teutonic).

For Brady, whose emotions were as fluid as a flowing river, few things raised his dander more than racism. He was, in fact, one of the few white men who had treated Peter Jackson—the black boxer who fought Corbett to a draw—with respect. "Black or not, he was as fine and intelligent a man as ever walked," he often said. As he did with Jackson, Brady reportedly fought on Taylor's behalf. He apparently pushed, shoved, and cajoled to get what he wanted. He contacted several men—probably including A. G. Batchelder, a race handicapper, future business partner, and future head of racing's governing body—and demanded they push their substantial heft around the racing board.

Whatever he said, and in whatever tone, it seems to have been effective. In short order, "one of the greatest innovators in entertainment," wrote cycling historian Peter Nye, "Brady helped Major Taylor obtain a League of American Wheelmen license to compete professionally in segregated America." The fighting man wasn't about to allow any racism toward Taylor without a fight. "He has sworn vengeance on anybody connected with those acts," a reporter later wrote. With a few turns from William A. Brady's persuasive Irish tongue, one of history's most controversial and celebrated athletic careers was free to begin.

With his hard-fought pro license in hand, all Taylor needed was his race jersey. Someone handed him a jersey that had been kicking around in the league's stockroom for ages; the one no one else wanted. Pro cyclists, like most athletes, are a superstitious lot; stenciled on the back of his new jersey was the number 13. Several riders who wouldn't come near the jersey surely snickered at the irony of the lone black man wearing the unluckiest number in the peloton. Taylor would wear that unlucky number for much of the next fourteen years.

With one hard slog behind him, an even harder challenge lay ahead. The race Taylor had signed on to was no ordinary event. It would, in the end, require every fiber of his being just to finish. He no longer had time for factory life. Taylor temporarily moved to Brooklyn where he joined the South Brooklyn Wheelmen and later the Calumet Wheelmen. In preparation for what would be a brutal and rather odd professional debut for a sprinter, Munger—perhaps wanting to astonish the broader world with his extraordinary find—laid out an equally brutal training routine. To help carry out his instructions, he set Taylor up with a noted trainer named Bob Ellingham.

Ellingham worked Taylor hard, watching daily as he racked up mile after mile on local roads and tracks. Some journalists, probably unfamiliar with the harsh nature of the sport, thought Munger's training routine bordered on abuse. "The training was rather rough but it has had an effect that is beneficial to the lad right now," wrote the *Sunday Herald* shortly after his initiation into the professional ranks. "Munger used to abuse the boy, some would call it abuse, but at the same time he was kindly to him and managed to make out of the lad a great rider."

On November 26, 1896, Thanksgiving Day, Taylor rolled his Birdie Special onto the hardened streets of Jamaica, Long Island. For him, the twenty-five-mile Tatum Handicap was merely a tune-up race, his last chance to put some competitive miles on his legs before the big international showdown at the Garden. One of the Vanderbilts was there; so was Pat Powers, probably wondering what Brady had gotten them into. A field of twenty-seven amateur riders lined up at what was then the heart of New York's commercial district. In recognition of his success in the amateur ranks, Taylor was placed on scratch by the always attentive race handicappers. A writer for the *Brooklyn Eagle* wasn't too enamored with the handicappers' decision. "Those men who were in the *supposedly* fast bunch," he wrote skeptically, "were Frank Munz, Fred Rich, and Major Taylor, the darkey rider who is entered in the big race in Madison Square Garden . . ."

The *New York Times* inked a few words about Taylor riding "a fine race," then moved on to the two amateurs they seemed to think were more "promising." Just out for a training spin and perhaps not wanting to draw the attention of the professional handicappers, Taylor finished behind thirteen riders, including John Rud of Newark, the overall winner.

At 1:30 that crisp fall afternoon, the curtain on Taylor's amateur career fell. The Tatum Handicap was not only his last amateur race, but apparently his last road race. It had been an eventful childhood for the atypical black boy from Indiana, one that saw him atop a bicycle at age eight and now, a decade later, ended with him atop a bicycle. Yet his life story was only just beginning. The Jim Crow era had been, and would continue to be, filled with struggles and intrigue. Fortunately, he hadn't had to go it alone. He had been helped by a handful of special men: his confidant Birdie Munger, his mentor Arthur Zimmerman, his athletic director Edward Wilder, and now William Brady, the fighting showman from the West. These caring men meant everything to him. Because, like most riders in the biking world at that time, he had no place else to go, no one else to lean on, nothing else he cherished. For Major Taylor, there were no train tracks leading back to Indy.

PART II

Chapter 7

SIX DAYS OF MADNESS

For years, Munger had been nurturing Taylor under his paternal wings. He had taken him into his home, trained him on seedy old racetracks, raising him up through the amateur ranks through a dilatory and careful development. It wasn't until the six-day race at Madison Square Garden under the glaring eyes of the sporting public, however, that Munger finally set him free.

With Arthur Zimmerman spending much of his time overseas, the nation eagerly sought a new hero. In the winter of 1896, America was in the third year of the most disastrous financial crisis in its history. The panic of 1893, which began around the time of Taylor's first race, had washed over American life like a hurricane. In some towns nearly 25 percent of the population had lost their careers, their investments, their farms. Violent strikes and riots wracked the nation and the middle class began whispering fearfully of "carnivals of revenge." A country that had grown supremely confident from its industrial success during the Gilded Age—when everyone was a potential Carnegie and success was celebrated as never before—was disheartened by rampant indigence. The strongest of citizens, including prominent bankers—more than five hundred banks had gone under—and Wall Street executives were overcome by feelings of hopelessness and trepidation. Their fears were not lost on politicians: Republican candidate William McKinley won the presidency with a simple promise to provide a "full dinner pail" for the unemployed.

Present-day writings often refer to the era as "the Gay Nineties," highlighting the extravagances of the Morgans, Belmonts, and Vanderbilts. In reality, eleven million of America's twelve million families lived below the poverty line, earning on average just $345 a year. The average income for blacks was considerably less.

Unlike the Great Depression, when more government programs were available to aid the impoverished, Americans were largely left to fend for themselves. Few areas, especially train depots, were without beggars. Some were content with finding their next meal; others too proud for handouts begged for jobs so they could fend for themselves; still others sought just enough money to afford temporary relief.

Relief came in many forms. In search of hope and encouragement, people filled churches to capacity. Entertainment venues like Wild Bill Cody's Wild West Show, The Magic Lantern Theatre, Barnum and Bailey's Circus, and ragtime music led by Scott Joplin also helped people cope. Though motion pictures were in their infancy, people were spellbound by them. From New Jersey to San Francisco, they scraped together twenty-five cents, turned a crank, and peered into Edison's kinetoscopes to watch *Bicycle Trick Riders* and Brady's six-minute production of a Corbett fight—the first big moneymaker the movie industry ever produced.

Americans also sought relief in sports. But with radio and television decades away, the only access people had to sports heroes either came from reading newspapers or magazines, seeing them on billboards, or attending live events. Americans eagerly awaited the morning paper for word on their sports hero or for any news of the big stars coming to their town, their moods ebbing and flowing with the successes or failures of their chosen idol. Live sporting events, the preferred medium, often provided the first opportunity for rural farmers to meet urbanites as they passed through the gates of the era's most popular sports: baseball, horse racing, boxing, tennis, and wrestling. But cycling arguably led the way. In 1896, the year of Taylor's professional debut, all facets of cycling were wildly popular: leisure riding, road races, outdoor track races, lantern parades, and the overflowing bicycle manufacturers' conventions.

In winter, no sporting event drew fans like the six-day bike races. As its name implies, the riders had six days—between Monday morning at 12:01 and Saturday evening at 11:59—to ride as many miles as possible. Around and around the steeply banked track they pedaled day and night, sometimes resting for only one or two hours a day. The rules were straightforward: after the final tally at the end of the sixth night, victory belonged to the man who had pedaled the greatest distance. The early version of the race was as brutal a sporting event as man had ever devised. But if a rider survived and won, the total winnings—$5,000 to $10,000 in the 1890s, $75,000 in the 1920s—was nearly enough to set up a man for life. Writers from most newspapers in America and Europe covered the race extensively. With one stroke of their pens, cyclists could gain unprecedented international exposure, instantly raising them from obscurity and poverty to fame.

In December 1896, cycling's broad-based popularity, Americans' need to escape, and the ruggedness of the era merged, greatly enhancing the spectacle of the race. The event, the stage, and the audience were set. It awaited only the lead actor, the new hero.

A t that extraordinary moment at the dawn of the "separate but equal" era, Major Taylor, the eighteen-year-old, largely unknown black man, walked past the Garden's Roman colonnades for the first time. That grand entrance off Madison Avenue, gleaming with lavender marble, must have been quite a sight for his pastoral eyes. It was the second of four buildings that have used the name Madison Square Garden and undoubtedly the grandest. No ordinary edifice, this was an indoor oasis so stunning the *New York Herald* considered it not just a building "but a state of mind."

After the first Garden, owned by William Vanderbilt, was torn down in 1890, its new owners, J. P. Morgan and a brilliant young architect named Stanford White, had erected a grand monument to the city's predepression taste and wealth. Extending 200 feet on one side and 485 feet on the opposite side, the building was an imposing structure of yellow brick and white Pompeian terra-cotta. On its roof was a popular observation deck that offered visitors a bird's-eye view of the city.

As grand as the building was on the outside, it was on the inside where Taylor would have been most awestruck; pale red walls enfolded an auditorium 200 feet by 350 feet, the largest then in existence, with seats for eight thousand people and floor space for several thousand more, all laid out beneath an eighty-foot-high ceiling.

And then there were the wine rooms, far and away the most popular, located in odd corners of the building. This is where enormous sums were wagered on races, and, as Brady recalled, people went "to get gloriously fried." Perhaps nobody more than he. "I must have been one of the best customers in the history of the old Madison Square Garden."

But Morgan and White, perhaps caught up in the excesses of the era, had spent too freely. By the mid-'90s, just a few years after its completion, they were having trouble meeting expenses. So Brady, Kennedy, and Powers were able to lease the building for years at a time at a substantial discount.

If, by finishing fourteenth in his last amateur race, Taylor wanted to come in under the radar of the professional race handicappers, it had worked. Early Saturday night, December 5, before the start of the six-day event, Taylor had signed on to the half-mile open handicap to touch off his career. He went largely unnoticed. While a few handicappers had vaguely heard his name, none had any reason to believe that he was anything more than an also-ran. He was, wrote one of the few reporters to recognize his name, nothing but "a Dark Horse." A Kansas City sportswriter referred to him as "a little ink-stained fellow." Their minds had been preoccupied by weightier American names like Eddie "Cannon" Bald, two-time sprint champion of America; his closest pursuer, Tom Cooper; famed world-traveler, Nat Butler; and the thick-legged powerhouse, Arthur Gardiner, among others. In recognition of his rookie status, the race handicappers positioned Taylor as limitman, with a thirty-five-yard advantage to the above scratchmen.

While he warmed up, and over the next six days, a melting pot of people would pour in by the tens of thousands, including the Vanderbilts and the Belmonts—Oliver and his new wife, Alva.

When the spectators entered, they moved through a long lobby entrance lined with polished yellow Sienna marble. They were greeted by the lively sounds of Bayne's Sixty-ninth Regiment Band as they emerged into the arena. New York's society folk were escorted to their red carpet suites. The commoners looked down from an upper level promenade that extended around the circuit of the arena. A catwalk arched over the ten-lap to the mile track where another thousand fans looked down on the riders. Hanging from the center of the track, a large electronic scoreboard allowed fans to track each rider's progress.

The night before the six-day race, the riders competing in the half-mile handicap entered the track individually to the deafening roar of the crowd. They glanced up at the throng, strapped themselves into their toe clips, and waited on the tape, their trainers holding them up. Brady's friend, a comely actress named Anna Held, squeezed the trigger, raising the curtain on Major Taylor's professional career.

At the sound of the pistol, Taylor's anxiety was quickly replaced with a massive forward push. He put his head down and stormed around the first lap of the track, his thirty-five-yard head start neither widening nor narrowing. After the second of five laps, some riders who had not yet closed the gap began to take notice of him. Others held their ground, figuring the new kid would eventually crack.

Eddie Bald, who'd probably never heard of Taylor but had a reputation to uphold, was the first rider to react to him. The man whose face appeared on cigarette packages nationwide and whose trading card was exchanged more than any other wasn't about to let "a runaway African," as one reporter called Taylor, beat him. Showing why he had earned the nickname "Cannon," Bald picked his way through the maze of riders, passing Cooper, Gardiner, and Butler. The champion of America was on a tear.

At the beginning of the third lap, as the handicappers had expected, Taylor's thirty-five-yard gap began dwindling; thirty yards, then twenty-five. The confident home crowd cheered New York's Bald on, waiting for him to overtake Taylor as he had everyone else that year. Smoothly, fluidly, Taylor rolled on, dipping and swerving around the steep wooden track. From their private booth, Brady and Kennedy could study Taylor's every move. They could see the grace of his cadence, the absence of wasted energy, the celerity of motion not unlike an eagle in flight.

From behind, Bald continued a relentless pursuit toward the speeding black man who looked like nothing more than a kid fresh out of high school. The rest of the field slid away, littered all over the track behind them. It was coming down to a two-horse race—the experienced Bald and neophyte Taylor. Pedaling with all that was in him, Taylor was alone on the lead, banking into the first turn of what he thought was the final lap. The half-mile race required five laps around the track. At the beginning of the fifth, suddenly, unexplainably, something happened. His right arm rose in a closed fist as though he was shaking it in triumph. There was a full lap left, yet he was celebrating as though he had won. Everything Munger had taught him about studying each track and staying calm had seemingly been lost. His lead was evaporating. Bald was closing. The crowd was shouting.

Perhaps he didn't know the track's length. Perhaps he had miscounted. Or the thunderous New York crowd, the web of international reporters, the grandeur of the garden, all combined to unnerve him. For a split second at the most significant juncture of his young life, Taylor wavered. The crowd, noticing his mistake, screamed themselves hoarse.

With less than three-quarters of a lap to go, finally realizing what was happening, Taylor dropped his head and lunged forward again. But under great pressure, his usual poise began unraveling. What had been a perfect matrimony between man and bicycle was now merely Taylor and his Birdie Special, struggling to regain their harmony. Craning his neck back, Taylor saw Bald charging at him. Looking ahead while ripping along at over forty miles per hour, Bald could see Taylor's form crumble. He shot forward drawing even closer: twenty-yards, fifteen-yards. He was eating away at Taylor's lead in chunks.

Bald stood up on his machine and pounced on his pedals, his legs straining, his long frame lunging to within yards of him.

Taylor was coming to the homestretch of his first professional race, eyes wide open, legs burning. Behind him were some of the greatest cyclists in the country. All around him, Madison Square Garden's plush interior thronged with thousands of howling fans. Above him, a catwalk of fans, their hands reaching out toward him. Ahead of him, an empty undulating wooden track and the glistening white tape of the finish line. And hot on his tail, the two-time champion of America.

The two men looked forward and saw the tape rushing at them. Just then, Taylor looked down at the track floor and saw nothing but his front wheel flying over the tape.

Ten days removed from his eighteenth birthday in his first professional race, Taylor had crossed the finish line ahead of America's sprint champion. All that remained of the crowd's vocal cords shrieked themselves out as he circled the track triumphantly. He grinned ear to ear as admirers tossed bouquets at his feet with the band wailing "Way down Dixie!" Stunned, Bald poked his head out from the infield, his mouth gaped open. Neither he nor anyone else could believe what had just happened!

With five fast turns around the Garden track, Major Taylor had thrust himself into America's sporting scene with tremendous force. In the press stands located in the center of the track, puzzled reporters leaped for their typewriters and began tapping away. Cables and telegrams went out. A group of managers, manufacturers, and promoters, including several from Europe, looked on quizzically from their booths—surely no one more so than William Brady.

Throughout the arena, fans who did not already have one shelled out fifteen cents for a race program and began thumbing through its pages. They mingled among themselves, asking the question: *Who is this young black man?*

Munger's slow cultivation of Taylor came to an abrupt halt one day after the half-mile race. Given Taylor's proclivity for shorter distances and the fact that he had never raced more than seventy-five miles, perhaps he should have taken his $200 purse and gone home. But for whatever reason, perhaps for the extensive media exposure, Munger signed him on to the six-day race. The total purse, $7,500, had attracted twenty-eight top long-distance riders, including several Europeans who made the long journey overseas. The race always began with the era's sports or entertainment stars firing off the pistol. In the early 1900s stars like Jack Dempsey, Jimmy Durante, Babe Ruth, Bing Crosby, and Mary Pickford did the honors. In the 1890s, it was actresses Anna Held and Lillian Russell, and President McKinley, among others. When Taylor took to the line, he looked up and saw Eddie Bald, the sprint champion he had just beaten, chewing on a toothpick and glaring down at him, pistol in hand. Given the heated battles these two men would have in the future, some later wondered if Bald had considered pointing down instead of up.

With the crack of Bald's pistol, around and around the twenty-eight riders went. Taylor stayed near the lead for the first few hours, but some of the more experienced riders were simply holding back in reserve. As the morning ticked on, the crowd began to thin. Some made the Garden their home for the entire week, cheering on the riders in the evening when the big crowds were there, then falling asleep in their seats in the early morning hours. After six hours of continuous riding, Taylor was holding up well, in second place, only a few miles behind Britain's Eddie Hale.

As time passed, few thought Taylor would survive. Some fans even "laughed and chaffed" at him as he circled the track. One particularly belligerent man who, according to the *Brooklyn Eagle*, "looked as though he had been up all night," had to be hauled outside and silenced by the police.

To keep crowd interest high, riders would occasionally compete in impromptu sprints. Fans repaid them by tossing money, called primes, at the winner. Over six days, a successful rider could add significantly to his overall earnings. No one seemed to understand the importance of entertaining the crowd better than Taylor, the only pure sprinter in the peloton. To please the speed-hungry crowd, he talked anyone who would listen into joining him in high-speed sprints. In so doing, fans and reporters began taking notice of him. "The star of the race thus far," wrote one journalist, "is Major Taylor."

But by day three, fatigue set in. Taylor drifted back to ninth place and the sprints became less frequent. Even his usually smooth form began sagging. To compensate, he got creative, fastening a pillow to his handlebars that he used to rest his chest on. Seeing this, the other riders joined in. Soon, nearly everyone circled the track with their chests buried into soft pillows, bringing chuckles from the stands.

By the end of day three, Taylor had logged nine hundred miles, but found himself one hundred miles behind front-runner Teddy Hale. While the more seasoned riders like Hale only slept for an hour or two a day, Taylor slept one hour for every eight hours of riding. At that rate, he stood little chance of an overall win. But he pushed on. Munger drifted in and out of the building, telling old racing stories and pitching the benefits of the Birdie Special to reporters. When he wasn't there, he left matters up to trainer Rob Ellingham. Ellingham tended to Taylor, acting as chief motivator, nurse, psychologist, and all-important chef.

One day blended into the next. With his total miles surpassing the one thousand mark, Taylor struggled to take in as many calories as he was using. During his short breaks, he'd sit down to a whopping feast: two fried chickens, four and a half pounds of red meat, pots of beef tea, and bushels of vegetables, all topped off with endless jars of milk. Yet he still rode away craving more food. But he was by no means the only glutton in the peloton. The food intake during a typical six-day race was astonishing: twelve sides of beef out of which were carved five hundred steaks, four hundred chickens, six hundred pounds of lamb chops, ten boiled hams, fifty pounds of bacon, three hundred dozen eggs, and fifty pounds of butter. In the cereal line, fifty pounds of rice, twenty pounds of oatmeal, six dozen boxes of cornflakes, and two hundred pounds of sugarcane. And to wash it all down, seven hundred quarts of milk, twenty-five pounds of tea, and to keep riders awake, seventy-five pounds of coffee.

These ample spreads did not always sit well. On one occasion following a particularly large meal, Taylor doubled over on his bike, his stomach so seized by cramps he could barely move. Suffering similar fates, others couldn't take it any longer. Attrition began thinning the field. By the end of day four, the original band of twenty-seven had been whittled down to fifteen ragged riders.

At that point, Taylor and a Canadian named Pierce were in a close battle for sixth place. Exhausted, the two men made a few halfhearted attempts at sprints. Sprinting against distance riders, Taylor nearly always won—"It's just too easy," someone heard him say. On one occasion, their wooziness caused them to lock handlebars. Taylor, whose arms and legs were by then like jelly, wobbled uncontrollably until finally losing control of his wheel, his bike bounding along the track, body tumbling head over heels for twenty feet. Ellingham ran over, scraped him off the floor, and carried him over to the infield. There amid his repeated cries to quit the race, he wrapped him in liniments, gave him a few words of encouragement, and nudged him back on the track.

By the end of day five, Taylor had logged 1608 miles, 153 behind leader Teddy Hale, but just three miles behind Pierce who was in sixth place.

Surprisingly, given the era, the crowd was connecting with Taylor. Besides his lively sprints, he entertained them by whistling loudly or swooping high up the steep bank and chatting with them as he rode passed. His victory over Bald, his pleasant demeanor, and his capacity to endure combined to make him a crowd favorite. "The wonder of the race is Major Taylor," announced the *New York Times*.

By day six, the word was already out. The crowds gathered en masse.

Even in the morning, despite ticket prices doubling to a dollar, six thousand fans had gathered. By six o'clock a massive evening crowd arrived. As they had the previous night, horse and man were backed up as far as the eye could see. Carriages of all types choked Madison Avenue. An extra force of police had difficulty keeping the avenue entrance clear. Ticket sellers were overwhelmed. The center of the track by seven o'clock was so thick with bodies, it was almost impossible to navigate. The rail by the track sagged under the weight of lines of shouting men and women twenty deep. Behind them, hundreds stood on tiptoe in a vain attempt to see the riders. By eight o'clock, every seat was sold, but because Brady and Kennedy, in those days before strict fire codes, were known to overbook, the crowd kept pouring in. Cots were set up along the upper railing for added seating. When attendants finally started turning away thousands of people at the ticket window, fights broke out and the police had to swoop in to simmer down the crowd.

On the inside, the ventilation system stood no chance against row after row of cigar-puffing fans, their smoke filling the auditorium and saturating the riders' eyes and lungs. On the track, the lack of sleep was sucking whatever life remained out of the riders. They were becoming "peevish and fretful," and the wear on their nerves and muscles was causing some riders to have terrible fits. Being the youngest and most inexperienced rider in the group, Taylor, in bike racing parlance, was among those cracking. During one break, he broke down in tears inside his tent, pleading with Ellingham to let him quit. "You fellows want me to stay here until my leg drops off so you can sell it to the doctor," he grumbled incoherently.

On another occasion he dismounted his bike, leaned it against a fence, walked across the track, sat down on a low rail, yawned, and fell asleep. Seeing this, a few fans stood up and tried cheering him back to life. Soon hundreds, then thousands joined in. "I cannot go on with safety," he mumbled near a reporter, "for there is a man chasing me around the ring with a knife in his hand." His face, according to a few reports, became "thin and emaciated," and "his naturally large lips became larger still with the condition of his face." Spectators thought he was finished.

Taylor wasn't the only rider losing his bearings. J. S. Rice, twenty-seven miles behind front-runner Hale, also became delirious, claiming that someone was throwing things at him. "He said he didn't care about bricks and stones," wrote one sportswriter, "but he objected to iron pillars being thrown at him."

Into this scene waltzed Teddy Roosevelt's men. As New York's police commissioner, he was responsible for leading a team of police surgeons into the Garden to check the pulse, temperature, and overall well-being of the riders. Human rights groups had been complaining about the race being inhumane. Knowing they were fighting an uphill battle against the immense popularity of the race, they sent in police surgeons as a temporary compromise. Brady, with his rawhide-tough upbringing, sneered at them. "It was nonsense," he later wrote, before lightheartedly telling the story of one six-dayer who was so damaged "he died, prematurely burned-out I suppose, just a month shy of ninety-one."

Inhumane or not, he and Kennedy stopped the race at ten o'clock, two hours before the scheduled witching hour. When they did, only four men remained on the track: winner Hale, sixth-placed Pierce, a rider named Maddox, and a thin, black teenager who was still trying to eke out a few sprints for an appreciative crowd.

Outside, horse-drawn floral wagons clopped up. An army of men hauled in loads of floral tributes, which were tossed at the riders as they circled the track. The crowd stayed until they left the building. Hale, mobbed by over-zealous well-wishers, needed a police escort to make it to his hotel across the street.

In the infield, someone uncorked a bottle of champagne. It was flat. Everyone went home.

They had witnessed one of the most remarkable demonstrations of human endurance ever displayed. Hale had traveled 1,910 miles, besting the previous record by 310 miles. Taylor was eighth with 1,732 miles. He too had shattered all previous six-day records. Given his age, fans were impressed with his fortitude. In this erstwhile unknown underdog, some saw themselves: alive but suffering, suffering yet enduring.

But it was a curious way to start a sprinting career. Taylor had survived an event that, because of its excessively taxing nature, would soon be forced to change. Though it didn't fit his racing style, the event fit the era. This was, after all, 1890s America. And it was, wrote author Ted Harper, "Six days of Madness."

On the morning of December 14, 1896, Brady, Powers, and Kennedy woke up in awfully good moods: $37,000 in net gate receipts and a similar number in concessions surely had something to do with their collective jolly. Waiting for them in the corridors of Hotel Bartholdi stood scores of haggard-looking men. The six-dayers, accompanied by their trainers and handlers, were looking to collect their shares of the purse. At noon, they were escorted into a reception room where they saw Kennedy and Powers standing behind a podium. Splayed out on a table sat rolls and rolls of gold. From his rostrum Kennedy congratulated the riders for their incredible fortitude, then called them forward one by one. Powers distributed the proper allocation of shining, double eagles.

In no physical or mental condition for an extended celebration, most riders accepted their money, then bolted for the door. But reporters stood near the exits, drilling them with questions while surveying their overall condition, which they reported on in illustrative detail.

Because the race only came to New York once or twice a year, the newsroom boys were going to have fun with this one. Winner Hale, who had slept twice as many hours the previous night as he had during the entire six-day race, could barely speak, his vocal cords lost somewhere in the Garden's haze. In true fighting-Irish style, he desperately tried pushing out a few words, but nothing came out, so he just bowed to the crowd and then walked away, red-faced. A few others ambled toward the table in a peculiar waddling gait, painful saddle sores rendering them nearly immobile. Even more riders were heavily bandaged or had surly scars on their faces and bodies, injuries obtained from countless high-speed spills. Rice, the second-place finisher, looked and felt empty. Though he had just consumed three whole chickens, several bowls of oatmeal, a loaf of bread, and a pot of beef tea, he couldn't satisfy his hunger. "I still feel half-starved," he said, somehow stringing together a few words. One top-ten rider who had to be carried across the street after the race asked Brady and company if they would please mail his winnings to him.

With trainer Ellingham watching, Taylor pressed forth on "swelled" knees, collecting $325 with little comment: $200 for his five-lap, half-mile win which took less than a minute, $125 for placing eighth in the six-day race that took 17,320 laps and 8640 minutes. Though this was equal to an entire year's wages in a factory, he would never again have to work so hard for so little.

The jolliness radiating from the promotional trio didn't end with presentations to the eleven scheduled prizewinners. Several riders who weren't supposed to receive anything were given $75 in gold. They expressed their gratitude to the magnanimous promoters. They "worked hard and had earned it," bellowed Kennedy in what must have been the understatement of the year, the smoke from his cigar further gagging the riders.

With that, the meeting adjourned, everyone scattering in different directions: the promoters to the bank, some riders straight to bed, and others—the more flush riders—to a Turkish bath or a local parlor for a deep massage.

Taylor wasn't able to leave so easily. There were promoters, manufacturers, photographers, and newsmen who wanted a piece of him. Though Hale had won the six-day proper and had received extensive coverage, sprinters were coveted by reporters because they competed more often. They were the men of the hour. "The highlight of the event was flashed in the bicycle world in the form of a veritable black diamond," *The Referee* said of Taylor, "he was all at once enthralled as the popular hero."

They had their subject. Their new hero, for the first time a black man, had come upon them. Major Taylor's seminal hour had begun.

In their desire to know everything, they would ask the obvious, the curious, and the absurd. Just how exhausted was he during the six-day race? Exactly how much did he eat? Did he plan to enter another six-day race? When? Where? One man seemed hell-bent on knowing how many times he had gone to the men's room during the race.

Taylor looked a little drawn in the face and sounded hoarse, remarked one writer, as he bounced from one reporter to the next.

"I feel very well, considering . . ." Taylor responded, perhaps holding himself in reserve for what would be years of reporters' inquisitions.

"Where are you going now?" asked a *Brooklyn Eagle* reporter.

"I am headed at once to Munger's home in Middletown to recover."

As Brady had assumed, Taylor was going to be all right. Save for a little stiffness in the knees, commented a surprised *New York Times* reporter, "Major Taylor was none the worse for his ride . . ."

Perhaps trying to one-up his counterparts, another writer claimed Taylor had succumbed to exhaustion and died from the race. Back in Indiana, Taylor's parents had to read that report in horror.

Within weeks of his first pro race, the news coverage already exceeded all previous years combined. That kind of coverage of a black man was unheard of. Some historians credit the great runner Jesse Owens with being the first black to be lionized by the American press, but four decades before, Taylor had somehow crashed through generations of racial barriers. "Men and women who normally did not care for blacks had cheered him on at the top of their lungs," wrote one reporter. "His game riding won for him many friends among people ordinarily opposed to the colored race."

In the coming months, the first of many nicknames would begin appearing. Sobriquets like Black Cyclone, Ebony Streak, Black Whirlwind, Ebony Flyer, Colored Cyclone, Worcester Whirlwind all found their way into the nation's papers. One journalist dreamed up the ultimate nickname, The Black Zimmerman—a superb but lofty claim for a young man with so many obstacles ahead of him.

The extraordinary coverage of Taylor would mirror that of the sport. Every major paper, many small ones, and several cycling-specific publications covered the sport at great length. The *New York Times*, *Boston Daily Globe*, *Brooklyn Eagle*, and *Washington Post*, among others, covered it nearly every day, including during winter, in special sections called *News of the Wheelmen*. *Bearings*, a twice-a-month cycling periodical, often spanned several hundred pages. Some papers had separate writers covering the cycling beat, but because the languages and sometimes the tracks were so similar, others doubled as turf writers covering horse racing, a sport that was also popular at the time.

Following behind the reporters came mustachioed photographers standing behind their cumbersome tripods, fingers pressed firmly against the flash lever, smoke puffing all around. Out came the earliest photographs of a man who would soon become among the most photographed sports figure in the world. The first known photo, a very grainy production, exposed his smooth baby face and his still-thin and short frame, around five-foot five inches and 125 to 140 pounds. One of the photos taken early in 1897 showing Taylor alongside several white riders was striking more for what it lacked than what it contained. In it were no signs of a meek black man cowering to the superiority of his white masters. Taylor blended in seamlessly as he had with Daniel Southard, his white boyhood playmate. Apparently it was all perfectly normal to him—he and his friends preparing to go out for another spin, neither white nor black, just young men sharing the same goals, the same dreams, all of them created equal. When blacks were expected to doff their caps and step aside for superior white men, Taylor, in his photos and his words, appeared neither conceited nor humbled, only modest and quietly self-assured.

While writers typed and photographers clicked, manufacturers scratched their heads: Would a black man using their bicycles be good for business, or turn potential customers away? Believing they knew the answer, many manufacturers refused to come near a black athlete. Others agonized over the issue. This was no small matter for athlete or manufacturer. Bike makers and tire, chain, and component companies hadn't batted an eye in their decision to pay Teddy Hale more than $4,000 for using their products during his six-day victory. But he, of course, wasn't black. It's likely no black athlete had ever been paid to endorse a product.

That is, perhaps, until Major Taylor entered Madison Square Garden. Taylor never revealed the financial arrangement between himself and Munger. Perhaps Munger paid Taylor's expenses in exchange for using the Birdie Special and the free publicity that Munger received from it. This seems likely considering Munger's dwindling reserves following Colonel Pope's decision to cut prices and consolidate the industry. For half the race, Taylor rode a Birdie Special. But for the second half of the race, he had switched over to a Stearns bicycle. Though he never revealed his agreement with Stearns, it is unlikely that he would have switched away from Munger without monetary compensation, making the six-day race possibly the first instance of a black professional athlete being paid to endorse a product.

Finally, race promoters and track owners would face similar questions. Like manufacturers, some promoters wanted nothing to do with black athletes; after all, it hadn't worked in baseball and was beginning to unwind in horse racing. But to any promoters who had seen or read about the six-day race, the racial question should have already been answered. Fans by the tens of thousands showed up to watch an event many writers claimed was being starred by a black man. But that event was held in New York. How would he be received in less friendly cities like those in the West or South?

For the time being at least, the desire for profit overcame possible prejudice. Taylor received an invitation to compete in the upcoming six-day race in Chicago. Since there were already rumblings of Brady becoming Taylor's manager, the offer likely came from Brady's group who controlled the Chicago Coliseum. But if Brady had already pondered being Taylor's manager, it would have to wait. Shortly after the six-day race, he lost his first wife unexpectedly to Bright's disease. Brady was grief-stricken. It would be months before he and Taylor would cross paths.

Meanwhile, Taylor analyzed the Chicago offer. He mulled over it, then discarded it along with the sensationalized article claiming he had died of exhaustion at the six-day race. His stunning victory over Bald in the half-mile handicap race had defined his future. His strong suit was short-distance races.

There would be no return to the six-day grind.

With all the attention surrounding him, the world seemed to be spinning under Taylor's powerful legs, slowly fixing the eyes and ears of the nation's sporting public on him. He would handle this newfound celebrity with an unusual amount of poise for someone his age, answering inquiries in a respectful, albeit laconic fashion. "He is fairly modest," commented one writer, "rather conservative, and not overly proud nor stuck up."

But in a world of finite resources, any attention given to one athlete had to mean taking away from others. For many years, the racing world had its heroes—dominant white men who had enjoyed considerable attention and wealth. These men had worked their way up the ladder slowly, earning their way to the top. Any novice trying to steal their spotlight was bound to meet with stiff resistance, especially a "lucky little black lad," as some claimed Taylor was after Bald purportedly slipped on resin during their half-mile race.

The six-day race had kicked off Taylor's professional career, but that was a sideshow to the main event. The outdoor racing season had arrived; the train stood waiting.

Chapter 8

BLACK AND WHITE, DARKNESS AND LIGHT

I n the spring of 1897, Taylor began the near daily travel routine that would be his life for much of the next fourteen years. It was a rootless existence that would see him logging tens of thousands of miles by rail, chugging up and down the eastern half of the country, pausing in one city after another. Taylor's goal, and that of all professional cyclists, was to win the American Sprint Championship. This championship was granted to the rider with the most points when the race season ended in the fall. Riders earned points, simply speaking, by winning races during the season. Riders earned the highest number of points by crossing the line first, followed by fewer points for second and third. The total points varied from one race to the next, but were usually 4-3-1 (a year later, in 1898, it would be 6-4-3-2-1). Events that were part of the national circuit provided riders more total points—and usually higher purses—than nonsanctioned events.

Though there were championship trophies for differing disciplines—the half-mile, two-mile, five-mile, and the overall—the most important championship was the one-mile. Thus Taylor's greatest strength, and indeed his main goal throughout his career, would coincide with the event that held the public's greatest interest.

As winter snow gave way to spring flowers, one big question loomed over Taylor. Despite his success in his first professional race, or because of it, many reporters believed that the long grind of the six-day race would "kill" his sprint. It seems to have been a common belief at the time; even his own trainers subscribed to it. Taylor set out to disprove this theory.

It didn't take long. In late May, he won the one-mile open at the popular Charles River Track in Boston. At the Manhattan Beach Track in early June, he won the quarter-mile race in a tight finish and was cheered wildly by the crowd. "The colored boy," imparted one track writer, "is already making a stir."

But Taylor's promising new career was sadly interrupted that June when he received word of his mother's passing from heart disease. Though his wanderlust had kept him on the move since childhood, a strong bond had nonetheless formed between him and Saphronia. He spoke of her often, kept her abreast of his whereabouts, and sent his race winnings to her whenever he could. Beginning with his earliest days on the farm, she had, in her unique and loving way, instilled in him a strong work ethic and had taught him to be kind and considerate to others. She was responsible for his amiable and modest manners—invaluable traits that helped deflect racism and were recognized and admired by everyone he met. Her lasting legacy would forever live on in him and would soon be shared with the world. Returning to Indianapolis on a June day, Taylor joined his mourning family at her burial. Already behind his rivals, he returned to the track with a heavy heart.

July arrived and on Taylor went to a packed house at a Providence, Rhode Island, track where he picked up a win in the one-mile open and placed second in the half-mile. Afterward, a reporter traveling with the circuit suggested the peloton put to bed any hopes they may have had about Taylor's sprint being "killed."

Weeks later in Harrisburg, Pennsylvania, Taylor took first place and set a long-standing track record for the one-mile. In front of six thousand fans in Reading, Pennsylvania, Taylor defeated Eddie Bald, the reigning American champion, in a heated head-to-head duel, once again causing a stir with sportswriters. "His coming out will cause a ripple of surprise," wrote one reporter. The following day at Wilkes-Barre, before a record crowd, Taylor humiliated Nat Butler, one of three famous Butler brothers, in the one-mile open race, and placed second in the half-mile. "Taylor is one of the pluckiest little fellows of his race that ever came before the public," announced the

Brooklyn Eagle. "There is no more grueling contest in modern athletics than a first-class bicycle race, and a man who shows such pluck in the terrific fight down the stretch with the acknowledged champions of the sport as Taylor has done is entitled to the admiration at least of all true sportsmen."

A few months into the racing season, Taylor's presence on the nation's tracks was already having an impact on the sport. Wherever he raced, large crowds were gathering. Though Bald still held a sizable lead in the points column, the battle between him and Taylor, who hadn't competed in as many races because of his mother's death, was drawing great fan interest. They were fast becoming the sports story of the year as bike racing was enjoying explosive growth. According to several sources, attendance at nearly every other sporting event including baseball, horse racing, tennis, and even yachting had been adversely affected. One very detailed report, issued at the end of 1897, stated that bicycle racing had become the most popular form of entertainment in the United States. Eight million spectators spent $3.6 million to watch 2,912 bicycle races. Promoters, led by Brady's group, took in $1 million. In July alone, one million paying customers had passed through the turnstiles at the nation's tracks. Thousands more massed at countless road races.

As the 1897 season pushed into August, attendance would continue to surge and Taylor would be part of it. An important event was coming up, the most significant of his young career. Since 1880, the highlight of the racing season had been the annual convention of the League of American Wheelmen (LAW). With fans pouring in from all over the country, cities clamored to host the event, using it to showcase their cities and often sparing little expense. Boasting over four hundred miles of paved roads, Philadelphia was selected for the eighteenth annual meet scheduled for August 7 and 8.

From the minute they were granted the honors that winter, Philadelphia had been busy. To accommodate what race organizers believed would be enormous crowds, tens of thousands of dollars were spent extending and widening roads. An army of extra personnel had been hired to install extra ticket booths, concession stands, and a new three-lap to the mile wood track made of special pine painted olive green. Grandstand seating was increased from twelve thousand to over twenty-five thousand. In the months leading up to the event, the nation's papers detailed every aspect of the upcoming races. Next to the World's Fair, the annual LAW convention was considered the greatest "get" for a city—the Super Bowl of sporting events at the time.

The outlay of the Philadelphia Wheelmen and Brady's company, which managed the track, did not go to waste. The clanging bells of rolling cyclers began arriving at six o'clock on the morning of August 7 and did not let up until the next day. Special bicycle excursion trains, League of American Wheelmen boats, ferries, and steam and trolley lines disgorged around fifty thousand fans near Willow Grove Track. Thousands more on "century rides" pedaled in from Baltimore, Boston, New York, New Orleans, and as far away as the West Coast and Mexico. It was the largest crowd for any sporting event in American history.*

Every railroad company flowing into Philadelphia had been strong-armed by the LAW into adding extra railcars to house thousands of bicycles free of charge. Every railroad depot, road approach, and waterway teemed with LAW staff members handing out souvenirs, medallions, and programs as fans thronged into the city. Large delegations chugged into town by special Pullman cars from Saratoga, Indianapolis, and Omaha, each armed with reasons why their city should be awarded the coveted prize the following year. Indiana even went so far as to send Supreme Court justices, along with Taylor's former employer Harry Hearsey, to plead its case.

By race time, Philadelphia and surrounding suburbs had become an endless undulating stream of rims and spokes and humanity festooned in knickerbockers, golf stockings, badges, and other cycling paraphernalia. Once in town, the fans found Philly decked out in all its grandeur. Every club, saloon, and hotel in the vicinity was "filled to the roof" with visitors and had been adorned with bunting in the respective colors of the visiting wheelmen. Unable to find lodging anywhere in the city, visiting salesmen had to turn around and find other cities in which to sell their goods. Several trainers had to sleep on tables and desks in overfilled hostelries. Presses broke down printing programs and papers. "The League of American Wheelmen" shouted the *New York Times*, "owned the town."

Because they could earn many times the usual points for winning at the annual convention, nearly all the top riders were present: Champion Bald, Tom Cooper, the famous Butler brothers, Arthur Gardiner, Earl Kiser, William Becker, Walter Sanger, Fred Loughead, Jay Newhouse—some four hundred from all over the nation.

---

* The paying crowd at the 1897 League of American Wheelmen convention in Philadelphia was reported to be the largest for any sporting event in American history. For more information, see the Notes section in the back of the book.

To whittle down the field to a manageable number of the best riders, a series of preliminary heats—like qualifying heats for the Indianapolis 500—were run off. Taylor won or placed high enough in each of them to qualify for the finals, a noteworthy achievement in its own right. The race handicappers, however, still viewed him as an underdog. With Bald leading in the overall standings and Taylor still a beginner, they placed Taylor as limitman, giving him a thirty-five-yard head start as they had at Madison Square Garden.

In the final of the one-mile race, only the strongest riders in the nation remained. Taylor, "his skin covered in perspiration and shining like polished ebony," looked up from the starting line at the mass of noisy humanity and couldn't believe what he was seeing. The grandstand and surrounding area looked as though it was one continuous spectator. Many visiting reporters couldn't believe that a black man was actually allowed to race. "The most startling feature of the meet," wrote the *Baltimore Sun*, "was the fact that a colored man competed with white men."

The pistol crackled in the riders' ears. Taylor preserved his thirty-five-yard lead out of the gate and still led as the entire field veered around the backstretch. Somewhere near the last furlong, Taylor saw three riders closing on him through the corner of his eye. He could barely make out their faces; it was three of the most dominant riders in the country—Bald, Loughhead, and Cooper—all whittling away at his lead. Taylor quickly spun his head forward and gave it all he had for the final stretch. Soon the three stars caught up to him. For a moment, they all bunched together in a furious forward thrust. The quartet of riders, matched pedal stroke for pedal stroke, blazed down the homestretch at a tremendous clip. Behind them, one by one, the rest of the field dissolved.

Up in the grandstand, the immense throng roared, shaking the wooden rafters. Screaming through a megaphone at the top of his lungs, the race announcer's voice gave way.

For Taylor, though he was in the final scrum of riders, all was not right. Watching near the paddock area, his aquiline nose protruding out over the railing, Birdie Munger must have noticed Taylor's rookie mistake. When competing against a field of this caliber, there was no room for error. Within yards of the finish line, in the most important race of his young career, Taylor, having spent himself too soon, faltered!

He was close, but he wasn't there yet. Crossing the line a whisker's length in front of him rolled Fred Loughhead, Eddie Bald, and Tom Cooper. Taylor finished in fourth place. The crowd settled back into their seats.

Even though he lost in the finals, Taylor's trip to Philly had to have been gratifying. He had qualified for the finals in a major national meet and had fallen within a length of winning. With more than half a season left, a solid finish could still challenge Bald for overall honors. His every move was closely followed by an admiring press and public. "Little Taylor the colored boy," wrote one reporter, "is surprising the whole country with his game riding."

It was time to celebrate. In the evening, it was "Wheelmen's Night" and Philadelphia exploded into several gigantic bashes. The Belmonts had offered their Fairmont Park mansion for a mammoth lawn fete and bicycle-costumed dance party. Their sprawling yard and every avenue adjoining the mansion was jammed with over ten thousand elegantly dressed women and their escorts. All over town, bands blared, cigars were lit—100,000 at one party alone—and mass quantities of alcohol consumed, keeping the local magistrates busy for weeks to come. "Yes, the wheelmen owned the town," quipped the *Philadelphia Press*, and "some of them seem to think they own the earth."

Taylor surely watched the festivities, including balloon chariots rising skyward while men in parachutes mounted on illuminated bicycles descended onto the track from thousands of feet up. Later, fireworks rose from the track synchronized to Walter Damrosch's New York Symphony Orchestra.

While Taylor had much to celebrate, some men were secretly gathering, plodding, discussing ways to extinguish the spotlight that was beginning to shine on him.

Dark clouds were already gathering in the distance.

The war between horsemen and wheelmen continued as the summer of 1897 rolled on. For centuries, before the arrival of the steel steed in the 1870s, horsemen singularly ruled the land. In the beginning, when the two sportsmen shared the same tracks, horsemen didn't feel too threatened, thus a fairly amicable relationship formed. But once the crowds for the bike races rivaled or sometimes exceeded the horse races, the reinsmen began hatching elaborate methods of extracting revenge. By 1897, many of the bike tracks were wooden or concrete velodromes built specifically for bike racing, but a few towns still had the shared dirt or grass tracks.

On August 20, the horsemen—relegated to late morning status—were scheduled to race before the wheelmen at the Rigby Park Track in Portland, Maine, an exceptionally fast horse track. A couple thousand fans massed to watch the little bay horse, Gazette, blow out the field. As previously agreed, the horsemen were then responsible for smoothing out the track and cleaning up any mess their beasts left behind. But following their races, the horsemen saw a huge crowd swelling for the bike races, including the governors of every New England state. Their anger began building. They first took their resentment out on Lee Richardson, an exceedingly popular wheelman specializing in trick riding. When Richardson was in mid-exhibition, they wittingly charged out onto the track on their horses, throwing him off balance and causing him to abandon his act early. "Horses and bicycles don't jibe very well," cussed one reporter. But Richardson, a real ladies' favorite, got the ultimate masculine payback; women hovered around for hours, batting their eyelashes and snapping photos of him, all but ignoring the jockeys. "The graceful young rider has captured the hearts of the fairer sex," raved an envious *Portland Evening Express* writer.

The two warring factions came face-to-face. The horsemen apparently had angry dogs on their sides, including a little fox terrier who rode on the backs of some horses and a host of choleric bulldogs who growled at anyone who invaded their airspace. Teeth-chattering snarls, raised fists, and bitter words followed—the type that could only come from the mouths of young jockeys whose masculinity had been challenged. Reporters, hankering to see a good, old-fashioned horseman-versus-wheelman duel, bent their ear to it. "The horsemen did not take kindly to the bicycle boys," one man wrote, "and some of the remarks that the jockeys and the pool sellers [bookmakers] passed to the riders were disgraceful." But the horsemen, clearly overmatched by the larger wheelmen, decided to use brains in lieu of brawn. They quickly gathered their belongings, loaded up their prized horses, and hightailed it out of town—sans the track cleanup.

Soon afterward, Taylor arrived by boat with several riders. When they lined up at the starting line, they couldn't help but notice a few things. First, they saw a record crowd of twenty thousand raucous fans—more than one-half the entire population of Portland, Maine—occupying every seat in the grandstand. Then, they saw a track that looked like it had been used to reenact the Battle of Antietam, everywhere pocked with the hoofprints of large animals. When the traveling cycling journalists who shipped into town with the peloton saw the awful state of affairs, they too began carping on behalf of the riders. The track at Rigby Park they claimed, "being owned by the horsemen who have no love for the wheelmen was left in a very rough state."

Hugging the inner rail so he didn't have to zig and zag around as many pockmarks, Taylor was once again "the hero of the meet," taking two firsts and one second and becoming "the star of the afternoon." Following his victories, Taylor was escorted to the podium where he was introduced to the ecstatic throng. During the ceremonies, with thousands cheering him on, a mighty stench apparently permeated the air, one he surely remembered from his days on the farm. The odor must have been near the awards stand. Perhaps *someone* had purposely opened the floodgates of horse manure on the wheelmen. Taylor "abashedly" accepted his prize money, bowed to the crowd, and, according to the *Daily Eastern Argus*, "hurriedly left the stand."

Meanwhile, somewhere out in Maine's high country, a trainload of horsemen in their wide berths must have keeled over in fits of laughter. The horse owners, joked the *Portland Evening Express*, had "roasted the boys pretty hard."

As the racing season rolled into September, Taylor continued closing in on front-runner Eddie Bald in the points column. At ten August meets, he had finished first four times, second twice, fourth once, and had moved up from eighth place to fourth. With his form improving daily, Taylor stood a chance of challenging the champion—or at least finishing in the top three— when the racing circuit finished in late November.

But as the honeymoon between Taylor and the public grew, so too did the animosity against him from his competitors. "The position of the Negro is a trying one," wrote *Bearings*, "for every rider is anxious to top him, owing to his color, and the battle to beat him is waged fiercely day to day." On the backstretch, as the circuit chasers prepared for the second half of the season, there were whispers that certain riders were out to get him.

Starting in early September, those whispers became reality. At a race in Worcester, Taylor was deliberately crowded into the fence by a group of riders as he led the field around the backstretch. With no room on either side to maneuver, his wheel struck one of the posts, heaving his body to the ground and badly tearing his arms and legs. Scraping himself off the ground, Taylor sidled over to the steward's stand to lodge a complaint against a big bus of a man named Charlie Wells for fouling him. The stewards agreed and disqualified Wells. Shaken, Taylor nursed his wounds for a week, then prepared to rejoin the circuit.

Upon his return, riders began working in two-man combinations against him: MacFarland and Aker, Johnson and Butler, MacFarland and Stevens (aka "I and Stevie"), and so on through the whole racing fraternity. Taylor was always alone. On September 9, when he caught up to one of the combinations in front of a packed house at the Waverly Park Track in New Jersey, he was shoved over the pole during one of the preliminary heats.

On September 10, also at the Waverly Park Track, Taylor won the opening heat in the one-mile race by two feet. But when it came time for the final heat, he was nowhere to be found. He felt terrified. "I have a dread of injury every time I race" he told a reporter. While thousands of fans hollered "Taylor! Taylor!" down in the locker room several riders were threatening bodily harm if he rode again. These kinds of threats were not to be taken lightly. Taylor told the stewards, but they didn't seem to believe him. Wanting to avoid serious harm, he switched tactics and insisted that he was too tired to finish the race. The stewards asked Taylor for proof of his claim, but since none of the riders were willing to confess, he was forced to ride in the final. "A little more exercise might cure you," said one steward.

At the starting line, Taylor looked to either side and saw a field of riders glaring at him. Despair and trepidation spread through him. Not his usual aggressive self, he deliberately tucked in behind the pack, puttering across the tape as the lanterne rouge—bike-racing slang for the man who finishes in last place. "I know of no reason the boys should be against me," he would later lament. "I try to do clean riding without receiving the advantage of anything or anybody. I only ask from them the same kind of treatment . . ." Jay Eaton, one of the few sympathizers Taylor had in the peloton, summarized the treatment Taylor was facing. "Considering the length of time he has been in the game, Taylor has shown as much speed as any other rider . . . yet he is treated as a pariah by the majority of his fellows on the track."

Dealing with increasing hostility chipped away at Taylor's finite energy reserves, causing him to lose out on valuable championship points. His rapid ascension in the championship standings suddenly froze. With fall right around the corner and time running out, his dream of becoming the American sprint champion was in jeopardy.

Taylor's train sighed into Taunton, Massachusetts, during the final week of September. He was slated for two days of racing against a field of twelve riders, including second-place Tom Butler and William Becker, a noted rider from Minneapolis. Becker was a big, strapping man and the proud holder of the five-mile American Championship title. To some, he was seen as more than that. Since bicycles hit the streets in the 1860s, a few quack physicians, jealous horsemen, and general doomsayers warned of ill effects from bike riding. Cycling, they claimed, would ruin your eyes, hands, gums, face, heart, wrist, feet, and even your mind. With his muscular body and dashing appearance, William Becker fought back for the cycling industry, becoming a poster child of the real benefits of diligent bike riding. Several newspapers plastered his photo front and center, arms folded, handsome face thrown back in a stately pose, broad chest pushed out, fists planted firmly under his bulging arms.

Journalists filled vast column inches with the virtues of bike riding while simultaneously describing the remarkable physical qualities of Becker. "It's a pity that the old fogies who rail at cycling and talk of its debilitating effects upon the human body," ogled one reporter, "have not a chance to see, feel, and examine the splendid muscular tissue developed by W. E. Becker, America's five-mile champion."

Since they had been on the same racing circuit all year, Taylor was aware of Becker's racing exploits and his physical prowess—he's "as tough as a pine knot," wrote one correspondent. Throughout the season, Becker, who because of his pathological need for attention, was known to "play to the crowd." He had watched with silent scorn as huge crowds cheered Taylor on at race after race. Initially his anger was like a pilot light—ever-present but out of sight. But when Taylor's intense following began stealing some of *his* thunder, rage, jealousy, and the desire for revenge bubbled inside him like boiling water.

His largest seed of anger may have been planted in Springfield, Massachusetts, a week before Taylor's arrival in Taunton. By then, Taylor's popularity had risen off the charts, especially with fans in New England, a region that seemed to be a tonic for his racial ails. Even on a weekday— Tuesday the fourteenth of September—around twenty-five thousand fans, the largest throng in Springfield history, had crammed into the local track. Every hotel and boardinghouse had been filled. Countless neighboring towns had been all but stripped of their citizens. Since the grandstand wasn't nearly large enough to house everyone, the entire infield had bubbled over with a mass of smothering fans. With Becker—who had been eliminated in the preliminaries—waiting on the sidelines, Taylor, who performed better near his home turf, beat Bald twice. "The black cloud led the way," wrote one witness.

Becker must have figured he'd seen enough. Until the last week of September, he had held back his fury. But as was often said, hell hath no fury like revenge.

The first signs of a declining summer hung in the air as the field lined up for the start of the One-Mile Massachusetts Open on September 23. Apprehension spread through the peloton. Taylor's nerves were frayed and everyone noticed it. Taylor's Life in Danger headlined several papers days before the race. "It's true . . . they have threatened to injure me," Taylor confessed, stating some of the most ominous words of his life, "and I expect before the season is out they will do so."

With the crack of the pistol, the field surged forward, Tom Butler leading the pack, followed by Becker, with Taylor a close third. The three men careened around the track at a terrific pace, the rest of the field slowly inching back, struggling to stay in contention. The positioning remained static as the three leaders veered down the midstretch. Then, Taylor swooped in behind Becker, harnessing the sweeping draft created by his large frame, hoping he would eventually wear out trying to chase down front-runner Butler. Being intimately familiar with Taylor's inclination to finish with a burst to the inside, Becker inched closer to the inner pole to close off any attempt by Taylor to take over the prized position. With little more than the width of a bicycle separating him and the inner rail, Becker believed he had the inside all but choked off. But behind, as if tethered to him, Taylor was stalking him, waiting for the slightest sliver to open. It did.

Swerving down the final stretch, Becker craned his neck back to gauge Taylor's position, causing his bike to veer ever so slightly toward the outside. Taylor, who could be utterly fearless on a bike, saw the slender opening and pounced catlike toward the inside, his weight sinking deeper into his saddle. As Becker snapped his bobbing head forward, he felt a strong gust of air, while simultaneously glimpsing Taylor's lean frame whisking past him on the inside. As he passed, on one side mere inches separated Taylor from the rail and on the other side, no more than the width of a bicycle spoke separated him from Becker. In a flash, Taylor was more than a length ahead of him.

Once again Taylor had broken Becker.

Pandemonium rained down from the grandstand. Thousands of fans shouted as he shifted his sights on front-runner Butler. Becker, recalling all the times this scene had played out throughout the racing season, surely had one thought: *It's happening again!* He became unnerved, his eyes swelling with rage. He was riding amok.

Noticing that Butler's suicidal pace wasn't fading, Taylor dropped his head down and tore after him. But it was too late. Taylor crossed the line a length behind Butler, with Becker nipping frantically at his heels, finishing third.

Taylor stopped and leaned over his bike, his ribs heaving in and out. Before he had fully recovered from the strain of the intense race, through the roar of the crowd came a loud, masculine voice. Behind him the long, muscular arms of William Becker stretched forward. His open hands lunged in Taylor's direction, a demonic look washing over his face, an eerie portent of things to come.

Looking forward, Taylor never saw what was coming his way. Becker grabbed him from behind and tried hurling him to the ground. Taylor quickly collapsed under the tremendous force generated from Becker's sturdy frame. Taylor lay prostrate on the track floor while Becker's pent up rage and jealousy clamped down like a vise grip around the crook of his neck. Within moments, the weight of Becker's body and the firm grip around his neck compressed Taylor's chest and trachea, cutting off the already reduced flow of air to his lungs. A few minutes passed and Becker's grip had not subsided. Short of breath even before Becker began choking him, Taylor gasped for air, any air. Out from under the jumbled pile, a low, muffled plea for help dribbled out of Taylor's mouth, dying before reaching anyone.

At first, no one seemed to notice. Then a handful of fans began screaming for someone to help. Soon, a chorus of catcalls spilled down from the grandstand. Before long, chaos ensued. Piles of angry fans trampled out of the stands and tore after Becker. Enraged and oblivious, Becker continued his assault, the sweat from his hair dripping onto Taylor's jersey. His face was fire engine red, his lips were quivering, and his thick hands were still sinking into Taylor's neck, seemingly trying to squeeze the life out of him.

The color drained from Taylor's face. His eyes flickered shut and all resistance halted. His body went completely limp. A pulse of terror spread across the velodrome.

Doctors say a choke hold held for a few minutes causes convulsions, after four minutes brain death. One question droned through the track: *Is he trying to kill Taylor?*

Within minutes, the police intervened, finally prying Becker off Taylor's still frame. Agitated fans jeered and lunged at Becker. "Someone ought to give him a sound thrashing," one man yelled.

Meanwhile, Taylor lay motionless on the track. The compression that at first cut off his breathing threatened to shut off the flow of blood and oxygen to his brain.

To the massed thousands, it must have seemed as if Taylor were dead. Ten minutes had passed and he still lay stock-still. After separating Becker from the angry mob, the police hunkered over Taylor's flaccid frame desperately fighting to revive him. Today, the rescue breathing part of CPR is a standard lifesaver for choking and drowning victims. But in the 1890s when 10 percent of all violent crime involved strangulation, this effective technique was fifty years away from being discovered.

The life of one of the most likable and promising American sports figures hung in the balance.

An excruciating fifteen minutes passed and Taylor still lay unconscious. The police probably employed all the traditional techniques known at the time—slapping, yelling, striking the soles of his feet, massaging his neck, chest, and diaphragm.

After nearly twenty minutes in a lifeless state, Taylor finally came to. The crowd sighed. With someone's help, he stood up groggy and discombobulated, hobbling to the locker room where he struggled to regain his senses. The race stewards huddled to decide how to handle the final heats. One of the stewards had the insolence to suggest that Taylor race in the final heat despite nearly having the life strangled out of him. But with his head still in a fog, Taylor was in no condition to even think of it. "I was too badly injured to race," he later remembered. The stewards eventually came to their collective senses and disqualified Becker. Taylor sat in the dressing room choked up with emotion.

With great apprehension, he later emerged from the dim interior and hobbled to the rail station where he boarded a train. As the throaty, mournful wail of his train clattered west, the sun disappeared.

Word of Becker's assault spread through racing channels. In a special bulletin, Albert Mott, the bespectacled chairman of the LAW, announced the immediate suspension of Becker pending a full review. Becker's booming voice barked back, claiming that Taylor had crowded him. Virtually no one who was there bought into his argument.

The newsmen caught wind of the story and lit up the sports pages. Nearly all northern writers were calling for a multiyear ban so that Becker could, as one man wrote, "recover the manhood he seems to have totally lost." In its daily section devoted to cycling, the *New York Times* wrote a long piece titled "The Negro in Racing," in which they first read Becker the riot act, then moved on. "Probably none of the circuit riders has stored up resentment against the Major personally, unless the defeats he has administered to nearly all the circuit chasers may rankle in the breasts of some of the surly disposed, for the little Negro has always shown a very sportsmanlike spirit." Then the unnamed writer got right to what he believed was the heart of the matter. "It is simply a matter of race prejudice, which is one of the hardest things to eradicate."

The verdict among the reporters—that Becker should receive a long suspension, possibly forever—was virtually unanimous. But one writer, who at first condemned Becker, suggested Taylor was to blame. "Becker will undoubtedly be punished with a lengthy term of suspension, which he richly deserves," reasoned a *Bicycle World* reporter, "but the colored man, the cause of the unpleasantness, will remain just where he is, with the added halo of martyr to stimulate his hearty ill feeling which prevails against him among his rivals."

A heavy atmosphere awaited the verdict. Everyone knew the outcome would be an important indicator of the league's feelings on the touchy matter of race in professional bike racing. By imposing a harsh penalty at this early stage of Taylor's career, one proportional to the gravity of the offense, the league would be setting the stage for what was not acceptable. Conversely, a light penalty would send a message to all riders that the LAW wasn't going to take the issue seriously, in essence giving the white riders a free hand on the lone black man in the future.

While his allies in the press carried on, Taylor had other reasons to believe severe punishment would be doled out. Just two weeks before, Chairman Mott laid down the law in front of a group of riders at the Manhattan Beach Track. According to the *Brooklyn Daily Eagle*, Mott vowed "to rule over the riders with a rod of iron." He explained to the riders that he intended to be tough on anyone who committed fouls, saying that "a mere disqualification from a race was too small a punishment for foul riding." He then warned riders that he would not only disqualify them but fine them severely.

Taylor, who remained strangely silent throughout the affair, must have been comforted by Mott's pledge. If elbowing or crowding would bring serious consequences, an outright assault causing unconsciousness would certainly remove someone like Becker from the tracks for a long time, perhaps even for life as some in the press were demanding.

Refusing to give up on his dream of becoming the sprint champion of America, Taylor scampered off to a race in Cleveland late that evening. By the time his train arrived the next day, he was late. The crowd was waiting. He bolted to the dressing room, tore off his traveling clothes, and changed into his racing togs. Running on raw adrenaline, he proceeded to ride the legs off everyone there.

Days ticked on and still no decision had been reached. All eyes remained fixed on Baltimore and Mott's office where officials hovered over Becker's fate. The *Washington Post* was becoming impatient: "When racing men begin to kill each other on the track, it is time for quick and decisive action on the part of the racing board."

Finally, on September 27, five days after the notorious assault, Taylor got word that a verdict was about to be rendered.

He could not have imagined what was about to take place.

Chairman Mott stepped out into the Maryland sun and issued the board's decree. Instead of a life sentence and a stiff fine, as many had predicted, Becker received no suspension and a paltry $50 fine. The floodgates had opened.

Publicly, Taylor remained mute, but internally he had to have been burning up. With his silence, it seemed as if he were trying to solve his problems by ignoring them, a strategy he would pay for later in life. Perhaps he believed he could do nothing about it. Or he thought if he kept improving and crowds kept flocking to see him race, his problems would go away.

Unfortunately, the worst was yet to come. Shortly afterward, Taylor received word that most of the fine had been picked up by a passel of sympathetic white riders, another slap in the face to him. These despicable riders, lamented one Philadelphia writer, "were willing to identify themselves with one of the most disrespectful acts ever perpetrated on an American track."

Taylor felt alone. Three decades later, memories of the '97 season and the Becker assault still haunted him. "I found that the color prejudice was not confined to the South entirely, in fact it had asserted itself against me even in and around Boston. It would be difficult for me to narrate all the experiences which I underwent . . . and also to call to mind all the vicious attempts that were made to eliminate me from bicycle racing."

The northern correspondents wouldn't let the issue die. In their sports pages near the close of the year, the *New York Times* concluded that the assault "caused more animated discussion than any event this year." Clearly Taylor had some important decisions to make about his future as the only black man in a sport ruled by the tight grip of white men. For him, the wheels of justice did not roll on; instead they had stalled one September day on a hardened Massachusetts homestretch.

Following his win in Cleveland, Taylor packed his bags in preparation for what was known as the Southern Extension. Since the American Championship was granted to the rider who had the most points, there was no way a rider could win without picking up points from this Southern circuit. It encompassed one-third of the season.

In October, with or without him, the circuit was scheduled to chug west through Wisconsin, Michigan, and Illinois, then move south through Kentucky and Missouri, finally finishing in the deep Southern states of Georgia and Florida on November 20. By then, despite the hostility directed at him, Taylor was still seventh in the standings. If given a fair shake and a good showing during the Southern Extension, he stood a decent chance of a top-three finish.

But the Southern states proved unforgiving for black men in 1890s America, especially one who had been "humiliating" superior white men all season long. If Taylor decided to join the circuit, it would be an audacious move, reserved only for exceptionally ambitious men. "The Southern meets would never stand his entry," warned one of the traveling cycling scribes, echoing the words of many columnists.

And so, on September 28, special excursion trains stood waiting at the Buffalo, New York, depot. To save on travel and lodging cost for the riders, the league had commandeered a couple of "palace" railcars. One car had a glass observation room stocked with a grand piano; the other was a dining car with waiters, chefs, and "little gyp Pete." A sawed-off vagabond of unknown origin, little Pete was a mascot-porter who had become popular among the riders because of his willingness to please and his mystical ability to hoist nearly twice his weight. Funded by manufacturers, advance teams arrived in each city before the riders, alerting racing fans of their pending visit.

After inspecting the riders traveling home, two thousand fans stood in a light mist watching Major Taylor, Eddie Bald, and the rest of the field board the *Iolanthe* and the *Pickwick*. A haunting tension gripped the train as they rolled west over the plains. In Detroit on the first day of October, one of the first stops on the tour, Taylor was allowed to race. But a certain reticence clung to his racing style—the same one that reared up when he felt danger lurking. He quickly drifted out of the money, watching cautiously as Fred Loughead won the day.

As the railcars loaded with journalists sputtered farther south, Taylor's worst nightmares were realized. In town after town, including Indianapolis, New Albany, Louisville, and St. Louis, his entries were either refused by racist promoters or shunned by riders who, in cahoots with one another, refused to race against him. After a coldhearted riders' protest at the bike track in New Albany, Indiana, that included open threats of violence, he was reduced to racing against a horse on a seedy horse track on the other side of town. Dejected and disheartened, he lost. "The colored boy," one reporter wrote of his decision to leave the New Albany bike track, "thought discretion the better part of valor." Louisville, the next stop, was a hopeless cause; the owners of the local Fountain Ferry Track not only barred blacks from racing but they wouldn't allow them to step foot on the track surface for any reason.

Some people were even calling for the color line to be drawn by the press. *Bearings* began receiving flack for including Major Taylor in their *Bearings* thermometer, an ongoing gauge of each rider's total points and win percentage. Taylor was now relegated to reading about the men he had raced against all season, winning purses before idolatrous crowds. "I shall go to France," he hollered to the *Boston Globe* in a fit of anger. "There, I can hold my own and will be thought something of, maybe."

Days passed, then a week, then a month, and Taylor's point total remained frozen. Meanwhile, Bald, Cooper, Butler and others all saw their point totals rise. When the circuit headed into the deep South, he compared his point totals with the other riders. The spread had widened to the point where there was no chance of catching them even if he was allowed to race. His once prominent name had suddenly gone dark in the papers and in the standings.

The speeding wheel of Taylor's life had come to a standstill, his dream of becoming national champion and the honor and respect that came with it scattered to the southern winds. Soon the newsmen would splash the news. Eddie Bald, the man Taylor defeated in his first race at Madison Square Garden, was again crowned National Sprint Champion. Taylor's train sped to Worcester. Out his window, the jagged countryside flickered past. Gazing out in deep reflection, Taylor felt hollow.

Birdie Munger was having the kind of year no businessman cares to have. While Taylor was competing at the annual convention in Philadelphia back in August, hundreds of his employees had gone on strike. The strike had been preceded by a pay cut, which had been preceded by another pay cut. Since the day that Colonel Pope had dramatically reduced the price of his bicycles, Munger had been forced to lower costs on his models to an unprofitable level. There simply wasn't enough room for hundreds of manufacturers. Without the means to compete against the massive Pope juggernaut, something had to give.

Standing in his Middletown factory office one summer day, Munger and his partner heard a loud knock. When they opened the door, in walked a large, uniformed man—the kind of brown uniform a person usually saw when he was in trouble. It was a Connecticut sheriff named Brown there to place another lien on his four brick buildings, this time for allegedly failing to pay on a $25,000 loan. Soon after, Munger's business was placed in the hands of a receiver. Like the auto industry decades later, the bicycle industry was consolidating. In the coming months, the once-thriving Worcester Cycle Manufacturers Company would pass into history.

For the ex-high-wheeler—the most important man in Taylor's life— the end of an era was near. He would have to find his way in a changing world. While weaving his way in that new world, Munger would have little time for anything else. Sadly, he and Taylor parted ways. Taylor was now without his patron, his surrogate father, his best friend for as long as he could remember.

From his room in Worcester, Taylor watched the clouds thicken. Outside, bright leaves swirled in the cool, fall winds. He mulled over his future.

With Munger's shop in receivership, his options outside of racing had further narrowed. Effectively banned from competing in the latter third of the season, his choices inside racing didn't look so good either. Over the years, he would see or hear of several cyclists who were either killed or seriously injured from racing. He knew that continuing in an environment so hostile toward him could prove suicidal. Or as some suggested, he could succumb to the intimidation, retreating to the confines of his parents' farm and the life of anonymity from which he came.

But since the carefree days of his youth, the bicycle was all he had known. On its leather saddle he felt alive and free, liberated from the menial toils of the farm and factory. He had already become a top-ten rider in America, but he wanted to accomplish much more, like someday becoming the fastest bicycle rider in the world, as Munger had prophesized. And there were many places to see, like those exotic, faraway lands Arthur Zimmerman spoke of back at Munger's bachelor pad.

Professionally, the odds were stacked against him. Baseball and boxing had already rejected the idea of blacks at the professional level. But this was bike racing and Taylor was no ordinary man. When he allowed himself to think freely, emancipated from all attempts to bring him down to where blacks were "supposed" to be, he dreamed big dreams. In those moments, he was not satisfied with mediocrity; he wanted superstardom now and for posterity.

But by the end of the 1897 racing season, no riders wanted a black man to humiliate them in front of thousands of adoring racing fans. Perhaps, as some reporters suggested, it would be best for all concerned if he just left the country. In his anguish Taylor probably lost himself in Zimmerman's book, a wheelman's bible at the time. In it were stories of the internationally famous bicycle tracks as well as bicycle row where much of France congregated, including the "pretty Parisian Mademoiselles." France, the mecca of world cycling, would, he had heard, welcome him with open arms.

In November, the *New York Times* picked up on his thoughts and highlighted them in an article titled "Taylor Yearns for France." But going to France now would conflict with his goals. He had always wanted to follow in the footsteps of Arthur Zimmerman, his childhood hero who had first conquered his own country before sailing overseas.

If Taylor was going to continue with his chosen career in the cold, hard world that was 1890s America, he would have to find strength and guidance from others. He needed someone who would shine a light on him when others tried plunging him in darkness—perhaps someone not of this world. Having neither the desire nor the time to manage his racing affairs, he would also need someone of this world with experience in such matters. Major Taylor needed the divinity of almighty God and the tenacity of William A. Brady. Sometime that winter while he lingered in the depths of despair, providence would unite them.

Chapter 9

GUIDING LIGHT

William Brady reentered Major Taylor's cruel world during the cold winter of 1897–1898. By then, Brady had become the nation's preeminent sports promoter and, in his own immodest words, "was written up in more newspapers then Teddy Roosevelt." After helping him get his professional license and then watching him at Madison Square Garden, Brady believed Taylor would fit in perfectly with his managing motto—"Always try to find a champion." Now that he had at least partially recovered from the loss of his first wife, he was ready to get down to business. He contacted Taylor. The two men met and discussed a contract. Before signing on the dotted line, Brady, ever the businessman, checked with Albert Mott, chairman of the League of American Wheelmen, to make certain Taylor would have unfettered rights to race on *all* tracks nationwide. Mott assured Brady and a contract was signed.

Brady was happy to have him on board. "Billy Brady has always had plenty of admiration for the colored boy," a *New York Journal* reporter wrote "and his quick instinct to push a good thing along led him to take the colored boy under his wings."

An avid boxing fan, Taylor was aware of Brady's reputation and must have known he'd expect nothing less than another champion. Never one to think small, Brady signed up around fifty other riders, most of them non-circuit pacemen, and immediately provided them with the best of everything. He housed them in a spacious cottage called "the homestead," near the famous Manhattan Beach Velodrome and Sheepshead Bay horse track. There, he employed full-time chefs to handle the riders' nutritional needs. Riders were given access to a gymnasium, handball court, and a stable of masseurs, personal valets, and the nation's best trainers—all innovations in sport. Large enough to sleep fifty people, the homestead was surrounded by vast acreage where the riders and their trainers could relax by riding horseback and shooting the breeze on nonracing days. Close to the Manhattan track yet far enough away from the main hotels where the mass of inquisitive reporters stayed, these idyllic surroundings would serve as their headquarters for the season.

Under Brady's organization, wrote one reporter, "Taylor will not lack proper encouragement to race, and if he is bound to become as much of a sensation as promised, this summer will develop all there is in him."

For Brady, Kennedy, and Powers, this sizable investment had the potential for big rewards. While Brady provided Taylor and his entire stable of riders everything they could have asked for, it was also ideal for him personally. He had purchased the Manhattan Theatre close to the track, making it easy for him to juggle his passions. It was not uncommon for him to oversee a Broadway play one moment, then dash down the street and fulfill his obsession for bike racing the next.

Despite the inevitable difficulties of managing a black man in 1890's America, Brady saw big things in Taylor and sent for noted trainer Willis Troy to round him into top shape. A quick-witted Italian who had helped Arthur Zimmerman achieve worldwide stardom, Troy was hailed as one of the best trainers in the business.

Following the rough treatment he had endured the previous year, Taylor was pleased with the first-class arrangement and motivated to prove himself to Brady. "Naturally I was somewhat disturbed by these conditions until I signed up with . . . Brady. I'm out to whip the champions this season," he excitedly told a reporter, "and hope to have better luck on the track, and I'll start out to make this my banner year."

With the security of a contract with Brady, his future looking brighter, Taylor began filling his closets with new garb. Gone were any remnants of farm life, the Sears & Roebuck denim overalls and work shirts, the heavy lace-up work boots, the newsboy-style cap, the bandana around the neck. He began appearing in tailored suits, pleated gambler shirts with suspenders, and various accessories like a gold gentleman's pocket watch, brass-headed walking stick, white gloves, and custom shoes. Crowning the impressive wardrobe was the popular black felt Earl of Derby bowler hat. Flitting from town to town, Taylor cut a dapper figure in his new raiment. So much so, he was often hailed by sportswriters as the best-dressed man in the peloton, a notable distinction against men like Tom Cooper and Eddie Bald, long known for their stylish appearances.

When 1897 became 1898, Taylor was all dressed up with someplace to go. To succeed in the competitive sport of track racing a rider must begin training early in the season, usually January or February. This challenged riders living in cold Northern states. To overcome this, professional riders had trained at Camp Thunderbolt in Savannah, Georgia, for more than a decade or at a handful of tracks in sunny Florida. It was widely accepted that any rider failing to go south for winter training would be at a significant competitive disadvantage when the regular season began. So, wanting to get the season off to a good start, Brady assigned Troy the task of organizing a southern trip.

But as everyone knew, the South wasn't known for rolling out welcome mats for precocious black men. Troy accepted the assignment with much trepidation. Taylor didn't seem too concerned. "I think the change to a warmer climate will improve my health," he said with surprising naïveté.

Around the time Taylor signed with Brady, he also made a deep commitment to the teachings of Jesus Christ. Following in the footsteps of his loving mother Saphronia, he became a devoted Baptist. On New Year's Day, he declared his faith through an adult public baptism at the Johns-Street Baptist Church, a quaint wooden church in Worcester. From that moment until the day he died, he and his Bible became inseparable. He immersed himself in its pages at every opportunity—on trains traveling from town to town, in velodrome locker rooms across the country, on ships, and at home in his spare time. It gave him a sense of love for himself and others as well as a feeling of assurance, warmth, and security. The lessons he learned from its pages were exemplified in the kindness he displayed to those around him. His close relationship to God, his caring nature, and his pacific personality would all be given a startling amount of space in newspapers throughout his career.

Taylor's deeply held belief in the Baptist faith was sincere. As the lone black man in his chosen sport, it gave him strength when others tried knocking him down both physically and emotionally. It helped guide him during his racing career and through the racism he faced in his personal life. Religion became an integral part of his life, as was his relationship with his pastor, Reverend Hiram Conway. He followed his pastor's teachings to the best of his ability and devoted Sundays, the Sabbath day, entirely to Christ.

Spiritual leaders of all denominations would come to cherish true believers like Taylor, but initially at least many of them were none too happy with the rise of the wheelmen. As a nation deeply Calvinistic in orientation, they had strict ideas about what was permissible on Sundays. Sporting events were not among them. Yet for many Americans who worked long hours Monday through Saturday, Sunday was the only day they had for leisure and to attend sporting events. Intense debates sprang up over the issue of Sunday racing and leisure riding.

Since the early 1880s, religious leaders had been using their pulpits to broadcast their concerns. There one heard cautionary tales against infidelity, drinking, murder, and . . . bicycling!? Because the bicycle boom had been eating away at their parishioner base, some pastors went to great lengths to get them back. One Connecticut chaplain terrified his parishioners by painting a frightening picture of a string of cyclists, all without brakes, of course, rolling helplessly down a steep hill to a "place where there is no mud on the streets because of the high temperatures." Religious leaders in Covington, Kentucky, who had tried banning bicycles altogether, voted over-whelmingly to remove "all members who had their teeth filled with gold or who rode bicycles"—a perplexing juxtaposition of sins. Their feelings against wheelmen were so strong, even Taylor had to apply twice before Reverend Conway, who kept a "watchful eye" on him for over a year, finally admitted him to "full brotherhood."

Unable to compete against the bicycle, most eventually shifted. Deacon Jenkins Lloyd Jones from the All Souls Unitarian Church in Chicago preached that the bicycle was a good thing spiritually and morally, even allowing his congregation to park their bicycles in his church basement. While recognizing that the bicycle was reducing attendance, he still credited it for its ability to bring its jockey into "a closer communion with God." In his desperate mission to bring wheelmen back, one deacon perhaps swayed too far into his former adversary's camp. "I would canonize the inventor [of the bicycle]," he shouted to a hushed parish, "if only I knew his name."

Theologians struggled with the best way to handle the influx of Sunday morning cyclists and the resulting decrease in churchgoers. But for Taylor there was no confusion. While he may not have opposed leisure riding for some folks after church, he adamantly opposed Sunday racing and insisted that his trainers, masseurs, and valets take the day off as well. "I have the satisfaction of believing, and the extreme pleasure in feeling that I am right," he would say of his stance against Sunday racing, "and I know that many Christian people have been pleased with my testimony . . . I have done it because I believed it to be pleasing in the sight of God . . ."

This insistence against Sunday racing would put him at loggerheads with other riders and race promoters, eventually igniting whole nations into impassioned debates over the issue. Along the way, Taylor became conversant with theology and seems to have read the works of many Christian thinkers. He openly discussed his faith when asked, but never pushed it on others. "I am glad to say that I am a Christian," he would tell a reporter, "and it doesn't make any difference who knows it. I don't make a secret of it, though I don't go 'round sounding a trumpet." Yet he was often mocked by other riders for his beliefs, which only further galvanized him to his faith.

As the years rolled on, the most important quality he gained from his religious teachings appeared to be his modesty. Elite bike racers at the time were lionized like today's auto racers, yet Taylor remained humble. He always had a soft spot for those less fortunate. The messages in the Scriptures would be his guiding light in a world brimming with darkness.

Trainer Troy had a sinister feeling. He had been procrastinating about going South, but the Manhattan winter winds eventually pressed him into action. He knew it was critical for Taylor to train hard that winter because most of his rivals had already headed down there. But Troy, who was in charge of finding safe, comfortable lodging and knew the South from his days as Zimmerman's trainer, couldn't get over his edginess about taking Taylor to a section of the country he knew was openly hostile toward blacks.

Troy telegraphed a number of acquaintances in a few Florida cities before leaving. But as he feared, he was told to look elsewhere; the white riders, he was warned, would have no part of any "uppity Nigger" on their tracks. He kept searching. With the aid of another friend, Troy eventually secured a boardinghouse near a track in Savannah, Georgia. But as a Southern training ground for blacks, Georgia was no consolation prize. Next to Mississippi, Georgia had the highest number of lynchings in the country, more than one a day.

Beneath a gray winter sky and not wanting to cause a stir, Troy shipped out before Taylor. He rented rooms at a boardinghouse in his own name and told other boarders that his black "valet" was on his way. His diversionary tactic worked for exactly one day after Taylor had arrived. Someone noticed bicycle cases sitting outside with the name Major Taylor emblazoned on them. This person put two and two together and began talking to his neighbors. When the other boarders learned that a black man was staying in the same complex, they complained bitterly to the management. Then they threatened to leave if the "darkey" remained. Eventually, the owner buckled under the pressure and kicked Taylor out.

Disheartened, Troy and Taylor scoured Savannah for alternative housing. At some point Taylor was forced to sleep in a squalid horse stable, all musty and bug infested. Finally, they secured lodging with a sympathetic black family on Lincoln Street. After settling in, they set off to the Wheelmen Park Track for much needed training. But when they arrived, Taylor and his pacemakers were immediately booted off the track by an angry mob of track owners and cyclists. Taylor had to consign himself to sitting idly by while his competitors rolled past.

With precious time wasted and the track off limits, Taylor decided to train on the road instead. Here, too, he ran into difficulty. Local wheelmen began complaining bitterly about a "Nigger" having the "gall" to pass them. Not content with just removing him from their tracks, the white riders began devising ways to get him off "their" roads as well.

One afternoon, Taylor was all alone on a drab side street heading northwest out of town. Rolling briskly along, he spotted a trio of riders flying up ahead on a triplet—or bicycle built for three. Like any competitive cyclist who spots riders in front of him, Taylor gunned forward to challenge them. When he caught up to them, he recognized their faces; it was Savannah's top triplet team. They were startled to see him still in their town. When Taylor slipped in behind them, the rearmost rider craned his neck back and began yelling at him. "We have no intention of pacing a Nigger," he frothed. "Take a hike." Taylor ignored him and continued charging down Waters Road. As miles ticked off, the barbs exchanged soon degenerated into outright threats of violence toward Taylor. Taylor offered to settle the dispute with the bicycle instead of with violence. But the Southerners had other ideas. "Alright then," Taylor retorted, "if you won't pace me, I'll pace you." Taylor stood on his bike and powered forward with everything he had.

What began as a light afternoon training session turned into a heated, heads-down skirmish with Taylor leading three enraged white men through the vertiginous backstreets of Savannah. Eventually, and only because of his brute strength on a bicycle, Taylor was able to distance himself from the angry trio and roll back to his quarters unscathed.

Taylor may have been a fairly well-read man. But he was not yet completely aware of, or simply chose to ignore, the intensity of the hostility toward blacks in the South. He was about to learn.

The following morning, he rose, ate a hearty breakfast, and limbered up for another day of road training. On his way out, he saw an envelope lying at the base of the door. He opened it. As he read the letter inside, the hair on the back of his neck stood up. It said: "Mister Taylor, if you do not leave here before forty-eight hours, you will be sorry. We mean business. *Clear out if you value your life.*" The letter was signed "White Riders." And just in case the threatening words weren't enough, next to them was a drawing of a skull and crossbones.

Troy received a similar letter, warning him that his alliance with a black man was unacceptable in that part of the country. They gave him the same amount of time to pack his bags and speed north. Letters like these needed to be taken as a shuddering statement of intent. A white man had received a similar letter for giving piano lessons to a black student from a group who called themselves "White Cappers" shortly before Taylor and Troy received theirs. This letter told the recipient to get out of town or face "tar and feathering." The man discounted the warning and even threatened to prosecute the authors of the letter. Days later, his body was found in his cabin riddled with so many bullet holes, it was difficult to identify him.

Taylor, probably thinking the training incident was nothing more than a hard-fought competitive duel, was aghast at the letter's tone. With less than a week of broken training behind him, he sent word of the incident north to Brady. Meanwhile, a writer drubbed Taylor in the *Savannah Press* newspaper. "Major Taylor de coon rider from de north is dead sore on the south," he wrote, dipping his pen in vitriol. "He does not like the way he was treated in Savannah . . . but the Negro has no cause to kick. It is lucky that he was not severely handled. He forced himself on the white riders and made himself generally obnoxious. Hereafter Major Taylor will give Savannah a wide berth." A civil war-of-words broke out between Southern and Northern writers. "Cowardly Writer," responded a Massachusetts reporter, "Writes Like A Midnight Assassin. As soon as evidence is found," he continued, "they will be prosecuted in the U.S. Court." Another newspaper printed a drawing of Taylor on his bicycle desperately speeding away from a sign saying "Georgia." On the same road sign was an arrow pointing toward the words "New York."

Back at the homestead, Brady—rarely one to shy away from a fight—received word of the threats and boiled over. But being all too familiar with the lay of the land in the South and wanting to protect his investment, he bit his tongue, then instructed Taylor and Troy to head north.

Immediately, they packed their bags, rounded up their pacemen and all their bicycles, and got the hell out of Georgia. "It is useless for a colored person to attempt to get along in the South," Taylor told a reporter. "The feeling is so strong only a race war will settle it."

On his way north, Taylor felt the warm Georgia sun give way to the cold New York snow. If this incident was indicative of the rest of the season, it would be another turbulent year. It made him search for answers and peace of mind. He thumbed through the Scriptures, pausing on messages like those of Luke, whereby iniquities are countered with kindness and understanding:

I say to you that hear,
love your enemies,
do good to those that hate you,
bless those who curse you,
pray for those who abuse you.

He drifted into a deep sleep, the Bible's pages fluttering to the ground. He woke to the sight of Manhattan's Iron Pier, charming Victorian brownstones, spires from the eight-hundred-foot Manhattan Beach Hotel, and the

Iron Tower whisking tourists three hundred feet up for a high view of Coney Island. Though the year's racial tensions were just beginning, a sense of calm washed over him.

But Manhattan was enduring one of the coldest winters in years. Before the racing season's first pistol had been shot, Taylor was already put at a distinct disadvantage to his rivals, many of whom continued training under the swaying palms for months.

When the winter weather finally lifted, Taylor began training on the Manhattan Beach Track. From his headquarters in Manhattan, Brady could do little about the Georgia riders. But he wasted no time warning the rest of the peloton. "He gave the circuit chasers to understand," stated the *New York Journal*, "that trouble would follow any underhand work or threats against the Major." Some riders took note. "The big men of the circuit appreciate the power in the racing game that Brady represented and Taylor was allowed to use the training quarters in peace."

The early season racial difficulties continued. In April, two men named Tom Eck and Senator Morgan, managers of Philadelphia's Woodside Park Track and owners of a rival racing syndicate, formally announced their plans to bar Taylor from their track. Taylor, they said, "must suffer with the others. Our entry blanks will be plainly marked 'for whites only.'" Coming from a supposedly tolerant Northern state, their harsh stance surprised many observers. What made it more puzzling was that Eck had been Birdie Munger's manager for several years. It's hard to believe Eck was unaware of the special relationship between Munger and Taylor before attempting the ban.

But as they were about to learn, they weren't dealing with Munger. They were dealing with an altogether different man. Though it had always been Taylor's and Munger's style to remain silent in such instances, hoping it would pass in time, this was not William Brady's style. "To step on Brady's toes intentionally was to get hit," the *New York Times* would write, "and not always figuratively either." Brady immediately got on his high horse, clopped down to the New York papers, stormed into the offices of his sports writing friends, and, with all 130 pounds of him, began crucifying Eck and company about their "unjust discrimination." After a long, largely unprintable verbal incendiary in which the tone of his Irish tongue matched the flame of his fire-engine red hair, he finished with a succinct warning to the duo. "I beg to assure the *gentlemen*," he hollered, his voice rising, "that *any time* the *Major* enters a race, the American Cycle Racing Association will see to it that he receives fair treatment."

Over in Philly, Eck caught wind of Brady's public harangue and began hedging. New York and Boston were okay, he said, but "about Philadelphia, I am not so sure." But when Brady continued his condemnation, bringing in every friendly newsman he could find, Eck buckled under the weight of his words. Claiming to have been misquoted by the press, Eck said that he would see if matters could be "adjusted." Eck then retreated into a complete about-face. "The promoter who could debar a good drawing card like Major Taylor does not understand his business," he said. "Although a colored man he may ride against my men when and wherever he chooses."

Senator Morgan, who seemed completely taken aback by Brady's strong reaction—not to mention the negative press he was receiving in nearly all Eastern newspapers—also backpedaled. "I am not in favor of barring Taylor from any races," he said, "on any of the tracks of this association . . . this is unfortunate as I think Taylor a gentlemanly little rider, however, Brady has seen fit to take the matter up. Eck spoke before he thought, that is all, and the matter will be righted."

Taylor sat back and soaked it all in. Never before had such a prominent man, white or black, stood up for him in such a potent public fashion. He took comfort in the strength of Brady's words.

The train carrying William Brady and Major Taylor whistled into Philadelphia's Tioga Track on the morning of July 16. Because of his shortened preseason training routine, Taylor found himself floundering in a distant fourth place when the heat of midsummer arrived. But with each passing week, Brady couldn't help but notice that Taylor was showing signs of catching up to his main rivals. The race handicappers apparently agreed. Whereas they used to position him as limitman thirty-five or more yards ahead of scratchman Bald in one-mile handicap races, they began moving him back to within fifteen or twenty yards. But the stronger he became, the more trouble seemed to follow in his wake.

While most of the hostility directed at Taylor had come from low-level riders, it wasn't limited to them. As he slowly inched up in the standings, more elite riders became concerned about his rising popularity. Even Eddie Bald, the top circuit rider, began developing a disdain toward

Taylor, reportedly threatening to "thrash" him if the opportunity arose. Taylor lived under the constant threat of riders teaming up to pocket, elbow, sandwich, or flat-out dump him to the hard velodrome surface. He began sheltering himself in the protective cocoon of the rear of the peloton where he could eye and stalk his competitors until an opening formed. When he made his jump through the thicket of riders, he was often forced into pitching his head and body deep into his handlebars to avoid the inevitable jab or elbow. He rides so low, commented rider Howard Freeman, "his nose touches his handlebar." While effective, his new tactics were by no means foolproof.

While Taylor warmed up, Brady watched seven thousand fans trample into Philadelphia's small Tioga Track for a series of championship-level races. He had Taylor signed up to compete in the one-mile open and the one-mile handicap races. Before the races, a heated argument took place between the riders and track management. Apparently nobody wanted to wear unlucky jersey number thirteen. With a hidden grin, Taylor ended the argument, proudly slipping the forbidden jersey over his shoulders. "They cannot outride me anyway," Brady overheard him say. Taylor wasted no time making an impression with the ardent Philadelphia crowd, which had become endeared to him at the national convention in 1897. In the one-mile open race, he defeated all his main rivals, becoming "the idol of the meet."

As the field lined up for the final of the one-mile handicap, the crowd rose and chanted his name. With most of the crowd cheering for him, animosity filled the ranks of the riders. His eyes trained on the track, Brady must have noticed riders sneering at Taylor as they broke from the line. Bald quickly caught up to Taylor, then shot out to the lead, with several riders in tow. Taylor tucked into the slipstream, waiting for the right moment to pounce. Just as the bell rang announcing the start of the final lap, Taylor saw what looked like an opening and uncoiled.

A wall of riders immediately formed in front of him. He rolled near the human barrier, body arching over his bike, eyes set, head down. Suddenly, like a flock of angry birds, the cabal of riders—out of the steward's view— swerved outward in unison, deliberately bashing him off-kilter. Up in the grandstand, the Taylor-friendly crowd gasped. Pinching a cigar in his fingers, Brady felt his fury intensify.

For an agonizing moment, Taylor fought with his swerving craft, frantically trying to keep it from crashing. With his bike teetering on the edge,

Taylor staggered sideways, clinging on for dear life while simultaneously trying to decelerate. For good reason; he was on a collision course with the press and stewards' stand lining the track. Perched high up in the boxes, scores of horrified reporters recoiled as they watched Taylor, seemingly out of control, rapidly approaching the hardwood structure beneath them. Taylor was on the verge of being maimed.

In an amazing display of acrobatic riding, Taylor somehow righted his bike at the last minute, shimmied back in his saddle, then scorched for the line. By then he was alone—in last place. Brady and the crowd exhaled. When Taylor finally caught up with the pack, it was too late. Owen Stevens had torn across the line in front of him with Bald by his side.

Acting as head race steward that day, Chairman Mott stared out through his double-barreled opera glasses. Surely aware of Brady's presence, he knew he had to do something. He immediately called an inquiry and demanded to know who was responsible. Mott had seen the commotion and knew something was afoot, but because of the large number of riders, his view of the infraction had been impeded. He conferred with the other stewards. He then summoned several riders to the stewards' quarters and one by one called them on the carpet.

None of them would talk.

Outside, the crowd stood in confusion. The ruling finally came down. Their silence had worked. Unable to prove collusion or pin the infraction on any particular rider, the race results were upheld and no fines were levied. Brady was incredulous. Down in the winner's circle, Stevens, who was no fan of Taylor, accepted the trophy and his purse with a telling smirk. From the sidelines, Taylor watched sober-faced. He had once again lost valuable points to competitors, clearly in cahoots with one another. "The nerve of the men in doing teamwork right under the eyes of the chairman," barked one race writer, "took the breath away from many."

Incensed, Brady bounded up the press box stairs to address journalists and to once again stick up for his rider. "Leave the boy alone and he will land a winner every time," he shouted. "Think of the odds he has worked under. Of course, it is humiliating to have colored boys win," he continued, his arms flailing, "but he does the trick honestly, and in racing parlance, there isn't a whiter man on the track. He's game to the core, and you never hear him complain." Nearly everyone agreed, including his previously dubious partner, Pat Powers. "He can beat any of them in a match race," Powers shouted, a lump of chewing tobacco swishing in the corner of his mouth, "and they know it."

On the train afterward, Taylor felt restless. Brady's mood mimicked that of his rider. Each unwound in his own way. Brady no doubt soothed his anger with a bottle of wine; Taylor drank water and slept. In the midst of a trying season, both men headed north.

They reeled into New Jersey's Asbury Park on the morning of July 28. When the railcar door slid open and Taylor stepped out, he caught sight of an old friend surrounded by admiring fans. Though it had been five years since they had first crossed paths, he recalled the man's features, the wide smile, the caring eyes, the towering figure, as if he'd seen him just yesterday. Waiting on the platform stood Arthur Zimmerman, the former champion of the world. Zimmerman raised his arm and offered his hand.

Hardly a day had passed without Taylor harking back to that memorable day when Zimmerman had wooed him with fantastic stories of races won at tracks across the globe. Zimmerman could not have known just how momentous that brief meeting had been for Taylor or how much the kindness he displayed toward this anonymous black boy had inspired him to carry on amid pervasive racism.

In the intervening years, Zimmerman had lost some of the jump in his legs, yet his legendary status with the American public, sportswriters, and every pro rider remained. Capitalizing on his popularity and his ability to boost attendance, Brady often invited Zimmerman to act as startman, the person who shot the pistol to begin a race. Since their last meeting at Munger's bachelor pad, Zimmerman had been following Taylor's rise to national prominence with great interest. Even though he was still recuperating from a near-deadly case of Mexican fever when he received word that Taylor was racing in his hometown, Zimmerman, who didn't have a racial bone in his body, greeted him at the depot and offered up his home while he was in town.

Familiar with the temptations pro cyclists faced—frequent invitations to late-night parties, the drinking, gambling, and womanizing—Zimmerman praised Taylor for his racing success and for abstaining from the vices that had burned out some of his competitors. Zimmerman escorted Taylor to the track as Taylor had escorted him to Munger's home years ago.

"I am very anxious to see you win the event this afternoon," Zimmerman said, "and I feel sure you will, even without a suggestion from me; however I have one to offer, which aided me in my heyday, and I trust you will give it consideration." Hours before the race, Zimmerman, who had a patriarchal quality about him, led Taylor out on the rain-soaked track where he gave him a lesson on the subtleties of winning on the Newark oval. The two men—one declining, the other rising—stood alone on the barren track and talked in the vernacular of bike racers.

"If you can lead the field into this turn," Zimmerman said, pointing to the backstretch halfway to the last turn, "nobody can pass you before you cross the tape. I made all my successful sprints from this identical spot."

Taylor marked the spot, thanked Zimmie for his sage advice, and limbered up. Watching the former world champion walk off the track, his best years behind him, Taylor must have viewed the incident as a passing of the baton. Later that afternoon, Brady and boxer Jim Corbett, his official time-keeper, wedged into the damp grandstand alongside a small and wet crowd of a couple thousand fans. Though it was a drizzly weekday race with a light purse, with Zimmerman and "Papa" Zimmerman standing by, it meant everything to Taylor.

Zimmerman pointed his pistol skyward. The riders, surely jealous of the attention the former star had given Taylor, glanced up at Zimmerman. "No group of racing horses," commented Taylor, "ever faced the barrier in a more nervous state." The field broke even and stayed bunched together until midway through the one-mile open race. As he rounded the far turn, Taylor eased up, dropping into the slipstream of the main field and surveying his rivals for potential weaknesses. Rolling into view of "the spot" on the track, Taylor experienced a unique sensation. Professional cyclists claim that on certain days they are so strong it's as if their bicycles have no chains. They feel little resistance; all things move forward effortlessly.

For Major Taylor, this was one of those days and Zimmerman's famous spot was upon him. At the precise mark, he channeled his surge of energy into a vicious sprint for the line. One by one, the rest of the field, trying with all their might to respond to Taylor's move, collapsed under the strain. The first to pop off the back was Stevens, then Gardiner, followed by Cooper. The last to crack, yards before the tape, was Champion Bald.

Taylor flew across the line in front and alone. Glowing like a child, he circled the track waving to the crowd. Zimmerman watched the crowd swarming around him, recalling his own glory days. "Our friend Birdie Munger was right about you," Zimmerman repeated several times as he, Brady, and Corbett doffed their caps and joined the celebration on the track. "He shared the honors with Major Taylor," wrote the *Boston Globe*, "the lion of the hour."

The victory and the resulting purse, however sparse, proved to be one of the most rewarding moments of Taylor's life. But it meant as much to Zimmerman as it did to Taylor. "I have never seen a more happy man in my life than Arthur A. Zimmerman as he shook my hand warmly at the conclusion of the race," Taylor remembered.

In the end, it wasn't the racing tip that had motivated Taylor. It was that a man of Zimmerman's stature cared about *him*, the despised black man. It would prove to be the kind of compassion that was redemptive and everlasting.

Somewhere out on that barren New Jersey backstretch before an otherwise forgettable race, a ceremonial baton was passed. Given the racial acrimony at the time, it was a unique exchange—passing from the wavering hands of a legendary white man who had lived a life of unprecedented fame and glory into the grasp of a persecuted black man who had previously moved in obscurity.

With that baton clenched in his hand, it was now up to Taylor to run with it—or watch it fade away.

Chapter 10

THE BOYS WOULD GLADLY MAKE HIM WHITE

By the middle of 1898, William Brady believed he had greatness in his midst. It was time, he reasoned, to expand Taylor's horizons. For race promoters, a top-flight match race could attract big crowds and equally large gate receipts. For riders, there was the potential for significant purses and increased notoriety. For Taylor, it would be time to test his mettle in something new. Beyond the profit potential, Brady had other reasons for wanting to involve Taylor in match races. In nearly every traditional race, he noticed Taylor's true talent had been impeded by other riders. Because he hadn't yet been allowed to soar freely, no one knew how fast Major Taylor really was.

A lot of people were eager to find out. So Brady put out a nationwide challenge to every pro rider, including the "big four": Eddie Bald, Arthur Gardiner, Tom Cooper, and Earl Kiser. "I will match Major Taylor with any man in America in a sprint race for any amount from $1,000 to $5,000," he announced confidently. Under normal circumstances, riders would have gone out of their way for a shot at that kind of purse. Brady employed all the promotional tricks he had learned from his days managing Corbett, yet no one seemed willing to come near Taylor. "I want to race these men," Taylor told a reporter, "but they choose to ignore me entirely . . ."

His rivals fired back with every conceivable excuse—too sick, too busy, maybe next week. Eddie Bald, who had just agreed to a match race against Tom Cooper for half of what Brady was offering, came right out with it, claiming that competing head to head against a black man "would affect him socially." Many observers read right through their explanations. Previously, those losing an open race to Taylor could explain it away by claiming they were pocketed or that something beyond their control had been responsible. But in match races, or "races of truth" as they are called, little room for excuses is available to the vanquished. In Taylor's case, none of the elite riders wanted to risk explaining to their friends and family why they lost a heavily publicized match race to a man born of an "inferior" race.

Believing it was racism pure and simple, Brady was furious at the American circuit chasers. But there was a reason why he was known as "The Fighting Man." After it became clear that none of the elite American riders would risk the potential shame and humiliation, he sent all the way to Wales for a tiny crumb of a man named Jimmy "Midget" Michaels, who was universally hailed as "the athletic marvel of the century."

Michaels was a boy-faced, twenty-two-year-old Welshmen who, even soaking wet, rarely tipped the scales at more than 105 pounds. His lithe frame would measure more than five feet but only if he stepped into his much taller wife's high heels. Michaels was so small and looked so young, a judge had recently kicked him out of a Calaboose because the court did not allow "minors" in the local jail. Yet in 1898, a few years beyond Zimmerman's peak, Michaels was among the most talked about, written about, and idolized athletes in the world. Along with Corbett and Zimmerman, he was also among the richest.

His initiation into the sport had apparently been inauspicious. "His opponents," explained Brady, "laughed out loud when they saw this pink-cheeked midget, hardly out of short pants, trotting his wheel around the track to compete with grown men. But once he was in the saddle and digging into the pedals behind his pace," continued Brady, "he turned into a streaking wonder."

Unlike Taylor, Michaels avoided the regular circuit races and specialized instead on one thing—paced match races. In this popular niche in which sportswriters judged him "invincible," Michaels had set many world speed records, defeating everyone he had ever faced. No one, including puzzled physicians who were brought in to analyze him, could figure out where, within his diminutive body, such incredible power came from. Some wondered if it wasn't just one giant lung. His global fame was such that before he agreed to ship overseas, he demanded a king's ransom from Brady—a guaranteed minimum of $22,500, plus purses and promotional fees from bike and tire manufacturers. One of only a few promoters able to underwrite such a venture, Brady, with his partners, agreed to Michaels's demands.

The timing was right. America was utterly obsessed with speed, and any minute advance in technology or human conditioning that increased a rider's speed captivated the public. Brady understood this well and was the man most responsible for bringing paced racing to America. In those days before reliable motorcycles, he had hired more than fifty strong "pace" riders to pilot super long bicycles built for anywhere between two to eight men. Paced racing was fast and dangerous. "Take a spill off a speeding bicycle on a hardwood track," commented Brady years later, "and you'd be better off if you'd stopped one of Joe Louis's punches."

Brady sat down with Michaels and Michaels's agent and ironed out a deal. Brady agreed to pit Taylor against Michaels in a one-mile paced match race, even though paced match races were not part of Taylor's normal routine. Michaels agreed, and even though he had set a world record for the one-mile, his preference was for middle distances. In mid-August, while waiting for his new Orient bicycle in Worcester, Taylor received a telegraph from Brady ordering him to get to New Jersey at once to prepare for the race. Upon arrival, Taylor worked out at Jim Corbett's sporting center, a resort nestled in among seven acres of pine trees near the Asbury Park bike track. The Farm, as it was called, had tennis and handball courts, dumbbells, pulley weights, pools, punching bags, masseurs, and Aunt Mary, a fabulous black cook who could prepare any wholesome meals he wanted. The world-famous training grounds had become besieged with so many visitors who wanted to meet the star athletes who worked out there, Brady required them to procure a special pass signed by him.

Though it was the ideal matchup, the match race with Michaels would have to wait until after Michaels responded to a summons to appear before one of his staunchest fans. At the White House waiting to receive him for dinner—along with Dave Shafer, James Kennedy, and William Brady—was First Lady Ida and President McKinley, who had recently given a rousing pro-wheelmen speech before a partisan group of three thousand riders. If it was like most of his meals, Midget Michaels pecked on a light salad. Kennedy, a pleasingly plump man of prime 1890's stock, surely devoured half the White House. Brady apparently kept his Irish tongue in check for one evening.

A fterward, William Brady paid a visit to the New York newsrooms to charm his old friends. The press, already fascinated with the match-up, didn't need a lot of prodding. With their coverage, including drawings of expected luminaries (with Zimmerman being one of them), the *New York Sun* and the *New York Journal* seemed to find the topic more interesting than the Spanish-American War.

Taylor kicked back and watched a master promoter in action. "I dare say," he commented after having competed in hundreds of races, "no bicycle race that was ever conducted in this country ever received the amount of space in the sporting pages that this one did."

On August 28, thousands of fans filed into the Manhattan Beach Velodrome. The only thing keeping it from being a sellout, one editor believed, was the inevitability of another Michaels's victory. With Taylor, the young black star, competing against Michaels, who women thought "was the cutest thing they ever saw," the place had a feminine air about it. All the female fawning had apparently gotten to Michaels. "He made so much money and received so much adoration from the ladies," Brady remembered in amazement, "that his head was badly turned."

All around the track, large sums of money changed hands, with Michaels as the favorite. Feeling surprisingly confident, Brady sidelined Dave Shafer, Michaels's manager, and offered to wager a large sum on Taylor's legs. "Michaels," said Brady, "will be up against the best man in the world." Shafer accepted the challenge with a knowing smile.

Without the typical wind gust swirling in from the Atlantic, an unusual stillness permeated the balmy track, causing the first of several signature products to appear. Ladies cooled themselves with silk accordion fans that featured Taylor prominently in the center and nineteen white riders, their arms folded, filling in each fold.

Defeating Jimmy Michaels would mean worldwide fame and fortune for Taylor, and everyone knew it. Tension filled the air. "I have seen enthusiastic gatherings at bike tracks all over the country," remembered Taylor, "but I never saw one more on edge than the assembly that witnessed the final heat in this great race."

Out of the gate, Taylor and Michaels broke even. They remained neck and neck through the first of three laps. Right before midstretch, conserving energy for the final push, Michaels purposely faded behind Taylor, hounding him like a dachshund nipping at the heels of a speeding greyhound. Noticing the gap widening and Taylor pressing forward at a relentless pace, Michaels gunned ahead, lopping yards off Taylor's lead with every turn of his crank. Bending around the final turn of the second lap, Michaels drew up near Taylor again. The hair-raising speed of both men was building and building, bringing the riders near exhaustion.

The two men winged down the final lap at a tremendous pace, one of the fastest in bike-racing history. Taylor glanced to his side and saw Michaels's tiny legs rotating at an astounding cadence. Mere inches in front of him he saw twenty powerful legs and ten straining pacemen on quintuplets leading them toward the tape. Taylor's eyes were riveted on the finish line ahead. Waiting there, "bounding about like a rubber ball," stood Brady, sweat dripping from his brow, stopwatch clenched in one hand, a pinched Cuban cigar in the other.

With a half-lap remaining, Brady noticed Michaels becoming unwound. His hips and shoulders began rocking side to side, legs revving like pistons in a four-cylinder engine. Up in the grandstand Arthur Zimmerman rose to his feet screaming, his temple puckered in sweat.

Taylor's merciless pace never wavered. His form, in contrast to Michaels's, remained smooth, graceful, sparrow-like, an eight-cylinder thundering toward the line. Brady then witnessed something he had rarely heard over the years: Taylor cried out to his pacemen for more speed! "Move along!" he hollered. "Move along!" But the pace was too much, and all five pacemen were completely spent. Taylor passed his pacers. Seeing this through his sunken eyes, "face pale as a corpse," Michaels sat up on his bike and capitulated. He too was spent. Taylor tucked his head down into his handlebars and rushed forward, crossing the line twenty yards in front.

The king of pace racing had been dethroned! At once, Manhattan Beach Track became a noisy, rumbling place, men and women leaping in the aisles.

For the first time in his career, Michaels was hissed by the crowd. Taylor circled the track triumphantly as flowers and women's hats fell near his feet, his stealthy form melting into the crowd, jersey number thirteen flapping in the wind. Brady was feeling emboldened. He ran over to the announcer's booth and ripped the megaphone away from announcer Fred Burnett. His stentorian voice cut out over the grandstand. "I am announcing a sweeping challenge for another match race between these two men for a purse of $5,000 to $10,000 for any distance up to 100 miles," he bellowed. "Do you want to see these men race again?" The wildly popular challenge was received with tumultuous applause.

Michaels slinked into his locker room.

Following the race, the crowds piled into streetcars and horse-taxis, stopping long enough to empty restaurants like Delmonico's and Sherry's of food and drink. Brady tracked down Taylor, congratulated him, and handed him an extra $1,000. "Just a little present from one good sport to another," he said.

Taylor was ecstatic with his win and Brady's gesture. Without any obligation to do so, he graciously shared some of his purse with his pacemen, all of them white. He was so thrilled, he even began thanking reporters. "I want to thank your paper," he told the *New York Sun*, "for the way you have treated me. No one knows how much I appreciate your good will."

Agitated, Michaels had made several unusual threats that became revealed in newspapers worldwide in headlines such as MICHAELS MAY QUIT CYCLE RACING FOR GOOD, WILL THEN BECOME JOCKEY–OWNER. Anticipating the potential publicity value, horseman Phil Dwyer grinned. Mindful of the significant investment he had in Michaels, Brady cringed. But after giving him the rough side of his tongue, not to mention the threat of a lawsuit, Brady eventually wrung enough of the obstreperousness out of Michaels to keep him racing a steel steed for most of the next half decade.

If Taylor's victory over Eddie Bald in his first professional race at Madison Square Garden brought him a degree of notoriety, his conquest over Michaels, known the world over, stopped the presses. The victory, said the *New York Sun*, "was like an electric shock to many who did not believe a colored man could win."

Taylor's stock was soaring. Back at the homestead, phones rang off the hook, letters clogged the mail, and overseas cables congested Brady's office the likes of which he hadn't seen since Corbett defeated Sullivan. The offers came from all over America and from the cycling meccas of Italy, Germany, Holland, France, and Australia. Promoters, manufacturers, and cigarette makers now wanted a piece of Taylor. Under his handling, Brady told a reporter, "Major Taylor will develop into a world-beater."

Taylor seemed to thrive under Brady's tutelage. With men like Michaels and Zimmerman raking in, by some estimates, healthy five-figure annual incomes—an enormous sum of money in the 1890s—Taylor suddenly had the potential to be among the world's highest paid athletes. Major Taylor's victory, proclaimed the *New York Sun*, "coming as it did just after the unsuccessful efforts of certain race meet managers to debar him from their tracks on account of his color, and for no other reason, has established fortune for him."

In the minds of many observers, it now seemed unlikely any track owners or race promoters would bar Taylor from their tracks or races. This belief seemed to be borne out the same day Taylor defeated Michaels. Brady received a dispatch from T. Laing, manager of St. Louis Circuit City Track, formally inviting Taylor to an important national meet being held there in October. Laing was the manager who had barred Taylor from his track in 1897, all but crippling his chances of winning the championships.

Putting all distractions out of his mind, Taylor stayed focused on the one goal that had eluded him, his dream since early childhood: to become the sprint champion of America. And that meant winning as many points as possible in the national circuit races.

It was the early afternoon of September 27, 1898, and the owners of New Jersey's Trenton House Hotel had become curious. Outside, amid a pouring rain, special trains unloaded carloads of riders, valets, and reporters from all over the country for a national meet. But when the doors of the railcars slid open and suited attorneys stepped out with them, it became obvious something bigger than just another bike race was going on.

There was.

Professional bike racing had been experiencing the same challenges professional baseball and horse racing had faced a few years before. Rumors trickled through the peloton that a few "rebels" were contemplating breaking away from racing's governing body, the League of American Wheelmen. As the season ground forward, the list of possible defectors had grown to a point where a full-scale meeting became necessary.

The movement surprised many racing fans. Sportswriters had raved about how well the LAW was run; some even suggested that bike racing was the best organized of the major sports. Knowing the sheer scope of the league's racing responsibilities—overseeing a multitude of clubs, riders, track owners, and big money promoters, all with their own unique interest—others weren't so surprised. The league, some believed, should give up control of bike racing and focus on the monumental task of expanding the nation's roads.

This September revolution wasn't the first time the league's authority had been challenged. But all previous rebellions had been quickly quashed by influential League leaders, often with strong political ties, and the press, who frequently condemned the instigators as naïve and underfunded. But this attempt had more weight behind it. Apparently some riders, promoters, and disgruntled former League employees believed they could do better, and the Trenton House was their staging ground to try to prove it.

Taylor listened intently to both sides, jotting down copious notes. Immediately, several top-level riders appeared poised to jump ship. Taylor decided to hold off until he was convinced the new organization would have the same quality of management and financial backing as the LAW. He had other reasons for pause; rumors that several riders wanted to use a "secret ballot" to anonymously vote him out of the new league began circulating. In the interim, the dark New Jersey skies unleashed buckets of rain on the track, washing out the scheduled races. The meetings carried on into the wee hours of the night. A knot of reporters and racing fans noised about the hotel. It was, one of them wrote, "the most historic day in cycling history." Because the hotel operator was "anxious" to bar him from its rooms, someone else booked a room for Taylor using his own name. Taylor, who had been kicked out of two hotels in Westbury, Connecticut, a few days before, snuck into the room and laid his head down on a pillow, enjoying one of his last restful nights of the season.

The following day, heavy rain still pounding the track, everyone sped to the Bingham House in Philadelphia for more meetings and a series of races, leaving the Trenton House Hotel gutted. By the morning of the second day of meetings, many riders had signed on to the new organization, which they named the American Racing Cycling Union, or ARCU. From this the National Cycling Association, or NCA, was formed. Taylor was still understandably undecided; the top positions in the new league were going to his chief rivals like Eddie Bald, Arthur Gardiner, Tom Cooper, Floyd

MacFarland—many of whom wanted to expel him from the sport. To some observers, it seemed as if the foxes were positioning themselves to watch over the lone hen. Taylor kept vacillating. If most of the top riders defected, he wondered, how exciting would it be racing against a softer field in low-rent races every day? But his treatment from the league had improved since the choking incident, undoubtedly because of Brady's presence. And he had other considerations. After defeating Michaels, he had been bombarded with offers from manufacturers. The National Board of the Trade of Cycling Manufacturers, siding with the league, announced they would only award contracts to league-sanctioned riders. In addition, Taylor had been working on a European racing junket and the European promoters, having enjoyed a long-standing relationship with the LAW, were not ready to recognize a rebel organization.

Then he had to consider Brady, with whom he was under contract for the entire year. Wanting more control over the sport, Brady's organization seemed to be siding with the rebel movement and had probably put pressure on Taylor to defect. After agonizing over his choices and seeing several top riders sign on, Taylor, in a move that surprised many, finally decided to join the rebel group. But he did have one condition before signing on: absolutely no Sunday racing. "It's against my religious scruples," he told his rivals with conviction. They assured him there would be none. With that, he was admitted to the new organization, despite the fierce objections of several riders, including Floyd MacFarland, Orlando Stevens, Arthur Gardiner, and William Becker, the man who had notoriously strangled him.

The new group set the dates for the final and deciding races. The champion of the 1898 season would be determined at a few key races in Missouri in mid-October. Even though Taylor had beaten Bald ten out of twelve times and had competed in five fewer races, he was just two points behind Bald in the point's column and led everyone in win percentage (.517). It was coming down to the wire.

As September gave way to October, the wires were clogged with gossip about the real intent of the rebels. This gossip turned into vociferous public finger-pointing. "There are a few followers of the colored boy's riding," railed a track writer for the *Brooklyn Eagle*, "who profess to think that Bald and Gardiner have taken the sensational course just made public to break up the championship table, which it was an even break for first place that Taylor would win, as neither Bald nor Gardiner are in any form to stop him at present."

Oblivious to the politics of it all, Taylor's train pressed on. A reporter for the *Boston Daily Globe* sat nearby. "It is now a case of black and white," he said.

The gossip chased Taylor west toward the mighty Mississippi. The backstretch at St. Louis's Monument Track was replete with anecdotes, primarily suggesting that when Taylor signed on with the NCA, he had indeed been hoodwinked. Arriving the day before the races, Taylor headed straight to the hotel where the rest of the wheelmen were staying. He stood fidgeting in a long line behind his competitors and a slew of visiting racegoers. When he finally made his way to the front desk, the attendant drew the color line, rudely telling him that he would have to find quarters elsewhere.

Agitated and humiliated, Taylor scoured the town for alternative lodging. But in one place after another, he met with the same fate. Given that hundreds of citizens had gone through the trouble of signing a paper demanding that the promoter accept his entry long before he arrived, Taylor was taken aback by this treatment.

Evening neared. Exhausted and hungry, Taylor slid under a swaying elm tree and drowsed, a heavy mass of charcoal clouds drifting overhead. Reduced to temporary homelessness, Taylor's search for a roof over his head resumed. After a protracted pursuit, he was eventually welcomed into the home of a sympathetic black family outside of town, a long monotonous journey from the track. As accommodating as his black hosts were, Taylor, who was on a strict bike-racer's diet, didn't feel it was proper to ask complete strangers to cook special meals just for him. So he trekked all the way to the restaurant at Union Station three times a day to satisfy his nutritional needs. But his stopovers caused a stir with management. On one occasion, he was forced to eat his meal alone in a hot and sweaty corner of the kitchen. By his third visit, they had seen enough of him. Shortly after Taylor sat down, the manager told him, rather curtly, that he was no longer welcome; his restaurant was for whites only. There was a long pause while Taylor internalized what was happening. Anger began building. The manager then ordered the headwaiter, also a black man, to refuse his order. But by this time one of the nation's most admired athletes, Taylor had become an inspirational force to other blacks. The near-daily stream of articles chronicling his successes as well as his clean, God-fearing lifestyle had an effect on his unfortunate brethren. Some African Americans began questioning their traditional societal position, their usual subservience. The black waiter, at a time when jobs were scarce, took the bold step of standing up to his white manager and refused to obey his order. Voices were raised and harsh words exchanged. The waiter was summarily fired, but his action spread a message far and wide. "I must say," snarled the *Syracuse Standard*, "that I think if Major Taylor is good enough to ride with, he is certainly good enough to eat with."

Despite the harsh treatment, or perhaps from pent-up anger because of it, Taylor found his way to the track and soundly defeated his competitors in the opening heat of the five-mile race. But moments before the peloton lined up for the final heat, with first place up for grabs, a torrential rain doused the track. The crowd scurried for cover. The pouring rain continued throughout the afternoon and into the early evening. As darkness fell, the race announcer's voice crackled over the track, postponing the final heat. The remaining crowd headed for the exits. Taylor waited patiently while racing officials conferred with some of the riders, the leaders of the new organization, to decide on the reschedule date.

The forthcoming decision would be the beginning of the end of Taylor's hopes for the national title. The finals, among the most important of his life up to that date, was set for the following day, a *Sunday*. Taylor was irate. He confronted the group and reminded them of their agreement to avoid racing on Sundays. They pointed to a never-used clause in the bylaws of the new organization: "Where local opinion permits, there shall be racing on *any day of the week*." Taylor, whose every waking moment was consumed with either racing or training, had apparently never looked over the fine print in the agreement. He had relied on the word of Bald, Gardiner, and others. "But we entered into a gentlemen's agreement," he argued repeatedly.

His argument fell upon deaf ears. The finals were on for Sunday, with or without him.

Neither what he viewed as deceitful competitors nor the splendor of winning the American Sprint Championship was going to break Taylor's deep-seeded stance against Sunday racing. He had, after all, promised his loving mother he would never race on the Sabbath. Feeling betrayed, he packed his bags for Worcester. Meanwhile, after contesting the final heat in

St. Louis on Sunday, the rest of the peloton pushed one hundred miles south to Cape Girardeau for the final major race of the season.

At the eleventh hour, it appeared as if Taylor's hopes would be revived. While he was preparing to leave town, Henry Dunlop, the race promoter for the upcoming event at Cape Girardeau, corralled him. He said he sympathized with Taylor over the rough treatment he had received at the hands of hotels and restaurant owners in St. Louis. He went on to say that he owned the hotel in Cape Girardeau where all the riders would be staying, and promised Taylor he would receive the same treatment as everyone else had. For Taylor, it was as if a lead weight had just been lifted off his shoulders; his dashed hopes came alive again. With these assurances and the knowledge that a victory could still clinch the title, Taylor sped south to the cape to catch up with the rest of the wheelmen. Long after the other riders had checked in, Taylor stepped up to the counter to register. There stood Henry Dunlop, his pronounced jowls jangling up and down, explaining to Taylor that he had arranged for him to stay with a black family outside town, ignoring his promise entirely. Taylor's shoulders slumped, and his heart sagged. He reminded him of their arrangement, but was shocked when Dunlop refused to change his mind. Testy words were exchanged. Taylor appealed to some of his fellow riders, but they merely laughed at him.

A horse-taxi transported Taylor on the long trek to the black family's house, every turn of its wheels intensifying his rage. Once he had settled in, his mind rolled back over the week's events. He had been lied to by his rivals and by a race promoter. He had repeatedly been denied access to conveniently located hotels, unlike the rest of his competitors. And his all-important diet, one of the keys to his success, had been disrupted after being denied meals. The crisis was escalating. He agonized over his choices. There was a lot more at stake than just the honorable title of Sprint Champion of America. Among the wheel, tire, gear, and bike manufacturers, the *Washington Post* estimated that Taylor would earn $10,000 in endorsements if he were to win the title.

But after careful reflection, he decided he'd had enough. While the rest of the well-fed peloton rolled out of their hotel en route to the track at six o'clock the next morning, Taylor walked off to the Union Rail Station, walked up to the ticket counter, and bought a seat on the first train for home. While his train stood waiting, Dunlop, evidently tipped off by someone at the train station, arrived to rub salt into his wounds. If Taylor refused to compete in his race, he warned, he'd be barred from the track forever. Taylor was overcome with feelings of degradation and humiliation. All the back-stabbing and inequities had sunk deep into his psyche. Taylor let Dunlop know in no uncertain terms exactly what he thought of his "word" and his "hospitality," and then stomped onto a train pointing east.

As the whistle sounded, Taylor saw Dunlop storm off. The train lurched forward, anger all around it.

In a scene eerily similar to the previous fall, Taylor sat in the swaying belly of an eastward train agonizing over what could have been had he been granted the same treatment as his rivals. Journalists would soon announce the name of the 1898 NCA champion to the nation. And it wouldn't be Taylor's.

Taylor brooded. Amid the rocking and clanging, he found a quiet section of the train and sat alone, staring out as the first wave of fall leaves dropped to the ground. As always, nestled in his lap sat the Scriptures. As he thumbed through the pages, perhaps ruminating on the calming message in the words of John, he thought about all the opportunities lost. He surely grasped for hope in verse 14:27, in which all earthly troubles seem smaller, more manageable:

Peace I leave with you;
my peace I give you.
I do not give to you as the world gives.
Do not let your heart be troubled
and do not be afraid. I am with you.

He finally drew into Worcester. As he emerged from the train, his sense of calm was replaced by a surge of energy, an undercurrent that needed attending. Though some sportswriters and prominent race handicappers considered him to be the unofficial American champion, Taylor felt incomplete, as if he had much to prove.

Upon his arrival home, he retrieved a letter someone had slid into his mailbox. It was a formal notice of his suspension from the rebel organization for abandoning the Missouri races. Any chance of reinstatement seemed improbable and would only be considered after payment of a lofty $400 fine. He tossed it aside apathetically. What's more, he would learn that Brady's mighty group, wanting to cash in on Sunday racing, was at the vanguard of the rebel movement.

He had only one avenue to go down. Taylor contacted Chairman Mott and applied for reinstatement into the League of American Wheelmen. If accepted, this would mean access to manufacturer's contracts. He prayed for the opportunity to prove to a nation of confused racing fans exactly who the fastest man really was. After careful review, Chairman Mott accepted his application for reinstatement. Taylor's prayer, in the form of a lucrative offer from a well-heeled manufacturer, would soon be answered.

Crisp fall leaves crackled across Philadelphia's Woodside Park Track. At the end of the previous season when Taylor had faced strikingly similar challenges, he retreated to Worcester to ponder his future as a professional bike racer. But for a few bone-chilling days in mid-November 1898, with most sports fans hunkered indoors for the coming winter, he decided to channel his anger on the track.

Because professional bike racing had broken into two separate entities, similar to the American and National leagues in baseball, the winner of the American Sprint Championship was blurred. A few riders put forth claims as the victor, including Bald and Taylor. Everyone had an opinion. One of the most interesting ones came from a gentlemanly, midlevel rider named Howard Freemen. "I am in a good position to comment on the relative amount of speed possessed by Eddie Bald and Major Taylor," he said after having had a unique view to the rear of Taylor throughout the year. "During the season, he has been blessed with almost superhuman speed . . . all the boys willingly acknowledge him to be the fastest rider on the track and also a splendid fellow personally, but on account of his color, they cannot stand to see him win over them. If it were possible to make him white," Freeman continued, "all of the boys would gladly assist in the job."

The official LAW record lists Tom Butler, a man who stayed with the league, as the 1898 winner. In accepting the trophy Butler must have felt unfulfilled; he was sixty points behind Taylor going into the final races right before the breakup.

So Taylor took up one of the many offers that had begun piling up in Brady's office following his victory over Midget Michaels. "There's no sense crying over spilt milk," he said of the Cape Girardeau incident. Harry Sager and the Waltham Manufacturing Company, manufacturer of the popular

Orient bicycle, offered to pay him $500 for each world record he set. He was also offered $10,000, a princely sum in those pre–income tax days, if he spun off the mile in less than one minute, thirty seconds. The current record for the one-mile was an impossible 1:32 3/5 set by Frenchman Edward Taylore, another Brady recruit who added an *e* to his last name to distinguish himself from Major Taylor.

Compared to the large animated summer crowds, Woodside Park Track had a frigid fall feel to it. Taylor didn't care. With several official clockers waiting at the line and a glaze of ice forming on the edge of the track, he proceeded to obliterate nearly every world record of note. The first to crumble to the weight of Taylor's fury was the quarter mile in an astonishing 22 2/5, followed by the half (45 1/5), three-quarters (1:08 2/5), one kilometer (:57 3/5), and two-mile record (3:13 2/5). He then lined up for the record everybody strived for—the one-mile flying start.

Five hundred diehard fans wrapped in winter garb fanned out around the track apron, blowing hot air into their palms. Taylor strapped himself in. Even with the November winds piercing through his cloth cap and blue silks, Taylor broke from the line at a bruising pace. At the half-mile marker, so used to having other riders ringing around him like a school of piranhas, Taylor, looking to both sides, felt a startling realization set in. For the first time in his career, he was alone. With no one to elbow, pocket, or choke him, he felt emancipated, energized, empowered.

His torrid pace continued as he bolted around the final turn, his blazing tempo suggesting to everyone that he was on a special ride. With seven furlongs behind him, the mile marker looming up ahead, he cried out for more speed to his pacemen. Their teeth "chattering" from the cold, they couldn't respond. Taylor took matters into his own hands. He ducked his head and rocketed past his pacemen.

Crossing the line, he and his bicycle turned into a black and blue streak.

The crowd, having just witnessed history, murmured among themselves and peered over to the clockers' stand. His ribs heaving in and out, Taylor also glanced over. The clockers clicked their fingers down on their stopwatches. The hands told the story: 1:31 4/5. The scant Philly crowd had just witnessed the fastest speed ever achieved by human power. The five hundred fans erupted in enthusiastic applause, sounding more like thousands. Taylor smiled.

If, after his first race at Madison Square Garden and then the Michaels's match race, there were fans who still didn't know who Major Taylor was, they surely did now. Newspapers worldwide trumpeted the news. Congratulatory telegrams poured in from every corner of the nation. His exploits, in fact, reached well beyond bike-racing fans. He had not only beaten the fastest man, he had also shaved more than three-and-a-half seconds off the world-record speed of the celebrated horse Salvator, an especially noteworthy accomplishment at the time. "It is a curious fact that last week, when the horse was monarch in New York," wrote a turf writer for the *Evening Democrat*, "its silent steel-framed contemporary, the wheel, was monarch in Philadelphia, and succeeded in establishing some records for time that throw all past performances of trotters and runners into total eclipse. Indeed," he continued, "the surprising exhibitions of Major Taylor, the crack colored bicyclist, at Philadelphia, have opened the eyes of wheelmen as well as of horsemen."

Now the fastest man in America, the former horse tender collected his money, hung up his racing togs for the season, and celebrated.

From their homes, many of Taylor's competitors read the news and winced. For the first time, those who had impeded his progress couldn't do a thing about it. Setting several world records without the possibility of interference was, for Taylor, supreme retribution. "With it," he beamed, "came the sublime thrill that was beyond the power of words to express." Given a clean trip around the track, remarked Brady, who was eager to have him back with the NCA, "he is simply the fastest man on the track"

Motivated by his year-end Philadelphia fireworks display, Taylor set his goal for the 1899 racing season. As was his style, he set it high. He wanted to go where no African American had gone before. In August, for the first time in several years, the World Championships would be in North America. With so many forces arrayed against him, even the thought of winning cycling's ultimate prize seemed a long shot. But as the weight of the depression softened during the waning days of 1898, it was abundantly clear that Major Taylor was no ordinary man.

Chapter 11

THE WEIGHT OF THE WORLD

For perhaps the first time in his life, William Brady, an exceedingly public man, did something important without much fanfare. After returning from a whirlwind tour of racetracks up and down the West Coast and joined by only a handful of his closest friends, he quietly slipped into New York's St. Thomas Catholic Church and married Grace George, the actress-comedian he had courted at the six-day bike race.

Despite minor squabbling during the season—the usual manager-athlete wrangling over who pays what expenses—Brady's contributions to Taylor's career had proved momentous. He sponsored and fought for his inclusion in races. "A real man," he often said, "should be known as a fighting man." By sticking up for him at every opportunity and providing the best trainers, chefs, and pacemen, he had helped propel Taylor to worldwide fame. But more than anything, Brady believed in him when Taylor's world seemed to cave in around him. Despite their polar opposite personalities and lifestyles, Taylor, reported the *Brooklyn Daily Eagle*, "had a soft spot for Brady, the man with many irons in the fire." During the summer of 1899, while the racing lords fought for overall control of the sport, the two men would part ways. Later, when the stakes were even higher, their paths would cross again.

That following winter Taylor donned his finest business suits and began a whirlwind tour of the nation's bicycle trade shows. Leveraging his stack of world records, he signed a lucrative contract with the Sager Company, which called for him to embark on a nationwide marketing blitz of its chainless gear set. Ads that claimed Major Taylor, the Great Colored Rider, Rides a Chainless ran nationwide. Excluding his undisclosed arrangement with Stearns Bicycles during the second half of the six-day race, the contract with Sager was almost certainly the first time a black man sponsored an athletic product.

In New York, Chicago, Indianapolis, Philadelphia, and various other cities, hard-core racing fans and casual riders alike flocked to browse the latest gear and meet the world's fastest man. Being an ideal role model for his race, blacks in attendance looked up to Taylor. "Every colored man and woman is proud of Major Taylor, the champion bicyclist," remarked one journalist.

In rare moments of racial harmony, whites who may have otherwise expected a black man to fetch their luggage or step to the side hovered around his booth to shake his hand and shoot the breeze. Taylor—whose booth was usually the first one visitors saw as they entered the various trade shows—handed out pamphlets and willingly entertained audiences in his usual unassuming manner.

Standing alongside the bike on which he had set the one-mile world record, he described the speed qualities of his Sager-equipped machine and spun tales of his racing exploits, just as Zimmerman had done for him years before. "He demonstrated he can talk wheel as well as he rides one," wrote one Philly paper. He was the center of attention everywhere he went and crowds responded; the Taylor-sponsored Sager-equipped bicycles were among the best sellers, putting to rest the much-questioned viability of using a black man to sell athletic products. "You cannot imagine," Harry Sager would say of his decision to sign Taylor, "how much good it has done me." With the winning combination of talent, dogged determination, and understatement, Taylor had knocked down previously impenetrable fortresses, blazing a trail for others to follow. While in Chicago, Taylor stumbled upon his old friend and mentor Birdie Munger. By 1899, the bicycle shows had taken on a new look. Many of the same men who made bicycles showed up at the shows with strange-looking contraptions called horseless carriages, or automobiles. Even before his Worcester Bicycle Manufacturing Company fell to the industry's consolidation wave, Munger had been working on a new type of automobile wheel and tire. His presence at the Chicago show suggested he was there pitching his new wheel to a rapidly changing world.

For Taylor, now without a manager, Munger's presence both calmed and reassured him. The two men lingered into the small hours of the night reminiscing about their Indiana days. Before turning in for the night, Munger agreed to assist Taylor with some of his affairs that summer. With his instinctive understanding of the sport, he cobbled together an ambitious plan for the 1899 racing season. They both agreed it was time to go all out, to shoot for the World Championships in Montreal. But they had their differences on strategy. Knowing Taylor's nerve-racking tendency to hover back of the field and then thread his way along the pole down the stretch, sometimes agitating his rivals, Munger strongly suggested that he tone down his aggressive racing style. But Taylor thrived on a certain amount of danger. For better or worse, that would be one command Taylor never obeyed.

With the security of his Sager contract and peace of mind knowing Munger would lend his support whenever he could that year, Taylor was so motivated he had trouble containing his excitement. "I do not get half enough sleep," he would tell the *Boston Globe*, "for I think all the time about . . . those Montreal races."

After completing his road show, Taylor swapped his business suits for his racing togs. In preparation for the 1899 racing season, Munger and a noted trainer named Bert Hazard drew up an intense training regime involving weight lifting, running, boxing, and, when weather permitted, cycling.

Across town, the rebel riders in the outlaw organization kept a keen eye on the daily happenings within the LAW. From the moment Taylor appeared on the nation's tracks that summer, word spread within racing circles that his body was finely tuned and his mind set on becoming the World Champion. His five-foot-seven-inch frame that had been a jockey-like 118 pounds in 1895 was now filled out to 160 pounds of rock-hard thighs, striated calves and arms, washboard abdominals, and well-defined, v-shaped back muscles. His new look added another imposing element for his competitors to ponder. Reporters and fans praised his appearance and looked forward to seeing him race. The rebels, having worked hard to get rid of him, wanted nothing to do with him.

In a preemptive strike designed to ease their concerns over a possible return of their black nemesis, riders in the competing league inserted a new rule into their union bylaws. They minced no words: *Blacks were barred.* But before the ink had time to dry, the press pounced, claiming cowardice and prejudice. Keenly aware of the obvious target of the new rule, a *Brooklyn Daily Eagle* reporter called the directive "the most unsportsmanlike move on record."

The split-up caused some interesting banter. With Gardiner, Cooper, Kiser, MacFarland, and Bald in the competing league and Taylor, McDuffee, McCarthy, and Tom, Frank, and Nat Butler leading the LAW, fans and sportswriters argued over which league was superior. The NCA clearly boasted more riders and had two previous champions in Bald and Cooper, but the LAW probably had the best riders for each of the three main disciplines—short, mid, and long distance. There was even talk of a world series of sorts at year's end to settle the matter.

One of the welcome effects of the separation was that the competitive forces caused an increase in the daily purse at some races. To entice riders to switch allegiances, the LAW offered purses as high as $1,000. Elite riders, Taylor included, could also command as much as 50 percent of the gate receipts at certain events, an amount that could rival the purse.

Taylor's painstaking attention to conditioning paid dividends immediately. After signing a lucrative contract with Stearns Bicycles in Syracuse with Munger's aid, he tore through the early season, winning a high percentage of races and lining his pockets in town after town: $875 at Charles River Track on Memorial Day, $1,000 a few weeks later in Boston and Westborough, hundreds in St. Louis in early July. But with success came realignment. Race handicappers slid him back to the scratch position. He would never again be among the limitmen.

He continued to draw crowds: ten thousand in Boston on May 27, fifteen thousand on June 18. Even in the sleepy town of Janesville, Wisconsin, teams of horses lined both sides of the streets for half a mile on opening day. But if anyone believed Taylor would escape prejudice with some of his rivals gone to another league, they were mistaken. While not as frequent as in previous seasons, the elbowing, pocketing, and intimidation continued. It didn't always involve outright physical contact. Sometimes suggestive "stare downs" were enough to sap his morale. While Bald, MacFarland, and Gardiner, who reportedly received aid from other riders when they rode against him, could no longer incite trouble, others stood ready to step in their shoes. The three famous Butler brothers were masters at teamwork and used it against Taylor at every opportunity. And he had Barney Oldfield to contend with, a future winner of the Indianapolis 500. Oldfield would become known for his desire to "restore the supremacy of the white race."

Taylor struggled to find shelter from the racial storm even in, of all places, the bucolic surroundings of Ottumwa, Iowa. A major railroad hub in the 1890s, Ottumwa was no place to hold a convention of Sunday school superintendents. Known as the headquarters of sin between Chicago and Denver, this raucous Wild West–like town had many times the number of gambling dens and saloons—called "blind tigers"—as it did churches. Once liquored up at their favorite watering hole, visitors sought inspiration at myriad houses of prostitution stretching from one end of town to the other. Given all the choices, these adventurers had difficulty making up their minds. Eventually middle-class visitors slipped into 303, a deceptive upstairs establishment on the northwest corner of town. The flusher ones and those needing discretion snuck in the back door of Auroras, a gothic red brick building on East Main Street. Those who didn't care one way or the other drifted into "The Road to Hell" on South Market Street, otherwise known as "Battle Row." Whenever someone tried reforming the bustling town—say an evangelist or the temperance folks—the "house of sin" owners simply grabbed their hammers and nails, charged down to the houses of worship, and pounded in new pews, effectively silencing their critics for a few more years.

The Klu Klux Klan lingered there as well. For a teetotaling, God-fearing black man, it could not have been a desired destination.

But to many people's dismay, Major Taylor happened through that not-so-sleepy town on July 26, 1899, snuffing out all hope his rivals had of running away with the field.

Once there, he won two races, took second in another, and set a track speed record. Soon afterward, a local writer let Taylor have it. "Taylor is a queer specimen. He is supremely arrogant and egotistical and does not readily make friends. He imagines he is the whole performance." The unnamed writer's diatribe went on to mention how Taylor was "marble hearted," how the crowd "did not like him," and how he "arrogantly" swung around his rivals to win.

It turns out the editor was also co-owner of the Ottumwa Track. He was incensed that Taylor hadn't told him of his entry sooner; having Taylor's name on the race card well enough in advance would have allowed them time to paper the town with advertisements. His star power, combined with a heavy marketing blitz, could mean the difference between crowds of a few thousand to as many as ten to twenty-five thousand.

Taylor's appearance in Ottumwa apparently caught everyone by surprise, including himself; he was supposed to be in Chicago trying to lower the world speed records with Munger, only to have the attempts postponed right before the Ottumwa meets. Like Savannah, Georgia, Taylor found the town and his rivals cold and inhospitable—"something on the order of that lawn-party and the skunk business," he remembered with a quiver. But after his unwelcome victories, he felt a little better. "I guess I spoiled their little party," he said, partially vindicated.

As the day rolled on, the hospitality didn't improve. When dusk fell over the Midwestern settlement, Taylor clopped off to the closest inn to eat and bed down for the evening. But like many times before, he was turned away by the proprietor because of his color. He kept searching—reportedly causing a rouse among innkeepers—but to no avail.

His was a bittersweet existence, one minute enjoying adulation from thousands of cheering fans, the next, on the streets, hungry, disrespected, and alone. In the darkness, the world's fastest man lay under the moonlit sky tired and hungry, eagerly awaiting the next train headed for safer ground. With a sinking feeling, he soon parted Ottumwa, never to return, even to collect his prize money. For that job, he sent Frank Gateley, a friend and part-time rider who occasionally traveled with him. Upon returning home, Taylor hustled to the bank to deposit his $350 winnings.

From "Little Chicago," as Ottumwa was called, Taylor's train clattered into the real Chicago for his first race in the Windy City since the Black National Championship in 1895. Chicago was a cycling hotbed, and Taylor wanted to show the fervent local racing fans how far he had advanced in the intervening years. Before a raucous crowd in the feature event, the one-mile open, Taylor crossed the line seemingly well ahead of the rest of the field. But the presiding steward called it a dead heat between him and a local rider named Jimmie Bowler, a man who would later play a role of paramount importance in Taylor's life.

Sportswriters were stunned by the ruling. Convinced of his victory and not too thrilled with the idea of sharing the winning purse, Taylor challenged Bowler to a rematch—winner takes all. But Bowler, overjoyed for having stayed anywhere near the Black Whirlwind, refused, irritating the crowd. For Taylor, it was just another day. "I have never received the benefit of a close decision," he vented as his train rumbled east.

For Major Taylor, every meal, training session, and waking moment was geared toward his number one goal: winning the World Championships. The title of world champion then, as today, wasn't about money. It was about prestige, notoriety, and national pride. To Taylor it meant even more: no native-born African American had ever won a world championship in any sport. More than anything, he wanted to prove to other blacks that, with hard work and an unyielding will to win, they could achieve anything they set their minds to.

July faded and D-day, August 10–12, drew closer. The papers were full of speculation about whether the outlaw riders from the NCA would be allowed to compete in the World Championships. To plead for their inclusion, NCA president A. G. Batchelder traveled tirelessly to and from New York and Montreal. Without the rebel riders, especially three-time champion Eddie Bald, Batchelder warned that the event would lack credibility. And the fans, he said, would shy away. Not everyone agreed. "Most of the outlaw men are has-beens," wrote the *Montreal Daily Star*, "and there isn't a one of them that Major Taylor could not give five seconds to in a mile and best him out."

While cycling's internal wars carried on in the press, many wondered about the status of Eddie Bald, the NCA's star rider. For whatever reason, since the sport had split into two separate leagues, Bald's lightning sprint lacked the zeal that had earned him the nickname Cannon Ball. Known as a lover of the "fleshpots," perhaps he simply wanted to enjoy more playtime, drifting into that familiar slipstream inhabited by other superstar athletes. Several reports had him frequenting the prestigious Eastern horse tracks, hobnobbing with famous jockey Tod Sloan, another athlete with similar passions. Maybe, as others speculated, it was simply being careful what to wish for as you might just get it. After rejecting Taylor for years, he had partially succeeded in ridding him from direct competition. But with Taylor now in another league, perhaps the absence of those intense, black-versus-white, nose-to-nose finishes had sapped excitement from his game. Some believed that Bald was well aware of Taylor's extraordinary condition that season and simply wanted nothing to do with facing him on the sport's largest stage.

In either case, Bald was never the same dominating rider after Taylor's departure. Days before the World Championships, without even telling his trainer Doc Morrow, the Cannon Ball, one of America's greatest cyclists ever, was nowhere to be found.

In preparation for the event scheduled for August 10–12 at Queens Park Track, Montreal went into overdrive. In its mission to create North America's most modern track and host one of the greatest bike races ever held, an army of workers had been doing yeomen's work for seven months. They added concession stands, seats, press boxes, electric lights, and bookmaking facilities. Ashinger Company, a noted track builder, installed a new wood track. In what may have been a first at a Canadian sporting event, Bell Telephone Company erected a large tent abutting the track and stocked it with rotary phones, a novel idea for those able to scrape together four cents for an outgoing call.

Keeping a close eye on the progress, Montreal's mayor, himself an ardent racing fan, deemed opening day a civic holiday and called for merchants to shutter their doors. Lord Minto, the governor-general of Canada, gave patronage to the race and stressed the enormous social weight of the affair. Race headquarters, the Windsor Hotel, as well as every other hotel in town, sold out in advance. Private families stood poised to help with any overflow. Gold and silversmiths had already cast shiny medals and trophies. Chartered trains were en route from every direction. Down at the Waltham, Massachusetts, rail station, more than one hundred riders from the NCA were packed and ready to board a special train. The city was abuzz in race talk.

Meanwhile, skeptical reporters crawled around race headquarters waiting for news on the rebel NCA riders. Would they even be allowed to race? If not, what would become of the event?

Just when everything seemed set, Britain's Lord Henry Sturmey, the reigning king of the International Cycling Union (now the UCI), a giant of a man in stature and disposition, rendered his decision. The outlaw riders from the NCA, he decreed at the eleventh hour, were not welcome in Montreal.

With that, the air went out of the organizers' sails. Many thought the event was destined to flop. Back in Waltham the rebel riders received the unfortunate telegram, unpacked their bags, and voiced their displeasure.

Having invested significant time and money, track owners, racing officials, and civic leaders gathered for a meeting behind closed doors inside the Windsor Hotel. As they paced inside room 21 slurping coffee and trying to figure out how to exit the scene gracefully, a lone man named H. B. Donnelly, secretary of the Canadian Wheelmen, strutted outside on the newly surfaced track. "Give us Major Taylor," he told a reporter, his voice jaunty and self-assured, "and we can run the meet without any other American professionals. I consider him the best attraction we can secure, and with him as an American representative, I do not fear."

No one else knew what to think.

Amid all the doubt of that important moment, one thing now seemed clear: a great deal rested on the drawing power of a certain twenty-year-old black man perusing his Bible on a slow train rattling their way.

Taylor's train pulled into Montreal three days before festivities opened. His first time on foreign soil, he had no idea how he would be received. It did not take long to find out. The minute the train doors swung open and he stepped onto Montreal's sun-baked soil, he found himself wandering into fans and reporters. "He is a very pleasing looking boy, especially when he smiles," boasted one of those reporters, "with looks as soft and as smooth as velvet." They tailed him to the track, where more than ever before, Taylor would learn the art of balancing his time between training and maintaining a symbiotic relationship with the press.

At Queens Park large white tents lined the perimeter of the track. Inside them stood over one hundred of the best riders from all over the world. Many had been congregating there for weeks. In the days before Taylor's arrival, hundreds of fans gathered to watch the riders glide through their training sessions. When Taylor arrived on the spanking new track for his workouts, fans began migrating en masse, the number jumping to around five thousand. They hung over the rails, showering him with applause as he hunkered over his bike and ripped across the track.

Opening day came and nervous racing officials braced themselves. Soon people rolled in from all directions. Swarms of business leaders, obeying the mayor's declaration of a civic holiday, shuttered their doors and scampered to the track. Scores of special bicycle excursion trains from the United States and Canada rolled in. Ships weighed down with racegoers steamed in from Quebec and Toronto.

The race organizers, peering on as fans continued to stream in, took a deep breath. Over the next few days, their early apprehension over the enthusiasm and number of fans vanished. All told, at a championship meet without any of the elite riders from the NCA, Taylor's star power helped pull in over forty-five thousand fans*, the largest paying crowds in Montreal sports history to date, at times overwhelming track personnel. There was simply no greater draw in all of sports.

Outside the track the lines of people trying to buy tickets—and those who already had tickets and were just trying to get inside—were backed up as far as the eye could see. More than five thousand angry fans, many of whom had traveled long distances, were eventually turned away.

On the inside, every seat was booked. Every inch of aisle space was clogged with bodies. Racing officials escorted the overflow underneath the stands, their chins level with the surface of the track, heads peeking out through the fence slats, making them look as one newsman wrote, "like a row of prisoners before the bar of the Recorders Court." One solemn figure sidled up on top of the roof overhanging the grandstand and dangled over the edge, scaring fans below. Bank accounts got slimmer as thousands were wagered on the race at special "deal tables," apparently legal in Canada.

Reporters from all over the world lingered in the press section conducting interviews and hammering out every detail of race preparations. There were so many scribes from so many countries an "official press organizer" from Mexico was employed to organize the chaos.

When Taylor emerged onto the track for the opening event, the half-mile race, the band played the American national anthem, sending an emotional wave of patriotism through him. What began as a field of more than one hundred riders had, through a series of preliminary heats, been whittled down to six of the world's best.

At the starting line, Taylor stretched his leg over his bike frame, then cinched his feet into his toe straps. He looked down the row of elite

---

* This attendance figure, like all others in this book, comes from published reports. Since attendance figures varied from one publication to another, the authors used a medium figure. At the World Championship in Montreal, some newspapers reported a total attendance of 40,000 and others as high as 50,000.

international riders and focused in on his greatest rivals, Nat Butler and Charles McCarthy. His main goal was winning the one-mile race, but if given a clean break for the finish line, Taylor believed he stood a good chance of wearing a half-mile World Championship medal as well. A loud crackle sounded, sending the peloton into a wild burst of speed. The grimacing cyclists bore down on their machines jockeying for position while the crowd rose and let out a deafening roar. Nat Butler immediately muscled Taylor to the outside, leaving a wide berth for McCarthy to blaze through. Right on cue, McCarthy came from the back to take over the lead, Taylor second with Nat Butler close behind. As they had done many times in the past, the two men had successfully wedged Taylor into a pocket. Having been pocketed throughout his career, Taylor knew exactly what to do. He remained calm and eased up a tick on his pedals. This surprised both McCarthy and Butler, causing them to ease up and look back at him. Just as they craned their necks backward, Taylor pounced. Before the riders had a chance to react, Taylor had found a minute hole and shot through it, taking the lead. McCarthy scowled, then dropped his head lower onto his machine. He stomped down on his pedals, retaking the lead. A seesaw battle followed.

Motivated by the animated crowd, Taylor gracefully yet mercilessly powered his machine past McCarthy. Racing pell-mell behind, the rest of the field dropped into the distance, becoming mere spectators. Looking forward down the stretch, Taylor saw nothing between him and the finish line. A thought surely kicked around in his mind: *Within seconds I may become the half-mile World Champion.*

But in his peripheral view, he saw a tall form gunning alongside him. He shifted in his saddle and glanced to his side; it was McCarthy rapidly gaining ground on him. He hadn't shaken him. Releasing the nervous force that had been coiled up in him all season, Taylor locked his eyes on the tape and powered forward with a potent push. McCarthy was right there. The two men felt the therapeutic rush of crushing speed as they exchanged leads, then rolled over the line together.

Convinced of Taylor's victory, the vast throng leaped and whooped, the grandstand trembling beneath them. Taylor, who was also certain that he had won, circled the track basking in the glory of the moment. Taylor wheeled over to the winner's circle and dismounted his bike. He looked toward the stewards' stand where a team of men huddled together. There was an awful delay.

In 1898, one year before the Montreal World Championship, W. C. Petrie, an enterprising racing fan from St. Louis, invented and patented a device that snapped photos of horses—next to a clock—as they left the gate and as they crossed the finish line. For whatever reason, this ingenious idea of a "photo finish," designed to aid race judges, would not see widespread use in horse or bike racing for many years.

Meanwhile, all eyes glared out on Montreal's Queens Park Track. A lone judge sauntered over to the tote board to enter the winner.

The winner of the half-mile World Championship was American Charles McCarthy.

Taylor's charcoal face turned pale.

Like air being released from a tire, a sibilant whir greeted the stewards' decision. A man near the finish line hollered, "Taylor! Taylor! Give the colored man a chance." A woman next to him joined in, followed by a third. Soon the entire grandstand, convinced of Taylor's victory, screamed his name. Even the mayor and the governor-general, who sat in president boxes straight out from the finish line, protested. Five minutes of relentless hissing and screaming passed. The racing officials, aging before everyone's eyes, huddled together again. The crowd suddenly grew unruly, lobbing names and hurling epithets at the judges.

Someone suggested that all those who were against the decision should stand up. With that, every single man, woman, and child, black and white, rose in unison. After thirty minutes of continued howling from the grandstand, William Inglis, the presiding judge, finally broke from their meeting and walked indifferently toward the race announcer. Behind a long black megaphone, the announcer, his voice catching in his throat, barked out the final ruling. The original verdict stood. McCarthy was the half-mile world champion.

What happened next was nothing short of sheer mayhem. Spilling down from the grandstand came popcorn, soda cans and bottles, race programs, cigars—anything that wasn't nailed down was sent aloft. The track resembled the center of a cyclone with everything swirling and raging and roaring while a mass of humanity shrugged and shrieked and anathematized. Officials struggled to get a grip on the irate crowd. Large teams of Mounted Canadian Police galloped onto the scene, trying to quell the boisterous mob. A gaggle of secret servicemen enveloped the mayor, governor-general, and a host of other suited luminaries. The crowd raged on. Deeply concerned about the raucous scene unfolding before him, Taylor rolled over to the stewards' stand, expressed his disbelief, then asked if that was their honest decision. After they said yes—that their decision was indeed final—Taylor walked over to the press stand and spoke. "Well, all right," he said calmly, his arms folded, "if that is your verdict, gentlemen, I shall have to abide by it." With that, the crowd simmered. Taylor pulled himself together and limped back to his dressing room. In the press section, reporters were unanimous in their incredulity. "There was only one mistake and it is extremely difficult to account for," cried the *Montreal Gazette*, "that was why Major Taylor was deprived of a race that he won."

Back in the States, the question on the lips of racing fans appeared in glowing prose on the front of a major paper's sports page: WILL MAJOR TAYLOR BE A WORLD'S CHAMPION? This question would be answered the next day.

A pea-soup fog greeted the dawn of the following day. In the afternoon, it lifted, replaced with blue skies and an August sun that bathed the fans in the summer heat. From an international field of thousands of pro cyclists, only twenty-one qualified for the main event: the one-mile World Championship race. Through a series of preliminary heats, this original group of twenty-one elite riders had been further culled down to five of the world's best athletes. After enduring fierce battles in the prelims, Taylor was one of those few men left standing for the finals.

In what was the most important race of his life, Taylor learned that he had more than race judges to fret over. The duo of Nat and Tom Butler, two brothers who had trained extensively for this one race, lined up next to each other on the inside pole. "My biggest concern," Taylor said, "was being trapped in one of their pockets." Next to the Butlers stood Angus McLeod, the brawny champion of Canada. Rounding off the grupetto, swathed in the red, white, and blue uniform of France, stood the imposing figure of the French National Champ, Courbe d'Outrelon.

The first big outburst from the fans, many of whom stood in aisles or the infield, could be heard when Taylor emerged from his locker room and circled the track during his warm-up laps. At five o'clock, Taylor rolled over to the starting line.

A hush settled over Queens Park.

The eerie silence was interrupted by the loud crack from the starter's gun, followed by the resounding chants of thousands of racing fans. The pace of the first half mile was nervous and tentative, each rider gauging the other's strength while jockeying for position. At the halfway marker, the pace quickened. The famous Butler brothers got down to business. Like eagles in flight, they swerved out in unison, tag-teaming Taylor to the outside and taking the lead. Staying composed, Taylor then gunned forward, passing Tom Butler before settling in behind brother Nat. Taylor powered toward the remaining brother, but Nat Butler, in the best form of his life, refused to let him pass.

Once again, Taylor found himself in the middle of one of the most formidable combinations in the world. Just as he began his move to overtake Nat Butler, he saw a figure coming into his side view. It was Tom Butler out of his saddle, weight forward, stomping on his pedals in a mad dash. His explosive burst propelled him past Taylor, putting him right where he wanted to be—alongside his brother Nat.

To everyone's surprise, Angus McLeod, the large Canadian who had sympathizers from the hometown crowd, put on an unexpected display of power, gliding his way alongside the Butlers. They leaned toward him, trying to drive him to the outside. As the field arced around the first turn of the second lap, Taylor stretched out in the back of the pack, drafting, plotting, watching the race unfold in front of him. A fine position.

On the backstretch of the second lap, the race tightened. Like a string of railcars trailing a locomotive, the quintet of riders blazed down the backstretch, one after the other. Rounding the far turn, the neat order of the formation disintegrated.

Grown men began to crack. The first to unhitch from the speeding train was Angus McLeod, the big Canadian. Shortly afterward, having spent himself too early trying to keep up with his brother, Nat Butler faded.

Taylor was in the third slot as the field veered around the far turn of the last lap. As he was being sucked along by the gathering momentum of the pack, many in the crowd wondered when or even if he was going to make a move. Taylor was biding his time, waiting for a clear opening in front of him. Another sixteenth of a mile ticked by and the positions had not changed.

Some observers believed Taylor had plenty left. But Taylor could not have been so sure. He was putting out nearly everything he had, yet he was still trailing Tom Butler and Frenchmen d'Outrelon.

From his position to their rear, Taylor saw a slender lane through the middle of the two men open. He had to act. Sinking in his saddle and bent over his bike as he streaked down the homestretch, Taylor was ripe for the kill. He pointed his front wheel at the gap, then punched his way toward the slender hole that had opened in the center of the track. Before long, he found himself splitting Butler and d' Outrelon in two. Within 150 yards of the finish, the three riders pedaled into a virtual dead heat.

As the field drew to within a football field of the line, the pace went from relentless to unsustainable.

Within yards of the finish line, the field of thousands of professional cyclists from around the world had been whittled down to just three men, Tom Butler, Frenchmen d'Outrelon, and Major Taylor. They forged onward, leaving everything they had on the track. They heard the distinct sound of chains gnashing, the whirling of wheels, and the hum of rolling tires. They felt the release of endorphins, and the ensuing rush of euphoria that only a cyclist blazing forty miles per hour under his own power feels. Out in front, nothing but a white line, open air, and a split second in time separated them from the title of the fastest bicyclist in the world. Butler lunged, d'Outrelon stretched, Taylor surged. There was no elbowing, pocketing, or intimidation—just three men at their limit, crossing the line within feet of one another.

The crowd rose to their feet screaming. According to virtually everyone present, Major Taylor had just become the first native African American world champion.*

The stewards grouped again. Several minutes ticked by without a verdict being announced. The crowd began to stir. Not again. The *Montreal Star* weighed in: "The crowd, fearing that their dark-skinned boy was going to get the worst of it again, began to be a little demonstrative." Canada had never seen such affection given to an athlete. "The hold which Taylor has taken upon the sympathies of the people in the grandstand," one reporter wrote, "is something wonderful."

William Inglis, the same presiding steward who had pronounced Taylor's defeat in the half-mile race, trotted over to the bulletin board with his verdict. Twenty-year-old Marshall W. "Major" Taylor had rolled across the line as champion of the world!

---

* George Dixon won the bantamweight boxing World Championship title in 1891. Dixon, however, was born in Canada, making Taylor the first native-born African American world champion in any sport.

The crowd was hysterical. All around the grandstand swirled a bewildering maze of men and women dancing in the aisles. From the infield came the strain of "The Star-Spangled Banner" scarcely audible above the chatter of thousands. On the track, with an American flag wrapped around his waist and a huge bouquet of roses in his arms, Taylor circled to thunderous applause. Even with all the racism he had endured over the years, even though next to the article in a Montreal paper praising him for his World Championship title was another about a lynching back home, Taylor's love for his country rang true. "My national anthem took on a new meaning for me from that moment," he beamed. "I never felt more proud to be an American."

But he was disheartened about one thing. "During that joyous demonstration, there was but one regret," wrote Taylor, "which was that Birdie Munger could not be present to witness his remarkable prophecy, that I would become the fastest bicycle rider in the world." Taylor would go on to win the two-mile championship race as well, cementing his position as world champion.

For a few fleeting moments during that summer of 1899, the wheel of Major Taylor's life had spun to unprecedented heights. On the top step of the awards podium, flanked by Butler and d'Outrelon, he stood poised in the regal stance of a world champion—head high, eyes scanning the adoring crowd, gold medal glistening in the sun. All things shining!

But three thousand miles across the vast Atlantic, a Frenchmen—said to be the most superior cyclist of all—read of Taylor's win and smirked: "The Major hasn't found his master on the other side of the water," the Great Edmond Jacquelin, who was unable to make it to Montreal, would say to reporters. "So hear this, that is going to change!" With those fighting words, the first seed of one of history's greatest sports showdowns was sowed.

The summer of 1899 yielded to fall. Taylor had somehow breezed through the rest of the season, winning an astonishing twenty-two out of twenty-nine races and walking away with the League of American Wheelmen Championship title. He was presented with a handsome gold medal struck from special dies made for the league. The Butler brothers received the silver and bronze. Across town, Tom Cooper outdueled Eddie Bald to win the American Championship in the rival NCA organization. Talk of pitting the two American titans against each other in a cycling world series was bandied about by the press. But because neither organization seemed willing to recognize the other's existence, the grand match-race idea withered and died. As a result, the reverence toward Taylor's accomplishments was partially muted. He became agitated that some people, mostly NCA riders, seemed reluctant to give credence to his title of American or world champion. Without the possibility of a grand showdown with Cooper, Taylor's restlessness over the lack of clarity on the subject of American cycling supremacy mushroomed.

While biding time with family and pitching the Sager-equipped Orient bicycle at H. T. Hearsey's bike shop in Indianapolis, Taylor was interrupted by a rap on the front door. A courier handed him an urgent telegraph from Harry Sager, his bike-parts sponsor. Taylor ripped it open. He paced around as he read. It was not good news. His reign as the fastest man in the world had come to an abrupt halt. The talented Bostonian Eddie McDuffee, who was also having a remarkable season, had dropped the one-mile world speed record all the way down to a shocking 1:21.

Taylor had read enough. Rather than viewing the news as a negative, he looked at it as a challenge—and the ideal way to silence remaining critics. After congratulating McDuffee, Taylor contacted Sager, Munger, and trainer Hazard, and asked them to pack their bags.

In November 1899, Team Taylor rolled west out of Union Station for Chicago's Garland Park Track, primed for an assault on the new world speed record. But this time in the luggage compartment of the train, nestled alongside his trusted bicycle, sat new weapons. Instead of the thirty or so burly pacemen who had paced Taylor to world speed records one year prior, Sager commandeered two mechanics and a crude-looking, steam-powered tandem motorcycle, similar to the device McDuffee had used to eclipse Taylor's record.

If recent history was to be any guide, the mechanics would come in very handy. Earlier in the year, following a promotional blitz, seventeen thousand fans snarled traffic and cleaned out concession stands at Charles River Track, hoping to see Taylor and McDuffee break records behind the new machines. After several hours of futile mechanical adjustments, the event was finally called off. The overflow crowd went home disgusted, seriously questioning this whole motorized bicycle scheme.

In the first few days of their arrival in Chicago, the mechanics were the most important men in attendance. Because the motorcycle was a new invention, they tweaked and adjusted and experimented and tweaked some more until it was finally reliable enough to pace the world champion for a one-mile sprint around the track. As they had earlier in the year, thousands of onlookers staked out their territories around the track rail and bleachers, peering on in bewilderment. Some traditionalists looked at the machine as an unnecessary nuisance while others wondered if they were witnessing the bicycle's replacement. Taylor was concerned with only two things—the new machine lasting long enough and being fast enough to keep up with the tremendous pace he pictured himself riding.

On November 15, eight official clockers stood on the side of the track braving frigid conditions. Taylor leaned over his machine at the starting line. All around the track, a hardy gathering of Chicagoans, hoping to witness history, chanted as the elongated machine whirled past. Taylor ripped out of the gate and tore around the first turn, trying to catch up with the speeding device. Somewhere along the backstretch, man and machine eventually drew even. Taylor clung on as if his life depended on it, drafting mere centimeters from the back of the machine. In a seat near the finish line, Sager couldn't decide what he wanted to watch more—a gorgeous young woman in the stands he thought was Taylor's wife, or Taylor's relentless pursuit toward a world speed record achieved on his bicycle components. Being a gentleman of remarkable multitasking abilities, he managed both.

Nearing his breaking point around the far turn, Taylor lunged to the fore with stunning rapidity. The machine, also on the rivets, steamed forward, draping him in a haze of miniature steam clouds. The dual battle of Taylor versus McDuffee and man versus machine was joined.

At the time, America did not know which was faster—man under his own power or this newfangled motorized contraption. Taylor answered the question. On the homestretch, somehow finding that little extra energy, he pleaded with the drivers to step on it. There was no reaction. Within yards of the tape, he veered around the most advanced machine America could throw at him and blitzed across the line at a never-before-recorded, knee-buckling speed of 45.56 miles per hour. The crowd looked on in amazement. The team of clockers looked down at their watches. One mile in 1:19. He had wiped out McDuffee's world record by 1 2/3 seconds. Watching from the sidelines, McDuffee charged home and retired from cycling.

And with that, the doubting Thomases were all but drowned out by the sound of editors singing Taylor's praises nationwide. In a long cover piece

dedicated to Taylor, the *Chicago Times* expounded on THE COLORED BOY
WHO HAS ASTONISHED THE WORLD. Back in the East, the *Brooklyn Daily
Eagle* would boast that "their" man "Major Taylor, The Wonder is Now Back
Home," even though Taylor had only lived in Brooklyn for a few months.
Taylor and Bert Hazard booked a train east for Worcester, pausing briefly at
Sager's Rochester headquarters where Taylor was treated like royalty. Seeing
dollar signs, Sager immediately began a national advertising push linking his
bicycle parts with Major Taylor, "the fastest man in the world."

As the curtain was about to fall on the 1800s, one sportsman stood a rung
above all others having overcome incredible odds, including apparent
attempts on his life. Having pierced through a seemingly impenetrable wall
of prejudice and bigotry, Major Taylor found himself standing on the top
step of one of the world's largest sports stages.

Back in Worcester, he could raise his window shades and scan the open
sky. Outside, a rapidly expanding nation that had been so profoundly affected
by the bicycle awaited the future. Henry Ford, Wilbur Wright, and Horace
Dodge tinkered in their bike shops. The twentieth century was coming, and
America tilted its highly industrious face skyward.

Gazing out his window, Taylor could run his hands over his World
Championship medals and crack a smile. But underneath the smile, he
would have felt a stab of apprehension. In the distant sky, a Nor'easter was
forming. With it would come turbulent times.

CHAPTER 12

UNDER THE CYCLE MOON

The year 1900 rolled in under thick, gray clouds. Swirling winter winds whistled across the Appalachians. Worcester, at a virtual standstill, struggled to shovel out. Horse-drawn plows and carts skittered about the streets, horses snapping their legs under the strain. Large teams of immigrant shovelers earning twenty cents an hour unearthed snowed-in businesses.

Never a lover of the cold, Taylor, who was caring for his very sick sister Gertrude, waited for a break in the weather. He would have to wait a long time. Substantial snowfalls continued throughout the Northeast, including five feet in neighboring New York, a one-day record.

The heavy snow kept falling. Over most of New England tree limbs snapped, toppling telegraph, telephone, and electrical wires, electrocuting horses on the streets below. Train and mail service slowed or, in some areas, halted altogether for the first time in forty years. For a fortnight, portions of the Northeastern seaboard were virtually cut off from the rest of the country.

Over in New York, amid the mounting drifts, a quiet stir was forming. Word leaked out that the League of American Wheelmen's racing board was holding secret meetings.

Rumor had it that the league was contemplating major changes that, if carried out, would directly affect Taylor's livelihood—or worse yet, eliminate it altogether.

Weeks passed and Worcester finally dug out. Feeling antsy, Taylor bundled up and rolled into town. There, he learned the world as he had known it had just come crashing down. After external pressure from the rival NCA and a crippling lawsuit from Brady's group, the League of American Wheelmen—that venerable organization that had overseen all things "bicycle" through one of the greatest crazes in American history—voted to give up governing the sport. The league, it was decided, would focus its resources on improving the nation's roads for cyclists, and the new horseless carriages that were popping up.

At the peak of his young career, Taylor found himself unemployed, a world champion without a guardian. With the league out of racing for good, the NCA's ban on blacks, and the heightened hostility toward him from the rival league's riders, there seemed no way out of his malaise. A Massachusetts paper, in bold type, highlighted his solemn mood: LITTLE HOPE FOR MAJOR TAYLOR. Sensing this as an opportunity, a French promotional concern tried luring him overseas with a lucrative offer. But because the contract called for Sunday racing, Taylor rejected it.

With the American racing season just months away, Taylor strategized means to get the union leaders within the NCA (ARCU) to drop their ban on blacks and reinstate him. Bike racing, after all, was his passion, the only thing he really loved. He sent out feelers, which fell on the deaf ears of the union's governing board. He grew more desperate with each passing day. Eventually, he hired attorney William Allen, a Worcester resident and a vice president of the NCA, but even he didn't seem overly confident. "I fear my sentiments do not meet with favor in the minds of the majority of the officials of that body," said Allen, speaking candidly.

February snows were followed by March showers. Like a giant iceberg, Massachusetts melted, sending torrents of water gushing into numerous tributaries, lakes, and rivers. Rivers overflowed, turning streets into flowing streams, some as deep as eight feet. Horses drowned in their stables. Boats floated down several roads. Electric streetcars sat idle. Unable to ride as often as he wished, Taylor's form worsened and his hopes dwindled. "Major Taylor's chances of reinstatement into the NCA," commented one reporter, "are just about one in a thousand."

But Taylor, Allen, and the press continued to push the issue all spring. Various newspapers printed conflicting reports: he's in, he's out; the Western riders were against him; the Eastern riders for him. Taylor was confused. The pressure was building. Finally, crossing the wires one spring day came word of a special meeting to be held in New Jersey. Nervous, Taylor immediately packed his bags. "If favorable action is not secured," warned a journalist, "Taylor's career as a racing man is ended . . ."

In mid-May, shortly before the start of the racing season, a collection of white riders amassed at the Continental Hotel in Newark, New Jersey, to discuss Taylor's lifetime ban and the broader issue of blacks in professional bike racing. Recognizing this as the most important race of his life, Taylor sped into town and stormed toward the hotel meeting room. Even though the meeting was about him, he wasn't allowed in. Taylor paced about the lobby, anxiously awaiting news from the men who controlled his destiny. Reporters swarmed the issue.

The executive session brewing inside that hotel conference room would prove to be one of the most fantastical in the 136-year annals of organized bike racing. Seven of the nine members of the Grand Council—with titles ranging from secretary to president—were present: the previous year's American champion Tom Cooper, Earl Kiser, John Fisher, Jay Eaton, Edward Spooner, Howard Freeman, and a westerner named Orlando Stevens, one half of the infamous "I and Stevie" combination that had caused Taylor infinite grief.

On their way to the hotel, these seven men had galloped under Major Taylor billboards, browsed ads for Taylor-sponsored bicycles, and read endless articles rehashing Taylor's accomplishments—world champion, American champion, holder of seven world speed records. They watched people cool themselves with Major Taylor fans, knew children who exchanged Major Taylor trading cards, had neighbors who smoked Major Taylor cigarettes and wore Major Taylor buttons. Firsthand, they knew he was kind and unassuming to a fault. Yet here they were, noisily debating his continued permanent ban from the nation's tracks. For what?

With years of pent-up hatred behind them, those opposed to his entry pounded on the table with what amounted to two objections—neither deserving of a lifetime ban. First, Taylor still owed the NCA $400 for abandoning the controversial Cape Girardeau race back in the fall of 1898. Second, he had black skin.

Shouting from his San Jose, California, soapbox against Taylor's inclusion stood a six-foot-four rider who held a hypnotic "influence" over everyone. His name was Floyd MacFarland, the other half of the "I and Stevie" combo, and a man who could start a fight in an empty room. Including Taylor would, he and others thought, hurt the sport's pure image.

Conceding that Taylor was the best drawing card in the business, someone reminded the assembly of biking's stiff competition from baseball, boxing, and horse racing, and that deep-pocketed promoters like Brady and Kennedy wouldn't stand for Taylor's exclusion.

The first reports were negative. "Almost certain defeat stares him in the face," reckoned one reporter.

For Taylor, time stood still. He moseyed about the hotel lobby displaying a combination of apprehension and confidence. He had always thrived on being an in-control perfectionist: rigid training routine, clothing always tidy and proper, bicycles maintained meticulously, handwriting neat and orderly, every penny spent entered in his diary. Yet here were nine men, many of whom burned with racial contempt toward him, controlling his fate without allowing him any say in the matter. Feelings of helplessness ran through him.

But he was well aware of his popularity and his ability to fill the stands. Surely this key fact would be considered. He also had, without even trying, powerful friends in high places. Taylor stepped outside for a breath of fresh air and let his allies in the press go to work. Before, during, and after the meeting, these newsmen—recognizing this as much more than a sports story—read the men of the Grand Council the riot act. "The riders have drawn the color line," wrote one columnist. "It is unconstitutional, un-American, unsportsmanlike . . . the color line will not be accepted by the American public as a valid excuse for the ruling off of a champion." Some writers were more forceful and no doubt caused the council, which tilted against Taylor, to pause. "If the NCA wants the endorsement of every fair-minded lover of sports in the country," hollered another reporter, "it had better strike out that word 'white' in its rules . . . and strike it out quick." All Taylor could do was wait. Finally, the leaders presented the council's ruling. In the end, the forces united for Taylor proved too much for the union lords. With payment of a $500 fine, Taylor was readmitted and American cycling had one unified governing body again. The news was cabled to the rest of the wheelmen. Back in San Jose, Floyd MacFarland plotted his revenge.

Behind in his conditioning, Taylor hopped on a streetcar outside the Continental Hotel en route to the rail station to catch a red-eye. He boarded the train a happy man. Waving to friends and reporters as the whistle sounded, Taylor's train ground toward Worcester and the one dream that still eluded him—the *undisputed* champion of America.

The life of a turn-of-the-century professional bike racer was inherently peripatetic. Some riders had grown so accustomed to the daily howl of a train's whistle, the hard feel of strange hotel beds, and the incomplete taste of restaurant meals that they occasionally forgot where they were. Competing in scores of races at different towns all over the country, several had lost the need to ground themselves to any one place. Many seasoned pros found it difficult to buy a home and settle into a normal family life. The more one could ignore or at least delay this familial urge, they reasoned, the more races they could win, the more money they could earn, and the more praise they could receive from the public. Some riders were torn between these two worlds. Others thoroughly enjoyed the sights, sounds, and feel that went with being a professional bike racer at the time of its greatest glory, sifting through wine and women as often as others chewed tobacco.

Most riders sought balance. It was this yearning for balance and his urge to feel rooted, not to mention flush accounts at several banks, that caused Taylor to shop for a home of his own early in 1900. With the exceedingly positive coverage he received from the local newspapers and Worcester's claim of being an open-minded community, it seemed like a good place for him, as a black man, to settle down. Like any home buyer, Taylor wanted his to be of a quality commensurate with his ability to pay. The only problem was that few, if any, blacks lived in those high-end neighborhoods at the time. In the areas Taylor had been shopping, the most "select" section of town, no precedent existed. But Taylor needed no precedent. After shopping all over town, he fell in love with a seven-bedroom home on Hobson Avenue on the north side of town and prepared to buy it. One of the benefits of spending so much time training and traveling was that it didn't leave a man a lot time to spend the money he had earned. Taylor, whose only real monetary indulgences involved his clothing, had amassed more than enough money to pay the $2,850 asking price in cash. He had found the home of his dreams and had the money. His American dream was in full swing.

Somewhere along the way, perhaps anticipating trouble, Taylor contacted Cornelius Maher, a local realtor, and asked him to close the deal for him. But the developer, wanting to keep the neighborhood an "ideal residential locality," had inserted certain restrictions to help keep out "undesirable people." So, unsure of the developer's position on blacks, they devised a plan to circumvent the usual approval process. Taylor gave Maher power to sign on his behalf and went about his business. But when Maher went to close on the property, he was grilled with questions about the buyer.

"Is he a good Yankee?" the developer asked.

"Yes," Maher responded.

"Is he financially viable?"

Maher said that he was well to do and, unlike most people who typically put down only a few hundred dollars, he was paying cash for the house.

"What's his name?" pressed the developer.

"M. C. Taylor," Maher replied coyly.

The seller, perhaps sensing something fishy, balked. He repeatedly asked for a meeting with the actual buyer present. At each subsequent meeting, Maher told the seller his client was an extremely busy man on the road all the time and would be unable to attend the closing. "You'll see him soon enough," he promised. Finally after several meetings, the seller relented. At the scheduled closing, Taylor apparently stood in the hallway waiting impatiently. The developer, a non-sports fan who apparently wouldn't have known the difference between a Kentucky Derby–winning jockey and a world champion wheelman, thought Taylor was just Maher's coachman. Maher signed for Taylor and the property changed hands.

When the 399 white folks living in Taylor's neighborhood caught wind of this transaction, some of them stormed the realtor's office claiming they were tricked and bemoaning the fact that a black man lived in *their* neighborhood.

"What do you mean by this outrage," one of them hollered, "this violation of confidence and agreement, *sir*?"

The seller also felt deceived. "I consider it an injury to me to have him come in and squat down on my plot against my will . . ."

Amid threats of lawsuits, the deal stood. After Taylor moved in, the seller's and the realtor's reputations fell through the roof.

For a city that often boasted of being open-minded, the incident was troubling. Apparently it was okay for blacks to live in *certain* sections of town, perhaps as a valet of a white man, but when it came to living next door in the finer part of town, that was another story altogether. Nervous and fearful, some neighbors gathered in clandestine meetings. They emerged with what they believed was a brilliant plan. They offered Taylor nearly double what he paid for the house if he would just move elsewhere. One resident even offered Taylor a deal he couldn't possibly turn down on a quaint home in a more appropriate part of town.

Unmoved by the offer and all the hoopla, Taylor refused. "I don't know why I haven't as much right to buy a little place as any man in town," he said defiantly, as though there was nothing unusual about his purchase.

After reminding locals that their ancestors had fought in the Revolutionary War and Civil War for freedom and equal rights, local journalists joined in a chorus of catcalls against the residents. "There must be Democrats out at Columbus Park," barked a writer for the *Worcester Telegram*. "They are making a lot of fuss because a good Republican is to be one of the neighbors."

Once the dust settled, Taylor began employing the unique communicative skills he had honed over the years. One of his most effective weapons against racism was his belief that people can be taught to treat you the way you want or expect to be treated. So Taylor lifted his chin, introduced himself to his new neighbors, and rolled through the very streets where monuments of him would one day stand, new furniture protruding out the back of his horse-cart. Over time, his strategy worked. One neighbor after another slowly warmed up to the idea of having the gentle world champion living in his or her backyard. So much so that when he needed them in the future, they would be there for him.

Many stood up and took notice. Like his fight with the NCA, the news was viewed as more than just a sports story. It flowed through the local papers and down to the black press before spilling out into several major papers. This unprecedented move would further elevate him in the eyes of those of his era—and those who, more than one century later, can view its import through the lens of history.

One of Taylor's motives for buying his new home likely went beyond having a nice roof over his head. For some time, the press had been snooping for information on his romantic life, but their intrusiveness only caused Taylor to tighten his sphinx-like silence on the issue. However, the pressure continued. "How about it, Major?" they kept asking. "How about it?" Uncomfortable with reporters poking their pens into his every move, he went to great lengths to ward off their scent into his romantic life, even to the point of fabricating stories.

He once told Harry Sager that he was married, just to get him and others to quit asking. It was all over the papers the next day. Worse yet, Sager insisted that he and his fictive wife come to his palatial Rochester estate for a formal sit-down dinner. Taylor now had to unwind what began as a jest. "If I was married I didn't know when it happened . . . Just the work of some of those paragraphers," he told a newsman, buckling over in laughter. "They are always making me married."

The truth was, around the time he bought his new home Taylor first set eyes on the stunning face and captivating eyes of Daisy Victoria Morris. The daughter of a black mother and white father, Daisy was born in Hudson, New York, in 1876, making her two years older than Taylor. Her sweeping beauty, refined grace, and sharp intellect turned heads at a private academy where she schooled in the mid-'90s. When her mother Mary died, Daisy moved to Hartford to live with a relative named Reverend Louis Taylor. There, she joined the esteemed Amphion Social Club, where she dazzled crowds at the dramas and concerts in which she performed.

Though she appears to have grown up on the rougher side of Hudson and under less than ideal circumstances, it did not adversely affect her comportment. Everything about her spoke of elegance. Beyond her striking beauty, people couldn't help but notice her fashionable velvet walking suits with vested fronts, her gored accordion skirts with silk taffeta at the hems, or her assortment of lovely Victorian-era hats trimmed with colorful silk flowers. In stark contrast to the usual hourglass shape favored at the time, Daisy carried an athletic, twenty-first-century figure. Her appearance even captured the attention of the society writers: her face stared out from the cover of a black society magazine that had found its way into Taylor's hands.

In 1897, Reverend Taylor was uprooted from his Hartford congregation and transferred to Worcester. Because Major and Daisy were both deeply religious, they may have met at a local church function. Or, like so many other couples of the era, perhaps they met on a leisurely Saturday afternoon bike ride on the streets of Worcester. A stroll through town on a "wheel" or on a visit to the local racetrack had become a fashionable way to meet potential mates.

In fact, few inventions had a greater impact on women—or stirred up as much controversy—than the bicycle. Since the Civil War, little had changed in women's clothing or in their general subservience to men. But once the bicycle came along, this "new woman"—and Daisy was most likely one of them—was free to go about as she wished and form her own ideas about what she wore. And since travel had become less cumbersome, women had a wider base of prospective mates to choose from beyond the traditional, pre-arranged match ups.

The press did its part in perpetuating this new belief. The *New York Herald* reassured all brides-to-be that a bicycle was a better matchmaker than a mother, and that more often than not, the tinkling of a bicycle's bell turned into the pedaling of wedding bells. The most effective way to elicit masculine approval, wrote cycling historian Robert A. Smith, was to take a short spin down a country lane "under the cycle moon."

But all this freedom concerned some groups. The radical Women's Rescue League believed that "bicycling by young women had helped more than any other media to swell the ranks of reckless girls, who finally drift into the standing army of outcast women of the United States." Several Kentucky newspapers carried out a deliberate campaign to discourage women's cycling by printing pictures of absurd-looking bicycle attire, combined with reports suggesting that women were incapable of controlling a bicycle. A medicinal company warned of many harmful effects to all those of the "weaker sex" who rode bikes. But just in case one succumbed to the peer pressures of riding, it had the answer to the inevitable "heating of the blood." All one had to do was drop $1.50 for a patented cure-all, Payne's Celery Tonic.

But these forces didn't stand a chance against cycling supporters, like Carlos Martyn, a flamboyant reverend who told a stunned congregation that a woman riding a bicycle would not destroy the home nor eradicate mother-hood or grace or delicacy. He suggested that "it would be just as sweet and just as pleasant to make love to a woman wearing bicycle bloomers as to one who does not." One New York doctor even seemed to credit women's cycling with the vibrancy of the country. "Cycling had come along just in time to rehabilitate the American woman." Until then, he suggested, women were in bad condition because their "nervous force was wearing out."

Somewhere along the roads of Worcester, the exact time and place left as their own intimate secret, Major Taylor and Daisy Morris first crossed paths. By all accounts, they were immediately smitten, flowing together like water until you couldn't tell him from her. Considered the best all-around female athlete at her college, Daisy shared Major's love of sports and often snuck into racetracks without any of the ogling men knowing she was the girlfriend of the world champion black man at whom they were either cheering or sneering. Taylor, with his good looks, gentle persona, ample finances, and worldwide fame, was a sought-after man. Daisy, with her striking beauty, elegance, and intellect, was a desirable woman. Together, they formed a class act. Early in 1901, they would become engaged. In the spring of 1902, they would wed, then move into Taylor's much fought-for home.

CHAPTER 13

AND THEN THERE WERE NONE

It was a June day in 1900 and the peloton was standing around, the riders' eyes fixed in glorious disbelief. In the distance, they saw a large black figure waddling toward them. It couldn't possibly be Major Taylor, they thought; this man was too large about the waist. But it was. After settling into his new home, reuniting with the NCA, and signing a contract with bike manufacturer Iver Johnson, Taylor popped up at his first race with around ten pounds of additional weight. And it wasn't muscle. For some, ten pounds here or there is insignificant, but for Taylor, who had the type of frame where excess weight congregated in one spot—his stomach—extra weight stood out like a sore thumb. "The Colored Whirlwind," wrote one reporter, "is almost elephantine." The NCA riders, many of whom hadn't seen Taylor for more than a year, couldn't believe their good fortune. Optimism ran through the backstretch.

At the Manhattan Beach Track starting line, with pinched lips and raised brows, they eyed him skeptically. Surely the startman, a long-time fixture at the track, even looked at him oddly before firing the pistol. The field broke in a trundled mess, riders scattering everywhere. Taylor trudged around the first turn, chugged around the far turn, and lumbered toward the homestretch. As he came out of the homestretch, fans watched in astonishment as a handful of also-rans rolled by, leaving him panting. Even old Johnnie Fisher, a middling rider from Chicago, sailed by him. The puzzled crowd, expecting a season full of torrential bursts of speed from the Black Whirlwind, hissed. One New England paper even spelled out his impending doom in bold print: MAJOR TAYLOR IS LOSING HIS LAURELS.

If the glare from his competitors and the less-than-glowing assessments from the press weren't enough to shake him into a higher state of fitness, reams of articles hailing the invincible new kid on the block certainly did. Several track writers who had been full of Taylor stories began singing the praises of a new rider many claimed was greater than all other Americans.

The man gracing those pages was a young powerhouse named Frank Kramer. Twenty-three months younger than Taylor, Kramer was a six-foot-tall, thick-boned, barrel-chested Indiana native. He was a staid man, with a personality not unlike a rose bush in January. He eschewed late night carousing with fellow riders, preferring instead a life of such rigidity that his neighbors could stare out their windows and watch his bedroom lights flick off at exactly nine o'clock each night. For the curly-haired Kramer, smiling was a superfluous imposition. His stiff gait had a walking-broomstick look to it, implying overcompensation for an old back injury caused perhaps by a run-in with a track pole or being on the losing end of a horse-bucking session.

On a bicycle, he had a mechanical quality about him as though he was a cybernetic organism, pedaling without a stitch of emotion. Although he would become well-liked, people often teased him about his banality and that ski-slope jaw of his. One tale suggested that the wayward jut of his chin—which earned him the nickname "Chisel-chin"—and his stoicism were so pronounced, people would pass by what they thought was a hat rack, toss their hats his way, only to be stunned when the seemingly inanimate object *moved*.

After coming down with tubercular symptoms in his early years, Kramer's parents rushed him off to New Jersey for its fresh sea air, propped him up on an old high-wheel bicycle, and watched with delight as it helped spin the sickness right out of him. His first race on a regular safety bike, which he lost because of his lingering illness, was one of the few races he would ever lose. After the once-frail youth had breezed through the local race circuit, his dominance in the national amateur ranks was so complete, one New

York paper predicted "he would earn as worldwide a reputation as Arthur Zimmerman"—a statement which bordered on blasphemy.

Kramer's extraordinary riding talent, combined with all the media hype, attracted big money. Pierce-Arrow, a large manufacturer of bicycles and luxury cars, opened its usually tight pocketbook and signed him to a lucrative multiyear contract. By the time he joined the professional ranks at the beginning of 1900, urban legends had already gained traction. Rumor had it that Kramer once outpaced a thoroughbred on an old high-wheeler, and that he had effortlessly passed a locomotive. A lot of people took these stories seriously. "Kramer," prophesized one track writer, "is expected to clean up the whole bunch."

Taylor's biggest concern was that, in the real world, Kramer had stood up to his top billing; although the season was young, he had soundly defeated nearly every pro he faced. Unfamiliar with Kramer, Taylor read all the hype with great interest, took the reports seriously, and began strategizing. He wouldn't have much time. Less than a month into the season, people began howling for a match race between the black world champion and the great white hope. On June 30, with little time for buildup, they would get their wish.

With the match race less than two weeks away, Taylor latched onto his new Iver Johnson bicycle, shooed away the press, went into seclusion at a quiet oval, and trained intensively with trainer Robert Ellingham. Meanwhile, Kramer continued to win and impress reporters. "Kramer," boasted one writer shortly after another of his victories, "was riding like the wind."

On the last day of June 1900, under a blanket of threatening clouds, Taylor drew up next to Kramer on the Manhattan Beach Track primed to settle the issue. Few races meant more to Taylor. Not only did he want to prove his superiority over Kramer on the track, but he also had a bone to pick with Pierce-Arrow, Kramer's sponsor. Taylor had made overtures at the Pierce headquarters to ride their bikes, but was quickly whisked away. "Frank Kramer," he was told, "is the king-pin of all bicycle riders in America." Being a proven rider and world champion, Taylor did not take rejection well. He retreated from the office angry. "If I ever meet Kramer in a match race," he grunted to himself, "he will have another thing coming." The entire earth seemed to be shifting toward Frank L. Kramer.

By carriage, bicycle, trolley, and open-air automobiles, crowds spilled out of the New York, Manhattan, and Knickerbockers Athletic Clubs, streamed down Neptune Avenue, and poured into the track by the sea. Throughout the day, the Long Island, Brighton Beach, and various other railroad companies dropped off thousands of racegoers. Coney Island sunbathers and amusement park visitors stopped what they were doing and walked to the track. Although they were not legally allowed at American tracks (bike racing tried desperately to avoid the same betting scandals that had rocked horse racing), bookmakers trolled neighboring hotels and the Coney Island Jockey Club. While Taylor had always garnered an enormous following from fans, both black and white, plenty were eager to see a white rider restore things to a "more natural order." They believed they had their man and expressed their confidence by dumping bundles of cash on Kramer to win. "Experts pick Frank Kramer," wrote at least one paper.

Taylor emerged confidently from seclusion having trimmed nearly all his excess weight. Kramer, stiff and upright, rolled his gleaming Pierce-Arrow bike to the starting line, threw his muscular legs over his machine, and stared forward. The noisy crowd rose to its feet. The band shushed. The race announcer shouted their names over a profusion of fedoras and colorful ladies' hats. The pistol cracked in their ears.

The race was over before anyone could blink. From the finish line, Taylor gawked back under his arm, straining to catch a glimpse of the man many deemed invincible. Everyone filed out. The amusement park filled up again. Coney Island food stand vendors were snowed under with hot dog–chomping racegoers once more. A contingent of Kramer bettors shook their heads, hopped aboard trolleys outside the track, and went home with lighter wallets. "On the whole," admitted the *Brooklyn Daily Eagle*, "Major Taylor is king-pin among the sprinters . . ."

This would not be the last time, however, that Americans would hear of Frank Kramer. Over the next twenty-two years, whether they wanted to or not, they would get an earful.

Since Frank Kramer had already conquered most of the elite American contenders and Taylor had soundly defeated Kramer, only one American had a realistic chance against him. For years, Taylor had tried in vain to arrange a match race against Tom Cooper, the NCA champion of 1899. Back in 1898, even William Brady, with his deep pockets and powers of persuasion, hadn't been able to convince Cooper to challenge Taylor in a match race. As treasurer of the NCA, Cooper also led the push to ban Taylor in '98, and had since done all he could to keep him there.

As June bled into July, track owners, race promoters, and newsmen hounded Cooper. As he had done before, Cooper ducked them. Only after racing fans joined in the chorus, calling him a coward and insisting the NCA strip him of his American championship, did he finally relent. A match race was scheduled for July 13, 1900, at Milwaukee's racetrack. Race promoters got busy placing ads all over town. They offered a $1,000 purse, which Taylor and Cooper matched with a side bet of another $1,000.

After years of waiting, it appeared as if Taylor would finally get his wish. While the two men were warming up, however, Cooper took a light spill. He got up, looked down at the track, and complained to track officials. An impromptu meeting with the race organizers was called. Cooper pointed to a splinter in the wooden track and demanded the race be called off. The officials asked Taylor if he was willing to proceed with the race. Taylor didn't seem to think much of it. Absolutely yes, he said, if Cooper was. All eyes fell on Cooper as he looked down at the splinter, then up at a confident Taylor. He declined. Just then, rain began falling, sending the crowd scurrying.

The calls for a replacement date from the media and the fans went out immediately. For the next five months, Cooper would duck and weave and delay until he could finally hide no more.

Taylor rumbled into Indianapolis's Union Station in the predawn hours of one July morning. The doors flung open and he paraded down the steps, rubbing the sleep from his eyes and surveying the landscape of his native city. Much like he had, the city had matured since the days of his youth when he roamed the meadows near the Southard estate. Intercity electric railways, called "interurban," and a handful of locally built Duryea automobiles rolled about town.

It had been years since he last competed in Indiana; on one of his last visits in '98, he was toasted at several smokers and banquets and had been presented with a medal by young black women. Newsmen stood around marveling at the hometown man turned internationally renowned sports star. They tailed him to the track on Central Avenue, retracing the route he and Arthur Zimmerman took seven years earlier. Taylor was surely struck with pleasant memories as they rolled by Hay & Willits Bike Shop where he once dazzled locals with his trick riding, and the streets where he won his first race at the age of thirteen. But not all memories were rose-colored; vivid still were recollections of his white friends playing without him at the YMCA and being banned from Indiana racetracks, all because of his color. The papers buzzed with news of the race. On July 18, amid inclement weather, a large crowd jammed the modern track to see the local-boy-done-good in the two-mile handicap race. From the paddock, alongside rivals Barney Oldfield, Owen Kimble, Al Newhouse, and others, Taylor scanned the vast throng, fixing his gaze on a familiar face in the front row. There, his father, Gilbert, who had never seen him race, sat perched in a booth along the finish line, his proud eyes gazing back at his son, his wispy, white hair blowing in the wind. With him sat a battalion of his old comrades from the Grand Army of the Republic, bedecked in their Civil War uniforms—blue Schuylkill sack coats, matching vests with shiny gold buttons, light blue Deering trousers, black Carter boots, all topped off with the stately kepi cap embroidered with the Grand Army emblem wreathed in laurel leaf.

By this time in his career, with a LAW American Championship and a World Championship title in his trophy case, Taylor was usually a deep scratchman at handicap races. Sometimes he was hung out so far behind the rest of the field some folks couldn't understand it. Unfamiliar with handicapping—the fastest rider starts the farthest behind—his father became agitated when he saw his son, the lone black man, lined up so far behind his white competitors, he may as well have started the race from across the street.

The pistol cracked in the air. Taylor moved up from his scratch position and, one by one, began picking off the limitmen who started well in front of him: at fifty yards, Newhouse; seventy-five yards, Owens; one hundred yards, the desperate long shot, Lew Gordon. Taylor was on fire, weaving in and out of traffic, burning up the white pine track to the delight of the crowd. As he sailed down the homestretch, his father and everyone else in the speed-crazed town rose and let out a thunderous ovation. When the hometown darling spun across the line three full lengths ahead of second-place Newhouse, fans emptied the ten-thousand-plus grandstand seats, ran out on the track, and mobbed him.

Everyone, that is, except his confused father.

In the midst of his son's resounding victory, something still gnawed at the senior Taylor. After the awards ceremony, he charged past the paddock and through a double tunnel winding into the dressing room under the stands. Negotiating past eighty-five massage boards, he cornered his famous son in his private locker, complained about his peculiar starting position on the track, then let him have it.

"Well son," he grumbled, "there is one thing I don't understand. That is, if you are the fastest bicycle rider in the world, as the newspapers say you are, why in time don't you beat those white boys out farther at the finish line?" A tongue-tied silence followed.

"Well," Taylor finally retorted, a puzzled tone to his voice, "I won by a couple lengths, didn't I?

"Yes," Gilbert continued, his voice bouncing off the locker room walls, "but I expected to see you leave them so far behind that you could get dressed and come out and see the rest of them fight it out for second and third money."

A gathering of startled wheelmen leaned in and eavesdropped, gaining a revealing glimpse into the source of Taylor's tenacity, competitiveness, and dominating mind-set. "The innocence of old age," penned the younger Taylor.

Major Taylor was having one of those days during which a man contemplates finding the nearest border crossing and leaping over. While lounging at his father's home on a Saturday afternoon shortly after his victory at the Newby Oval, he stumbled upon a letter that had been slid under the front door. He immediately recognized the sender's name. As he tore the letter open, his mind drifted back to another day shortly after winning his first race when he received a letter from the same man summoning him to appear before him.

When Taylor, then a jumpy thirteen-year-old, arrived at the man's office, he was quickly whisked in by a white, middle-aged businessman who proceeded to grill him with a barrage of questions and overt threats.

Where had he acquired the name Major? Was this his real Christian name? "You can't use *my* name," the man said, "and furthermore, if you do, I will see to it that you are interned in the Plainfield boy's reformatory."

Taylor bolted out of the building, nearly sobbing.

And with that, the thirteen-year-old black Major Taylor and the middle-aged white Major Taylor, both somehow living in the same city at the same time with the same unique name, parted ways.

Some months later, after young Major Taylor's name started appearing in newspapers because of his racing victories, he received another summons to appear, this time from an Indianapolis law firm.

And so Taylor, by then fourteen or fifteen years old, journeyed into town and sat around a conference table with suited attorneys. The life of Major Taylor—the white executive—young Taylor was told, was being adversely affected by all the articles in the papers saying he had converted from a prominent business man into a bike racer.

"You will go back to using your real name of Marshall and immediately refrain from using Major," they insisted. And just to be sure they got their message across, they upgraded his potential sentence to time in the "Michigan penitentiary," a reform school for incorrigible boys. Taylor, frightened, agreed to immediately cease and desist from all use of the name Major. But as he was leaving the law offices, he turned his face to them and muttered, "I can't stop all the kids in town from using my name, but I'll try."

When Taylor, now twenty-one, received the latest summons at his father's new home in town, he thought that since the name "Major" had appeared in nearly every newspaper in the world, the executive and his attorneys were ready to send him up the river.

But when black Major Taylor arrived at white Major Taylor's house in the summer of 1900, he found a cheery executive standing there with his arm extended in a handshake.

"You have performed on the racetracks of the country in such a sportsmanlike manner," beamed the merchant, "that you are now free to adopt the name Major Taylor."

Instead of losing customers, apparently all the positive international publicity had brought about a "Major" up-tick in his business.

"I want to congratulate you as champion and wish you every success," he continued.

"I will do my best to uphold the proud name Major," replied Taylor, wiping the sweat from his brow.

It was a melancholy season for nearly everyone whose name wasn't Major Taylor. During August, September, and October of 1900, Taylor went on a rampage. The warm summer winds blew him through Montreal, where another huge crowd vividly remembered him from the World Championship of the previous year; in Vailsburg, where ten thousand fans watched him crush Frank Kramer in another match race; in Hartford, where he was "greeted with a storm of applause" by a large crowd; in Worcester, where a new Taylor-inspired velodrome was built; in Buffalo, where he blew away the field and "astonished cycle fans"; in New Bedford, where he set a long-standing track record and was hailed as "the neatest rider who sits in a saddle." "If America is to have a white champion this year," wrote a New England reporter, "Major Taylor is the man they have to defeat."

Defeat him they would not. In the end, the 1900 outdoor season proved to be one of the most dominating in the history of American cycling. By the time Taylor arrived in Peoria, Illinois, in mid-October, the race for the American Championship title was a mere formality. There, as he had done all year long, he simply ran away from the field and, with double the points of his closest competitor, Frank Kramer, won the title Champion of America. These victories, wrote the *Brooklyn Daily Eagle*, "showed very plainly why the pros of this country took such care last season not to permit him to mettle against them."

But like '97, '98, and '99, a few asterisks hung out there by his name. First, since the World Championships held in Paris were run on a Sunday that year, Taylor did not even try to uphold his World Championship title. Second, the Frenchman who took his title—a man unable to compete in Montreal in 1899—was hailed by many throughout Europe as the greatest rider the world had ever seen. Third, midway through the summer, Tom Cooper, the 1899 NCA champion and a man Taylor had been clamoring to square off with for four years, had accepted a large contract to ride overseas.

Sometime in November, Cooper returned with deep pockets and a few medals around his neck. For some fans and reporters, the issue of American supremacy hung out in perpetual debate. As if they were two heavyweight prizefighters, the press once again began calling for a match race to settle the question once and for all.

And no one knew prizefighting better than William A. Brady and his partner James Kennedy. A late-fall sun hung in the New York sky as William Brady stared out his window in deep thought. When the sport split into two leagues, wheelmen became concerned over what they had been reading in the press. Being a good friend of famous horseman Phillip Dwyer, who had helped Brady finance the Corbett-Sullivan fight, rumors that he was leaving the wheelmen for the dreaded horsemen had swirled through the sport. But as much as Dwyer pressed the issue of thoroughbred racing, Brady's passions lay elsewhere. In interviews with a few reporters, he said he was happy to see the sport governed by one body again, then put an end to all the speculation. "I've been all wrapped up in cycling, boxing, and the theatre and haven't the time or the inclination for horse racing." Besides, he later wrote of animals in general with his legendary sense of humor, "they're just smelling machines."

But as he sipped brandy and watched the leaves fall outside his Manhattan window one day, something ate at him. Wanting to kick things off in his customary grand style, he and Kennedy had leased out Madison Square Garden and were preparing for the indoor event of the season: New York's six-day bike race. But because human rights groups claimed the race amounted to cruel and inhumane punishment, the state legislature had threatened to ban any athletic event that exceeded twelve hours. While the ban included horse races, it was clearly aimed at the six-day bike race. Brady's hardened past didn't allow him to fully grasp the extent of the rider's suffering. With tens of thousands in gate receipts on the line, the former bowery brawler lobbied against the ban with all his powers of persuasion. It was no use. The legislature banned the race anyway. "The politicians were simply not getting theirs out of the big money in cycle-races," he griped.

The event, almost certainly the most heavily attended sporting event in the country, was at a crossroads. And Brady found himself in a promotional pickle. But he did not give up altogether. Surely his rough riding friend and New York governor Teddy Roosevelt, a cycling fan and follower of Taylor's career, would veto the bill. But then Roosevelt signed the bill, and with that, it was thought, the race was finished. "I will never understand," wrote a disconsolate Brady, "why Roosevelt signed that bill since he was both intelligent and a lover of sport." The events had been so successful, wrote the *Brooklyn Daily Eagle* in a six-day postmortem article, "they were veritable mints for their promoters."

But their declaration of the event's demise would prove to be greatly exaggerated. Refusing to let the highly profitable event die Brady retreated into one of his private brainstorming sessions. He eventually emerged with a brilliant proposal whereby there would be teams of two, with each man riding no more than twelve hours in a day. The legislature was okay with it. A senator named Collins slapped his name on the bill and bragged to his constituents about *his* idea. Brady's face-saving six-day race, now universally called "Madison's," was on.

Unsure how the public would take to the new format, he and Kennedy knew they needed the strongest possible headliners. By 1900, even the greenest promoters knew who that was: Major Taylor versus Tom Cooper. When Taylor was asked to headline the event with a one-mile match race against Cooper, he salivated at the idea. Known as the Blond Adonis from the West, Cooper, fresh off a moderately successful overseas voyage, was only lukewarm. But after extensive arm-twisting, a $500 initial purse, and a strong Irish talking-to, he finally relented. The two men would skip the long six-day grind, but the question of absolute American supremacy in the one-mile sprint would finally be answered.

On their way to the track, Cooper's trainer, a silk-suited man nicknamed "Mother Web," tried intimidating Taylor and his trainer Bob Ellingham. "Well, Bawb," he bellowed in a fractured syntax, "Tawm will now proceed to hand your little darkey the most artistic trimming in his young life. However, Bawb," he continued, "I have cautioned Tawm that in the best interest of the sport and for the good of all concerned, not to beat the little darkey too badly." Without saying a word, Taylor laid down his Bible and carried on.

Before the strike of midnight, on that same track where he had defeated Eddie Bald in his professional debut exactly four years before, Taylor waltzed out to a rafter-shaking ovation. Cooper, a wily veteran and one of the wealthiest (he would finance a then-obscure man named Henry Ford), most confident athletes in the country, rolled alongside Taylor. Cooper, his championship emblem embroidered onto his silk uniform, stripped off his colorful bathrobe, stared over at the man he had successfully evaded for so long, and smirked. Taylor looked back at the long imposing lines of the man who, as treasurer of the NCA, had done everything in his power to ban him from his beloved sport. "If ever a race was run for blood," Taylor recalled later, "this one was."

Knowing Cooper was among the fastest closers but a slow starter—"He starts as a crayfish," one rider remarked—Taylor got down to business. He pressed into the lead, twisting the screws into his evasive rival. In the stands, there was no doubt about the crowd's loyalty. New Yorkers stood and cheered frantically for Taylor. Feeding off their energy, he bent around the dangerously steep forty-five-degree track, his body and his craft angling out nearly parallel to the ground, inertia the only thing keeping him from cascading to the floor. Cooper lay in behind, stalking him. In front, Taylor's black legs bound up and down, gathering rhythm and peeling away. Cooper was already falling back. A length. Length and a half. Two.

From their booth, Kennedy and Brady could look out and see Taylor storming by at more than forty miles per hour. They remembered the graceful stride, the absence of wasted energy, and the mysterious uncoiling of power from '96 when their paths first crossed and '98 when the world first took notice of Taylor. A few booths down from them, a stately French promoter who had been keeping a close eye on Taylor for years twisted his whiskers and sipped a drink.

As the bell signaling the last quarter mile rang out, Taylor pressed down on his pedals and felt a certain correctness in his cadence, a confidence radiating in him and pushing out through his legs. He looked under his arms and saw Cooper becoming unhinged, wagging and wigging and spinning farther and farther away. The Blond Adonis was overheating.

The crowd was in a frenzy. Fans reportedly stood on benches, tables, chairs, and railings to see the finish. A few booths down from Brady and Kennedy, a contingent of European promoters sat alongside European reporters. "Taylor," one French journalist said in amazement, "was simply toying with Cooper."

In the final lap, by now largely ceremonial, Taylor glided past a blur of faces and a sea of noise, crossing the line well ahead of a humiliated Cooper. The crowd, knowing no one was left for Taylor to conquer in America, shouted him home.

Hopping off his bike, Cooper's face was long and drawn. Sweat seeped out of his cloth bandana, giving him the appearance of a melting candle, drooping under the weight of his ignominy. He left the track in anguish, retreating to the riders' room without shaking Taylor's hand or uttering a word. "I have never seen a more humiliated pair of 'toms' in my life," one man wrote, referring to Cooper and his trainer.

After the race, Taylor slid into the crowd and took on the role of genial spectator. The press circled him with questions such as: With no competitor left in America, are you going overseas? Tell us about the match race. What do you think of the tempo of the six-day racers? "It is a fearfully hot pace," he said, keeping his plans close to his vest. Eager to keep large crowds streaming in throughout the entire event, Brady and Kennedy cornered Taylor and asked if he would headline each of the remaining five days with stabs at various speed records—"name your terms," they said. Taylor did, and promptly repaid them with two world speed records in the one-half- and one-third-mile sprints.

All told, somewhere between fifty and sixty thousand fans showed up to an event that was supposed to have died.

Over the previous four years, the nation's riders had tried with all their collective might to impede Taylor's remarkable ascension. But on one chilly December evening, he had finally conquered everything they could throw at him. He now stood as the undisputed champion of America. But there would be little time for respite, as much was happening in the vast world beyond her shores. In the cycling meccas of Europe where bike racing began, millions of impassioned fans and several high-powered racers who had been hearing tall tales of him for years eagerly waited.

With his standing in America absolute, Taylor was eager to steam east and give the Old World a few lessons on Yankee supremacy. There were goliaths to spear across the pond in the spring of 1901. Among many others were Willie Arend, the uber-cyclist from Germany; Thor Ellegaard, the tall Danish powerhouse; Grognia, the champion from Belgium; and Momo, the champion of bike-crazed Italy. And there was another, a giant among men. As Taylor walked toward the Garden's exits, two European riders named Gougoltz and Simar approached him. The Great Frenchmen Edmond Jacquelin, they said with absolute certainty, "will beat you as he had beaten all cyclists." Taylor's competitive blood boiled as he walked outside and out of the nineteenth century.

Chapter 14

EDMOND JACQUELIN

Victor Breyer, one of the race promoters eyeing Taylor at the Garden, was the model of what Frenchmen wanted to be like—and the man with whom Frenchwomen wanted to be. To American observers, he had all the appurtenances of a prosperous Frenchman—a white, straw boater hat, flowing handlebar mustache, refined demeanor, and the quiet confidence that comes from success and popularity. Educated in Great Britain and fluent in English, Breyer strolled about with a relaxed, charismatic propriety, as though he knew people were looking at him. There was a decided omniscience about him, leaving the distinct impression he had advanced knowledge of things.

Thirty-eight years old in the winter of 1901, Breyer was a rakishly handsome, smooth-talking sportsman from the Bordeaux region of France. From his days as a founding member of the sport's international governing body, L' Union Cycliste Internationale, Breyer had learned to spot racing talent from a mile away. Sometime in the 1890s, he stepped into race promotion and sports journalism at the French daily *Le Velo*. His outward appearance was mirrored by the elegant flow of his written and spoken words. He described the world poetically in a visual, tactile, aural way, creating that tang of feeling that drew people to him. Breyer teamed up with fellow journalists and former pro racer Robert Coquelle and began actively recruiting cyclists to race on the tracks of Europe. After a few fits and starts, their fortunes turned when they successfully enticed several well-known Americans to make the long voyage, including Eddie Bald, Tom Cooper, and the Great Zimmerman. Before long, it became known in cycling circles that if you wanted to race on European tracks, you would likely have to go through Breyer and Coquelle. By 1901, they *ruled* European racing.

The French duo thought they had seen the best of them until the mid-'90s. That's when men, women, and children began gathering at velodromes throughout France, peering up at the winners' podiums with a look of awe normally reserved for those witnessing the second coming of Napoleon. Twenty-five years old in 1901, Edmond Jacquelin, the mercurial superstar grinning back at them, was simply the most extraordinary cyclist Europe had ever seen. A prototypical French rider, he was a Gallic mix of charm, breathtaking speed, and brute force. Foreign riders who had competed against him returned to their native lands and immediately pronounced him "the fastest sprinter in the world." Also a skilled boxer and former soldier, Jacquelin's appearance alone put fear into his rivals. He had powerful tree-trunk thighs, thick, striated calves, and the same commanding manners as the early French racing legends George Cassignard, Paul Bourrillon, and Constant Huret. Other riders didn't dare cross him; he once clobbered a rival in a velodrome locker room for the unforgivable offence of "getting in his way."

On the track, he was a chameleon. One moment, usually the first half-kilometer, he was like a greyhound—graceful, polished, poised. The next, usually down the homestretch, he was athletically incorrigible—bucking, rocking, swerving violently side to side. Rival wheelmen swallowed hard at his intense competitiveness. The suddenness and swiftness of his effort, one man marveled, "surprises, paralyzes, demoralizes his adversaries." "When I have beaten everyone in speed," Jacquelin would tell a rapt reporter, "I feel the need to take on the rest of them, to find out what they have *in their guts.*"

But it wasn't just his incredible speed that filled European racetracks. It was his raffish demeanor and his intolerance for authority figures. With judges and handicappers he was a hellion, an early John McEnroe, delaying matches with his brashness. At one race, he was such a verbal menace, he was fined for "incorrectness of attitude." In Jacquelin's confrontational psyche, raising the startman's pistol was akin to a rodeo clown raising his red flag to a raging bull. But once on wheels, he tore across the tracks, leaving his rivals strung out behind him while fans pardoned him for his transgressions.

Strangely, Jacquelin's only weakness came *because* of his strengths. When he sensed there was no rider worthy of his energy, he was wont to occasional bouts of laziness. At night, he was known to indulge in the "unusual pleasures" of the Parisian nightlife. During the day, in an era when few had autos, he'd motor around Paris in a twelve-horse Fournier while Parisians looked on.

After thrice defeating American star Tom Cooper as though he were a "second-rater," some believed the only way America stood a chance against this Frenchmen would be to turn back the clock and send over a youthful Arthur Zimmerman. In 1900, when Jacquelin felt like it, he exhibited such devastating speed he rarely even trailed in the homestretch of a race. When on form, he had no peer. His victory in the famous Grand Prix of Paris race came with little effort. His second of three French National Championships soon followed. The World Championships, the final leg of bike racing's prestigious European Triple Crown, etched his name in the history books.

As Jacquelin's managers, the names Breyer and Coquelle had become perhaps the most widely known in European sporting circles. With him in their stables, they knew they held greatness in their grasp. But they had arrived at a quandary. Since Jacquelin had ridden the legs off everybody in Europe as well as top Americans he had faced, many believed no one was left who could make him crack a sweat. Others, including William Brady, thought maybe, just maybe, there was one exception.

A few short years before, no one would have guessed that that one exception would have been Major Taylor. When he escaped rural Indiana and came east in the throes of a depression, he was a smallish, completely broke, largely unknown amateur trained by a washed-up former rider. His contemporaries had called him nothing but a little "pickaninny." But by the winter of 1901, after filling out his frame and fighting his way through a wall of racism, the whole world knew who Taylor was. They also knew that the devout Baptist and one-time horse-tender would be a tough nut to crack.

Any European race promoter interested in signing him faced the sticky subject of Sunday racing, which first had to be overcome. This was no simple matter: *Avoiding* Sunday racing was as important to Taylor as racing *on*

Sunday was to Europeans. In Europe, following morning mass, Sunday afternoons were often all about bike racing. Sports fans throughout the Old World poured out of their gothic cathedrals, paused for coffee at one of their ubiquitous cafés, then fought over front row seats at the velodromes. In France, where bike racing was (and still is) not so much national pastime as a state religion, Sunday racing was hugely popular. After watching the incomparable Jacquelin dominate his rivals at the famous Grand Prix of Paris, Brady was astounded by the French enthusiasm toward their hero and cycling in general. It is *the* big sport he told a *New York Times* reporter when he returned. "They go wild over cycle races in Paris. Why, there were more people at the Grand Prix cycle races than we turn out to a Suburban," referring to the popular Suburban Handicap, part of horse racing's Handicap Triple Crown.

But weekday races, usually reserved only for preliminary heats, rarely drew the same large crowds.

For Breyer and Coquelle, breaking decades of deeply entrenched tradition was not something they cared to tackle. Rather than trying to change the sporting habits of *millions* of European purists, surely, they reasoned, it would be easier to get *one* man to change his ways. For some time they had been trying to do just that. Their obsession with Taylor started in '96 after his victory over Eddie Bald at the Garden. It picked up speed during his ill-fated season of '97 and multiplied when he beat Jimmy Michaels at Manhattan Beach Track in '98. Toward the end of the 1899 World Championship, the overseas offers had begun appearing in newspapers nationwide. TAYLOR, shouted one headline, REFUSES $15,000 OFFER FROM FRANCE.

The numbers changed often, but the reports kept coming, although some people were skeptical of the validity of the offers. To mollify the skeptics, a consortium of French cycle makers and track owners hired Mark Braun, a Chicago-based representative of *Le Velo*, to corroborate the reports.

Hardly a week passed without another headline in another European paper claiming TAYLOR'S COMING or TAYLOR'S NOT COMING. The rampant speculation invariably caused confusion. Taylor was occasionally asked for comment on some overseas voyage he was supposedly going on, of which he knew nothing. For differing reasons, Taylor had rejected all offers. First, much of his career had been spent riding in the shadow of his mentor Arthur Zimmerman; he mentioned him constantly. Like Zimmie, he was determined to assert his right to race against, and beat, America's elite stable of riders before venturing overseas. "Unless it be as Champion of America," he had told a reporter in 1898, "I shall never race on the other side."

Second, the World Championships, which he would not have missed for the life of him, were in nearby Montreal in the middle of the 1899 racing season. Finally, his close sister Gertrude, who temporarily lived in his home, fell ill with tuberculosis. Having recently lost his mother, Taylor wanted to stay stateside to take care of her whenever he could. Gertrude was delighted to stay there instead of in the sterile confinement of a hospital. But she was so ill, she was only strong enough to leave the comforts of a special room that Taylor set aside for her just once. Sadly, Gertrude lost her battle with the disease in the spring of 1900 and was buried near her mother at the Crown Hill Cemetery in Indianapolis.

In the winter of 1900–1901, with those issues behind him, a seemingly impenetrable wall still stood between him and the Old World. It concerned, as the French like to say, his *raison d'être*. And it appeared in nearly every paper in the world at one time or another: Major Taylor Won't Ride on Sunday.

These headlines were often followed by counterheadlines, perhaps planted as feelers by Breyer, Coquelle, or Brady, suggesting that Taylor was softening his stance against Sunday racing. A lot of people believed them; even Birdie Munger hustled down to the *Boston Globe* to express his shock at Taylor's supposed change of heart. When Taylor saw these headlines, he wasted no time putting the rumors to rest. "I stand today just where I stood a year ago, and hope to stand a year hence," he growled, "I am irrevocably opposed to Sunday racing."

The Frenchmen, both eternal optimists, had never come up against such a deeply entrenched objection. Taylor wasn't the only, or even the first, rider who came out against Sunday racing, but most had a price at which they could be persuaded. Like others before him, Breyer kept thinking that by upping the ante, Taylor would eventually crack under the weight of his expanding wallet. No cyclists, save perhaps Zimmerman and Michaels, had ever received offers as large as those Taylor was discarding.

But having grown up penniless on a small farm, the offers were exceedingly difficult to walk away from. Taylor agonized over each and every decision. Several papers headlined his anguish: Taylor's Conscience Still Troubles Him. "I have given up France," he announced during a long interview. "I shall not race on Sunday and I will not do so as my inner self would not be satisfied. Although there is a fortune over there for me, I would not desecrate the Sabbath. It looks as though racing for me is out of the question in this country." But even the *Boston Globe*, which had always been fair in its coverage of Taylor, bet that he would eventually acquiesce. "The above is all right," wrote one of its race reporters, "but a long shot would be pretty safe that the dusky whirlwind will choke or drown that inner self and look for French gold."

With the nation's most catastrophic economic downturn still fresh in their minds, many people reading these headlines couldn't believe anyone, especially a black man, would turn down what amounted to some thirty times the average American's income for an entire year's labor. Some thought he was foolish. Others stood firmly behind him, including a Boston reverend who wanted Taylor to be "immortalized in Carrarra marble."

One Christian reader was so impressed with Taylor's stance, he told him so in a long heartfelt letter that was published in several papers. Taylor was so inspired by the letter, he responded with a long letter of his own that appeared in newspapers large and small. "I am pleased indeed to know," read a small portion of his epistle, "that there are still a few Christians left who possess the courage of their conviction, and who are not afraid to come out on the side of truth and stand up for what is right." But the allure of the almighty dollar had tested him, and he wasn't afraid to admit it. "I am laboring under the greatest temptation of my life, and I pray each day for God to give me more grace and more faith to stand up for what I know to be right." If he didn't get his way, Taylor told another reporter, he would go to Europe on his own and ride when he pleased.

Nearly every day, Taylor rolled into town to pick up another cablegram. Nearly every night, he poured over another offer from another overseas promoter. All of them called for Sunday racing.

All of them were turned down.

Eventually, nearly all the top wheelmen, horsemen, and boxers found their way under the bright lights. For Taylor, with his growing international celebrity, it seemed long overdue. While waiting to see if Breyer and Coquelle would break from their long-held traditions, Taylor decided to have some fun. One of the most popular forms of entertainment at the time was vaudeville. So Taylor, a good pianist, singer, mandolinist, and all-around natural entertainer, teamed up with Charles "Mile a Minute" Murphy for several weeks of racing theatrics. Murphy had gained worldwide fame in 1899 when, in a death-defying act, he rode his bike at the remarkable speed of sixty miles per hour behind, of all things, a locomotive. Matching up the two cycling celebs on stage seemed natural.

Over the years, a few high-profile athletes had met with enormous financial success in vaudeville while others had flopped. Hoping to add to his considerable wealth, Eddie Bald had formed his own vaudeville company called A Twig of Laurel and then planned a national tour. The *national* tour, however, barely made it out of his home state of New York. He had worked hard at it, though, dutifully rehearsing his lines, eventually getting to the point of committing them to memory. But at his first big production without using notes, the show, which had gained national attention, took an awkward turn. When Bald reached the point of breathing words of love and telling the heroine how fast he would ride for her sweet sake, "a solitary and silent figure," wrote the *Brooklyn Daily Eagle* "loomed up in the gloom of the auditorium in the middle aisle." It was none other than showman Billy Brady.

Bald's once-promising career in vaudeville apparently ended the moment the "stage-struck" wheelman spotted Brady in the crowd. "I collapsed," he told an *Eagle* reporter as he tried to explain why his lines departed from his memory, laughter-induced tears of embarrassment dripping down his cheeks.

But other athletes made fortunes in vaudeville, the most prominent being Jim Corbett, the heavyweight boxing champion with whom Brady had traversed the Wild West.

Now it was time to set Taylor off on his debut. Perhaps wanting to avoid an Eddie Bald–like embarrassment, they decided on a simpler act, and one that avoided Sunday performances. The mandolin stayed at home and bike trainers were ordered instead. Theatergoers didn't seem to mind. At theaters in Pittsfield, Springfield, Hartford, Worcester, Rochester, and others, wedged between various other acts, Taylor and Murphy plopped two oversized home trainers down side by side on the stage and spun like mad until the first man completed five miles. Next to their machines hung colorful flags and large dials that kept the crowd abreast of each man's progress. Though brief, the cycling tandem was a success. Everywhere they went, full houses paying top dollar fixed their eyes on the dials and shrieked themselves hoarse.

For Taylor, the vaudeville act fit perfectly. With it, he was able to stay in decent shape in the dead of winter, further line his pockets, meet some of his fans, and have a rip-roaring good time.

He would need it; the coming months would be among the most intense of his life.

The thoughts of everyone in racing narrowed down to one topic: Major Taylor and Edmond Jacquelin had to meet in a match race. Taylor had defeated everyone America had thrown at him, had set many track records and several world speed records. Jacquelin had beaten everyone Europe had to offer, had also set track records, and had won the Triple Crown.

Across the pond, track writers continued pleading for a definitive match race. Long multipage dissertations comparing the strengths of the two titans were set to fly off newsstands. The only problem, of course, was that there was no contract. Having waited years, racing fans were getting frustrated with the stalled negotiations. So were Breyer and Coquelle. While they had landed nearly every other top rider, they hadn't been able to bring home the mother lode.

A few days before the close of the nineteenth century, Breyer threw up his hands, boarded a ship, and steamed back to France growling to himself. Coquelle, a few years older and a bit more patient, lingered. In a last-ditch attempt before he too set sail, Coquelle hustled off to Boston. There, Taylor and Murphy were lighting up another sold-out crowd at Keith's Theater. Coquelle sat back and watched Taylor with one eye, the frenzied crowd with the other. He knew he had to lure this natural entertainer over to the Old World.

After the show, he cornered Taylor and asked him to engage in further negotiations. Taylor consented. The duo moved to Taylor's home, where Taylor's father showed Coquelle portraits of Booker T. Washington and Teddy Roosevelt in his Rough Rider pose. In his living room, Taylor's fingers rolled across his piano while Coquelle and Gilbert Taylor bantered back and forth.

"How do you like America?" Gilbert asked.

"Oh wonderful, magnificent," beamed Coquelle.

"Is Paris as beautiful?" Gilbert queried.

"Oh, much better," Coquelle boasted. "Major will be able to tell you all about it later on because I hope very much to be able to take him over to France."

Eventually the piano went quiet. Taylor drew up a stool and negotiated. Coquelle threw out a figure of $10,000, with prospects for much more. Clearly, he hadn't been paying attention; again the offer included Sunday racing. Taylor looked up, fixing his gaze on a photo of his deceased mother, Saphronia, with whom he had made his pact to never race on Sunday. "I believe in the saying that 'a mother's prayer will last forever,'" he would say, "and I honestly believe it is my mother's prayers that are standing by me now."

The room filled with an uneasy silence. They all stared at one another for a long, drawn-out moment. Coquelle broke the silence, once again explaining that fewer fans attended weekday races in Europe. There was simply not enough money in it, certainly not enough to support the cost of an athlete like Taylor. If Taylor insisted on no Sunday racing, Breyer said, all he could offer was a comparatively scant $3,000.

Taylor didn't have to do a lot of math. Knowing he could make a healthy income riding in America, he refused. Where was the incentive? The room turned electric. Clearly, coming to Taylor's home and chitchatting with his father wasn't working. Reacting in a manner typical of someone used to having things go his way, Coquelle got visibly angry. He then played the Jacquelin card, telling Taylor, with sharp overtones, that he was cutting off all negotiations with him. He was, Coquelle told Taylor, going to devote all his energies toward managing his French legend.

Taylor wouldn't budge. "All sorts of people have come to me—learned, clever men—and have tried to argue with me that riding on Sunday is not wrong," he would later tell a reporter. "But it was of no use. I listened respectfully to what they had to say, but when a man fears God, he has no other fear, and fears nobody else."

They broke without reaching an agreement.

Somewhere along the line, William Brady reportedly stepped into the middle of the stalemate. The price eventually went up: $5,000, plus purses, a share of some gate receipts, $2,000 from Iver Johnson, and no Sunday racing*. To protect the interest of the NCA and other American track owners, an ironclad clause was added: Taylor had to return in time to race in *every meet* on the American grand circuit.

By then, European newsrooms had fallen into a state of near hysteria. Since Taylor hadn't even arrived yet, they sought the next best thing. The

---

* Reports of the agreed-upon dollar amount varied widely from one source to another.

minute European riders tramped down their ships' gangplanks after returning from racing at Madison Square Garden, they were grilled by reporters. Their inquiries centered around one topic: Major Taylor. What's he like? Is he as fast as everyone says he is?

Coquelle, mortified at the prospect of crossing the Atlantic without *the* prize, swallowed hard. As darkness fell over the city of Worcester on January 2, 1901, the men stood up, raised their chins, and shook hands. The deal was sealed. Coquelle exhaled.

The long-awaited European invasion awaited only its chief actor. The May 16 International Match Race, widely touted as the greatest ever, was on.

Taylor may have been a box office and press wonder in America, but in the prestigious cycling meccas of Europe, his pending visit may have been the most heavily marketed and highly anticipated arrival of a sports figure in its history. Coquelle immediately cabled Breyer in Paris. Breyer leaped for joy, then fired up the presses, setting off months' worth of extraordinary media coverage. Papers all over the world sang with the news. A giddy *Worcester Telegram* cycling editor, who seemed to have the inside scope on how often Taylor visited the men's room, was the first to break the headline news in America: TAYLOR ON CONTRACT! GREAT SPRINTER IS TO RIDE ALL EUROPE.

Thirty-six-hundred nautical miles to the east, the winds blew. Looking supremely confident, Edmond Jacquelin, who had been training indoors at a hippovelodrome, settled into one of his luxuriously furnished Parisian apartments. While handling his gigantic Mastiff, his servant handed him the news. "Let him come," he would say. "He will not triumph so easily as he thinks. I will lead him on a hard trip." Someone asked him what name he planned to give to his new dog, said to be the size of a donkey. His aristocratic face arched up in a wide grin as he answered. "Major," he blurted, before ordering his dog to heel.

After collecting his $1,800 advance payment in early March, Taylor geared up for the long voyage on the *Kaiser Wilhelm der Grosse*. Wanting the best trainer and one who could break away for several months, Taylor sought a topnotch black man named William Buckner. Well-known and highly skilled, Buckner had experience with several top riders, including Charlie Miller, a friend of Brady's and the winner of a six-day race, and the Colburn brothers, a famous quintet from St. Louis. While black trainers were widely accepted and used by several top white riders, strangely, this was a first for Taylor. With all the difficulties he had faced booking hotel rooms and getting restaurant meals, Taylor apparently preferred using white trainers in whose name hotels could be booked and meals ordered. But now that he was going overseas where he expected fewer racial difficulties, Buckner would be a good fit.

Having recently returned from France and having leased the Manhattan Beach Track for the entire year, Brady stayed in New York to manage the national circuit races. On March 4, Taylor said his good-byes at the New York pier before boarding the ship he would spend part of the next decade on. Knowing she wasn't going to see him for several months, Daisy gave her fiancé a protracted hug. "As the champion's fiancée," wrote an emotional French society writer, "a charming mulatto saw with apprehension the departure of her fiancé for the modern Babylon."

Pushing off from the New York pier, the 650-foot luxury vessel steamed into the Atlantic, swishing over the very waters in which it—as the first ship to go down in the First World War—would eventually meet its doom.

The accommodations on board the *Kaiser Wilhelm des Grosse* were breathtaking—so much so it caused controversy back home. On the first day of the six-day voyage, Taylor strolled through the world's largest moving object in awe. In his quest to outdo his British rivals at the Cunard and White Star line, the German Kaiser had spared no expense on the *der Grosse*, creating the fastest ship on water, the first to install a wireless system, and the first to employ four giant steam funnels on the outside. On the inside, Taylor looked up at the high ceilings and ornate wood carvings prevalent throughout the first-class section of the ship. As he moved through the six-hundred-person, titanic-like first-class dining area, people either chatted about him in private or recognized him as the ship's "most universally admired passenger," despite the presence of world champion boxer and friend Kid McCoy (aka "The Real McCoy"). In his stateroom, a colorful surprise awaited him, compliments of "his New York cycling friends." It was a large floral arrangement in the shape of a racing wheel.

Back in the States, inquiring minds wanted to know about black passengers on luxury vessels. A curious reporter from Wisconsin, having never heard of a black man traveling first-class on a luxury liner—especially one as grand as the *der Grosse*—launched an investigation into the matter. The reporter first interviewed several people who were at the pier. He then apparently contacted Norddeutscher Lloyd, the ship's builder in Germany, to see what they had to say on the delicate matter. After a thorough inquiry, he was unable to find the name Marshall Taylor or Major Taylor on the ship's manifesto.

Rumors of his apparent desertion spread to France. The rumors hardened into sheer panic. Frantic cablegrams raced under the ocean floor, reaching America in the form of pithy questions. Where is Major Taylor? Did he or did he not board the *der Grosse*? The reporter eventually published his conclusion: just as he had done when booking hotels, Taylor, unsure how he would be received in first class, had booked the voyage under an assumed name. Since no one the reporter spoke with could say with any certainty whether Taylor was onboard, France bit its collective tongue.

Back onboard, a black man looking a lot like Major Taylor began losing his sense of equilibrium. Queasiness was setting in. He tramped onto the deck to shake off his wobbliness, but the constant swaying and the steady hum of four thirty-one-thousand horsepower engines was getting to him. In the ship's smoke room below, men and women danced, tossed money into the ship's pool, and clanged glasses. For one black man, however, things were coming to a head. While his shipmates reveled and Europe waited, one of the world's fittest athletes—a man they called "the bronze statue"— grasped the ship's railing, dropped to the deck, extended his head over the side, and threw up into the Atlantic.

In the decades surrounding the turn of the twentieth century, bicyclists, called wheelmen at the time, fought against horsemen for equal rights to roads.

Arthur Zimmerman on the left, his trainer, Joseph McDermott in the center, and Zimmerman's father, T. A. Zimmerman, on the right (photo retouched).

A portrait of Louis D. "Birdie" Munger.

In the early days of bike track racing, before effective helmets, riders endured many hardships, including crippling injuries or even death. Pictured above is a battered and bruised rider named Alphonse Goosens, shortly after being patched up by his trainer.

Worcester, Massachusetts, in 1898 (from the collections of the Worcester Historical Museum, Worcester, Massachusetts).

Munger faced fierce competition in the bicycle manufacturing business, primarily from Colonel Albert Pope, New England's largest employer. Above, Teddy Roosevelt rides in a Pope automobile, flanked by secret servicemen on Pope bicycles (credit: The Connecticut Historical Society, Hartford, Connecticut).

A portrait of William A. Brady.

Fans file into the second of four buildings named collectively Madison Square Garden. This one, built during the Gilded Age, right before the economic depression of the 1890s, was undoubtedly the grandest.

Undated photo of a velodrome (credit: from the collection of the Indiana State Museum Historical Sites).

An artist's rendering of Taylor's dramatic night races under colored incandescent lights.

In the lonely world in which he lived and raced, Taylor sought strength from the soothing words of the Bible and the tenacity of William Brady (photo from *The Cycle Age and Trade Review*, July 21, 1898).

Claiming their social lives would be adversely affected, many of Taylor's rivals avoided man-to-man match races against him (photo from *Bearings*, July 29, 1897).

Despite racism from fellow countrymen, Taylor stands proudly wrapped in a red, white, and blue sash (photo from Taylor's autobiography).

A Major Taylor accordion fan (photo from Taylor's autobiography).

Major Taylor

Taylor met Daisy Victoria Morris sometime around 1900, thrilling society writers around the world (photos from the collection of the Indiana State Museum and Historic Sites). In one of his letters to her, Taylor wrote:

> . . . sweetheart, when a man is married and has a good wife as I have, and a nice baby girl, he will take a good deal, and stand for many things that he would not, were he not married. . . . I stand for many things now that I never thought I could put up with, and for which I never would stand up before I married.

Taylor stands next to French writer and race promoter Victor Breyer in 1901.

Shortly after the remarkable 1900 racing season, Taylor stands outside a velodrome locker room (photo from Taylor's autobiography).

Photographed here by the French newspaper *La Vie au Grand Air,* Taylor became the most widely followed person in Europe (photo from Taylor's autobiography).

Cold and shivering, Taylor walks onto the Parc des Princes track ahead of French Triple Crown winner Edmond Jacquelin. Their match race would be remembered more than a quarter century later (from *La Vie Illustrée,* May 24, 1901).

Taylor's appearances in France generated enormous profits for track officials, allowing them to substantially upgrade the Parc des Princes track, shown above, and later secure the Olympics held there.

After snapping a photo of him with his Kodak Brownie camera, Taylor extends his hand to Jacquelin (credit: Jules Beau collection, Bibliotheque Nationale Paris).

Shortly before leaving Europe, Taylor accepts another award (credit: Jules Beau collection Bibliotheque Nationale, Paris).

When Taylor returned to America he faced intense hardships, and fierce competition from men like Frank Kramer, pictured above (credit: Bibliotheque Nationale de France).

Daisy and Major pictured together during their 1903 honeymoon in Australia (from the collection of the Indiana State Museum and Historic Sites).

A packed house at the racetrack in Sydney, Australia. According to race promoter Hugh McIntosh, when Taylor raced, gates of 50,000 to 60,000 were commonplace.

Taylor's archenemies, Floyd MacFarland and Iver Lawson, surface in Australia in 1904 (photo from *The Referee*, December 30, 1903).

During his hiatus from bike racing, Taylor often drove his Renault along Worcester's tree-lined roads (from the collection of the Indiana State Museum and Historical Sites).

Taylor and Jacquelin in a match race in 1908 (credit: Bibliotheque Nationale de France).

Daisy, Major, and their daughter Sydney pictured around 1907–08 (from the collection of the Indiana State Museum and Historic Sites).

Before a packed house in New Jersey, Taylor competes in the 1917 Old Timers' Race (photo from Taylor's autobiography).

Champion Bike Rider Dies

MARSHALL W. "MAJOR" TAYLOR
World champion bicycle rider, who died in the county hospital here Tuesday, June 21, of heart disease after three months illness.

In the last known photo ever taken of him, a thin Taylor reads a book, which is probably the Bible (from the *Chicago Defender*, July 2, 1932).

After taking ill, Taylor looks away from a cameraman sometime around 1926 (from the *Worcester Telegram*, December 18, 1926).

Chapter 15

"THE MESSIAH"

Taylor staggered down the gangplank and onto the shores of Cherbourg, France, on the overcast afternoon of March 11, 1901. A large cluster of European photographers and special correspondents, conversing in a polyglot of foreign tongues, escorted him to the rail station. Flashbulbs popped in his ashen face. They hopped aboard a train pointed east. After the usual pleasantries, someone made the mistake of asking him how his first voyage across the beautiful Atlantic had gone. It had been perhaps the most miserable days of his life; he had spent four of the six days dangling over the ship's railing or the nearest toilet, and had hardly eaten a morsel. His bloodshot eyes rolling in his head, Taylor mumbled something about how he had wanted the captain to turn back to New York, or better yet, to just throw him overboard.

The special train chugged out of the ancient fishing village, past the hedgerows, and into the city of lights, arriving in Paris at one in the morning. At the Gare St. Lazare rail station, every customs official and customs employee—none of whom had bothered to declare Taylor's blue varnished bicycle case—formed a circle around him, ignoring all other passengers. Taylor learned that he wasn't the only one feeling a bit woozy. Greeting him there, fresh from Coquelle's wedding reception, was Breyer, anesthetized by an evening's supply of vintage champagne. Delighted to hear someone speak fluent English, slurred or not, Taylor greeted him with a handshake. He told him how excited he was to finally be in France, and that he looked forward to seeing the beautiful country he had heard so much about.

As he would be for the next few months, Taylor was grilled for comment about his chances against World Champion Edmond Jacquelin. "They say he's the best man in the world," said Taylor, his voice starting to come around. "Well, when I'm in form, we'll see how I measure up to him right enough." The ubiquitous question about whether he would ever break his stance against Sunday racing brought a laugh, a shrug, and a classic Taylor reply: "Before I left home, I swore to God that I would never race on the Sabbath, and I don't like the idea of going to hell." Taylor seemed surprised when someone asked him if he sailed under an assumed name. "Why would I bother with a fake name?" he asked. "Everybody on board knew who I was."

At three in the morning, veiled under a thick fog, the woozy party stumbled into the fabulous marble and gilt Hotel Scribe where visiting royalty often stayed. Breyer headed for the bar. Taylor, dying for rest in a motionless environment, went to bed.

Paris rocked.

The Paris Taylor entered that spring was a glittering thing. The final years of the 1890s brought forward so much prosperity, enterprise, and freedom, the French dubbed it La Belle Époque—the beautiful period. Life was humming along so well a pamphlet titled *Right to be Lazy* made the rounds, promoting three-hour work days and a healthful "regime of laziness." Some took it seriously, demanding more pleasurable locales where prosperous Parisians or visitors could spend their newfound wealth and free time. To fill this void, racetracks, circuses, and operas sprang up all over. Plus there were the twenty-seven thousand cafès that, when combined with all the wine bars and cabarets, gave Paris the notable distinction of having more drinking establishments than any place on earth. France drank as never before.

All the fancy watering holes and eateries were splendid, but what really kept wheelmen, horsemen, and politicians coming back were places like the large stone building down on 12 rue Chabanais, near the Louvre Museum. On the outside, it was disguised as just another French cocktail lounge. But it wasn't the façade that drew people to it. On the inside, excited men—some women too—were handed a green alcoholic drink called absinth and then escorted down a long corridor that wound past elaborate rooms lined with velvet, ormolu, and tiger skin. But it wasn't the elaborate interior, either. Not until they arrived at the "selection salon," where gorgeous women were dressed in scant lingerie and gesturing in velvety French accents was the real inspiration for their visit finally unmasked.

The building was the home of Le Chabanais, the world's most famous and luxurious *maison closes*, a French euphemism for brothels. It had none of the cavorting monkeys like the Moulin Rouge, just some of the world's most beautiful women in the grandest possible settings—*ne plus ultra*, as the French called it.

In later years, Ernest Hemingway, between visits to the six-day bike races, drew inspiration there or at neighboring cabarets, as did performers Humphrey Bogart, Marlene Dietrich, and Cary Grant.

Artists found themselves so captivated they lived there—literally. The famous French painter Henry de Toulouse-Lautrec, an avid bike-racing fan who sketched several portraits of Arthur Zimmerman, deftly juggled his passions, drifting to and from the racetracks and his address of record: Le Chabanais. Many politicians and visiting royalty insisted that it be a part of any visit to Paris. At the 1900 Paris Universal Expo attended by Tom Cooper, Eddie Bald, and Floyd MacFarland, the visitors were so thrilled they gave the Japanese room, with its hanging rhino horns and exotic overtones, an award for, of all things, "best design."

And the place swarmed with athletes. Given that the proprietress, a one Madame Kelly, was a member of the high society Jockey Club, her equestrian friends, including prominent Americans, wore out the winding path leading to its doors. And wherever horsemen went, wheelmen were not far behind. Endeavoring to make visiting wheelmen feel at home, the Madame and her wealthy partners, who used *nom de plumes* like Pointy Nose and George the Cavalryman, had rooms fitted with Eroto-cycles, a half-bicycle, half-sex toy—a bizarre-looking contraption that only a turn-of-the-century wheelmen and willing courtesans could possibly figure out. Some people came there or to neighboring establishments like the Moulin Rouge just for the musicals, while others indulged in carnal pleasures. The faded notation for just such an establishment found buried in Taylor's vast scrapbooks reveals nothing about the reason for his visit.

The "storm" that commenced at six o'clock on the morning of March 12 would not subside until late June. The moment Taylor and Buckner stepped onto the streets of Paris for what they thought would be a peaceful early morning stroll down the Avenue de l'Opera, shopkeepers, fashion designers, photographers, and journalists were at the ready asking questions such as, "How did you sleep last night, Major? How will you fare against the Great Jacquelin? How was your trip over?" For hours, Taylor shook the hands of fan after fan as he and Buckner wound down the long avenue. "It had been three years that the cycling season has passed without having seen this transatlantic star whose name has crossed seas and continents," raved one reporter. "But this time," he continued, "we have him!"

Perhaps from years of watching Brady's handling of Corbett and many theatrical stars, Taylor had learned how to handle the press. He also knew how to keep his name in their papers. "Major Taylor," wrote one American journalist who was shocked he didn't have a press agent, "has a happy facility of keeping in the public eye about as prominently as any theatrical star ever did." But in France, the birthplace of world cycling, no effort would be needed. Everywhere he went he was mobbed, talked about, or written up.

The French press, convinced his seemingly innocent early morning walk was worthy of a breaking news story, retraced his movements in their papers. One writer even issued a special dispatch, informing his readers that Taylor had actually "crossed the street." Another reporter came dangerously close to crossing that historic line in the sand. "Taylor's arrival in France ... the heroic guardian of the Sabbath," he said, "can only be compared in importance to Zimmerman's visit of eight years ago." Up to that point, such talk among reporters was considered sacrilege, so he carried on gingerly. "Taylor arouses curiosity all the more, and is surrounded by mystery because of the color of his skin."

Because he was being covered by some writers who knew nothing about bike racing, many reporters focused on him personally, delving deep into his childhood like inquisitive therapists. They also appeared to be competing for the preeminent physical description of him. In their unique 1901 French way, they described his v-shaped back muscles, broad shoulders, muscular legs, and washboard abdominals ad nauseam. But their greatest fixation seemed to gravitate toward his ankles and calves. If there were a hundred ways to describe calf muscles, the esteemed French writers coined them; they were cat-like, effeminate, powerful, shapely, and beautiful. "No man," wrote one French journalist, "had ever been presented to the public in a more flattering fashion."

While they certainly profited in a big way, the obsession wasn't the exclusive purview of the reporters who massed at the Hotel Scribe seeking interviews: the nation's cycling-crazed *tifosi* were insisting on it. So much fanmail poured in demanding to know everything about him, newsrooms became overwhelmed. What was he wearing? What does he look like? What did he eat? Where did he go? And surely the favorite of the ladies: Is he married? "Major Taylor," one of them gushed, "is one of the most beautiful athletes you will ever meet." When front page stories weren't enough, they published a four-page excursus with photos of him flexing and Daisy, "La future Madame," coiffed elegantly.

Taylor had grown accustomed to the singular life of fame, but this was a different strain. In America, it was less personal. In France, where Major Taylor posters were being hawked for five francs and countless people gathered at the Grand Palais to stare at his life-sized photograph, it was a penetrating, in-your-face infatuation. At first, he seemed to favor the American model. Preferring a fair amount of airspace around him, Taylor was, he said, a bit annoyed with all the people "who came to see me and looked at me right in the eyes." "Are blacks not seen in Paris?" he asked a reporter, feeling as though he was the only black man in the country.

Mustachioed photographers in frock coats tailed him, setting up their heavy tripods and capturing his every move, mood, and nuance. As he was without a doubt Europe's most newsworthy subject, images of him in everything from his briefs to a tuxedo would appear in newspapers. Everybody wanted to be in the picture. The leaders of France's expanding automobile industry, Henri Fournier and Count de Dion, made sure their faces were seen in papers all over Europe sitting proudly next to the visiting megastar in their early machines.

Because the number of automobiles in France outnumbered those back home, Taylor was slow to warm to them. He even told a reporter he couldn't stop laughing when he saw those heavy cars Parisians called omnibuses "wandering pitifully on the Champs Elysees." But later, after the two automotive magnates invited him to lunches and fought over the promotional currency his endorsement would bring, Taylor thrilled them by announcing his desire to buy an automobile and bring it home with him. "The people of Worcester," he said, "will be rather surprised to see me come back on a 16-horsepower."

Trainer Buckner had seen great fame before but even he couldn't believe what he was witnessing. He sat back and watched European nobility toss calling cards his way, inviting him to dinners and horse races. "The Europeans were absolutely crazy over him," he would tell an American reporter. Only days off the *der Grosse*, before he had even stepped on a racetrack, France and Europe were full of Major Taylor. Had the girls of Les Chabanais modeled string bikinis on the Avenue de l'Opera during his stay, few would have taken notice.

On the Avenue de la Grande Armee, where the gates open to the fortifications into Neuilly, stood the trendiest resort for wheelmen and wheelwomen in the world. The café *de l'Esperance*, one of many Parisian cafés for ardent sportsmen, was a bicyclist oasis where riders sat around sharing big, fat lies about their storied racing days. The place was so thoroughly enjoyable, people practically lived there. One rider reportedly hadn't missed a single day in nearly a decade, leading some to wonder if he really had that wife he said he had.

A predecessor to today's sports bars, its attractions were numerous. On its walls were pictures and murals of all past French greats—Bourrillon, Huret, Cassignard, and others. Maps of all the best cycling routes were strewn about. On race days, after struggling just to get in the place, avid wheelmen gathered in the main room, sipping wine and staring at a large pillar on which were pinned telegrams announcing the results of races from across Europe. At all other times, people hovered either inside, in the midst of its Bohemian smoke and noisy poolrooms, or outside, where, like the rest of Paris, tables and chairs sat on a wide sidewalk.

On the happy occasion when elite riders happened through the place, a wide path cleared, and caps were doffed. When its most revered foreign guest Arthur Zimmerman first strolled through its doors eight years before, the encomiums and the flatteries that were heaped upon him scarcely knew a limit. In the colloquial of the Café de l'Esperance, wheelmen hadn't stopped chatting about Zimmie since that first visit.

On a cloudy late March day in 1901, all such talk temporarily halted. In an unannounced visit, Major Taylor stopped by, nearly bringing the place to a standstill. Everyone gathered around, including former greats Bourrillon, Huret, and Morin, eyeing him up and down and asking for autographs. Newsmen, having already abandoned all their professional objectivity, joined in, giving the café the look, feel, and sound of a papal visit. Few men fit into such a place better than Taylor. Bring up gearing, tires, wheels, or that race he won back in '97 and he could talk a person's ear off.

While surrounded by that entourage, conducting interviews, and reminiscing about his early racing days, Taylor's attention was suddenly diverted. In the distance, he spotted smoke billowing from an automobile as it puttered down the long cobblestoned road leading to the café. The car, a spanking new Fournier two-seater, sputtered to the curb. The hazy sketch of a man materialized out from its wind-whipped interior. Through the fog, Taylor saw a majestic man, heavily muscled, placing a white straw hat over his mussed hair.

It was Edmond Jacquelin, the Triple Crown winner and champion of the world. The gathering, unable to believe their good fortune, tossed confetti on the boulevard and quietly cleared a path. The two men—one black, one white, one from the New World, the other the Old World, one brash, the other reserved, both skilled boxers—circled each other like two heavyweight prizefighters. Jacquelin's taller frame towered over Taylor, his steely eyes gazing down at him. Taylor looked up and offered his hand. There was a long pause. Finally, with a pained smile, Jacquelin shook Taylor's hand. The world's fittest men locked hands firmly together.

"I did not expect to find a very large man," Jacquelin then said, "but you are really smaller than I was led to believe."

"I was led to understand that you were a very large man for a sprinter," said Taylor, "but did not expect to find a giant as you are."

Someone tossed a tape measure at them. They began to take measurements. Laughter interrupted the seriousness of the occasion.

"You have remarkably big legs," said Taylor, in a relaxed jocularity.

"Yes, but yours are much prettier," laughed Jacquelin.

"That's not the point," said Taylor. "I am afraid yours might be quicker."

"But suppose yours prove quicker than mine. What then?" retorted Jacquelin.

As the two racers continued their exchange, the café owner brought out a bottle of vintage champagne and popped the cork. Jacquelin, born in Santenay, a well-known appellation of Burgundy wine, raised his glass and looked on in astonishment as Taylor sipped his glass of water. Flabbergasted at his ability to abstain, a reporter later asked him how he did it amid so much peer pressure.

"A man comes to me and says, 'Have a glass of beer. Have a glass of wine. Have a cigar.' I decline and I don't feel anything. I don't miss them," Taylor said, "because I have never had them."

The two men then clinked their glasses together while enjoying a few laughs inside the two-wheelers' sanctum. With their match race—which was already selling for ten times normal cost—only a month and a half away, this Franco-American détente would be short-lived.

On another overcast morning in late March, Taylor and Buckner set off for the Parc des Princes Velodrome in the Parisian suburb of Auteuil to begin training. Buckner had been growing concerned; the abysmal spring weather had kept Taylor from his much-needed preparation and he suddenly found himself behind schedule. Somewhere along the line, someone tipped off the public; a steady stream of horse carriages, wheezing automobiles, and rolling bicycles followed them to the track.

Once there, Taylor and Buckner looked into the grandstand and saw a large crowd staring back at them. Since it was just a light, early morning workout on an ugly spring day, Taylor was shocked at the large showing. "There was such a big crowd on hand," one reporter overheard him say, "I thought there was a race meet on." A thick phalanx of European correspondents, including those from political, general news, society, and sports publications, hovered around the track apron hounding him at every opportunity. Several reporters practically camped out there, not missing a single workout. To them and a group of European riders who peered on, Taylor's riding style and his position on his bike seemed abnormal. In the insular world of European pro cycling, riders maintained a more upright position. So when they saw Taylor bent over in an aerodynamic crouch almost parallel to his top tube, some veteran riders told him his posture was not appropriate for sprinting.

Others didn't know what to make of it. "On a bicycle, his position is not disgraceful," stammered a writer for French newspaper *La Vie au Grand Air*. "He doesn't arch his back like a donkey, leaning over his steering wheel, his posture is not exaggerated." But the more they saw, the more they began warming up to it. "His style is supple, at ease, regular, mechanical, never jerky no matter with what speed he progresses and he has a perfectly harmonious strength. He becomes one with his bicycle better than any other compatriot."

His unorthodox training regime also had them baffled. While Europeans trained plenty hard, many of them rolled through essentially the same routine day in and day out. Like Zimmerman, Taylor constantly varied his routine; one day short violent sprints, the next day longer, slower miles, the next behind motorpace. "I do whatever pleases me," he told a surprised Frenchman.

The backstretch had long been a gathering ground for men with deep-rooted superstitions and rigid beliefs in old wives' tales. The Europeans were perhaps the most superstitious of them all. Wearing jersey number thirteen ever since he obtained his professional license, Taylor was a sweeping departure from traditional riders in this regard as well. The European riders, who Taylor believed were inflicted with a silly case of triskaidekaphobia, stood perplexed while Taylor spoke of his contrarian ways. "I am not superstitious," he told someone before relaying a story about how he once raced on September the thirteenth, stayed in hotel room number thirteen, then raced against a field of thirteen, wearing, of course, jersey number thirteen. "And I won it," he said laughing, while everyone stared quizzically at him. His diametric ways irked some and mystified others. "Taylor," one man wrote, "is said to attract the greatest delight from his association with the number thirteen and other uncanny things that tend to freeze the blood of his countrymen."

So when he was given the keys to cabin number thirteen, one of the quaint buildings set aside for riders close to the track, he was unfazed. But the minute he opened the door, he was unceremoniously attacked by a smattering of brooms and wheelbarrows and old bicycles that had been stored there for the winter. The pile fell at his feet outside the door. He looked down, kicking the debris to the side. Someone then handed him the key to cabin 57. He took it. Buckner unloaded his bicycles and clothing, set up a massage bench, and installed a punching bag on the ceiling. Then they settled into the place they would call headquarters for portions of the next few months. Curious Europeans peered in, fixing their gaze on the strange punching-ball, wondering what in God's name he was up to. "It strengthens the muscles and increases considerably the breathing," he told them wryly.

After settling in, they stepped out their door on the way to the track where they planned to train at ten in the morning and three in the afternoon each day. They couldn't help noticing a sign, embossed in gold trim, hanging on the door of cabin 56—right next to theirs. The words stood out like the Eiffel Tower: Edmond Jacquelin Champion of the World.

The trip to the track was as much about settling in to his new training digs as anything else, and with the weather growing nastier as the day progressed, Taylor wasn't keen to do any more training. But with a large animated crowd leaning up against the track rail, he decided to entertain them instead. Harking back to his early days as a trick rider, he mounted his bike backward, then rolled across the track with his hands grasping the handlebars behind him, feet on pedals, pointing south. It was all that was needed for the crowd to rid themselves of their hats and handkerchiefs all the while hollering hysterically, "Vive Taylor!" "Vive Taylor!" The wild cheering carried on long after he walked off the track.

It started to snow. Taylor left the track to take in the sights, which included the Automobile Club of France, the luxurious Palace de le Concorde with famous sportsmen René Boureau, and a comedy. People tapped each other everywhere he went whispering "Look, it's Major Taylor." Reporters shadowed him, including one Frenchman who made the preposterous claim that Taylor was one of them because his parents hailed from African countries under French control. He then met with a host of tire manufacturers who were jostling over his endorsement, eventually choosing the le Paris Tire Company. Buckner was stunned at the monetary rewards. "They were throwing all kinds of money at him," he told an American reporter.

On the evening of April 6, 1901, the train carrying Taylor, Buckner, and Breyer pushed east from Paris's Gar du Nord rail station. Looking out the window of lucky sleeper number thirteen, Taylor watched them roll past picturesque medieval castles before settling into downtown Berlin. When Taylor's weary body stepped out into a waiting carriage, a reporter announced that "The earth under Germany shook." They clopped off to the unfamiliar surroundings of the Friedenau Sportspark Velodrome to take part in his first European race. Taylor looked out at a field of European riders circling the damp, windy track as if it were a sunny summer afternoon. He was about to face several new challenges.

First, he had to deal with European cyclists, a very hardy bunch. For whatever reason, they and their fans seem to thrive on early spring races, both road and track, in some of the harshest conditions. Thousands gathered at famous races like Paris-Roubaix, set out over grimy, wet cobblestones, while Americans trained in the deep South. The American track-racing season, in fact, usually didn't start until after Memorial Day. But since Taylor intended to defend his American championship title later in the season, he was obligated to begin outdoor racing much earlier than he was used to. An admitted fair-weather racer, he despised racing in the cold or even being out in it. The cold weather had reportedly been one of the factors keeping him from crossing continents sooner.

Since he was scheduled to race in Europe for a few months, he also had to become intimately familiar with a different style of racing. American fans, being an impatient, high-strung lot, demanded knee-buckling speed from start to finish. Any deviation from this brought heckling from the stands. To mollify Yankee racing fans, American cyclists usually employed a put-your-head-down-and-ride-like-hell-from-beginning-to-end strategy. It was an unsophisticated game plan, but effective.

European fans, on the other hand, were in no hurry for anything and often showed up fashionably late. They fancied themselves a more cultured lot who preferred more strategizing. As a result, European pros crawled around the track for the first three-quarters of a race, jockeying for the best position in a cat-and-mouse game before finally uncoiling in a vicious sprint down the homestretch.

Then there was the language barrier. European pros, because of their extensive travels throughout the continent, have always been remarkably multilingual. Other then stringing together a few words in butchered French, Taylor spoke only English. The politics within the international peloton were complex; riders who were bitter rivals one day would work in tandem to outmaneuver a favorite the next. No one had been the subject of more team-work than Taylor, but in America, he could at least hear his rivals' tactics and react to them. In Europe, he was stripped of one of his primary senses. "If Americans are to go to France in numbers," Taylor would joke to Buckner, "they might petition the managers of the track meets there to demand silence at the races." Finally, though the Europeans respected Taylor, some noted that he had done all his racing on the questionable terrain of the New World. "They are not of the same class as the top four or five French flyers," boasted one returning European rider, summing up European opinion of most American riders. Having invented the sport, they wanted nothing more than to dethrone the much-ballyhooed black man from America. After scouring the continent for its best trainer, Willie Arend, the champion of

Germany, had gone into virtual hiding in Hanover to exhaustively prepare for his race against Taylor.

Together these challenges—combined with unfamiliar racetracks and enticing nightlife—had spelled doom for nearly every American rider who had crossed the Atlantic, save Zimmerman. When the American "aces" got near Europe, wrote Coquelle, who had grown pessimistic over the years, "they vanished like smoke." Going into his first European race in cruddy weather, Taylor was clearly up against it.

As the pistol cracked before a large and cold German crowd, which included the German chancellor and high military personnel, the cunning field of riders, employing the European method of racing, crawled out of the gate. Taylor watched and listened as the riders, knowing he couldn't understand them, began openly strategizing with each other in their native tongues. Suddenly Willie Arend, a former world champion, swooped around Taylor and stormed for the line. Laboring coldly along the pole in a full-length cotton sweater, Taylor paused slightly before he realized what had happened. He eventually reacted, lunging forward, trying to catch Arend's rear wheel. It was too late. In the best shape of his life, Arend crossed the line ahead of Taylor.

Taylor wasn't altogether prepared for what happened next.

In a jubilant celebration, an animated throng of Arend supporters practically tripped over one another as they trampled out of their seats. They scaled the fences and charged onto the track, waving their handkerchiefs, tossing their hats into the air, and roaring in an animated and sustained bellow. Every bleacher, grandstand seat, and booth had been vacated. Even racing officials found themselves caught up in the excitement. The crowd sought out Arend, hoisting him on their shoulders, and carrying him around the track. The entire crowd then joined the band in singing "Watch on the Rhine," while their short-sleeved national hero, wreathed in a jumbo-sized horseshoe of roses, wheeled around the track in triumph.

Facing enormous pressure to succeed against the men Jacquelin had already defeated, Taylor tried to wriggle his way through the noisy labyrinth to shake Arend's hand. It was no easy task: the sheer size of the celebration overwhelmed him. "That's one of the greatest demonstrations I have ever seen on a bicycle track . . ." he would say. Before long, posters of Willie Arend, Champion of the World, were being pinned up in bike shops around Berlin.

Having his money and his reputation on the line, and fearing any loss may take the zeal out of the Jacquelin match race, Breyer removed his straw boater hat, wiped the sweat from his brow, and fretted. "The sky seemed to be against our shivering son," wrote one of his nervous *Le Velo* journalists. Knowing Taylor well, Buckner slipped through the crowd unmoved.

Being an intensely competitive man, losing never sat well with the Major. It gave him an unsettling feeling in the pit of his stomach. Three days later, deciding he loathed losing more than he despised the cold, Taylor made mincemeat out of a stunned Arend, winning by a length—the length of several attached railcars that is. Breyer and Buckner smiled. Believing they had the man who would unseat the much-heralded American, Germany had been silenced. "Jacquelin," someone muttered, "is the only man who can even pretend to defeat the man."

In the dark of the Teutonic night, more than five hundred star-struck fans, many of them Americans, followed Taylor, Buckner, and Breyer back to the train station. The whistle blew, his admirers yelled their approval, and the train lurched ahead. In the coming weeks, the train would scatter across the continent, passing a sea of followers and reporters en route. With each visit, word that the great black man was coming hummed through the telegraph wires. Somewhere along the way, darkness would turn into light. One of the most remarkable followings in sports history had begun.

Their train twisted through the Black Forest and on to Paris for a week's worth of legging up at the Parc des Princes. Stopping in Paris was of little use; the weather was cold and dreary again. Buckner, worried because Taylor's training was still behind schedule, tried to encourage him. Watching the rain turn to sleet and then snow, Taylor brooded.

One week later on a red-eye coach, they shoved off from Paris in the darkness, rolled out over the vineyards of Northern France, still cold and dormant, and into the town of Roubaix in the early morning hours of April 22, 1901. This being Taylor's first race in France, the town was waiting for him. The minute he sprang out of the railcar doors, he was mobbed by fans. Flowers were tossed at him and endless praise heaped upon him. "Nothing," Taylor later told a reporter, "was missing to make me happy." An elegant black carriage picked them up and whisked them off. Along the dirt road winding into town, thousands tossed their hats, hollering "Taylor! Taylor!" as they rolled by.

At the Hôtel Moderne, Taylor asked for and received room thirteen. At the track, every seat and close-by tree limb was filled with humanity. Among others, Louis Grognia, the talented Belgian who had twice won the prestigious Grand Prix of Roubaix, awaited him. Taylor scorched out of the gate, leaving everyone in his wake. When he reached the exceptionally steep final turn, blazing along at a murderous pace, his heart nearly jumped out of his chest. Unfamiliar with the angles and flow of the track, he had cut it too sharply, causing his left pedal to scrape the concrete surface. The brief brush with the track threw him off-kilter, sending him scurrying catawampus to the outside. Grognia and a rider named Dangla, who would soon die from a tragic track accident, clawed by him on the inside. But in a remarkable display of wheelmanship that brought gasps from the crowd, Taylor somehow righted himself, then scorched rubber to the finish line just in time to win by a nose.

With evening falling over Roubaix, their train skimmed along the River Meuse before cutting through the Ardennes Forrest and into Verviers, Belgium, perhaps the most bike-crazed nation on earth. "Room thirteen, please," Taylor asked at the front desk of his hotel. Though room thirteen was normally used for first aid, he was told they would make it available for him—an extraordinary response for a black man accustomed to being turned away by hotel owners.

Morning, noon, and night, crowds would gather outside his hotel hoping to catch a glimpse of the visiting dignitary. When one race had to be postponed because of rain, thousands charged out of the track—forgetting their refunds—and swarmed his hotel. They stayed there, refusing to leave until he poked his head out his window King Leopold–style.

Living vicariously through Taylor, Buckner adjusted his Texas-sized cowboy hat, stared out his hotel window at the waiting horde, and shook his head. He was loving every minute of it. Most people, including Buckner, were at least as impressed with Taylor's warm, genial character as they were his athletic skills. "I have never before met such a gentleman in every respect of the word," beamed a Dutch track owner. With few exceptions, he referred to his rivals as "my friends." He treated people the same whether they were valets or famous dignitaries, an admirable trait he learned from Zimmerman and from the lessons in the Bible, which he passed through as often as other men imbibed. He made a point of introducing Buckner to people, making him feel, perhaps for the first time in his life, special—someone more than a black servant. "I have the greatest confidence in him," he often told journalists.

Verviers was also the hometown of Grognia, the Belgium national champion who enjoyed superstar status among Belgians. Because he was undefeated there, a lot of local fans were predicting another Grognia win.

To their dismay, they would have to watch Taylor beat the competition again. "Alas," exulted *Cycle Age*, "America has found the new Zimmerman for whom we have awaited." One prominent European track owner said that people had never seen anyone like Taylor. "They gazed at the little Major and seemed not to understand whether he was an ordinary human being or a man having some kind of 45 horsepower motor in his body."

From Verviers, their train snaked toward Antwerp, passing by sixteenth-century castles not yet scarred by war. Thousands amassed in the rain at the 400 meter Zurenborg Velodrome. "That part of the world hadn't seen such fanaticism since the tulip craze," one man later cracked. Coquelle surely looked at the wet crowd and began questioning the long-held belief about weekday races not drawing well in Europe. Taylor put on another show for the crowd, mowing down Momo, champion of Italy, and Protin, champion of Austria, before pipping champion Grognia at the finish line again. The crowd, drenched to the bone, roared. Recognizing his manifest superiority, Taylor had eased up down the stretch. "He didn't care to make his defeats too apparent," giggled one reporter. Grognia, whom the *Referee* was now wittily referring to as "GROGGY," threw in the towel. "He's the most marvelous racing man I have ever seen," declared Grognia. "If he wanted he could have won by as many lengths as he desired."

But as they had in every town, people asked the same question. Do you *really* think you can beat the Great Jacquelin? A skeptical reporter for the *Boston Globe*, who had just written a gushing article about the Triple Crown winner, went right ahead and answered the question for him. "Major Taylor will have to ride faster than he ever did in his life. Taylor can sprint, but the Frenchmen, when he turns loose on the last eighth of a mile, he whizzes around a track like a meteor dropping from the skies."

The train backtracked, pausing in Verviers, Roubaix, and countless small European towns before arriving in Paris in the still of the cool April night.

Upon his return, it became clear that Major Taylor had really arrived in life. He began opening letters from home addressed to: *Major Taylor Paris France*. Since nearly everybody knew who he was and where he was at every waking moment, no address was necessary. The young black man had his own zip code! "Major Taylor," gushed Victor Breyer, echoing the sentiment of others, "was awaited like the Messiah."

On May 2, the train carrying Taylor, Breyer, and Buckner pushed out of Paris's Gare de Lareze rail station. It cut through the emerald vineyards leading into Bordeaux. Next to Paris, Bordeaux was France's most cycling-crazed city. Fans stood around the rail station waiting in lively clusters for the coming hero. The trio pressed out into a flock of fans that had been sipping the local flavor and discussing his pending visit.

The three were immediately whisked into a waiting Dorsey automobile by local track owner Henri Barbareu-Bergeon and his personal chauffer. Taylor stared in reverence as the open-air six-seater passed the marble monument of the revered French cycling hero Georges Cassignard, who died young after being thrown off his horse. They continued rolling by a picturesque string of grapevines along the Gironde estuary before wheeling into the dish-shaped Velodrome du Parc. It was all quite a sight for the twenty-two-year-old from Indiana. "Neither the living nor the dead," wrote his friend Arthur Zimmerman, "could take exception to taking residence in Bordeaux."

Like most of his races in Europe, people arrived from all corners of the continent and wedged themselves into every available square inch of the track. It was the largest crowd ever seen in Bordeaux. Fans in a medley of shades pushed up against the rail, waving the tricolors of the republic. Busy concessionaires crisscrossed the velodrome, making sure the dense pack was sufficiently topped-off with their favorite beverage. "The French," Zimmerman told the *New York Times*, "enjoy themselves at the races in grand style. People sit around the grounds drinking, smoking, and discussing the races." They resembled picnics, he continued. "Everyone is in good humor."

As the sun fell over the city, Barbareu-Bergeon flipped the switch on the newly installed night lights; unfortunately, the only thing staring back was the moonlight. Unable to safely see the track, the riders waited for the lights to be repaired. After a half hour under the moonlight, some of the fans in the one-franc or "democratic" upper-section—an area that attracted heavier drinkers—started to stir. Forty-five minutes in the stir turned into a steady stream of profanities, their anger building and building.

The humiliated track owner, working frantically to repair the track lights, started getting a bit panicky. After an hour, flying objects appeared. Riders scattered. Bergeon's voice wafted out over the packed grandstand. "Due to a problem with the lights," he announced, "the race is off." The crowd was irate. They stood and hollered their disapproval in every conceivable language. Bergeon tried pacifying them, saying he would kindly issue a full refund and that he would simply reschedule for the next day.

Now, the good cycling fans of Bordeaux, having waited patiently for years and having paid a generous premium to see the "Flying Negro" had reached a boiling point. In an act of destruction that would have been the envy of the most unruly Wild West American crowd, the frenzied Frenchmen tore the track asunder—mowing over and breaking up the track railing, tearing lights down from poles, busting tables and chairs, and setting the place ablaze.

As a plume of smoke blew across the track, a ripple of horror spread through the peloton. Riders ran out into the street and bolted for cover. They glared out in astonishment as the crowd took out their anger with fire glinting in their eyes. With portions of the edifice crackling in the night, the fire brigade and local gendarmeries appeared out from under the smoke. With guns and sabers at the ready, they hauled the perpetrators off to jail and hosed down the inferno until midnight. Taylor could not have said he hadn't been forewarned. "A French crowd is the most amiable thing, extant" his mentor Arthur Zimmerman wrote in his 1895 autobiography, "up to the point where it becomes convinced that an imposition is being practiced. Then, of course, quite Jacobin-like, it pulls up the stakes and makes a bonfire on the spot."

A local reporter, who had probably been planning a literary tour de force for months, had few words the next day. "Utterly deplorable," he reported, pithily.

The following afternoon, Taylor reappeared amid the remaining ruins before what must have been a hungover crowd. He proceeded to ride the legs out from under an Italian cyclist named Ferrari, then immediately retreated to his quarters. The sellout crowd would have none of it. They cheered continuously, waiting and waiting for him to make a curtain call. When he didn't reappear, Bergeon, frantically trying to avoid another pyrogenic incident, hustled into his locker room and talked him into a solo exhibition ride. Taylor mollified the crowd by riding one lap around the track, 333 meters in 20: 1/5 seconds, a new world record. Later that day, after being mobbed as a spectator at the famous Paris-Bordeaux road race where even more alcohol was served, Taylor quickly hotfooted out of the city.

It was wet and miserable again. Through much of the weeks before the 1901 International Match Race, the air sang with the pattering sound of rain. Paris, enduring one of the wettest and coldest seasons in years, seemed like an endless string of wide open silk parasols. At Parc des Princes, a dark cloud hovered around cabin 57. At times, Taylor had been visibly despondent. "Besides five or six days that were passable," he had moaned, "it rained constantly."

Buckner had watched as a shivering Taylor looked sullenly out at the moist cabins and soggy racetrack. Having trained six-day race winners, Buckner knew a thing or two about keeping exhausted men motivated, but he had his hands full with the warm-weather Taylor. At first he tried humoring him. Then he poked and prodded and cajoled. Some days his persistence worked and Taylor either mashed a punching ball hanging from the ceiling or made a cameo appearance before a crowd of hardy Europeans burrowed under umbrellas. On other days when he couldn't get Taylor to budge, he lit a fire and the two men wrote home, took photographs, strummed the mandolin, or read the Scriptures in silence. On one particularly gloomy day, Breyer looked at Taylor's sad disposition and droopy eyes and said he'd never seen anyone so morose. In ninety-degree heat, Taylor was spry, smiley, and alert. But since the only thing April showers brought were May showers, he just couldn't get used to the cold, damp Parisian spring. "I'm an African, not a European" he snapped, as the rain continued dancing off cabin 57.

The weather was having such an effect on his mood, even photographers and the press, who couldn't find enough good things to say about him, occasionally set him off. The atmosphere alternated between being mildly amusing and openly truculent. One day, when yet another photographer wanted to take yet another picture alongside yet another fan, an angered Buckner shooed them all away so Taylor could have some privacy.

It was of little use. Mystified by the black Horatio Alger who had turned away so much money to avoid Sunday racing, fans continued showing up. Railroad companies even began organizing special "spectator" trains to haul in carloads of people wanting to view him as if he was a rare panda at a zoo. Reporters continued pecking away. They really had no choice in the matter. "He is," one of them wrote, "as much talked about as the premiere."

Jacquelin was also growing agitated with the press. Like most superstar athletes, superhuman feats were expected—and reporters had a love-hate relationship with him. When he won, they practically prostituted themselves to get an interview with him, always following it up with gushing praise. When on the rare occasion he actually lost, no matter the circumstances, he was but a washed-up has-been. "What would I have to do to convince these half-dozen stubborn journalists who enjoy doubting me every year, always looking for someone better than I?" he barked to a reporter. "Now they were going to unearth a Negro?"

After losing a few races to a couple of middling riders at Turin, Italy, in mid-April, some reporters all but wrote him off. "He will have to undergo a miraculous change in form," wrote *Cycle Age*, "if he expects to defeat Major Taylor." There was even talk of plucking the Great Bourrillon, a former French rider who had become an opera star, out of mothballs to take on Taylor in his place. For a flicker in time, Jacquelin's subpar showings made Taylor a 5 to 1 favorite.

But it was all just Jacquelin being Jacquelin. In early May, shortly before the International Match Race, Jacquelin strapped his feet into his toe-clips, bound his hands in tire tape, and utterly incinerated Louis Grognia at the prestigious Grand Prix of Nantes in Nantes, France, winning by an embarrassing number of lengths. In a move that completely silenced even his most hardened critics, he then defeated Danish strongman Thor Ellegaard in the International Sprint Race one day later. Ten thousand mouths gaped in the grandstand. No one was more impressed than Major Taylor, who had wriggled into the stands after being enveloped by spectators. Ellegaard, one of the fastest men in the world, leaned against his bike and marveled at the Frenchman. He walked over and shook Jacquelin's hand. "You will eat that American up next week," he said humbly. The crowd yelled, "Yes! Yes!"

After the race *Cycle Age* backpedaled; Jacquelin, they wrote, "could not be had at even money." "If you think this Darkey scares me with his airs of wanting to swallow everything winner-take-all," Jacquelin told track director Henri Desgrange, "you can tell him I accept what he proposes [Taylor, as always, had demanded that the winner receive the entire purse]. We'll see who is the chocolate guy."

As race day neared, a gripping tension swept across the backstretch. The race was becoming a global fixation, sucking up all the media oxygen. "Interminable calculations" were being made in editing rooms across Europe. The cablegrams and papers reaching the States were thick with notices and photos of Taylor. The muscles of Jacquelin and Taylor had been studied by doctors and reporters in astonishing detail. The French populace, one American paper decreed, "has gone practically crazy over the coming meets."

Regardless of the weather, hundreds if not thousands amassed around the track daily. Next door in cabin 56, the Jacquelin camp was outwardly confident. Jacquelin and his brother, who was also his trainer, looked out at the inclement weather and sneered.

Underneath the certitude, an enormous amount of pressure was being placed on him by the vast number of adoring French racing fans. "Those who are familiar with Jacquelin and understand the pedestal pose in which he has been placed by the enthusiastic French," proclaimed the *New York Sun* on race eve, "say that it will about break his heart and nearly be his ruin if he loses."

Taylor seemed to be aware of his place in history, an awareness that began early on. Before bedding down, as he had done since his first races, he cut out newspaper articles about himself and his races, had some translated, and then glued them into a large book that he carried with him always.

Parked inside his cottage on May 15, an apprehensive Buckner surely looked at the forecast: *cloudy and cold again.*

He kept his mouth shut.

Paris didn't care. All across town, lively race-eve gatherings sprang up. The Moulin Rouge, Le Chabanais, and the Café de l'Esperance entertained an unprecedented number of visiting racegoers throughout the night. Race tickets selling at twenty times face value changed hands. Press coverage reached astronomical levels.

Chapter 16

THE FIRST WORLD WAR

Below a dull bank of clouds in the early morning hours of May 16, 1901, track director Henri Desgrange, co-creator of what is now the most heavily attended sporting event in the world—the Tour de France— sauntered onto the frigid Parc des Princes Velodrome. A brisk, cutting wind whipped across the track. Desgrange blew hot air into his chilled hands and gazed out at the swaying trees lined with spring foliage only grown to half-mast. Above him, black clouds bubbled over, threatening to unleash their liquid contents all over the city again. An army of concessionaires crisscrossed the grounds, stocking up on food, drinks, race programs, and souvenirs. A handful of amateur riders preparing for undercard races rolled past while an early crowd gathered outside the track.

Desgrange surely had mixed feelings about the threatening clouds and unseasonably cold weather. After months of intensive buildup and having already collected unprecedented gate receipts, part of him was no doubt deeply concerned that a heavy rain might cancel what the press was calling one of the most anticipated sporting events in history. But as long as it didn't rain hard, he reasoned, the inclement weather may actually help keep the crowd at the eighteen-thousand-seat track within controllable levels.

As race director, the decision about whether to run the race rested squarely with him. Following an agonizing moment, he made his decision; barring a heavy rain, he announced, the race was a go. His words spread like wild-fire. Back in the States, Taylor's American challengers eagerly awaited cables with the results. "Major Taylor is having little trouble to trim the riders on the other side of the ocean," wrote the *Daily News*, "and the sprinters on this side are beginning to wonder if the Major will return and sweep everybody."

Already preparing for Taylor's return, Brady's newsroom friends down at the *New York World* set the stage for the grand match. "All interest in cycling awaits the result with the keenest interest. To both men the result means everything. It will be as if they are gambling with their last dollar. For the winner there will be worldwide renown, for the loser the reputation of being a defeated champion."

Back in New Jersey, Arthur Zimmerman, the man whose insight and friendship had inspired Taylor to his current heights, surely read the fren-zied overseas cables with a great big smile. Some writers had come close, but now, except for a few hardened traditionalists, most elevated Taylor to the top of the world's most popular list. "Taylor is already more popular then Zimmerman was," wrote one veteran racetracker. "Should he defeat Jacquelin, I cannot venture to predict to what length people will go."

People began congregating around the entrance as early as six o'clock in the morning. All morning and early afternoon, bicycles, special trains, and elegant horse carriages disgorged thousands of passengers from every major city in Europe. On harrowing sojourns over dusty roads, enduring flat tires, clogged carburetors, and shotgun fire from angry farmers, primitive automo-tive caravans puttered in from the most remote provinces of France. A flotilla of boats drifted down the River Seine, dropping off thousands more at the track's gates.

Just before noon, nearly four hours before the race, Desgrange flung open the ten access gates, loosing a cavalcade of humanity. People who didn't know the difference between a bicycle and a horse cart—and normally didn't care—waved one hundred francs in the air, pleading for tickets. In the boxes along the tape where tickets sold for $16, many times their normal cost, nearly every nation in Europe was represented by a baron, duke, duchess, prince, king, or prime minister.

The money being wagered was almost certainly a record. William K. Vanderbilt, owner of the first Madison Square Garden and an avid cycling fan who attended Taylor's first race, dropped $3,000 on Taylor to win. Pennsylvania railroad tycoon Harry Thaw and gold rush millionaire William

Moore bet $20,000. World famous artist William Dannat and the Countess Castellane, daughter of wealthy financier Jay Gould, sunk their thousands on Jacquelin. A supremely nervous Pennsylvania senator named Clark kept his monetary allegiances to himself. It was now any man's race: of the twelve major Parisian dailies, six picked Taylor, six Jacquelin.

By one o'clock, the grandstand was jam-packed, so Desgrange opened portions of the infield, charging $20 for the privilege. The horde kept coming. By one forty-five, not knowing how far to push it, a nervous Desgrange began turning fans away. "No more," he kept hollering to his attendants. "No more." The track was bursting at the seams. On a threatening, bone-chilling Thursday, and at a time when the population was one-quarter its current size, twenty-eight thousand people—one of the largest crowds of any *single day* sporting event—wedged into the famous but somewhat neglected track. Five thousand fans stood along the rails.

Outside the track, thousands upon thousands more, including some of Paris's elite, unable to get in, congregated in thick formations around the gates, fences, and neighboring areas hoping to catch a glimpse inside. A solid row of French gendarmeries fanned out around the infield, preparing to keep the throng off the track. Over in the press area, journalists from all over were penning their prerace reports.

At three-thirty, the two men emerged onto the track to an eruption of noise normally reserved for opposing battleships, all but drowning out the wailing band. Like a prizefighter, Jacquelin had a superstition about entering the stage first. So Taylor, cold and frowning, walked ahead of him in a full-length African cloak, hood over his head, hands in his pockets, head down. Right behind Taylor, with his perpetual grin and bulging muscles, waltzed the supremely confident Jacquelin. Amid a gripping tension that enveloped everyone at the Parc des Princes, the Triple Crown winner exuded utter insouciance, strutting in with a look of a proud prince, eyes glaring down, but chin up.

They rolled up to the starting line of the one-kilometer, or five-furlong, race. Taylor took off his white cloak, handed it to Buckner, and rubbed his shivering body up and down, number thirteen visible on his purple and black silk racing togs. Seemingly oblivious to the crowd and the cold, Jacquelin, hot-blooded like most European riders, looked over at Taylor with clinical coldness. "I do remember getting a kick out of seeing my adversary buried in his long coat, looking miserable under a cold sky," he would remark in true Jacquelin style.

Each man raised one leg over his bike frame and cinched his feet into his toe straps. Buckner held Taylor up at the line, Jacquelin's brother doing the same for him. A tall man with a handlebar mustache slowly raised a pistol toward the sky, his fingers clasping around the trigger. The vast crowd drew its breath. All over the stands, reported Breyer, men and women were gritting their teeth, turning pale, biting their tongues and lips, and clutching themselves in unbearable suspense. An eerie stillness filled the air. It was so quiet, said one witness, "one would have thought that only a single man was the spectator—the silence was sublime."

After years of intensive negotiations and unprecedented international buildup, a loud crack finally rang over the heads of Major Taylor and Edmond Jacquelin at Paris's Parc des Princes Track.

In line with the European style of racing, the fastest men in the world rolled across the tape at a snail's pace. Craving the prized rear position for drafting and strategic purposes, Jacquelin, thriving on this style of racing, crept forward so slowly it appeared as if he were stationary. With his experience as a trick rider, Taylor matched him snail's pace for snail's pace. The European crowd, loving this cat-and-mouse game, stood up and erupted. The battle over who could go slowest was joined, each man struggling for balance, teetering on the brink of falling over. Someone had to give. Someone did.

In the biggest race of his life, before the largest and loudest crowd of his life, Jacquelin teetered and tottered and fell flat on his side! The fans, who had been biting their tongues and clenching their fists seconds before, buckled over into hysterical laughter.

As if nothing had happened, Jacquelin remounted his bike and the race quickly restarted. The crowd gathered themselves. Not wanting a repeat of this embarrassing scene, the pace of the restart increased slightly. With the first turn in front of them, Jacquelin rolled up the bank and surveyed his American rival below, dangling the lead position in front of him, tempting Taylor to seize it. Taylor wouldn't bite. Instead he steered his bike up the bank, settling in right behind the burly Frenchman. The crowd roared.

They hovered along the upper rail rimmed in faces, waiting for the other to drop down and make a move. Neither did. Instead, they reached out, grabbed the top rail, and glared at each other. As they dangled motionless, the crowd again erupted in a combination of pensive laughter and outright hysteria. They pushed off simultaneously and slow danced into the backstretch, their measured pace only deepening the agonies of anticipation and the decibel level of the crowd. They continued rolling side by side out of the backstretch, the haze of bodies along the barrier diluting then disappearing altogether, the commotion from the throng becoming a faraway roar. Jacquelin and Taylor were alone eyeing each other, scanning for signs of weakness.

They tiptoed out of the backstretch and pedaled together into the last turn, their strokes still rising and falling in unison, their eyes trained on the track ahead. The three remaining furlongs became two, one and three-quarters, then one and a half. The lead seesawed back and forth. No one knew what to expect.

With just three hundred yards remaining, Jacquelin stood on his machine and pounced. Energized by the sight and sound of twenty-eight thousand screaming fans, he vaulted forward at an infernal pace, the sinuous muscle on his calves, hamstrings, and quadriceps protruding under the strain. Underneath him, the metal on his monster gear (104) began bending, the violence from his frantic surge pressing his tires deep down into the concrete oval. Slowly losing ground to his side and spinning a much smaller gear (92), Taylor was astonished by the Frenchman's pace.

Like a gladiator, Jacquelin had muscled into a slight lead, seemingly trumping Taylor's much-celebrated late sprint. Taylor, who had been in this position before but never alongside a reigning world champion, must have thought Jacquelin would eventually crack. But he was showing no such signs. Taylor was getting nervous.

On the sideline, trainer Buckner, knowing Taylor's fickleness in the cold, gnawed on his nails and knelt down as if deep in prayer. Waves of amazement pressed through the crowd. Straining with all he had, Taylor began losing more ground. Jacquelin's front wheel forged past, then his crank, then half of his rear wheel. With only a half furlong remaining, France went shrill. Taylor's graceful form remained steady and poised, but the cold breeze shivered through him and in him, engulfing his entire body.

Jacquelin was a contrast in form and function. He lunged forward so rapidly, his hips swung wildly side to side, his knees thumped upward toward his chest, and his eyes stared forward demonically. But could he possibly maintain such a pace? An original thought surely pressed into Taylor's mind: *Maybe this Frenchman is faster than me, as many said he was.* In the French quarters of the press area, men roared.

With the finish line rushing at them, the 1900 and 1899 world champions stretched out over their machines. Their raw speed reached historic proportions*, their hips and legs cranked up and down in unison, and their heads and necks stretched and bobbed from the exertion. Along the rail, screaming masses waving hats, handkerchiefs, canes, and umbrellas clipped by them, blurring in their side view. Taylor looked forward and tried to answer Jacquelin's surge, but for the first time in an eternity, a competitor was actually outgunning him—a wheel, a wheel and a half, two wheels, a full length. The crowd was levitating!

Jacquelin looked back: he saw Taylor uncoiling nearly five feet behind, still laboring toward him. He knew he had him. The Great Frenchmen sat up as he rolled over the tape, crossing the line at his hometown track a little more than a length in front, riding strong.

What followed, one British reporter wrote, was "a scene which beggars description." After a brief pause while they recovered from shock, the crowd erupted into prolonged applause. They knocked over railings and barricades and tore after their "prince of sprinters" with all the force of a tidal wave. Some of them, one eyewitness remembered, "acted as though crazy." Others were so stunned, they couldn't move, yell, or utter a single word. Concerned over Jacquelin's safety, a posse of police and dragoons tried forming a human chain around him, but were no match for the onrushing mob. Behind him, Jacquelin's rolling wake sucked in thousands of men, women, and children. Hand in hand with common folks, normally staid dukes, barons, and duchesses in their finest attire went ballistic. "There is no way to describe it," said one witness. "It was as if some strong electric battery was being pressed in the feet and hands of these thousands of people who yelled in every possible manner."

France carried its megastar triumphantly around the track like Napoleon at Austerlitz. Jacquelin's eyes shone with the joy of it all, the band blaring with the sweet sound of "La Marseillaise." Lost in the revelers, Taylor and Buckner stood near the finish line bewildered and crestfallen. Trying to console him, Buckner handed Taylor his cloak. Taylor warmed himself in it.

Jacquelin's glorious moment in the international spotlight may have remained unbroken if not for what happened next. When the celebration rolled near him, Taylor inched toward his victorious rival to extend a

---

* Jacquelin's pace at the end of the first race was indeed historic. He covered the last 100 meters (109 yards) in five seconds flat, beating the previous competition record by a full second.

handshake. The right thumb of the man known for his brash, sometimes vulgar disposition rose to his nose in a crude and arrogant gesture, staying there as he continued his whirl around the track with a "villainous grimace."

Hearing a chant of "Down with Taylor! Down with Taylor!" Taylor boiled over. He was so shaken, he quickly retreated to his cabin, slinking by a sea of strangers. Flashbulbs popped all around, showing him in a state of abject dejection, his head down, body slumped, the ugly moment seemingly multiplied by his shadow visible in the picture. He hunkered down on his sofa and sobbed. "In all my experience on the tracks of this country [the United States] and Europe," he remembered later, "I have never before suffered such humiliation . . ."

Buckner, failing to console him, joined him in his glumness. Jacquelin eventually swaggered to his cabin, his footprints surely audible inside Taylor's cabin next-door. The photos of him exiting the track were a study in contrast. His broad chest was pushed out, his face was all smiles, and his hands were pressed into his sides. His brother stood next to him, laughing and smiling and bubbling over.

Track director Desgrange, along with Breyer and Coquelle, agreed to hold a revenge match on Monday, May 27.

In the intervening days, France would hang in suspense again.

That evening, Parisians danced and sang and drank with happy abandon, their world supremacy assured for a fortnight. "The Flying Negro Beaten" boasted one paper. The race, said another, "was the most perfect speed event in the history of cycle racing." All over town, wine and champagne went in through racegoers' lips and the name Edmond Jacquelin poured back out, their satiety spilling out of the racetrack into the cafe's and onto the streets.

As darkness fell over the Arc de Triumph one evening shortly after the match race, a chilly spring breeze whipping across the hushed oval, a solitary figure was dashing around the track. He was black, lean, and mad as hell. "Listen carefully," Taylor muttered to a reporter while pointing to the sky, "Jacquelin thumbed his nose at me and he will be punished up there for it. I will be very surprised if I don't beat him the next time we meet."

All he wanted, he would say, "was a warm day."

Chapter 17

THE SECOND WORLD WAR

May 27, 1901, rolled in under a haze. Eager to gauge the day's weather, Buckner rose early and raised the shades in his room. A thin trace of clouds impeded his full view of the early morning sun. He cinched open the window and put the flat of his hand against the screen. The air temperature was moderate, nondescript.

At the Parc des Princes Velodrome, a small crowd was already hovering around the outside perimeter of the track, chitchatting about their hero. The race they came to see almost didn't happen. After Jacquelin's victory over Taylor eleven days before, some had questioned the need for another match race. The Jacquelin crew remained tremendously confident, and nobody more so then Jacquelin himself. "I thought I had beaten Taylor so convincingly," he had boasted to a host of jolly reporters, "there would be no question of a revenge match." Though Taylor had committed to a second match before the first, Jacquelin had apparently left his options open. But with everyone hounding him to commit, he finally agreed. "If he (Taylor) wants one," said Jacquelin, his voice buoyant and cocksure, "I am at his disposal whenever and wherever he wishes."

The French lionized Jacquelin to such an extreme that some quickly forgave him for his nose-thumbing incident. But others, probably the majority, were disgusted. "There was no more likable athlete than Taylor and he did not deserve that kind of treatment," barked French journalist Maurice Martin.

Some people wondered whether anyone would even show up for a rematch. "The French promoters calculate," wrote the *New York Sun* a day before the first race, "that if Jacquelin should defeat Taylor, as he has all others, it would be impossible to get a crowd of any size to a return match . . .what's the use of going?" the paper asked. "It will be a walkover for Jacquelin." Desgrange knew better. When he walked out on the track that Monday morning, there was already a sizable throng circling the place.

By noon, the number of amassed thousands was greater than at the same time of the first match. By one o'clock, the grandstand was bulging. By two o'clock, the seats, aisles, railings, and press area were so crammed with white boater hats and spring dresses, the stands were barely visible. Several scores of "pretty" French actresses, fascinated by Taylor, occupied seats along the finish. The number of people inside and outside the track, many thousands more than the first race, may have been the largest throng ever to show up for a *single day* sporting event.* The overflow either waited outside the gates or thronged into myriad cafès throughout Paris.

At the famous Cafè l'Esperance waiting for *the* telegram to be pinned into the "pillar," people were crammed in wall-to-wall. "Had they been around at the time," remarked 104-year-old honorary hall-of-famer Jack Visceo, "the whole continent probably would have had their ears pressed against a noisy vacuum tube radio, listening to the race." "Never," wrote one European reporter, "had a sporting event provoked so much enthusiasm."

Over three thousand miles to the west, a nervous stir was forming. In New England, where the first mention of a statue honoring Taylor began circulating, Daisy was fidgeting, eagerly awaiting an overseas cablegram. In Washington, DC, Teddy Roosevelt was "especially pleased" to have Taylor "carrying the stars and stripes" while racing abroad. In New York, Brady was

---

* Several events in which Taylor competed—Montreal in 1899, Philadelphia in 1898, Madison Square Garden in 1896 and 1900, etc.—drew larger crowds, but these were multiday events. Had the track been large enough, some people believe the crowd could have been double the reported size.

preparing a new race with a $5,000 purse modeled after the Paris Grand Prix, and was sketching an offer to Jacquelin for its inaugural running.

The American press and most American riders had expressed surprise at Taylor's defeat in the first race. But in a rare moment of patriotic harmony, even some who were normally out to get Taylor started predicting and pulling for him. Much national pride was on the line. This was war, America versus France, being fought on a bicycle track. One New York paper had apparently drawn this conclusion after polling several riders, probably including Zimmerman. "It is believed on this side of the Atlantic," wrote one cycling scribe, "that he [Taylor] can ride the legs off of anyone who has ever sat on a bicycle saddle." But they had a few caveats and one strong recommendation. First, it had to be over seventy degrees. The second one Taylor had a little more control over. "The cycling athletes of this country still have faith in the ability of Major Taylor to defeat Jacquelin if, instead of complying with the French sentiment," the newsman continued, echoing the words of the riders, "'he will get on a bicycle and ride the stomach out of the Frenchmen.'"

As Taylor and Jacquelin prepared in their locker rooms the heavens relented. At last the wind stilled, all clouds dissipated. A bright sun lit the trees and shrubs in a profusion of color. Buckner handed Taylor the Scriptures. Taylor thumbed through it while Buckner pressed his palms into his lower back, kneading out the tension. Taylor got up and walked toward the track, the pages left open.

Have I not commanded you?
Be strong and courageous.
Do not be afraid:
Do not be discouraged,
For God is with you wherever you go.

As if his mood was inextricably connected to the weather, Taylor bounded onto the track smiling and jovial. On his way in, lines of photographers clicked away, the light from their cameras dancing off his face. Buckner looked up at the clear sky and thanked the heavens.

The two goliaths cinched in at the line. Jacquelin's upper body, in all its athletic symmetry, leaned over his bicycle. Surprisingly, given his previous defeat, Taylor was a lesson in quiet confidence. Several reporters looked at him in bewilderment, wondering if this was the same glum, shivering man who showed up at the previous match race.

Right before the startman drew his pistol, Taylor shocked everybody by suddenly leaping off his bike. Fashioning himself a skilled amateur photographer, he grabbed his Kodak "brownie" from Buckner and began snapping pictures of Jacquelin. At first puzzled, the crowd then chuckled. Jacquelin looked on with complete indifference. They lined up again. "The Frenchman," recalled Taylor, "had the same arrogant smile as he mounted his wheel." "For the first time in his life," jibed one American, "someone had to wipe that big smirk off his Gallic face."

In a show of confidence, Taylor leaned toward Jacquelin and extended his right arm in handshake without looking at him. Startled, Jacquelin raised his hand grudgingly, gazing at Taylor and mumbling something in French, perhaps details about how he was going to ride him into the ground again. Deep in thought, Taylor ignored him, setting his eyes on the track ahead. The crowd ground their teeth.

The Second World War was on.

Perhaps angered by Taylor's curious start-line tactics, Jacquelin eschewed the traditional European loafing and moved out of the gate taking the early lead. Taylor tailed him closely, sucking along in his vacuum, keeping his front wheel fastened to the rear of Jacquelin like a horseshoe to a hoof. The pace remained steady through the first turn and into the backstretch. The crowd, surprised by the tactics, let out a steady yelp. Out of the backstretch, black and white forms dashed forward, their flowing cadence increasing, their speed slowly rising.

Jacquelin rode confidently over the track, his tires rolling over the same circular route as eleven days before, his legs spinning piston-like, drawing the backstretch under his wheels and forcing it back behind him. Taylor looked forward and saw the arched back of his rival—and his broad hamstrings and calves pumping aggressively up and down, sweeping him along in his mighty slipstream. With two furlongs to go, they both saw the outline of the wailing crowd pushing up against the rail. They ramped up the pace, preparing for a heightened dash to the far turn and the onrushing throng. Jacquelin angled his craft outward, making a vicious push up the banking. Taylor tracked him. The massive crowd, nearly close enough to touch, reached forward, their hands flailing, feet stomping, faces an image of mayhem. Taylor, still trailing, moved forward ever so slightly. Fans gasped. Some of them fainted, dropping limp into the aisles.

Up in the grandstand, the large American contingent pleaded for Taylor to make his move before the Great Frenchmen ran away with it again. His mind drifting back to the unforgettable thumbing incident, Taylor inched up along his brash rival and ground his teeth. Through his binoculars, Buckner could see Taylor's anger. He knew it was now or never.

In a celebrated career spanning hundreds of professional races dating back to 1896, through the 1899 World Championships, defeating everyone America could throw at him, rarely had people seen the full wrath of Major Taylor. With one and a half furlongs remaining to the finish line, he set his jaw, bent down, and unleashed a ferocious forward assault. He slashed high up on the bank, curved his body around the final turn, and steered his machine down into the belly of the track's homestretch. Jacquelin, already gunning at a torrid pace, looked to his side in shock. He watched as Taylor inched up alongside him, then around him—first his wheel, then his crank, then his rear wheel. Within the space of a few seconds, the lead had changed hands, Jacquelin now swooping in behind Taylor's purple and black silks. Over in the press section, the French contingent sagged, their faces a rictus of apprehension.

Amid the merciless tempo, Taylor actually accelerated. The gap between him and Jacquelin began widening—a half-length, a length.

Along the tape Buckner stood chewing his fingernails down to the bone. With such a ruthless pace he, Breyer, Coquelle, and everyone else in the crowd knew one of them had to give. The first to show signs of cracking was Jacquelin. He looked forward and saw Taylor's back and hamstrings floating through the warm air like an eagle, seemingly effortless. "There is something mysterious about his power," wrote a European columnist, "and that mystery is itself a potent force."

Trailing, Jacquelin refused to give up. He stomped down on his pedals, his knees nearly thumping into his chest. Ahead, he heard the metallic sound of chain links stretching and cranks bending, and the familiar hum of metal spokes whirling at forty-plus miles per hour. With just under a furlong to go, his face took on the pained look of man nearing his limit.

Taylor was flogging the world champion, his one-length lead becoming two, two and a half, then three. Behind Taylor, Jacquelin was red-lining, his body zigging and zagging in an irregular sideways thrashing movement, his usual erratic form further degenerating into a scene of man banging against machine. The speed—the last 200 meters was run off in twelve seconds— seemed way too much for him.

Taylor dropped his head and body parallel to his top tube and rode for all he was worth. His world compressed into a few thoughts, sights, and sounds: out in front, the sight of the finish line rushing toward him; Buckner waiting at the line; Daisy in New England writing another love letter to "Major Taylor World's Greatest Cyclist"; in Washington, DC, Teddy Roosevelt, a follower of his; Brady in Manhattan, preparing for his return; hundreds gathered around the famous pillar at Café l'Esperance waiting for *the* telegram; around sixty thousand eyeballs looking down from the stands. Now it was just him, his bicycle, and an open span of track.

In the backdrop, it was all over for the proud Frenchman. Jacquelin felt the deadening buildup of lactic acid pushing through his legs, the limiting experience of oxygen debt, and the humiliating feeling of another man out of reach. For the first time in as long as reporters could remember, during a race he really wanted to win, the Triple Crown winner was being cut to pieces.

For Taylor, there was a sense of tranquility. He felt the penetrating warmth of the Parisian sun, the exhilarating tenfold high of man wedded to machine, and the sweet sense of revenge.

Major Taylor glided across the line a convincing four lengths in front, riding high over the world.

The entire American expatriate community leaped from their seats. They charged down through the aisles, passing heaps of stunned Frenchmen, tore right past the police cordon, and lunged after Taylor. They hurled their hats in the air and slipped a large bouquet of roses around his neck. Jogging along his side as he circled the track, they watched as he waved an American flag toward the French sky.

Jacquelin disappeared quietly from the roaring group of celebrants, his stomach still collapsing in and out from exertion. According to some, he would never be the same that year. It was, they believed, his Waterloo. "The redoubtable Jacquelin has been vanquished," claimed one reporter months later. "He has been taking back ever since Taylor took his measure . . ."

During the ceremony, with "The Star-Spangled Banner" playing in the background, Taylor was handed a beautiful silver loving cup donated by Delancey Ward, an American artist living in France. Buckner stood proudly nearby. Taylor looked forward, his mouth curled up in a reserved expression. Breyer and Coquelle looked on, their eyes green with profit.

Back at their *Le Velo* offices, the presses were churning out newspapers in unprecedented numbers. Before Taylor's visit, an average day's circulation at *Le Velo* was around twenty-five thousand. In a handful of days before and immediately following the second race, nearly three-quarters of a million copies of *Le Velo* alone flowed out of their presses and into the streets, cafés, and homes of Paris. A number made all the more amazing considering the *New York Times* had a circulation of around one hundred thousand at the time, up from twenty-five thousand in 1898. Even the heavily publicized death of Madison Square Garden architect Stanford White at the hands of Harry Shaw (who lost $20,000 betting on Taylor over Jacquelin), that resulted in the trial of the century increased circulation by fewer than one hundred thousand. With the aid of the world's greatest drawing card, Breyer, Coquelle, and Desgrange were rolling in money.

And the frenzy was only just beginning.

At some point, Taylor and his wide grin hopped into a Renault automobile, rolled out of the Parc des Princes, and sailed through the streets of Paris. In his state of giddiness, he apparently forgot that Paris had speed limits. A local gendarme flagged him down near the Arc de Triumphe. He got out and walked up to Taylor's car with a speeding ticket in hand. When he got close enough to see who it was his eyes widened and his hand reached up to doff his cap. "Oh, my God. It's *Le Champione*," he said as he waved Taylor off, sans the speeding ticket.

Taylor eventually made his way to the Chalets du Cycle, a popular outdoor café in the Bois de Boulogne frequented by wheelmen and their admirers. On his way in, he noticed a crowd thick as plankton milling around someone. He walked in to see what all the commotion was about. The crowd cleared an opening for him. There in the middle of the gathering stood none other than Jacquelin. Taylor walked toward him. The normally chatty crowd shushed. The two "knights of the track" drew up next to each other in silence.

Jacquelin was the first to break the silence. With a stern look on his face, he muttered something in French. Taylor, who was just learning fragments of French, could barely pick it up. A man dashed through the crowd, emerging with a bottle. A loud *pop* was heard. Suds sprayed into the air. Someone handed each of them a glass. Champagne was poured. Jacquelin raised his glass and spoke.

"Do the honor of sharing a drink with me," he said.

"With pleasure," retorted Taylor. "But you know very well I only drink water."

"Oh," Jacquelin said assertively, hoping to lure him in, "for once have a little champagne."

There was a dreadful silence. The crowd pushed inward, locking their gaze on Taylor. For what may have been the first time in his life, Taylor raised an alcoholic drink up to his lips and took a sip. He choked on it. "Awful, terrible," he complained. "Abstinence," wrote French paper *La vie au Grand Air*, "gives him spiritual pleasures."

After the thrashing he had endured, one wheelman later joked, Jacquelin probably finished the bottle himself.

June dawned warm and glorious for Major Taylor. The turning wheel of his life was spinning forward splendidly, and he couldn't conceal his *joie de vivre*. He was in peak condition, all things right with the world, and the cold, wet spring was giving way to summer. Since those first gusts of warm weather blew across the Old World, he had felt a smooth cadence in the saddle, a feeling of quiet invincibility, a desire to take on all comers. And while he was at it—to see the world. While Paris reeled, he and Buckner clattered across the vast European continent for several weeks of nonstop racing and sightseeing.

In ancient towns all over Europe, he either visited or passed by a cornucopia of historic sites. Their train, moving at all hours of the day and night, whistled into Antwerp, Hanover, Berlin, Lyon, Toulouse, Agen, and Bordeaux, each visit and race a special story in its own right. Posters, billboards, and newspaper ads promoting his visit lit up the continent. In Leipzig, someone drove all over town for days in a sputtering Mercedes Benz holding up an oversized portrait of him. Reporters welcomed him to their cities with long, tasteful poems. As before, fans greeted Taylor with profound reverence everywhere he went and, good weather or bad, rarely was a velodrome seat left unoccupied. On the way to and out of each track, hundreds if not thousands followed him enthusiastically. Luminaries continued to invite him to sporting events and elaborate social functions.

It was a following unlike any before, but it was the freedom from bigotry that Taylor would cherish most. Barring a few minor exceptions, from the moment he stepped on foreign soil, the bitter racism he had faced from riders and hotel and restaurant operators in the States had been checked at the ocean's edge. On one occasion, he nearly broke down as he discussed the treatment he had received in Southern American states, clearly stoking old wounds. There could not have been a more remarkable adventure for him or for his black trainer.

In each city, his dominance continued. In twenty-four total races, his only losses were to Jacquelin in the first match race runoff in the cold, Thor Ellegaard because of a flat tire that he immediately avenged, his first race to Arend shortly after stepping ashore, and a couple of races against two men on tandems. An urgent call went out for a third match race between Taylor and Jacquelin. But because of his tight, prearranged schedule of non-Sunday races, it never took place that summer. Taylor fans would have to settle for watching him thump Jacquelin in an open race. "It was a victory from which there is no appeal," wrote a prominent French reporter, "and I must now recognize that Taylor is the better man. He is '*it*' without a doubt."

By the beginning of June, Taylor was basking in the European glow so much—and Breyer and Coquelle were rolling in so many francs—he was asked to extend his stay. Taylor agreed. But with this ill-advised move, he and the French tandem infuriated some powerful men on the other side of the Atlantic. In New York, A. G. Batchelder, chairman of the NCA, fired off a flood of cables reminding Taylor and the parochial Frenchmen that Taylor was under contract to ride back in the States. Failure to return immediately, he threatened, would mean suspension and heavy fines for each race that he missed. Having leased the Manhattan Beach Track for the entire season, William Brady also expressed concern with Taylor's extension. Perhaps a bit more diplomatic in his choice of words, he also fired off cables asking Taylor to jump ship. He then sent lucrative offers to Jacquelin, asking him to join Taylor in his voyage back to the States: first $2,000, then $3,000, then $4,000, as a down payment for a few weeks of racing. Jacquelin, perhaps a bit Eurocentric in orientation, and a man who seemed to enjoy living as close to the pulse of Paris as possible, did not commit. After a delay that he'd pay dearly for, Taylor finally responded. Brady received his cablegram; he would head home on June 28, a few weeks later than his contract called for.

Taylor rounded off his racing engagements and then said his good-byes to his new friends at elaborate farewell ceremonies. At one large gathering he was showered in American flags—"I received enough flags to tapestry my bedroom" he told reporters. Women approached him, batting their eyelashes and wreathing him in colorful bouquets. William K. Vanderbilt was there, trying to wriggle into the gravity of the moment. But with Taylor present, reported the *Chicago Tribune*, one of the world's richest men went completely unnoticed.

As he prepared to leave on that late June day, he felt like a new man—proud, elated, and emphatically free.

On an evening before setting sail, Taylor strolled through the lobby of the Malesherbes Hotel where he was staying at the time. There in the center of the lobby sat a black Steinway piano staring at him, tempting him. Being a lover of music and a fine, self-taught pianist, Taylor, because of his hectic schedule, hadn't found the time to play it as often as he had wished. But on this night, being in a particularly melodious mood, he drew up a vacant stool, set his bowler hat on top of the piano, and sat down. Initially a small crowd noticed and gathered around him. Taylor played tentatively. The small crowd grew. Warming to the gathering, Taylor started singing "Hullo My Baby," an American song made popular during the 1900 Paris Expo. The crowd joined in.

. . . tell me I'm your own, my baby
Hello my baby, hello my honey
Hello my ragtime, summertime gal
Send me a kiss by wire, by wire
Baby my heart's on fire, on fire
If you refuse me, honey, you lose me
And you'll be left alone, oh baby . . .

"Remarkable singing voice," opined one journalist in the entourage. Taylor's hands poured across the piano, feet stomping on the pedals, voice wafting throughout the room. Champagne was brought out, and people listened and sang.

If man could freeze time during the moment of his greatest joy, Major Taylor may have lowered his thumb on his timepiece in that Parisian hotel, on that night, during that glorious season of 1901.

During his fourteen-year career, Taylor competed in hundreds of races. At each meet, several preliminary heats were run. Nearly all match races, including both against Jacquelin, were two out of three affairs. So as to not overburden the storyline with endless race descriptions and to maintain an even reading flow, the authors have described only the deciding heats of Taylor's most important races. It should be noted that in the first match race, Jacquelin won both heats, the first by a half-length and the second by under two lengths. In the Second World War race in warmer weather, Taylor won both heats by around four lengths.

Chapter 18

THE LAST BLACK FACE
IN AMERICA

The luxury liner *Deutschland* steamed into New York on the muggy but festive afternoon of July 4, 1901. Like his trip to France, the return voyage was a rocking, rolling, heaving affair. Sea travel, Taylor was now certain, simply did not agree with him. For four days, he had eaten almost nothing. During the other two days, whatever went in, came right back out. "I am such a wretched sailor," he would tell a reporter, "that a sea voyage leaves me knocked up." Had it not been for his commitment to Brady, he likely would have gone straight home, curled up in bed, and lay motionless for weeks. Instead, he and Buckner hobbled off the ship, jumped on a tram, and went straight to the Manhattan Beach Track.

Brady had the famous track all decked out for Taylor's reentry into America. Major Taylor banners and balloons hung from the grandstand, a large military band played in the infield, and a pyrotechnic display stood ready for a huge Fourth of July post-race soirée. He had even installed a new track surface. It was typical of the former peanut butcher. "Brady," wrote the *Trenton Times*, "always does things on a big scale ..." Down in the locker room, Brady must have taken one look at Taylor and wondered what the Europeans had been feeding him. Both men knew Taylor was in no condition to race, but outside, an early afternoon crowd was already milling about the grandstand. Brady was hoping Taylor would compete in the evening races, but after a quick huddle they apparently decided he would charm the crowd with a quick exhibition spin around the track. So he raised his sea legs over his bike and rolled around the track where he had gained worldwide fame by beating Jimmy Michaels three years earlier.

Even though the main races were during the evening and Brady had little time for marketing his name, five thousand raucous fans showed up mid-afternoon. They pushed up against the rails, hurling their hats in the air, yelling "Taylor! Taylor!" as he circled the track. The wild cheering continued for nearly ten minutes, all but drowning out one of Brady's bands playing "Way Down in Dixie." Long after Taylor had retreated to the locker room to prepare for home, the crowd remained standing, hollering his name until he reappeared, doffed his cap, and waved his appreciation.

But Brady would have to celebrate the Fourth of July without him. Immediately following his exhibition spin, Taylor charged home and contacted a physician. A Dr. Comey stopped by to look over his gaunt, bleary, dehydrated form. He immediately shot him up with a vaccine before demanding that he rest for at least two weeks. Taylor mentioned his commitment to chairman Batchelder, but his doctor was unmoved: "Rest and rehydrate or face the possibility of a more serious illness," he said. Dr. Comey promptly wrote up a certificate explaining his condition. Buckner sped off to race headquarters in New York and handed the note to Batchelder. He read it, glared at Buckner, pushed his chair away from his desk, and boiled over.

The bright light hovering over Taylor during his four-month European excursion was, for much of the balance of the 1901 racing season, replaced with shades of darkness. The doctor's letter that Buckner had dropped off at race headquarters was met with complete mistrust. Chairman Batchelder, a rummy, intemperate man who one reporter said could not "shake hands without a look of agony on his face," tossed it aside, then told Buckner to tell Taylor that he had to appear at every race "sick or not." Failure to comply, he said, would result in a $100 fine for each and every race that he missed. "Tell him he must ride at once," he frothed in Buckner's ear, "or he will be blacklisted." As they had many times before, Taylor's allies in the press counterattacked. One reporter reminded Batchelder and his readers that when Zimmerman returned from overseas in a similar condition a few years before, no one dared question the returning superstar. Another writer warned of a potential backlash from racegoers. "Public sympathy seems to be with the rider and not the National Cycling Association, which is troubling the colored rider. If the facts of the case have been correctly reported," he continued, "Taylor will certainly have the sympathy of the sporting public."

When Buckner delivered Batchelder's peremptory demands, Taylor became irate. "You can put this down," he wailed to a reporter while rolling over on his pillowed couch. "Batch has got about all the fines he'll ever get from me!" He then decided to strike back with the sporting currency everyone knew he had. Knowing that his mere presence more than doubled attendance, Taylor petrified the nation's track owners by threatening to quit American racing altogether. A group of concerned track owners, probably led by Brady, contacted Batchelder and asked him to tone down his rhetoric a few notches. But by extending his stay in France, Taylor had indeed broken his agreement with the NCA. His contract was ironclad and unambiguous, and therefore a penalty of some sort was in order. But during the summer of 1901, Batchelder seemed to blame him for everything save the stock market meltdown and President McKinley's assassination. "Taylor," he blurted out, "was just being arrogant and pigheaded." A real champion, Batchelder told the *Brooklyn Eagle,* "has got to put up with such things." A heated spat between the king of cycling and cycling's boss continued to play out in the press.

After returning from his exhibition ride, Taylor felt so ill he did not leave his house for more than a week. His doctor checked up on him every day. But the pressure to race nonetheless kept building. In mid-July, he was summoned to appear before Batchelder at the Hotel Hueblein in Hartford to try to bridge their differences. Taylor was introduced to an ecstatic and welcoming crowd at the Hartford Velodrome, no doubt reminding Batchelder of his transcendent hold on sports fans the world over. Taylor sat in the stands alongside his fans and watched the races before their meeting.

The hearing after the scheduled races carried on until one-thirty in the morning. With all the pressure on Batchelder from fans and track owners and Taylor's desire to join the race circuit already in progress, a compromise was agreed on. Reluctantly, Taylor paid a reduced fine of a couple hundred dollars. He then wired Brady, telling him he was prepared to join the circuit in Syracuse, New York.

Trouble awaited him there, and at nearly every other turn.

On the soft summer day of August 1, 1901, Taylor's train rolled west out of Worcester and into Syracuse. A streetcar dropped him off at the Vanderbilt, the same hotel where he had stayed several times before. Having a few letters that he wanted to dispatch, Taylor went straight to a writing table in the hotel lobby and drew up a chair. The minute he sat down, a bellhop began walking toward him. After all the attention he had received in Europe, Taylor probably thought he was just another autograph-seeker. Far from it. The bellhop walked right up and told him to get out of the Vanderbilt Hotel.

"You have the alternative of being kicked out or walking out quietly," he was told. Puzzled and confused, Taylor ignored him and kept on writing. Soon afterward, the hotel clerk walked over and joined the bellhop in excoriating him.

"What are you doing there at that desk? Get out of here," he yelled.

"I guess you don't know who I am," replied Taylor. "I've stopped here several times before and if you will let me explain, perhaps you will be more friendly."

The clerk wasn't interested in his explanation. "Get out of here or you will be kicked out!" he hollered, his voice echoing throughout the lobby.

Still on an emotional high from his triumphant European trip where hoteliers greeted him like royalty, Taylor was shocked and frozen by the demand. The clerk then latched onto his chair and pulled it out from under him. Taylor tumbled to the ground, looking up in horror at the two angry men.

"Now, get the hell out of here," the clerk repeated.

Taylor, a committed pacifist, shook his head in disbelief as he walked out onto the street a dejected man. Eventually he hopped aboard a streetcar and jumped off at the Yates Hotel. There, after looking him up and down, an apathetic clerk then offered up a room at what was clearly an inflated price. What's more, he was told he would have to "take his meals in his room," presumably to spare everyone the indignities of dining with a black man. Reading through the clerk's malevolent intent, he refused the offer and stormed out onto the streets again.

He found a park bench and stooped over, heartsick. "In all my travels over this country and Europe," he told a reporter, "I have never been hurt more personally."

Dusk was falling over Syracuse and Taylor still hadn't found a place to lay his head. Then he recalled a few riders saying they were staying at the St. Cloud Hotel farther away from the track. He jumped in a horse-cab, got out at the steps of the St. Cloud, and walked up to the receptionist. Once again a clerk combed his eyes over Taylor's black face. Just then one of his rivals noticed him and started chatting with him. Seeing this, the clerk finally offered him a room. Before retiring into a dark night of the soul, Taylor told the other riders of his odyssey. In a rare moment of harmony, most of them joined him in his outrage.

But Taylor's rage lingered. He eventually cabled his attorney Sam Packard and told him to prepare a discrimination lawsuit against the Vanderbilt Hotel for $10,000. Given that much of Taylor's time was spent training and racing, this bold act, very rare for blacks at the time, was one of the principal ways he could use his international clout to stand up for his race. The nation took notice. Word of his pending lawsuit was splashed in several major newspapers, certainly causing much discussion among blacks and whites. Win or lose, it sent a strong message that such indecent and illegal acts would no longer be tolerated without a fierce fight.

By the time Taylor was healthy enough to join the race circuit, Frank Kramer, the young Indiana powerhouse Taylor beat out for the championship in 1900, already had a thirty-point lead in the standings. Racing fans began calling for match races between the "Black Whirlwind" and the "White Flyer." Brady tried filling the void, challenging Kramer—or any rider who felt he was up to the test—into a match race with Taylor. As he had done back in 1898, Brady hung out lucrative purses, but no one immediately came forward.

Meanwhile, Taylor jumped headfirst into the circuit races. Sizable crowds continued to congregate wherever his name was on the race card. At the Buffalo Exposition in August, more than thirty thousand fans watched him—despite a thirty-yard handicap—defeat Iver Lawson, an up-and-coming star in the two-mile race. With the grandstand filled to bursting, hundreds stood in the aisles and upper railings. As Taylor's train sped *out* of Buffalo, a train carrying the last breath of President McKinley before his assassination sighed into Buffalo—shot dead by an Iver Johnson handgun— made by the same company that sponsored Taylor. Before long, Taylor—a staunch Republican—and the rest of the nation went into mourning.

Major's reappearance into the all-white American peloton was not a proud chapter in the annals of American sports. Perhaps jealous of his immense overseas success, Taylor's rivals pocketed, elbowed, walled, stymied, and ganged up on him with an intensity not seen since his early days as a professional. At several races, riders agreed in advance how they were going to "trim the nigger" and split the purse in the end. Several riders who openly admitted to receiving money from Kramer said that they liked Taylor, but the money was simply too hard to turn down. "Many times," claimed Taylor, "the toss of a coin would decide which one would bring me down."

Brady and other track promoters, who heavily advertised his appearances, became agitated with their antics. "None of the track owners," wrote one reporter, "were satisfied with the way Kramer had acted and did not believe the riders had given him a fair shake." On two occasions, riders nudged him headfirst into track railings, causing injuries that temporarily removed him from competition, setting him further behind Kramer. When Iver Lawson dumped him on another occasion, Taylor, who was already walking with a "perceptible limp" from previous spills, had to be escorted to his locker by the police. This had all been prophesized by several reporters before he left France. "When he gets back to the United States," wrote the *Daily News*, "there will be many a knife whetted for the Major's scalp this year."

Amid the bitterness, Taylor somehow hung in there, took his licks, and on the rare occasions he was left alone, continued his winning ways. But after coming off the high of Europe to the "whetted knives" of his American rivals, life weighed heavily on him. Increasingly, he was finding that the colors of the world around him were fading to black and white. It was him versus the world. He searched for answers.

This search—and his isolation from his fellow wheelmen—drove him even closer to God. He grew so disgusted with his rivals' race tactics and their continual stream of foul language that he often rented a room far away from his competitors in search of solitude. Before and after every race, Taylor curled up by himself in the corner of the locker room. There, sequestered with his *New Testament* open wide, his lips could be seen moving up and down in silent prayer. For every instance of myopia displayed by his rivals, he searched for light, strength, and guidance in its words. It had become the currency with which he expressed his views of the world. After one race at Madison Square Garden in the presence of an East Coast reporter, some of his rivals chided him for his deep religious beliefs, using their customary invectives. Taylor waved his well-worn Bible at them, imparting words that stood in stark contrast to theirs.

> *Do not let any unwholesome talk come out of your mouths, but only what is helpful for building others up according to their needs, that it may benefit those who listen . . . Get rid of all bitterness, rage and anger, brawling and slander, along with every form of malice. Be kind and compassionate to one another, forgiving each other, just as in Christ forgave you.*

August gave way to September. Taylor posited a gallant fight and was set to tie Kramer in the standings when his toe clip broke as he veered down the homestretch of a handicap race in Hartford. "Just hard luck," wrote the *Daily News*. Because of his illness, injuries, and late start, Taylor competed in only twenty-three of the thirty-seven circuit races that summer. Frank Kramer therefore became the sprint champion of America, winning by a close margin over Taylor, who took second.

But given the adverse circumstances Taylor had competed under, some reporters questioned whether Kramer deserved the crown. This question was echoed by Brady and other track owners. "The track promoters," wrote the *Hartford Times*, "do not believe that the man lives that can defeat Taylor in an honest match race with only one other man on the track beside himself."

Brady's offers for a match race still hung out there. As the season progressed, he continued a full-court press, ratcheting up intense pressure on Kramer to prove his superiority. When he involved the press, it became too much for Kramer to walk away from. Finally, a match race between the 1900 and 1901 American champions was arranged for September 27 at Madison Square Garden. After all he had been through, Taylor really wanted to win this race. "There was ill will between Kramer and myself," he admitted. Kramer concurred. "It is the one ambition of Kramer's life to trim the colored man," wrote the *Trenton Times*. "He has never forgotten the beatings Taylor gave him in the days gone by."

The night of September 27 rolled into New York with pitch blackness. Horses and streetcars dropped off thousands and thousands of fans along Madison Avenue. Inside the Garden, people could feel the tension.

As Taylor eyed Kramer's big ski-slope of a jaw at the starting line, "he had blood in his eyes," recalled Robert Coquelle.

Kramer broke rapidly, immediately taking the lead. After the first of ten laps, Taylor rode up to Kramer's rear wheel, drafting in behind his rigid form. For several laps, he clung to his rear wheel, limpid-like. For a while, the two men drew even. The battle persisted.

Several times before on that steep garden oval with thousands of New Yorkers watching, Taylor's pedals and legs had spun out over the wooden track, pushing his tires deep into the thin pine slats, carrying him forward at more than forty miles per hour. Rarely had he wanted victory more than he did that night. Venting months of frustration, Taylor crouched down over his machine and pounced forward with all the grace and force of a black panther. With every revolution, some 1,800 watts of energy—enough to light a bank of light bulbs—pushed down through his crank, bottom bracket, and wheels, propelling him forward at record speed. Kramer and Taylor, two of the fastest men in the world, leaned together into the infamous "Dead Man's Curve," where another rider was killed just days before, hummed through the straightaways and tore past the howling throng.

Brady was a nervous wreck. In his red satin booth along the track, he could holler at Taylor to take the lead. With one lap to go, as though he could hear his command, Taylor, flashing back to all the cruel treatment he'd received throughout the year, bore down as never before. Kramer, realizing his reputation as sprint champion was more or less at stake, looked to his side and watched in horror as Taylor ripped alongside him, then past him: a wheel, two wheels, a full-length. Watching Kramer's form disintegrate from under his arm, Taylor knew he had broken him. "Whenever his knees began to wobble," Taylor remembered, "I knew he was in trouble."

Down the homestretch, America's new champion stretched out in supreme effort. But there was nothing he could do other than watch Taylor's lead continue to widen: a length and a half, two lengths.

Taylor sat up and rode over the tape riding proud and hard.

New York racegoers, always diehard Taylor fans, shook the rafters in voracious applause. "The spectators were obliged to admit," Coquelle added, "that the real champion was not the one to hold the title."

Brady scanned the screaming fans. All the harsh treatment directed at Taylor, he and other track owners reasoned, was sure to drive him overseas and away from the American tracks possibly for good. With the world's best drawing card spending much of his time thousands of miles away, Brady knew his days of seeing Taylor race were coming to a close.

Taylor would miss the man who had done so much for him and his favorite sport. "My good friend," Taylor wrote years later, "William Brady, the present theatrical producer in New York, stood ready to make good his offers . . ." Late that September night, one of Taylor's staunchest supporters said his good-byes and slipped out of the old Garden.

One man's loss was another man's gain. A few months later, in December 1901, the French tandem of Breyer and Coquelle knocked on Taylor's door again. Given the praise heaped on Taylor the year before, their visit was inevitable. European sports fans, Breyer told a New York reporter, "demanded the presence of Major Taylor and, as a result, I made this trip to America to get his signature to a contract for another tour of Europe." Following such a regrettable American season, little arm-twisting was needed this time. On the spot, Taylor signed a contract guaranteeing him $5,000 plus purses. There was no need for them to even discuss Sunday racing: Taylor made sure the contract excluded Sundays.

Taylor did have one more demand. Hoping to steer clear of the miserable weather of the previous spring, he insisted on a shorter two-month stint, starting in mid-May instead of in the cold of April. They agreed. Breyer was downright giddy. "I consider Major Taylor the greatest racer and drawing card of them all. I am delighted to sign him up again and I will set sail for Europe one of the happiest men in the world."

There was one pressing matter that needed Taylor's attention before embarking on that second journey across the pond. On a windswept day in mid-March, he and Daisy were positively elated as they hopped aboard a northbound train. Hand in hand, they jumped off in the charming, clock-making town of Ansonia, Connecticut, where they were wed at a private ceremony at Reverend Taylor's home on Grove Street. By that time, Major had made a bundle of money and, considering Daisy's fine taste in clothes, he undoubtedly put some of it to good use, bedecking her in the finest Victorian wedding gown. In the quiet of Ansonia, far from the usual crush of reporters, Daisy and Major Taylor shared their special day with their friends, relatives, and pastor.

Major's nomadic occupation allowed for little time to celebrate. At New York's Grand Central Station a few days later, he said his good-byes to his new bride and several hundred fans, including W. E. B. Du Bois, the famous black leader, before shoving off on the fabulous *Kaiser Wilhelm der Grosse*. For two months, May and June 1902, Taylor rumbled across the European continent. As he had the previous season, he dominated his European rivals, often before sold-out crowds, while adding to his growing wealth in city after city.

Fred Johnson, the bike manufacturer Taylor still had a contract with and one of the greatest beneficiaries of his success, had stopped by Paris to promote the bicycle ridden by "the world's fastest man." Johnson's agents in Europe and America were told to query customers about why they chose his models. Their overwhelming response: "We want the kind Major Taylor rides." For ongoing bragging rights, Johnson also made certain his agents received cablegrams within one hour of every Taylor win.

Three thousand miles to the west at one of his shops in Fitchburg, Massachusetts, three thousand customers had backed up onto the streets to see the latest models, despite dreadful weather. He had spared no expense, decking out the shop with popular Taylor posters, American flags, colorful flowers, and even an orchestra to keep the throng entertained. Despite a general downturn in bicycle sales, his models with Major Taylor emblems on the head-tube continued selling well, even as far away as Japan. Previously skeptical of using professional racers to promote his bikes, Johnson had become a Taylor convert. "I am absolutely convinced," he had told *Cycle Age*, "that his riding of our wheel was a most profitable advertising investment."

Taylor's remarkable physical condition and the vastly improved weather made for a lethal combination. In every man-to-man match race in which he competed, he came up victorious. It was almost as if he was toying with his rivals. It wasn't on purpose; some victories just came easily to him. Since the World Championships, held in Rome that year, took place on a Sunday, Taylor refused to compete. But just in case anybody had doubts, two separate match races were scheduled against Thor Ellegaard, the new winner. A few days later, exulted *Le Auto-Velo*, "Taylor literally annihilated" the freshly crowned world champion. Watching soberly from the sidelines, Jacquelin refused a match-race challenge from Taylor, saying he couldn't possibly get in good enough condition to defeat him.

When the *Kaiser Wilhelm* steamed west for New York that June, he was still the most acclaimed athlete in the world. His name was indelibly stamped in the minds of sports fans all across the continent. "He was looked upon as an idol," beamed Breyer, "and when he took departure for his native shores, it was with universal regret." The popularity of bike racing reached new heights in France and much of Europe because of his visits. "The pastime," proclaimed Breyer, "took on a new lease on life." And since Henri Desgrange first discussed the Tour de France at that same time, Taylor's revival of the sport in France may have helped sow the seeds of the grand tour in his mind. At the very least, Desgrange, track director at Parc des Princes, had considerably more money with which to launch the immensely popular race. Before Taylor embarked, Desgrange offered him a large sum—potentially as high as $20,000—to race at another track he managed in Buenos Aires, Argentina. Taylor turned him down.

Months later, the first Tour de France was unveiled. The total purse: 20,000 francs.

D aisy greeted Taylor at a pier in New York on a June day in 1902. Being athletic and a lover of sports, she was elated to see her new superstar husband, and looked forward to accompanying him to the American races that summer. She may not have known exactly what she was getting herself into. The remaining season would again be racially charged and tumultuous. This time, Taylor saw it coming in advance. Wanting to avoid the same pressures as the previous season, he hesitated to sign a contract with the NCA. Batchelder had tried every inducement he could think of to sign him before he whirled off to Europe, including sending a representative to Grand Central Station with a pen and contract in hand. Taylor, in effect, freelanced that summer, accepting whatever offers he wished from individual track owners.

There was little chance of winning the 1902 Sprint Championships because Frank Kramer already had a thirty-point lead in the standings when Taylor joined the circuit. In addition, Batchelder had changed the rules to allow four men in the finals instead of two, a rule some believed was directed specifically at him, referring to it as the "Taylor rule.'"

The bitterness displayed by his American rivals may have reached a climax that summer. Taylor's tires mysteriously went flat right before or during races and his rivals knocked him around often. But when given half a chance, he kept winning a high percentage of his races. The press continued to bark dissent. Following a series of races in Baltimore, New Jersey, New York, and Boston, where he was repeatedly pocketed, elbowed, and knocked around the tracks, a letter sent to the editor of *The Sun* openly expressed one reader's disgust. "Is there no way to prevent such detestable tricks as are repeatedly put up by some riders who would secretly rejoice if they could upset Taylor and cripple him for life?" Such riding, the letter continued, "is unworthy of decent, self-respecting and sport-loving people, and makes a white man blush with shame to know that a colored man is today . . . the banner man for clean sport and gentlemanly conduct."

Despite the callous treatment, or perhaps because of it, crowds continued to adore him. When he popped up at a race in Ottawa, he was embraced by a delegation of Canadian officials, reporters, and sporting celebrities as soon as he stepped off his train. Having lost his bike in transit, he rewarded their flattery by winning handily on an ill-fitted, borrowed bicycle. When Taylor was overseas, attendance had dropped in North America. "However," proclaimed the *Colored American Magazine*, "as soon as it was announced that Major Taylor would ride, standing room was almost at a premium."

Taylor's plight received a lot of press that summer. The tone of the reporters had to open the eyes of commissioners in other sports. "Whether the skin color should be white or black, he is entitled to what he is worth," wrote one journalist, "and to defeat him the winner should be able to prove himself the better man, which should hold true in cycling, prize-fighting, wrestling, baseball, or any other sport."

On a summer day, Major and Daisy rolled into Revere Beach Track in Boston. Daisy sat alone in a front row seat, watching as Taylor rode away from the trio of Kramer, Lawson, and MacFarland, winning the half-mile race by more than two lengths. "With anything like a fair show," claimed one observer, "or an equal chance and the honest observation of the rules of bike racing, Major Taylor would be Champion of America again." Afterward, Floyd MacFarland, one of Taylor's chief rivals that summer, rolled up alongside him, waving his fist and barking out a string of obscenities intertwined with a fountain of racial slurs followed by outright physical threats. Taylor quickly retreated to his locker room, grabbing a two-by-four on his way just in case. MacFarland's rage moved over to the judges' stand where he complained that Taylor had fouled him. As Taylor was nowhere near him, the judges told him to watch his tongue and then shooed him away. MacFarland gathered the peloton together, huddling with them in the middle of the track.

In her seat along the finish line, Daisy bent her ear toward the group, then looked on in horror as the three-horses-of-the-apocalypse stormed toward the locker room where Taylor waited. A pang of panic rippled through the grandstand. Sensing trouble, Taylor peered out from the locker room door and saw them sprinting toward him. Outnumbered and physically threatened, Taylor latched tightly onto the two-by-four, reared back, and unleashed a vicious swing at them as they invaded his locker room.

He missed.

There was a brief moment of disbelief. The gang lunged after him, but Taylor, who ran as fast as he rode, dropped the lumber to the ground, scampered out of the room at lightning speed, and dove into an adjacent locker room where his trainer stood. They barricaded themselves inside and waited for the police to arrive. Outside the door, there was kicking and pounding and renewed threats of violence. Out on the track, Daisy shivered alone in her seat. Just then the police, who were never far from sporting events at the time, arrived to pacify them with a few persuasive whacks of their billy clubs. Taylor, who had all his weight pressed up against the door, slid to the ground and exhaled.

Racism was the main cause of Taylor's troubles, but a track writer for the *New York Daily News* picked up on another major source of strife among his rivals. "When it is considered that he divides his winnings with no man, nor teams up with anyone, as the others do, the reason for his unpopularity by circuit riders is quickly detected."

No blood was shed that afternoon. But that incident, combined with others throughout the year, shook Taylor, sapped his spirit, and caused him to question his future as a professional cyclist in America. Taylor's gentle disposition and pacifist nature didn't allow him to act violently without feelings of guilt. "That was the first time in my racing career," he remembered with a twinge of remorse, "that I ever lost my head to the extent of planning to fight for my rights at all cost."

At the foggy launch of daybreak one late summer Friday, Taylor and Daisy trained out of Worcester on the way to a race in Newark, New Jersey. Assuming there would be food on the train, they left home without eating breakfast, only to learn that there was no dining car on board. Their train paused in Springfield momentarily, but they had only enough time to grab a cup of coffee. When they finally arrived in Newark shortly after noon, they were famished. They hopped off the train and scampered to a restaurant on Broad Street, close to the depot. According to the *Boston Daily Globe,* they waited at their table for half an hour while waiters "developed nearsightedness," serving everyone else but walking by them as though they didn't exist. Taylor kept trying to alert them but they remained "deaf to his summons."

Tired of waiting, they left, each with a "forgiving smile," jumping on a trolley car to another restaurant on Market Street. This time, a waiter asked them to get out immediately or face being thrown out. Taylor stood there, speechless.

As time passed, their hunger grew and their frustration deepened. Again, they hopped a streetcar and whirled off to a different section of town. At a third restaurant they were again rudely turned away, this time by the manager. Taylor was beside himself with rage. His eyebrows squinted down over his eyes, his face reddened, and his teeth ground together. When Daisy was by his side he had a lower tolerance for putting up with racism. He dropped his head in sorrow, his features disappearing under the shade of his black top hat.

Disgusted, hungry, and enraged, he latched on to Daisy's hand, sprinted off to the rail station and bought two tickets for the next train out of Jersey.

Back at the track, people began asking the question, Where's Major Taylor?

Somewhere along the line, Fred Voight, manager of the Vailsburg Track, received word of their sordid odyssey. He hustled to the rail station in hopes of staving off their early departure. He found them there fuming. A long, animated conversation took place with Voight pleading with them to stay while expressing sympathy for their plight. At first, Taylor would have none of it. Voight then explained to him that the grandstand was already swelling with fans waiting to see him compete against a large field, including local hero Frank Kramer. He continued pleading his case, telling Taylor of the extensive marketing he had already done, including lithographic displays in windows throughout the city. With race time just hours away, Taylor reluctantly agreed to join the peloton, empty stomach and all.

But the damage had already been done.

When he appeared on the Vailsburg Track, which was becoming the epicenter of American racing, announcer Fred Burns barked out his name through the megaphone. The crowd roared its approval. As he cinched in at the line, Taylor didn't even hear it. All he could think about were the indignities his new bride had just experienced. Daisy squeezed into a seat that Voight had set aside for her. Sitting with her fingers crossed, she could not have known that this would be one of his last circuit races on American soil. The pistol cracked and Kramer tore across the track at a relentless pace. Taylor plodded forward reservedly, quickly drifting out of reach. He looked forward and saw Kramer cannonballing down the homestretch in the presence of his hometown crowd. For the first time in recent memory, he limped across the line out of reach. Daisy slumped in her seat. The crowd stampeded past her, vaulted down onto the track, tossed their soon-to-be 1902 American sprint champion on their shoulders, placed a wreath of flowers around him, and whooped. Their shouts could be heard for blocks around, drowning out sounds from passing vehicles and trolley cars. In the firehouse opposite the track, bells clanged, whistles blew, and firemen leaped for joy. In a rare display of exuberance, the normally calm Kramer lobbed flowers back at the crowd, smiling and blushing like a schoolboy.

For a brief moment, Taylor watched the revelers. Then he gathered his belongings, gently cinched the tips of his fingers into Daisy's hand, and walked out of the velodrome in silence.

After six turbulent years of professional racing on American soil, getting bounced around by the "whetted knives" of one competitor after another, dealing with threats of violence, refused meals and hotel rooms in town after town, Taylor had reached the end of his rope. "I was satisfied," he wrote with an edge to his words, "I could never regain my American Championship title . . . with the entire field of riders combined against me." With a tone of finality, an *Atlanta Constitution* reporter made a prediction that would largely hold true for nearly a century. "His will be the last black face probably ever seen in the professional cycling ranks in America."

He was only halfway through his racing career, but for Taylor, the long national nightmare was over. After boarding a train for home, he and Daisy sat down in the dining car and devoured their first real meal of the day. Neither of them could think of anything to say. The whistle sounded and the train ground forward, wending its way out of New Jersey, through Connecticut, and into Massachusetts. Daisy and Major gazed out the window, hearing the plaintive sound of wind and rain buffeting the train as it clattered under the cover of darkness. Both of them felt empty.

Chapter 19

ROYAL HONEYMOON

In the fall of 1902, the pall hanging over 4 Hobson Avenue was interrupted by an intriguing overseas cablegram. Taylor read it curiously. Standing at a telegraph office on the other side of the world was a thickset man, built low, with short black hair, laughing blue eyes, a tanned face, and a close-clipped Ronald Colman moustache. The twenty-six-year-old Australian awaiting Taylor's response was Hugh D. McIntosh, soon to be known among sports fans as "Huge Deal" McIntosh.

An acquaintance of Brady's, the flamboyant, fast-talking McIntosh had his nose in everything. In the early decades of the twentieth century, he owned the Tivoli theaters, oversaw many notable plays, and managed prizefights, including the racially charged fight between Jack Johnson and Tommy Burns. "Never before and never since, anywhere in the world," wrote one sportswriter, "had one man poked his prodigy fingers into so many pies."

Possessing a volcanic personality, McIntosh also held the defects of his qualities. He swore like a longshoreman, kept no opinion in moderation, and had a habit of underscoring his adjectives in conversation. He also had a mind so full of wild visionary thoughts no one knew what to expect next. He was, said one observer "a distinctive blend of charlatan, genius, dreamer, and bandit." Before the big money and the Bellevue Hill mansion that followed, McIntosh grew up in Broken Hill, a barren, fly-infested region when

Australia was young and imagination and hard work got you further than education and class. He ran away from home when he was nine, lived in an iron-roof shack, picked ore in the stifling heat, ate food covered with red dust, and considered a shower with clean water a luxury. "It was the nearest approach to hell on earth I've ever known," he remembered.

McIntosh moved about the colony working as a penniless farm laborer, boxer, tarboy, stagehand, chorus boy, and waiter. He got his first real break when he sold pies at Melbourne racetracks, eventually married the baker's widow, turned the bakery into a catering chain, then completed the circle by taking control of some of the same tracks where he once sold pies.

Like Brady, McIntosh had fallen madly in love with the fast-paced sport of bike racing. In 1900 and 1901, he dabbled with competitive bike racing but quickly learned he was a better boxer, manager, and entrepreneur. "I began as a rider," he later admitted, "but if there ever was a case of misapplied strength, it was me on a bicycle." Instead, he became assistant secretary of the League of Wheelmen of New South Wales in 1902, then president of the Australian Cycling Council, giving him tsar-like control of bike racing throughout Australasia.

Acting as a partner representing a syndicate of Australian track owners and businessmen called the Summer Nights Amusement, McIntosh cabled offers to Taylor. The attractive proposals tugged at him. He surely recalled Zimmerman's stories of his glory days racing on Australian tracks in front of crowds so large they perched atop overflowing grandstands to see him. And the time Zimmie was invited to demonstrate bike riding in the ballroom of the Victorian Palace by the Australian Premier. This, combined with the realization that his days of getting a fair shake on American tracks had all but faded, made him receptive to the idea. Australia, like Europe, was a hotbed for bike racing. With the backing of enterprising men like McIntosh, it also boasted the largest purses in the world.

Numbers were bandied back and forth. Taylor, by now a shrewd negotiator, surely mentioned something about how far away and expensive Australia was. Weeks passed and still no agreement was reached. Knowing the leverage he had, Taylor was simply playing hardball. But he was dealing with a man who was an absolute bulldog in form and personality. "McIntosh was not adverse to a good stoush," proclaimed the *Melbourne Punch,* "and positively bristled with energy and nervous force." McIntosh kept upping the ante, but Taylor kept hesitating.

But when McIntosh offered a guarantee of £1,500 (somewhere between $5,000 and $7,500) plus a share of gate receipts, plus purses—some as high as $5,000—and no Sunday racing, Taylor's eyes opened wider. On October 1, 1902, wanting to avoid burnout, Taylor cabled McIntosh: £1500 Okay, Number of Races too Many. Wasting little time, McIntosh agreed to lessen the number of required races to no more than three per week. Taylor finally cabled back his approval. McIntosh wired a $2,500 down payment. *The Referee*—a newspaper McIntosh would one day own—spread the news to what they thought would be an ecstatic public: Major Taylor Is Coming! All Doubts as to the Coming of Major Taylor, the Wonderful Black Rider, Are Now at Rest!

With his signature, Taylor entered an intriguing new chapter in his life and his career, one that would be given more space in his memoirs than any others. It would also further include his wife. Since they had not yet shared a real honeymoon together, Taylor broke the news to Daisy in the form of a honeymoon proposal. Wanting to see the world and her superstar husband compete in what she believed would be a friendly environment, Daisy immediately set about stuffing suitcase after suitcase with new clothing for the long journey that lay ahead.

In late November 1902 amid a puff of light snow, a porter hoisted seventeen suitcases into a Southern Pacific baggage car, then watched the train push out of Worcester's Union Station. Major and Daisy spent the first five days of their honeymoon rocking in the middle of a transcontinental train as it twisted west through the plains, over the Rockies white with snow, before steaming into Oakland's long wharf. They ferried over to San Francisco. When Major called for his steamship tickets at the Ferry Building, the agent paused, looked him over, then glanced at Daisy who was standing behind him. "I'm assuming the two of you are aware of the rigid color line in Australia," the agent stated. There was a long pause. After becoming a Federation in 1901, Australia did indeed have a "White Australia policy" that specifically "excluded coloured races." Taylor was caught completely unaware. "I somehow figured that race prejudice only flourished in this country," he lamented.

The honeymoon glow on Daisy's face quickly disappeared. "My first thought upon getting this information," Major remembered, "was to cancel my Australia tour . . ." The agent pressed the issue. "Do you want the tickets or not?" Major craned around and saw a look of confusion on Daisy's face.

But having signed a contract, he had no choice. With much trepidation, he bought tickets for the next day's trip.

Hungry, the newlyweds flagged down a horse-taxi and asked to be taken to the nearest eatery. But in 1902 San Francisco, racism was not only prevalent, it was city policy. Like in Newark, they were turned away at restaurant after restaurant. Because their steamship wasn't scheduled to leave until the crack of dawn, they asked to be dropped off at the nearest hotel. Once again they moved up and down Market Street, this time getting turned away at hotel after hotel. As dusk fell over San Francisco, the Taylors, standing with heaps of luggage, still hadn't secured lodging. Hungry and humiliated, Daisy and Major apparently spent the night together under the stars.

The next morning they boarded the *RMS Ventura* at Pier 7. No sooner had the steamship pushed off from the dock before a crewman draped in a white pressed uniform and a sailor's cap walked toward them.

"Are you Major Taylor?" the man barked.

"Yes, I am," answered Taylor hesitantly.

The man smiled, offered his hand, then started chattering with a thick East Coast accent. It turns out the ship's purser was from Westborough, Massachusetts, a small town in Worcester County only miles from the Taylors' home. It was a happy encounter. For the next few weeks, Major and Daisy bantered with the purser, listening in amazement as he spoke of Taylor's seven world records, his World Championship victory in Montreal, defeat of Jacquelin in France, and a few races even Taylor had to stretch his mind to remember. The camaraderie helped the days slip by. They paused in Honolulu before steaming by an endless string of tiny islands. Somewhere along the vast South Pacific, winter turned into summer. Each day, the purser pulled aside passengers, proudly introducing them to the world champion and his newlywed. Surrounded by a tropical sun and pellucid waters, endless racing stories were spun. At one point, a Catholic priest, wondering what all the commotion was about, joined the conversation.

"What church or denomination do you belong to?" asked the clergyman.

"Well, sir," Taylor replied, "I guess I'm a Baptist."

"Oh, well," remarked the priest, "I think you've got a chance."

"Yes, sir," Taylor said proudly, "I think I have got a chance and a very good chance, too."

Seven thousand miles slipped by. But as the ship inched closer to Sydney, the uplifting conversation switched to the ugly subject of the color line in

Australia. The purser confirmed that what they heard from their agent was true. But, he added, he wasn't sure if the racism was directed at blacks or the influx of Asians who were desperately trying to emigrate to the United States and Australia.

Daisy remained apprehensive. Major tried reassuring her, suggesting that a shrewd promoter like McIntosh wouldn't have coughed up a fortune if he believed they would be rejected. Unsure of his own words, Major's voice fluttered like the waves beating against the bottom of the ship. Daisy nodded her head unconvincingly. A spasm of fear spread through them. "It certainly was a distressing outlook," he would later write.

O n the afternoon of December 22, 1902, under blue skies, the captain of the *RMS Ventura* steered the six-thousand-ton ship into Sydney Harbor. Daisy tilted her white Victorian hat lined with silk flowers and purple ribbons upward, then pressed a pair of double-barreled opera glasses against her eyes. In the distance, she could see the faint silhouette of another vessel pointed in their direction. As they inched forward, one ship became two, three, then four—all headed right for them. She lowered her glasses, wiped the lenses clean, and peered out again. This time she saw flags waving, followed by a whistling noise. Major slid open a bronze sailor's telescope and looked out. He wasn't sure exactly what he was seeing. Perched behind the ships Daisy had spotted sat dozens more with signs hanging over their rails. More tooting sounds were heard, each growing louder as the *Ventura* cruised deeper into the harbor.

Puzzled, the purser peered through a maritime telescope.

For the next few miles, starting at the entrance to *Jackson Head,* leading all the way up to the Sydney pier, awaited one of the most sensational displays of athletic adoration ever seen. Everybody on board the steamer stood in amazement, running their eyes back and forth along both sides of the harbor. Facing them were hundreds of boats of all makes and models, both steam and naptha launches, filled with men and women yelling "Taylor! Taylor!" from behind long megaphones. Steaming through the harbor, which Taylor called "the most beautiful in the world," Australians leaned over the sides of their vessels waving American flags, blowing their whistles, and screaming themselves hoarse. "Welcome Major Taylor, welcome!" There, probably in his yacht *Mabel*—which would later famously capsize due to too much champagne on board—was McIntosh, leading the celebration.

Pointing over the railing, the purser, having never seen anything like it before, yelled to the honeymooners. "Look, look," he said, his throat choking with excitement. "Do you see all those American flags, do you hear those whistles and horns?" Major looked over the side of the liner, tears streaming from his eyes. The purser glanced at them and smiled. "Now do you think you will be allowed to land in Australia?" he asked.

At the pier, an army of newsmen, track owners, and racing officials joined thousands of fans cheering wildly as they went ashore. Daisy's anxiety over the possible drawing of the color line was quickly replaced with tears of joy as she walked down the plank.

The animated procession trotted off to the Metripole Hotel where thousands more massed, including city officials, prominent Australian cricket players, jockeys, and footballers. McIntosh had the hotel's best luxury suite reserved for them. That evening, McIntosh, who entertained with legendary munificence, held an elaborate outdoor banquet, giving Daisy, who carried herself with remarkable social ease, an opportunity to wear her spectacular new garb. The Lord Mayor of Sydney gave a rousing speech to their good health, telling the crowd that Taylor had "defeated everyone in America and Europe," and asked him lightheartedly if he would kindly go easy on the Australians.

The next day, the newlyweds strolled about Sydney, taking in a harbor excursion and a shopping spree while shaking off their sea legs. Everywhere they went, they elicited stares. "Hey mate, look it's the Maja, there's Maja Tayla." When they returned to the hotel each night, they were deluged with offers from civic leaders, executives, and sports figures to attend social functions. But because of his commitment to the syndicate, and the fact that he had not been on his bike for some time, Taylor had little time for socializing.

After a few days of sightseeing, Taylor rushed off to the Sydney Cricket Grounds and Racetrack for some serious training. He was greeted there by Sid Melville, his syndicate-appointed registered trainer, one of the finest in the business. Melville bore a startling likeness to the man in the American Gothic painting, minus the pitchfork. He was a thin-as-a-rake, spindle-legged, craggy-faced veteran racetracker who had a habit of not smiling. When he did force out a smile, it usually synchronized with that split second when one of his riders crossed the finish line first. Mindful of his substantial investment, McIntosh ordered Melville to watch over Taylor with eagle eyes. He took his job seriously. When an amateur walked into Taylor's locker room puffing joyously on a cigarette, all one-hundred-something pounds of

Melville chased him out. "No one, it seems," wrote a sportswriter known as Wheeler, "may smoke in the presence of a cycling chieftain."

The Sydney track where Taylor was scheduled to compete over a handful of dates was the most modern racetrack in the world. Much of the concrete track, which was three laps to the mile, was surrounded by grandstands that included a separate ladies' pavilion, members-only section, smokers' pavilion, bar and restaurant, and a shilling pavilion, otherwise known as cheap seats. Then there was "The Hill," a steep enbankment where rowdy hellions could imbibe at will, and fight without cause. It was a 35,000-seat racing seat Xanadu, that when combined with the large Australian purses, attracted riders from all over the world.

Every day, thousands of fanatically devoted Aussies paid just to watch Taylor go through his twice-daily workouts, dissecting his every muscle twitch. A gathering of amateur wheelmen gaped at him. Taylor's main professional rivals—Australians Joe Megson, Arthur Gudgeon, Bob MacDonald, and Don Walker, champion of Australia—watched his workouts with a degree of awe. They had never seen anyone train with such intensity. Nor had they seen such a gathering of spectators and reporters flooding the track for training sessions.

Slowly, Taylor's form, stunted from the long trip over, started to take hold. The public and the press watched every incremental step feverishly. "The sole topic of conversation yesterday," wrote one Australian reporter, "was the visit of the World Champion Major Taylor . . . tremendous interest is being taken in his performances." Their fascination with Taylor all but squeezed the hugely popular sports of cricket, football, and horse racing out of their usual position of prominence in the Australian newspapers. Nearly every day, papers provided extensive coverage, sometimes multiple pages, with several photos of Major and a few of Daisy.

Australia's religious papers, which had historically shied away from writing about athletes or encouraging sports, made an exception for Taylor. The *New South Wales Baptist*, which had taken heat for giving a few inches to the results of innocent cricket matches, devoted five entire columns in large type to a special interview of Taylor titled THIRTY THOUSAND DOLLARS FOR CONSCIENCE SAKE. The writer, clearly impressed with Taylor's life story, wrote about all the money Taylor had given up because of his refusal to race on the Sabbath day and his transcendent value to his sport. "For years this man of deep and strong convictions has been preaching to the sporting world a silent but eloquent sermon of example."

"I have always tried to live as a Christian," Taylor explained in the long interview. "I attribute most of my success entirely to the fact that I have tried to do what was right—live truly and squarely by every man—and any man who follows those principles is bound to succeed."

Not everyone was happy, however, with this unprecedented degree of attention being directed toward one man. After being denied access to the grounds for several important matches, the cricket association sued the tracks trustees. With revenues from the bike races vastly exceeding what they would have made from cricket matches, the trustees argued that they were merely doing what was in the best interest of the track. A heated, well-publicized trial would play out in the high courts of Australia for half a year after Taylor's arrival.

The Sydney portion of Taylor's Australian racing circuit, officially dubbed "The Major Taylor Carnival," began on January 3, 1903, only eleven days after his arrival. He didn't waste time before making an impression. In his first race, the Half-mile International Championship, he defeated Australian champion Don Walker with a sensational burst that had the crowd standing in the aisles. Trainer Melville shifted his kangaroo-leather cowboy hat at the finish line where someone swears seeing the outline of a smile forming on his face. The report could not be verified.

Despite losing the Walker-Plate Five-Mile Scratch Race to Don Walker that same night, it was obvious Taylor's form was already coming around; he knifed through the last quarter-mile in twenty-six seconds, an Australian record for the last quarter of a five-mile race.

The carnival continued. While no one event in Sydney stood out from a pure racing perspective, the Aussies couldn't get enough of the spectacular evening events. Having recently installed colored incandescent lighting over the track, McIntosh thrilled the crowds at race time. He switched off all other lights, silhouetting the grandstand in multicolored fire, leaving only the track illuminated in a green tint by clusters of electric arc lamps hanging high on track poles.

Being a new concept to the Aussies—and with the mysterious black man from America lighting up the track—these events were described as having a surreal, almost ethereal quality to them. Sketching a meticulous drawing of elegantly dressed women in their pinks, greens, and purples, and the riders ripping across the track, one unidentified artist captured the dramatic evening scenes as well as any of the era. The scene, wrote the *Town & Country*, "was almost like fairyland."

Reporters described the crowds as being nearly hysterical. At one race, nearly thirty thousand fans showed up in the rain. "Never before," wrote one reporter, "has enthusiasm been so prolonged." Before the Major Taylor Carnival shoved off to Melbourne, the large seating capacity of the Sydney Track would be needed. During a handful of race dates, more than one hundred thousand fans showed up to watch him race, a number equal to nearly one-quarter of Sydney's population. The excitement Taylor had ignited in sports fans spilled into other races. At twelve meetings in and around Sydney, a quarter of a million fans taxed local transit, ate McIntosh's track food, guzzled his refreshments, and cheered long into the night. Nearly every night, the separate ladies' pavilion, normally closed, was packed on both the upper and lower decks with "representatives of the world of fashion." Many of them were no doubt clamoring to be seen next to Daisy, whom one Australian reporter described as "one of the most fascinating of a fascinating sex."

McIntosh prowled the stands keeping his eye on Taylor, the continual stream of fans pouring through the turnstiles, and all the women who, because of his targeted marketing methods copied from Brady, often made up around half the audience at bike races in Australia. A consummate womanizer, McIntosh was in his element. "Put away the brooms boys," joked one of his caterers. "Here comes Mac; he'd go after anything with hair on it." But with his Clark Gable good looks and charisma, women had a tendency to flock to him. "Sometimes so many women surrounded him," wrote Wheeler, "that H. D. himself could not be seen."

Women aside, what McIntosh saw could not have pleased him more. Even though Taylor had three stops left (two in different cities), concession revenue alone—which he controlled through his catering company— was already more than the high cost of bringing him across the Pacific. "He would have been cheap at double the price," joked one reporter.

For the honeymooners, everything was clicking. In contrast to the cold Massachusetts winter and the bitterness of Major's American rivals, they were finding the temperate Australian summer and the warmth of the

Australian people enchanting. Gaining many new friends because of her "pleasant and attractive manners," Daisy, known as a "brilliant conversationalist," was having the time of her life. Major was winning races, making good money, and being universally praised by newsmen and fans alike. After enduring so much anguish back home the previous season, they were feeling good about life again. "I cannot emphasize too strongly," Major expressed, "the pressure off my mind upon learning that I would have no worry from the color line."

Their train chattered six hundred miles southwest toward the sports-crazed city of Melbourne. The honeymooners looked out and saw the emerald glow of the Tasman Sea on one side, and koalas, wallabies, and kangaroos bounding about the countryside on the other. The *Sydney to Melbourne Express* whistled to a stop on January 23, 1903. When the railcar doors slid open, Daisy, Major, and Australian champion Don Walker wiped the cobwebs from their eyes before stepping into the Spencer Street Train Station. They looked around and couldn't believe what they were seeing. Despite little publicity, people stood in the thousands waving American flags while shouting "Tayla, Tayla, welcome Maja." "The Star-Spangled Banner" blared in the background.

Daisy and Major shimmied their way through the throng before melting into an elegant "reserved" honeymoon-like carriage. Along the route to the Grand Hotel, fans lined the road in thick formations, tossing wads of confetti at the carriage as the couple rolled by. Flatteringly called a "dusky belle" by Aussies, Daisy must have been overwhelmed by the scene unfolding before her eyes. From the rich burgundy interior of their Victorian carriage, she could look forward, past the coachmen dressed in black frock coats and top hats, and see two regally beautiful white Percheron horses, plus rising balloons, flying confetti, and thousands of adoring Australians. In her wildest dreams, she could not have possibly fathomed a grander way to celebrate her honeymoon.

The chairman and secretary of the League of Victorian Wheelmen, assigned to greet them at the rail station, found themselves choked off by the growing multitude. The crowds were so thick, their coachmen had difficulty steering their horses in and out of the "surging crowd" that awaited the Taylors at their hotel. That evening, nearly everyone of note in Melbourne showed up at the Port Philip Hotel for a "monster welcome reception" held in their honor. McIntosh, who considered it his primary calling in life to keep everyone happy and in drink, strutted around making sure champagne glasses were topped off at all times. "McIntosh," someone joked, "gave away enough champagne to christen every battleship in Europe."

Melbourne's Lord Mayor Jeffries made a toast to Taylor's worldwide fame and his reputation as a true gentlemen and first-class sportsman. Following a thunderous applause, Taylor took to the podium and told the audience how overwhelmed he was with the hospitality and kindness of everyone in Australia. He added that while he knew everyone had heard of his exploits on the tracks throughout the world, "no one present," he felt sure, "had heard anything of his ability as a speaker." His persiflage brought laughter all around. Daisy looked up at him, smiling demurely while batting her eyelashes.

Rundown from all the traveling, riding in the rain, responding to press attention, and overall excitement of his honeymoon, Major took ill with a nasty flu and fever. At one point his temperature exceeded 104 degrees. For the better part of two weeks, he hunkered down in his Melbourne hotel room to recover. While he may have been relegated to his room, his inactivity didn't dampen his celebrity. He was the talk of the town. Throughout the day and night, Australian newsmen hovered in the lobby of the Grand Hotel in curious bunches, clamoring to be the first to scavenge any tidbit of news about his condition from Daisy or his doctor. When there was nothing new to report they simply elaborated on the previous day's story, which was, in essence, an elaboration of the day before.

Taylor's fame was so widespread even theatrical promoters tried piggybacking on the public's fascination toward him. "What Major Taylor is as a record-breaker in the cycling world," trumpeted Old Dreary, a theatrical promoter, "so 'Zaza' promises to prove in the theatrical sphere." Cigarette manufacturers, of all people, also tried leveraging his wide-reaching fame. Has Major Taylor heard, asked the makers of Home Cigarettes before fibbing to their readers, "our cigarettes do not injure one in training?"

By mid-February, Taylor had recovered. In front of crowds at the St. Kilda Cricket Grounds, similar in size to those in Sydney, he put on a clinic, winning the International Scratch Race and the Grand Match Race, among others. "It's no use," remarked Joe Morgan, one of his Australian rivals. "He's just too good."

Between the Melbournian public and the press, there was no end to the superlatives heaped on him or the descriptive nature of his physique. "Major Taylor is a very cleanly built, neatly packed parcel of humanity," claimed one reporter before moving on to the ubiquitous comparison of him to a racehorse. "No comparison of his build would be better than perhaps that of a thoroughbred racehorse . . . being highly strung, alert, nimble, quick to take advantage of an opportunity, and with an indomitable determination to pursue to the very end."

Before leaving Melbourne, Taylor took part in the Racing Men Association's inaugural Benefit Race. Profits from the race would help support cyclists injured from racing. With Taylor's name on the race program, it seemed a certain success. Yet despite the weather being so atrocious that one reporter deemed "it being nothing short of heroism to venture out at all," eight thousand fans showed up, helping to bankroll the fund for some time to follow.

Taylor, always a fair-weather rider, was having a bad-leg day, losing to a talented Aussie named Joe Morgan. Always the gentlemen even in defeat, Taylor rolled over to Morgan and shook his hand. "Just the fortunes of war," he said graciously. When asked by a reporter if the race was fair, Taylor replied, "I didn't congratulate and shake Morgan's hand for show. I meant it." But Morgan could not suppress his feelings. "I feel as sprightly as a punching bag," beamed a waterlogged Morgan. Beating a legend like Major Taylor was enough to make a man the talk of his town for the rest of his life. Feeling as though he had just slain Achilles, Morgan scampered home, then surely spent his remaining years reliving the moment to everyone who would listen. "It was the proudest moment of my life," he said later, his eyes welling up.

Despite his slow start, Taylor was pleased with his stay in Melbourne. "Although I was a sick man when I reached Melbourne," he later remembered, "I left that city in a blaze of glory . . ."

From Melbourne they sped northeast on the Great Southern Railway back to Sydney. Major was scheduled to compete in the lucrative Sydney Thousand Handicap beginning on March 7, 1903. Considering that the average annual income at the time was a couple hundred dollars, the huge purse—at $5,000, the richest in the world for a nonmatch race—attracted professionals from all over the world. For many riders, winning meant financial salvation, and with 114 cyclists competing in the event, collaboration among them was a certainty. With all these forces mitigating against him, Taylor knew he stood little chance of winning.

The semifinals were scheduled to start in the evening under the newly installed arc lights, but as race day dawned, sheets of rain dropped out of the Australian skies, soaking the grandstand and muddying up the infield. A convention of cyclists stirred nervously in the riders' room, listening to the rain ping off the roof while waiting for the weather to stabilize. It didn't. Hour after hour, the rains kept falling.

Meanwhile, anticipating perhaps the largest crowd ever to attend a sporting event, the railroad commissioners held emergency meetings to discuss the best way to handle the influx. Australians were so eager to see the races that when the rain finally relented at seven o'clock that evening, newspapers were "besieged" by fans demanding to know if the race was on. But by then, the city was saturated and the race called off.

Days later, under sunny skies, a relatively unknown American named Norman Hopper, given nearly a football-field's head start by the handicappers, won the event by a nose. Sensing collusion, a reporter howled his disapproval. "Taylor has proven himself a clean sportsmen and the adoption of the tactics of the cricket hoodlums, instead of impressing the visitor, must oppress him." Taylor had the opportunity to join in combinations with other riders, but as usual, he chose not to. "I could have bought a place in the final of the Sydney Thousand," he said, "but I'm here to win races not buy them."

The alleged collusion stirred up a hornet's nest in Sydney. The newsmen printed story after story for weeks after Taylor's departure. Regardless of the outcome of the race—which crystallized the nickname "Huge Deal" for McIntosh—it was a resounding financial success; an astounding fifty-five thousand fans showed up, quite possibly a world record.

At the end of March, following their stopover in Sydney, Daisy and Major turned around and rolled nine hundred miles southwest, past Melbourne and into the city of Adelaide. The city was ready for them. At the train station, they were engulfed by another eager throng, then entertained at a reception party at their hotel on par with those in Sydney and Melbourne. McIntosh roamed about the place, smothering guests in broad smiles and sneering at his caterers who failed to top off champagne glasses. "McIntosh turned on the parties as though there was no future," one of his friends recalled.

By this time, Taylor was peaking. Unfortunately, the astute Australian handicappers knew it. At one event, the two-mile Adelaide Wheel Race, Taylor's lonely figure hung so far back of the rest of the field he may as well have started from the outback. One of his fourteen rivals, an Aussie named John Madden, the designated limitman, bent over his machine some three-and-a-half football fields ahead of him. Taylor must have had to strain his eyes just to see him.

It didn't make any difference. In front of a crowd of twenty-two thousand, among the largest in Adelaide history, Taylor mowed down twelve other riders before somehow blowing past Madden right before the line. It was an amazing display of raw speed. "Experts here are now satisfied," confessed one previously agnostic Australian reporter, "that he is really the marvel that the continental and American press proclaimed him to be."

Days passed. Record crowds continued to pour into the track, even in the rain. Taylor continued to win races, including the prestigious Sir Edwin Smith Stakes and the Walne Stakes. "He simply won as he liked," grunted one of his rivals before stalking off the track

At a ceremony after the Smith Stakes, a photographer gathered a contingent of "titled aristocracy" for a photo shoot. Taylor, looking modest and contemplative, sat on his bicycle, the colorful winner's ribbon draping from his shoulder down to his feet. Trainer Melville straddled Taylor's rear wheel, his scarecrowish figure merging flawlessly with his forlorn countenance. "Sir and Lady something," wrote one American reporter, referring to Lady Smith and her noble husband, stood next to Taylor, covered from neck to feet in heavy Edwardian garb. Thick-set Macintosh, perhaps ruminating on how best to spend his profits, was the only one exhibiting any semblance of a smile. He had his reasons. Taylor's visits, one man raved, "puts the league on velvet."

Before leaving town, Daisy and Major paid an unannounced and heartfelt visit to a private hospital. There, they expressed their sympathies to a rider named Wayne who had been seriously injured during a race that Taylor attended. Lying there in despair and agonizing over his future as a cyclist, Wayne felt overwhelmed by their compassion.

On April 16, 1903, under a blue moon, Major and Daisy left the land down under, having turned the place upside down. In twenty-seven races stretched out over nearly four months, Major had won an astounding twenty-three. At track after track, he had gained the admiration of thousands of Australians. "The events," wrote one reporter, "aroused a pitch of enthusiasm that has never been witnessed here before."

Back in the states, a *New York Times* editor who had been following the Taylors' overseas odyssey was amazed at the attention the honeymooners were receiving as well as all the money being made. "Major Taylor, who combines cycling with preaching in the Methodist chapels on Sundays, is far on his way to making a fortune . . . far more than the best-paid editors, university professors, or nine-tenths of the legal profession."

In the years after Arthur Zimmerman's visit, cycling had lost some of its popularity in Australia. Taylor's tour dramatically changed all that. "It will be many long years," wrote a track scribe with a twinge of nostalgia, "before the American's phenomenal rides are forgotten."

Having signed a contract with the French tandem of Breyer and Coquelle before going to Australia, the Taylors' ship steamed out over the Indian Ocean toward the Suez Canal en route to Europe. Somewhere along the way, the ship experienced mechanical problems and had to be serviced in India, stretching out their voyage to over a month. Though Major had never been anywhere near India before, people certainly knew who he was. While idling there, he was lionized by the press and the public. They presented him with an elegant ebony cane handcrafted by Indian artisans, a high-status Victorian walking stick often used by barristers assigned to the high courts of India. It was an unexpected gift that he prized highly.

When they finally arrived in France, the European cyclists were in prime condition and Major had lost his edge. What followed was the same old pattern: lose early, gain form slowly, then defeat the natives on their home turf. Before leaving, despite sleeping upright in ordinary day coaches nearly every night, he took twenty-eight firsts, twenty-one seconds and seven thirds. And as he had done the year before, he defeated Thor Ellegaard on a Monday—the day after he had been crowned 1903 champion of the world. Large crowds continued to flock to see Taylor race, including more than eighty-five thousand at a meet in Paris.

This four-month European excursion turned into a romantic and nomadic haze that neither of them would forget. Her first time experiencing the diverse sights and sounds of the Old World, Daisy was in awe as reporters and sports fans mobbed them at every stop. For her, each day was a European postcard: fields of lavender, lavish chateaus, centuries-old farms and churches, everything steeped in history.

Before setting sail from Cherbourg, Daisy and Major finished their long honeymoon with a shopping spree. They kicked a few tires around Paris, bought a French car and motorcycle, then rode them onto their departing ship. A sizable crowd saw them off in grand style. The society writers in the Parisian dailies launched into a frenzy. In fine detail, they described Daisy's elegant "up-to-date" raiment and Major's "gentlemanly bow with cap in hand" as they smiled and waved good-bye to their European friends. All told, the Taylors would go home with $40,000–$50,000 that season, worth well into seven figures in today's money. It would be nearly twenty years before a baseball player, a man named Ruth, made that kind of money. A penniless horse-tender not so many years before, Taylor was now one of the wealthiest athletes. "Of all those people who used to poke fun at the Major," wrote sportswriter Charles Sinsabaugh, "how many today are able to show the bank account that this colored boy might expose? Not one."

A bright ray of sunlight hovered over the *Wilhelm der Grosse* as it carried the Taylors and other dignitaries—William Rockefeller and Cardinal James Gibbons—west across the Atlantic. They were on their honeymoon, they were in love, and they were the talk of the civilized world. Over an eight-month period, the young couple had met countless celebrities, civic leaders, royalty, and sportsmen. They had been invited to elaborate social gatherings at the finest establishments on three continents. They were feted and praised by religious leaders in town after town. At every turn they had set an example of class, elegance, and dignity for all to see and follow, especially African Americans who looked to them as role models.

But they had also traveled more than twenty-five thousand grueling miles. Upon his arrival on September 23, Major unloaded his new toys, turned the hand crank on his Renault, and announced his retirement to the press. "I am satisfied I have done enough," he said.

PART III

Chapter 20

GOING DOWN UNDER

At no point during his twenty-seven years had Hugh McIntosh been taught the meaning of the word no; maybe his inability to understand the concept began when he was a penniless teenager pedaling pies at racetracks throughout Australia. The moment he received word of Taylor's retirement, he scurried to a telegraph office and fired off a barrage of cablegrams.

McIntosh wasn't the only one after him. Astounded by the number and enthusiasm of the fans in 1902–1903, several Australian promoters wired competing offers. But Taylor, who had probably never been serious about retiring or signing with anyone other than McIntosh, got better at the negotiating game each year. Leaving time for rival promoters to up the ante in their bidding war, he surprised locals by storming around Worcester at the dizzying speed of fifteen miles per hour in his new Renault, the tousled hair of his poodle whipping in the wind.

No doubt taking Taylor's retirement threats seriously, perhaps McIntosh slid a quote from an Australian paper into one of his cables. "*If* I ever ride again," Taylor had said, "it will be right here in Australia."

Still in an unpacking mode and busy renovating his house, Taylor stalled. Once again backed by a well-heeled Sydney syndicate that his rivals called "a school of sharks," McIntosh offered a contract on par with the previous season, again no Sundays. This time, however, he wanted Taylor to stay longer and race more often. But after eight years of nonstop travel, Taylor was concerned he might start wearing down, if not physically, perhaps mentally. In his cabled response, he not only rejected more frequent racing but asked for £500 more than the previous season. "... will not guarantee to race more than three times weekly for £2,000 exclusive of prizes," he wrote.

Acceding to Taylor's demands for a thinner racing schedule, McIntosh sent over a contract for his signature. Suddenly, wrote the *Worcester Telegram* of his short-lived retirement plans, "Taylor had a change of heart." To not accept such an offer, remarked Taylor, "was like passing up too good a thing." On October 28, 1903, just weeks after returning, Taylor signed on, making his perhaps the shortest *retirement* on record.

But had he been paying close attention, Taylor may have sensed something different in McIntosh's tone this time around, as if he were omitting important details.

Oblivious to it all and still beaming over her honeymoon experience from the previous season, Daisy scurried through the house, stuffing the luggage she had just unpacked. At 10:12 on the morning of November 13, 1903, they boarded a California-bound train, pausing in Indy for a long interview with reporter Milton Lewis, who once tutored Taylor's siblings. From Oakland they ferried over to the Broadway wharf and then steamed across the Pacific on the *Sonoma*, stopping briefly in New Zealand before arriving seasick in Sydney.

But this time, Sydney would have a different feel to it. Already lurking at the Sydney Cricket Grounds stood a calculating man who had often been at the center of Taylor's greatest distress.

People often say that everyone has a polar opposite somewhere in the world. If they are right, the man waiting onshore was, for Taylor, just such a man.

Floyd MacFarland was not a typical bully; most bullies are more bark than bite. With six-foot-four inches of sinuous muscle, MacFarland could—and occasionally did—take matters into his own hands. Twenty-six years old in 1904, one year older than Taylor, the long, linear San Jose resident was a blunt man with a low, insinuating voice and clawlike hands. He was a dyspeptic man—fighting, raging, and hauling off at racing officials, rivals, promoters, even spectators at the drop of a hat. Ever since he first materialized on the prestigious Eastern tracks in the mid-'90s, he was at times such a nuisance, officials didn't know what to do with him. While his torrential outbursts and remarkable racing skills helped fill the stands, racing officials grew concerned that his antics, taken too far, may harm bike racing's image. No matter what they tried, MacFarland continued to cause trouble, eventually becoming among the most heavily fined and oft-suspended riders in the peloton. During one six-day race in Boston, he lunged and cussed at paying customers, becoming such a holy terror the NCA rehabilitated him with a six-month sentence for "rioting."

Even Edmond Jacquelin, known throughout Europe for his feral temper, squirmed in his saddle at the mere presence of MacFarland. At one race scheduled to take place between them, MacFarland decided he didn't like the weather and simply walked away. When the racing officials told him he had to return, he let loose a retaliatory tongue-lashing that caused even the hardened Jacquelin to cower, earning him another track suspension.

His language was a peculiar collage of sophisticated speech, unbridled expletives, and racial slurs. In Taylor's eyes, he was a cancer metastasizing within the peloton. During races in which both men competed, MacFarland committed every foul short of detonating an explosive device inside his bicycle, often pocketing, elbowing, or threatening Taylor with violence. When he wasn't personally involved in a race against Taylor, MacFarland tutored other riders on how to "trim the nigger," developing into a sort of racetrack-svengali.

When he failed to block Taylor from being admitted into the NCA, he set his sights on Woody Woodspath, one of the only other black pro cyclists. He tried achieving this by invoking his own "exception rule," which stated that only one black rider could be allowed in a race at a time.

Described as an autocrat, MacFarland also had contempt for authority figures. One day, when he came across a particularly rough patch of road during a road race in the Australian outback, he threw his bike to the side and stormed off. When he never arrived at the finish line, race organizers scoured the countryside. They finally gave up, drifting into some eatery for dinner. There he was, stabbing his fork into a plate of roast beef, tipping back a glass of beer, chatting with locals. When they asked what in God's name had happened to him, he stood up, looked down at them, and asked, surely to the repugnance of the waiting reporters, "What do you take me for, *a God damn kangaroo?*" He was dreaded and beloved for his audacity and back-alley boxing skills. At a champagne reception in Camperdown, Victoria, one summer's night, he walked up to a horse of a man, some nineteen hands high, and, for no apparent reason deliberately mouthed off at him. Unaccustomed to having nonboxers challenge him, "Bull Williams," a noted professional boxer, reared back and gave MacFarland his best shot. MacFarland took the punch, laughed it off, slung his six-foot-four frame forward, and knocked Williams senseless. *No one* messed with Floyd MacFarland. "His word," recalled one former racer, "was law."

On the track, he turned his rage into raw speed, winning consistently in short, middle, and long distance races, giving rise to nicknames like "Human Motor," "Warhorse," and "Handicap King."

Floyd MacFarland was tough as nails, a first-rate rider, and a civic menace all wrapped into one long frame. Mild mannered, deeply religious, and soft-spoken, Taylor was the antithesis of MacFarland. "Floyd MacFarland, my arch enemy of many years standing," Taylor remembered, "was the kingpin of all the schemes against me." "Oh," MacFarland liked to say of Taylor, "that damn nigger . . ."

Some people claimed Floyd MacFarland had a kinder, gentler side to him. If he did, Major Taylor had rarely seen it.

Huge Deal McIntosh knew a thing or two about what sports fans wanted to see. Even though Taylor had the grandstand overflowing nearly every day in 1903, McIntosh sensed Australians wanted to see someone who might actually make him crack a sweat. The previous season, excepting Don Walker, Taylor had faced a fairly soft field and, according to one journalist, "had made hacks out of Australia's best." So, besides Taylor's archenemy Floyd MacFarland, McIntosh had also invited MacFarland's comrade Iver Lawson, with little forewarning to Taylor.

As a competitive cyclist, Lawson was among the world's elite; he took second place in the 1902 American Championship and was one of the favorites for the 1904 World Championships. His personality was reportedly a bit more enigmatic. Dubbed "the melancholy Dane" and a "sober-sided athlete," there appeared to be something incomplete about him, something not quite ripe. While he wasn't the agitator that MacFarland was on the track, Lawson had been suspended for interfering with Taylor and knocking him down and out of racing for more than a week. "He carries the brand of the track yet," remarked the Australian *Referee*, referring to Taylor's ingrained scars.

Working in tandem, MacFarland, with his oversized wind-breaking figure, and Lawson, with his potent closing sprint, were nearly unbeatable in handicap races. And neither of them was fond of Taylor. Beyond the obvious racial element, MacFarland and Lawson found further reason for resentment. Taylor was the only rider who had received a large down payment to come to Australia as well as appearance fees at many tracks. Win, lose, or draw, Taylor was guaranteed a highly profitable voyage. "His legs and riding capabilities," joked the *Australian Cyclist*, "have been sold to a syndicate that negotiates for him." MacFarland and Lawson, on the other hand, had to win to profit.

On a quiet antipodean morning, two men and two bicycles materialized from under the morning haze, filleting across the Sydney Cricket grounds before coasting to a stop near the ladies' pavilion. It was MacFarland and Lawson on their super-light Cleveland and Columbia bicycles, riding tall. When Taylor first saw the famous tandem, he must have become deeply concerned; escaping racism was, after all, one of the main reasons he ventured overseas. From the grandstand, Daisy surely felt concerned as she ran her eyes down the list of wheelmen. Clearly, this wasn't going to be another honeymoon.

The tension would become palpable. Australia's rabid cycling fans braced for the internecine warfare to follow. They would not be disappointed. "The visiting Americans," race writer Wheeler wrote of MacFarland and Lawson, "have brought their prejudice with them, and they also want to atone for past defeats by Taylor."

McIntosh had been busy. He had set up a series of handicap races for January and early February, wedging the three American powerhouses in with the top Australians. Right out of the gate, his tactics worked. Fans poured into the Sydney and Melbourne tracks by the tens of thousands, snarling traffic at nearly every meet. The three men exchanged victories; one night MacFarland, the next Taylor, then Lawson. Each night there was the usual jabbing, elbowing, and all-around roughhousing, sometimes just part of normal track racing, and other times degenerating into verbal backstretch brawls. Either way the fans ate it up.

At one race in mid-January that Taylor won by a nose, twenty thousand fans attended on a rainy, frigid Monday evening—a day that normally drew only a few thousand. The following Monday, twenty-five thousand fans showed up in similar weather and watched Lawson, who had the night of his life, win three out of four events. Taylor won only one, the five-mile. "No man in the world can have a chance against Iver Lawson," claimed one writer, "when he has MacFarland working in his interest."

With each passing night, the teamwork and the tactics of Lawson and MacFarland became harsher and more obvious. "It was as plain as a pike-staff even to the palest-faced laymen," railed one reporter.

In early February, Lawson and MacFarland, who appeared to be joined at the hip, went too far. At the starting line of a half-mile handicap race, MacFarland rolled his six-foot-four-inch frame alongside Taylor's five-foot-seven-inches, glaring at him through his steely eyes. As the field straightened up for the backstretch, Lawson and MacFarland, with all the synchronicity of a school of sharks, bulled down the track and swung inward, bashing Taylor into the infield. For a dreadful moment, Taylor and his Massey-Harris bicycle staggered sideways, teetering on the brink of falling. In the grandstand, Daisy gasped. For forty circuitous yards, Taylor swerved in and out of fans, racing officials, and band members. Miraculously, somehow he righted himself and rejoined the race, finishing second to last. The crowd booed and hissed as MacFarland crossed the line ahead of him.

MacFarland was hauled before the board of inquiry and slapped with a one-month suspension. For days, he had an existential meltdown, cussing and fretting in the richest tones. Taylor, he hollered, rode onto the grass of his own accord. Not wanting to be on his own, Lawson threatened to pull out of several races if MacFarland's suspension was upheld. Eventually he got his wish; after an appeal, MacFarland's suspension was reduced to a small $125 fine for "abusive language."

The tandem of Lawson and MacFarland felt emboldened by the board's leniency. The public and the press felt the tension between the two camps heating up. "There is no love loss between the two factions here just now," wrote the *Australian Cyclist and Motorcar,* "and every time Taylor meets his compatriots, the curry is very hot."

The clock had hardly struck midnight before MacFarland caused trouble again. At one race attended by the prime minister and several other high-ranking Australians, he and Taylor stormed down the homestretch neck and neck. It was a drag race to the line. When they crossed the tape, most fans thought MacFarland had won and cheered him on as he looped the track, waving his hands triumphantly. But a judge inserted "dead heat" up on the tote board. Rigid with rage, MacFarland stopped his bike in its tracks. He rolled over to the stewards' stand and looked down at them, unleashing a profanity-laced tirade that scared the hell out of everyone within earshot. The stewards waited for him to calm down and shut his mouth, but he kept right on bellowing.

The Australian press corps had never met anyone quite like Floyd MacFarland. "How would a jockey get on," one sportswriter wondered, "if he thought he had won and abused the judge and stewards that way?" The stewards held their ground. According to them, MacFarland's giraffe-like neck stretched out ahead of Taylor's shorter frame, but his front wheel, the only thing that matters, had not. The race, they said, had to be run over.

Perhaps they were unaware of the fact that no one told Floyd MacFarland what to do. Instead of lining up for the rematch, he simply slammed his bike down, donned his street clothes and left the racetrack—leaving over twenty thousand fans stirring in their seats for a half hour, unaware of his departure. Fearing the crowd stampeding the track en masse, racing officials called for a veritable battalion of additional police to line the oval. They had valid reason for concern. When a gentlemanly umpire had the audacity to delay a recent cricket match because of light rain, over ten thousand raucous fans showered him with watermelon bits, apples, and beer bottles—"Ready your coffin," they warned. The head referee then issued an order for MacFarland to return at once and answer to the charge of disobedience. Having seen MacFarland's antics before, Taylor could retreat to his locker room in the member's pavilion and read Biblical passages. Hugh McIntosh was in no mood for theology. Agitated, he combed local streets trying to find MacFarland's scalp. He came up headless. A reporter finally tracked MacFarland down the next day, sprawled out on an easy chair. Thankfully, his mood had simmered. "It was a big event in my life to defeat Major Taylor," he said, perhaps wanting to savor the moment, real or imagined.

Following the handicap races, Australians began demanding to know the truth: Who among the Americans really was the fastest man? McIntosh seized the moment. He set up match races for February 17 in Melbourne. The first was to be a two-mile race between Taylor and Lawson, followed by a one-mile match between Taylor and MacFarland.

In the days leading up to the match races, Australia was a cauldron of nervous anticipation.

Nearly every afternoon Major and Daisy listened to raindrops tapping off their hotel window. In the mornings they heard the same tranquil sound. Wiping the sleep from her eyes, Daisy looked solemnly outside, blinking at the cold rain as it turned into sleet. They waited for the weather to turn. It refused. Several training sessions and a few prep races had to be delayed or postponed. Australians secreted away in their homes. "Instead of watching the struggles of the World's Champions," moaned one reporter, "cycling enthusiasts sat before a cozy fire, listening to the howling of the wind and the pattering of sleety rain on the roof; fires in February!"

After losing three handicap races to Lawson with MacFarland's aid, Taylor was clamoring for the opportunity to show Australians who the faster man was in a clean, one-on-one match race. Unable to remain idle any longer, he taxied to the track and slopped around in the cold rain. "If this is your summer," he once grumbled to a reporter, "I guess I would not like to have one of your winters . . . you have to be a gypsy fortune teller to get square with the weather." From the sidelines, trainer Sid Melville, the rain tapping off his crocodile cowboy hat, pressed down on his stopwatch as Taylor hummed by. Underneath his rain-soaked hat, he actually smiled. Again and again, the press hounded him. "He's as fit as a fiddle," he muttered.

Meanwhile, Australian papers were swamped with inquiries about the status of the match races. Fans had already begun pouring into Melbourne from all quarters of Australia. On trams and trains impassioned debates between diehard Taylor fans and MacFarland-Lawson fans carried the day.

The rain kept falling—on one day for twelve hours straight.

Amid the downpour, newspapers continued singing of the races. In the days preceeding the matches, entire pages in bold print were devoted to the events: TONIGHT—TONIGHT CYCLING CHAMPIONSHIP OF THE WORLD, boasted one paper, MEETING OF THE WORLD'S CYCLING GIANTS!! Beneath the banner headlines and advertisements were sketches of the three men followed by a heavy dose of prerace saber rattling. Publicly, MacFarland and Lawson expressed confidence. "Major Taylor is not invincible," they reminded everyone. Privately, they must have questioned their own words. Underneath the headline, Taylor's record in match races was posted: 200 wins, only 12 losses.

As race day neared, Daisy emerged from her hotel room in the middle of the afternoon, looking up at pitch-black skies. A clap of thunder crackled throughout the city. Melbourne braced for fireworks.

February 17, 1904, race day, rolled in under azure skies and a warm penetrating sun. Before noon, as they had at New York's Madison Square Garden in 1896, Philadelphia in '97, Manhattan in '98, Montreal in '99, Paris in 1901–1902, and all over Australia in 1903—thousands upon thousands emptied out of restaurants, stood in long lines at turnstiles, and then wedged into every bleacher, booth, grandstand, and press box seat to watch Major Taylor race. Trams, omnibuses, horse-carriages, ferries, bicycles, and special "Major Taylor Carnival" trains scurried all over Melbourne. Tramway authorities had made special arrangements to handle the extra traffic. Extra turnstiles and entrance gates had been installed. The most "influential" people in the country were turning up. Around seventy-five bookmakers trolled the place. By dinnertime, the Melbourne Exhibition Track was an endless sea of colorfully dressed racegoers. In the members stand near the finish line, Daisy slid in alongside Don Walker.

Taylor's first match race was against Lawson in a best two out of three.

In the first heat, before the throng even had a chance to settle in, Taylor jackrabbitted out of the gate. He got rammed twice by Lawson before ripping down the homestretch, winning by a convincing two lengths. The crowd roared. The newsmen wasted little time getting on Lawson's case. "With MacFarland out of it," one of them wrote, "Lawson's feeding bottle was dry . . . he seems to be useless without him."

Given a clean trip around the track, there was little doubt in Taylor's mind that he had Lawson's measure. He felt confidence bulging in him. "I felt doubly sure I could defeat Lawson on even terms every time we started." But Lawson, being the type of rider who got stronger as the night stretched on, surely didn't see it that way. No one left their seat.

Before the second heat, Daisy could glance out and see MacFarland, who had placed a large bet on Lawson's legs, privately conferring with Lawson. "Whatever you do," Sid Melville overheard him saying, "do not let Taylor win." A man named Toe-clip, Australia's preeminent track writer, tracked down MacFarland and asked his opinion of Taylor and who he thought would win. "He's a fine, game nigger," he scoffed, "he won't come out in this race."

Daisy and Major had become all too familiar with the anxiety that surfaced on race days, but this day had a gloomy, more sinister feel to it. The tension was tangible. Don Walker tried distracting Daisy from her trepidation with light humor. She pushed out a forced smile. The crowd, sensing the tension between the two camps, stirred in their seats. Lawson slipped out of his pink racing gown and cinched into his toe-clips at the starting line. A loud crack echoed over the city. Lawson, still fuming over his loss in the first heat, broke from the gate with a massive forward assault. Taylor immediately found himself trailing by several lengths, looking forward as red jersey number 65 pulled away. He mashed down on his pedals with his forward leg while pulling up with his rear leg, the light poles lining the track flickered by, spinning out of sight. A quarter mile in, Lawson peeked back under his armpit and saw a black, heaving mass charging full-tilt toward him. After a huge outlay of energy, Taylor finally drew even at the one-mile mark. For the next half mile, the two men exchanged leads, neither willing to give up any ground. Lawson rammed against him a couple of times, bullying him, practically undressing him. Taylor felt uneasy, too close for comfort.

Australia stood on its feet and let out a deafening roar, the crowd's decibel level growing exponentially with every turn of the riders' wheels. Lawson, who had surely never felt such intensity coming from a crowd, stood on his pedals, extracting every last erg of his power. He and Taylor were feeding off the crowd and the crowd fed off of them.

Lawson, back bent, bobbing-head down, eyes set, rode in front hugging the pole, the track surface droning up through him and whirling past. Taylor's front tire was shadowing Lawson's rear tire so closely it appeared as if they were one.

As though he had it blueprinted down to the millisecond, right as the bell rang to signal the final turn, Taylor pounded down on his pedals, steered out to the center of the track, and scorched around Lawson. His tongue burrowing deeper into his mouth, Lawson looked to his side and saw the familiar silhouette of Taylor's dark form sweeping by him in a blind terror. Having seen this play too many times before, Lawson seethed in his saddle. From the sidelines, in his deep baritone voice, MacFarland barked commands to Lawson, his words vanishing in the thunder.

Unable to take it any longer, Daisy squeezed her eyes shut.

What happened next would rock the cycling world for months to come. Lawson powered up alongside Taylor by the aquarium corner, gripped hard on his handlebars, and steered his machine aggressively toward the middle of the track—right into Taylor's pathway. There was no time to react. Lawson's rear wheel crashed into Taylor's front wheel, setting off an ugly scene. There was the blur of a helmet-less black body and a riderless bicycle catapulting through thin air at forty miles per hour followed by the crashing thud of man meeting earth and the screeching sound of metal wheels and pedals sliding across the track. Taylor's helpless form somersaulted uncontrollably across the track for fifteen yards before coming to a dead stop, the wheels of his bicycle whirling silently in the still air. His world twisted upside down, all light and color warped. Then everything went dark, still, and silent.

Major Taylor lay unconscious on the track floor. The grim realization shook through the throng. In an instant, horrified fans, track officials, and trainers threw their drinks to the ground, poured out of the grandstand, and ran helter-skelter onto the track, screaming "The Major's down! The Major's down!" Daisy, a look of sheer horror on her face, dashed through the mob, her skirt whipping in the wind.

Horrified, trainer Sid Melville trudged out to the track, dragging his bad leg with him. Racing officials joined him. "That's the most treacherous thing I have ever seen," one of them said. "Lawson will go out for life for this." "It looked like murder," one man wrote. All around Taylor's lifeless form pandemonium ensued. Wheelmen, doctors, and racing officials dashed everywhere, scurrying for bandages, ice, liniments, and a stretcher.

The Ambulance Brigade hovered nearby.

Up in the press box, reporters banged out their stories in shock. Coming from the crowd, claimed one reporter, there were "yells, hoots, groans, and threats of dismemberment." Perhaps fearing for his safety, Lawson disappeared into the night. Out on the track, the current of people converging around Taylor hoisted his limp body up off the track, then lowered it down onto the infield grass.

The shocked fans watched him being carried off the track presumably on a stretcher. Somewhere along the way, Taylor came to, his cataleptic state replaced with painful muscle spasms. Some of the flesh from his legs, buttocks, shoulders, arms, and forehead had been ripped away, exposing bone and giving him the appearance of a burn victim. His purple and white shirt and racing shorts as well as parts of his body became a crimson streak, as gouts of blood spewed forth.

Outside, a lone steward entered "no race" up on the tote board. A dour procession of racegoers marched out of the grandstand. The Ambulance Brigade eventually hauled the suffering hero to the hospital. Doctors hovered over his bleeding head and body, stitching and bandaging away.

Back in the States, a race reporter penned an ominous article. "Major Taylor's injury in Australia is likely to deprive the track of another great cyclist . . . it is the first bad fall Taylor has ever had. And," he wrote, before finishing his remarkably prophetic piece, "the first severe accident usually affects the *nerve* of the cyclist."

In the aftermath of the heavily publicized match race, Iver Lawson was a wanted man. To escape a proverbial hanging at the hands of angered Melbournians, Lawson jumped a train and rolled six hundred miles southwest to the relative safety of Adelaide, where he was popular. Floyd MacFarland joined him. With Taylor out of the way, the two men won everything in sight, including six races in a row, pocketing thousands in prize money. Back in Melbourne, fan letters poured into the papers lambasting Lawson, demanding his permanent suspension, and questioning MacFarland's role in the affair.

At the track, racing officials, trainers, and several riders examined the scar marks and the blood and flesh extending over fifteen yards of track.

The League of Victorian Wheelmen held an emergency meeting at the Port Phillip Hotel in Melbourne. They called in twenty witnesses for testimony. Eventually, Floyd MacFarland showed up, and became the only person to claim Taylor had pushed Lawson and was therefore responsible for his own predicament. Few bought his story. "What rubbish the public is asked to follow," wrote one witness.

In the interim, radiograms—a form of x-ray technology that was still in its infancy—were apparently taken of Taylor. They came back cloudy, indistinct.

After a thorough review, the chairman of the League of Victorian Wheelmen summoned Lawson to appear before the panel. Down in Adelaide while preparing for a race, Lawson watched a steward enter "scratch" next to his number 65 on the tote board. Soon afterward, the track owner hauled him off the track and escorted him to the train station. Lawson hopped on the *Melbourne Express*, sweating bullets the whole way.

A great deal was riding on the verdict. A long suspension would mean missing the World Championships scheduled for August in London, at which he was considered one of the favorites. There was also the upcoming $5,000 Sydney Thousand, the main reason for his twelve-thousand-mile journey to Australia.

After a heated civil war between Northern and Southern Australian racing leagues, Chairman Callaghan sat Lawson down and threw the book at him: he was suspended from racing anywhere in the world for one year. Lawson stooped over in his chair and pleaded for mercy. "All things considered," wrote one reporter, "Lawson may consider himself lucky . . . he is not wanted in Australia." If it happens again, he continued, "a sentence of life will be about fit for the occasion." McIntosh escorted Lawson to the pier and watched him go. To an American reporter upon his return, Lawson, a man for whom words seemed to be a struggle, muttered something about it being Taylor's own fault he was thrown.

In Adelaide, MacFarland read the news and barked his dissent to every reporter he could find. "And this is what they call justice," he growled.

Days passed. Taylor's shoulders, thighs, and forearms were still so badly lacerated, he was having difficulty moving. An ugly row of stitches crisscrossed his forehead. Standing was painful, but with the flesh of his buttocks torn off, sitting was even more agonizing. He was, according to one report, "taking meals off the mantelpiece." "Taylor's injuries are even more serious then we at first thought," confessed one man. Taylor's doctor, a Dr. MacGillicuddy, recognizing the national significance of his patient, had several of the best physicians from around Australia speeding in on trains to further examine him for possible broken bones or internal injuries. "He will carry the sears in his buttocks and arms for life," one of them said.

Track owners from Adelaide, where Taylor was scheduled to appear next, hopped a train to pay him a visit. They found him reclining on a Victorian settee in his room with Daisy and his doctor nursing his injuries. He was so heavily bandaged, Daisy, who was six months pregnant, struggled getting clothes over the angry welts on his body. After first expressing their sympathy for his plight, the track owners reminded him how much attendance had fallen because of his absence. When one of them put a guilt trip on him, pleading with him to race, injured or not, Taylor's doctor expressed outrage at the suggestion.

Days slipped by. The track owners showed up again. When they continued to press the issue—attendance was cut in half, they emphasized—Daisy became enraged, chasing them out of the room.

Hours became days; days, a week. The pressure to race continued to pour in from all quarters—racing officials, reporters, track owners, and expectant fans. Taylor was becoming uncharacteristically edgy. He emerged from his bed, stabbing angrily at the ground with his crutches and moaning. Daisy grew concerned.

February turned into March.

Physically, Major Taylor eventually made a full recovery that antipodean summer. He even won some races, including a few against MacFarland. But they were merely pyrrhic victories. Mentally and emotionally, he returned to the track a changed man. His cool demeanor and sense of equanimity that had heightened his fame the world over began slipping out of his control. In the past, he had let negative judges' decisions and requests from aggressive track owners roll over him with few words and little emotion.

Now he began snapping back. On one occasion he surprised a reporter at the South Australian Hotel by thumping him on his knee with his hand while simultaneously stamping his feet on the ground. "Some of your officials," he hollered, "have all along entertained a disgusting prejudice against me." The track owners, he howled to another writer, "have regarded me as a revenue machine and nothing more."

To him, it was as if everyone expected him to show up with a smile on his face and work his magic every day without fail. "I am a not a petrol machine," he had told a reporter. "I am flesh and blood like the rest of you."

As March became April, his anger turned into paranoia. He scratched out of some races because he was afraid of being "dealt with." When he did race, he often visited the stewards to warn them of potential foul play. "Keep your eyes open," he said fearfully, "keep your eyes open." He scratched out of one race in Adelaide because he claimed "the entire field was going after [him] with a vengeance." "I am frightened to race," he confided to another reporter. "After what happened at various times, it is no wonder that Taylor is scared," the reporter responded.

Even the race handicappers, who had a difficult and thankless job, bothered him. They continued placing him so far away from the limitmen, he often stood little chance of winning. When he uncharacteristically complained to one of them, the handicapper told him flat out "we just can't have the same man winning all the time."

Large crowds continued to show up—including thirty-two thousand one day at the Sydney Thousand—but the flattery no longer had the same meaning to him. The frantic yells, the bobbing heads, the waving handkerchiefs all looked and felt the same. The whole world worshipped him, yet he felt disillusioned.

Australians had apparently seen enough of Floyd MacFarland. Following a few losses to Taylor, he backed out of a heavily advertised match race at the last moment and without explanation, infuriating nearly thirty thousand waiting spectators. "Rather than submit to a licking by Major Taylor," lamented one reporter, "he has taken the rather undignified course of backing out of the match altogether." And Hugh McIntosh had had it with him. Like Judge Kenesaw Mountain Landis in Major League Baseball, McIntosh had been hired to stamp out corruption in Australian racing. It was a job the one-time amateur-boxer-turned-sports-muckracker took very seriously. "While the giants were still winded after their ride," *Smith's Weekly* once wrote of his treatment of a few crooked riders, "he would lay them out one at a time."

When MacFarland once again became the chief architect of chicanery against Taylor in the all-important $5,000 Sydney Thousand, McIntosh alertly disqualified the man MacFarland helped win. Losing a fortune as a result, MacFarland rushed toward him with vengeance in his eyes. A show-down of the big Macs seemed imminent.

"I'll kill you, you bastard," hissed MacFarland, his voice carrying out over the din of thirty-two thousand spectators.

McIntosh, who was intimidated by no man, seethed. His eyebrows rose as if powered by hydraulics, his eyes grew larger, and his tongue slid between his teeth as though he was about to bite down hard.

No one moved.

"Keep your fist to yourself, MacFarland," he snorted in a deep guttural tone that backed MacFarland off. "You can't fight any better then you ride."

For perhaps the first time in his life, MacFarland, retreating from a lock-kneed, gunslinger pose, backed down. McIntosh saw him to the Sydney pier, shoved him on the mail steamer *Sonoma*, then booted him across the Pacific with a three-year suspension. Weeks later, MacFarland got off in New York, ran to the *New York Times*, and began blurting out every adjective in his vocabulary. "It was injustice!" he barked.

Of the five American cyclists in Australia that year, three were sent packing with long suspensions: Lawson and Downing, one year; MacFarland, three years. Their departures, while a welcome reprieve, did not end Taylor's frustrations. Several Australian riders were also slapped with long sanctions, including a one-year suspension to a rider named Cameroon. "If these are carried out much further," one sportswriter wrote, "nearly all riders will be disbarred."* Taylor felt MacFarland's tentacles stretching all the way across the Pacific like an elongated octopus, even after he was long gone. "It was a strange revelation for me," he remembered, "to note how MacFarland's victorious campaign of propaganda had taken root among the Australian riders ..."

In May, Taylor left South Australia for good. "I will never race in South Australia again," he growled as he boarded a train for Sydney.

For a brief moment in early May, a small ray of light shined through the clouds. At her urging, Major rushed Daisy to a hospital in Sydney. "Mrs. Taylor," he said, "had been awaiting certain interesting developments." The Taylors had been discussing the name of their first child for some time. Since Major was the world's fastest man and Daisy was also athletic, they seemed to be the ideal pedigree for another world champion cyclist. Wanting a fast-sounding name that would, as Taylor wrote, "start him on his fast career to championship fame and glory," they settled on the original first name of *Major*. And, in honor of their favorite city, they selected *Sydney* for a middle name.

Consequently, their well-laid plans—foreseeing a new lad who would dominate future rivals on bicycle tracks—predated his grand entrance into the world. "Of course," boasted Major, "he was going to be a champion bicycle rider." When, on May 11, 1904, in the bustling city of Sydney, Australia, Major heard the first cry of a little baby coming from Daisy's hospital room, he rushed in and asked the doctor just how great a rider the little one was likely going to be.

"Is the baby perfectly developed?" he asked nervously.

The doctor, sensing his expectations of a boy, paused before speaking. "This child can never be the great sprinter that you are," he said hesitantly.

Major gulped. "Why, doctor, why?"

"Because," he said, "it's a girl!"

Boy or girl, Major was thrilled. "This wonderful little stranger," he wrote, "would make me the proud recipient of the greatest prize of all ..."

---

* Every sentence handed down to the American and Australian riders was later reduced. After several inquiries and a great deal of pleading, Lawson's one-year suspension was eventually reduced to three months, making him eligible for the 1904 World Championships in London, which he won.

Instead of Major, they christened her Rita Sydney Taylor. Eventually the name Rita was dropped. Everyone referred to her by her middle name of Sydney.

She would live for more than a century.

On June 6 Major, Daisy, and Don Walker watched in silence as Captain Houdlette steered the *S.S. Sierra* away from the Sydney pier. For the Taylors, it would be their last sight of Australia. Hugh McIntosh, along with members of his syndicate and a smattering of dignitaries, waved good-bye and wondered if they were seeing the last of the exotic black man from America.

Beginning with Arthur Zimmerman's visits, Australia had developed into a major player in the sport of professional bike racing. Despite a long and storied history in the sport dating back more than 132 years, those two years in which Major Taylor took center stage are still remembered with great reverence. "1904," wrote one Australian author nine decades after Taylor's visit, "was the single most amazing season of cycle racing in the history of Australia."

Having bought a small menagerie of cockatoos, parrots, and an exuberant wallaby, Major bided his time playing with them and his new baby during the long cruise home. But there was a restlessness about him that surely caused him to roll around in bed and stare at the ceiling. He tried putting on a brave face, but the roughhousing on the racetracks that year, especially his fall at the hands of Lawson, had scared him and made it hard for him to cope.

Back in Australia, several writers felt his anguish and expressed remorse at the harsh treatment he had endured. "It is all such a disgrace," one of them wrote after he set sail. "Major Taylor is one of the most genuine athletes that strode for victory in any country . . . there is not a shadow of a doubt that he has not had fair play in Australia."

The *S.S. Sierra* splashed across the Pacific, enduring hurricane force winds for nearly thirty hours. The grand reception and high-energy bantering with the ship's purser from the royal honeymoon of one year ago was replaced with solemn musing over his future. Major was falling into a dangerous emotional slipstream. Things that used to give him pleasure no longer had the same importance. His life, as he looked back, had lacked balance. He couldn't recall the day when his life hadn't been framed by a picture of him on the leather saddle of a bicycle, tearing around one track or another.

On the hazy Monday morning of June 27, they disembarked from the *Sierra* at the port of San Francisco. Exhausted from the long voyage, they decided to shake off their sea legs with a few days of relaxation in the city by the bay. They stopped at a nearby hotel, but were immediately turned away. "No blacks allowed," they were told. They moved farther down Pacific Street. With Daisy holding their crying infant, they were summarily booted off a hotel bus. "No use taking you up," bellowed the hotel bus runner, "there will be no room for you at the hotel." They jumped on another bus, but heard the same insulting refrain: "No blacks allowed!"

Hungry, they set off in search of a restaurant with the same outcome. For hours, they circled in vain with their bulky luggage and new pets, getting dropped off at different restaurants and hotels. A sympathetic police sergeant named Mahoney handed them a list of hotels that accepted blacks. But Taylor would have none of it. "Not my kind of hotels," he said with a angry glare. Don Walker, on his first visit to America, was appalled at what he was witnessing.

"So this is America about which you have been boasting in Australia," he asked quizzically. "From what I have seen, I cannot understand why you were in such a hurry to get back home here."

The afternoon pressed on. Major became tired, hungry, and angry. Just then, he heard a stranger harassing Daisy, who had light skin, for socializing with a negro. For a brief moment while Major's blood boiled, a hush permeated the air. Major edged toward the anonymous man, his eyes squinting. Walker, a rugged Aussie who was also becoming agitated by the whole affair, inched forward. Major shooed Walker away. He wanted to handle this one on his own.

For what may have been the only time in his life, Major, who normally boxed a half hour a day as part of his training, stepped back and launched a punishing punch toward the man's jaw. The fight was over before it started. There was the perfect connection of his clenched black fist to a stunned white face, the sudden press of severe pain, and the thumping sound of man meeting gravel. For a brief moment, there was complete stillness. Daisy and Walker stood back with their mouths gaping.

Major's message was clear. Someone might get by verbally harassing him, but he would never tolerate someone bullying his wife.

So instead of relaxing for a few days in San Francisco, they pulled themselves together and stalked off to Oakland. There, a midnight sleeper, stocked for a lengthy sojourn to the East Coast, stood waiting. As they sat waiting for their train to snake over the Rockies toward Worcester, Major glared out the window at the dark sky.

He had reached a breaking point. Eight years of nonstop travel, racking up nearly one hundred thousand miles on hot trains and wobbly ships, living out of a suitcase and sleeping in strange beds in cities all over the world, denied meals, hotels, and access to certain tracks—all this, wrote the *Worcester Telegram*, "took the heart out of him."

The overland sleeper ground forward. By the time it wound out of Oakland, Major was sound asleep.

S omewhere in the heart of the nation that had both idolized and rejected Taylor, Daisy could rest her head against his shoulder and slide the tips of her fingers into his palm. Major broke down. "I suffered a collapse," he confessed in one of the few moments where he admitted to a weakness. "This was caused," he wrote, "by my recent strenuous campaign in Australia augmented by the incidental worries of life."

When he returned home to the shocking news that his father had been killed by a speeding train, Major Taylor slipped into a long-lasting depression. His therapy would consist of his faith in God, his caring wife, and his beautiful new child.

For the better part of the next two and a half years, the shades were lowered on 4 Hobson Avenue while one of America's brightest lights went dark.

Chapter 21

LAZARUS

The fall of 1904 became the fall of 1905. In a separate room inside 4 Hobson Avenue, Taylor's bicycles, medals, trophies, and newspaper clippings gathered dust. Between 1895 and 1904, his movements could be traced on a near-daily basis through the press. From late 1904 to 1906 while he at times remained hermetically sealed, his name nearly vanished, making reports of his movements sketchy.

His days spent on the world's tracks had brought him both tremendous highs and extreme lows, but now he certainly struggled to recall anything except those moments of gloom. Sadness filled the hallway as he ambled by his trophy room each day. And he had no desire to come near his bicycle. To make matters worse, in the fog of his depression, he had all but forgotten, or chose to ignore, a contract he had signed with Coquelle to race in France that season. Breyer and Coquelle refreshed his memory, suing him $10,000 for breach of contract. NCA Chairman A. G. Batchelder, hell-bent on getting back at Taylor for not racing in America over the past few years, sided with the Frenchmen. Eventually the suit would wear on him, but now his body and mind were too jaded to care a fig about it. Besides, his doctor had issued a stern warning: stay away from the racetrack; your mental health is at stake.

"Little did they [his friends] realize the great physical strain I labored under while I was competing," Taylor later confessed. "Nor did they seem to realize the great mental strain that beset me in those races, and the utter exhaustion that I felt on the many occasions after I had battled against the monster prejudice, both on and off the track."

Daisy's spirits reflected his. But she began working on him, nudging him out of the darkness of their cloistered interior and into the crisp Worcester air. Knowing his love for automobiles, she surely pleaded with him to take her for rides in their new French car. Eventually, Taylor obliged and turned the crank on their Renault. They must have been quite a sight for the locals to see, whizzing along at the blistering speed of ten–fifteen miles per hour, Daisy struggling to keep her Victorian hat from flying off, evoking curious glares from everyone in town.

Since the ten-mile-per-hour speed limit was considerably slower than he was used to going on his bicycle, Taylor challenged the restrictive law. After receiving one speeding ticket, the local police seemingly began stalking the world's fastest man. On one occasion, Taylor, who spoke of becoming an automobile racer, found another mischievous car owner, and together they surely became public nuisances, discharging smoky exhaust, spewing up dust storms, angering horsemen as he had in his youth, and raising a deafening dissonance that scattered horses. These antics, combined with having the audacity to exceed the speed limit again, caused one incensed local magistrate to reform him with a $35 fine.

Unfortunately for all those who came near him, Taylor seemed to be more adroit at bike racing than auto racing. On one June day in 1905, probably while ignoring the speed limit again, he had rammed into a horse carriage carrying two elegantly dressed Back Bay ladies out on a leisurely weekend canter. Their carriage in shambles, a $1,000 lawsuit followed. But this incident did nothing to curb his irresistible penchant for speed. On another occasion, he and a well-known local businessman hit head on coming out of a corner. Surprisingly, they both emerged uninjured, but Taylor's mangled car had to be taken to an "auto hospital," a makeshift shop comprised of former bicycle mechanics who were basically winging it as auto repairmen. On occasion, he tossed little Sydney in the car, hopefully slowing down a bit so she might live to see her third birthday.

Somewhere on those dusty New England roads lined with colorful maple trees, Taylor started to feel alive again. Though he may not have known it then, the healing process had begun. Daisy felt as if every moment with him was on borrowed time. She had seen what had happened to him after eight years of professional racing and worried about his health. She nurtured him, picked fresh vegetables from their backyard garden, cooked him hearty meals, and watched over him. Taylor ate and ate to his heart's content. His frame filled out.

Time passed. Amid the soothing rhythms of Worcester far removed from the racetrack and the insistent press, they watched their daughter Sydney grow before their eyes. In the evenings, while stroking the muzzles of his poodle and wallaby and listening to his red-plumed parrot caw "Major! Major! Hallo Boy," Taylor could finally relax.

The year 1905 blended into 1906. Taylor began pausing as he passed by his special room, peering toward his memorabilia. With each passing week, the pause grew longer. Eventually he stepped into the room, probably reading a few newspaper headlines he had in his scrapbook: Taylor Defeats Midget Michaels. Taylor Is World Champion. Taylor Avenges Loss to Jacquelin.

As 1906 entered its final months, Taylor immersed himself in his collection, at times surely tarrying for hours. He eventually wiped the dust off one of his bicycles, for which he would later write a poem:

Now as a reward for faithfulness
My trusty bike has earned its rest
But not in the attic all covered with dust
Nor in the cellar to get all rust
But in my den on a pedestal tall
Or better still upon the wall
Where I can see it every day
And it will keep the blues away
We rode to win in every race
Fairly we played in every case
If life grows dull and things break bad
Just think of the days we've had

Avid cyclists often say that the passion for riding never goes away; it just lies dormant at times. The sport may in fact have the highest recidivist rate. "You may take a break, but you'll always come back," explained one professional rider. "You need the competition, the adrenaline, the endorphins.

You'll miss the flush, relaxed, satisfied feeling when you're heading home after a long ride with friends on an early summer evening at sunset."

For Taylor, this was the first period since his youth that he had been deprived of his life's passion. He began missing the howl of thirty thousand fans, the drug-like high that only a bicycle race can bestow. Standing alongside his trusty, record-setting machine, he felt something form in him, a sensation he hadn't felt in years. Since his last racing days in Australia, his fortune had reversed. Physically he had declined, but emotionally he began feeling better. Subconsciously, he'd hung on to the idea that he might compete again. All he needed was the right circumstances.

In December 1906, he heard a rap on the front door. It was Coquelle. He was in the States for the Madison Square Garden six-day race, looking for an amicable way to settle their lawsuit. Taylor invited him in and drew up a chair. They talked long and late about the good old days of 1901, especially the Jacquelin match races, still on the tongues of sports lovers in Europe.

Given that they had enjoyed a harmonious relationship before the lawsuit, Coquelle had surely agonized over his decision to sue the beloved black man. So he put an end to all the reminiscing, then made a startling suggestion: Why didn't Taylor try a comeback so they could drop this silly lawsuit? For Taylor, the idea was at once brilliant and frightening. The lawsuit—which named Daisy as well—had hung over him like a rain cloud, so he rejoiced at the thought of watching it disappear. "I wanted the worry of the suit ended," he sighed, "and to be free from the chance of losing such a sum of money." Though Taylor hadn't pedaled a bicycle in over two and a half years, the old friends quickly came to an oral agreement.

Taylor seemed set to return to the land of his greatest glory.

But during his absence, the racing world had moved on without him, producing several young stars who were lighting up racetracks. Could he possibly compete in this new environment? The press got wind of his pending return. Some newsmen thought the idea was preposterous. The comeback, if fruitful, would be unheard of. Several elite cyclists tried, including Arthur Zimmerman, Eddie Bald, and Tom Cooper, but they had met with more humiliation than success. Before the year was out, Taylor would be a comparatively elderly twenty-nine year old, several years older than most of the young bucks he would be facing. And his body had already been subjected to hundreds of grueling races strung out over thirteen years. In today's world, he would be near his prime, but in 1907, when the average life expectancy was forty-six for white men and only thirty-two and a half for black men, twenty-nine was considered beyond prime.

Before signing on the dotted line, Major put the ambitious proposal before the chairman of the board: Daisy. At first she appeared to be terrified at the idea of his going back to the racetrack, the very source of his troubles. But after seeing him mope around for much of the past few years, she seemed all too happy with the idea of getting him out of the house. "I advised him to do it . . . I urged him to take up cycling again," she told Coquelle "because I don't think it's good for a man to be idle."

On a brisk day in March 1907, Major, Daisy, and their daughter Sydney took a train to New York. They boarded the *La Touraine*—the French liner that would warn the Titanic of icebergs—and set out on the seemingly impossible mission of regaining his former glory.

It was like 1901 all over again. Before they had even arrived, the European press corps slipped into overdrive. They reignited the passions of longtime racing fans by reprinting many of Taylor's past exploits. For new fans, they painted a picture of coming divinity, a Lazarus they were about to bring back from the dead. The Resurrection of the Negro trumpeted Desgrange's *L'Auto*, a sports daily made popular in part by Taylor and the fast-growing Tour de France.

Europe geared up for the return of the legendary black man. Peugeot, Taylor's new bicycle sponsor, splattered the continent with ads and billboards boasting of its affiliation with the world-famous negro. All across the continent, people sang the words of a new song titled "*Le Negre Volant*" (The Flying Black Man). A book about him hit shelves. When a group of American tourists staying at the same hotel insisted those "niggers" get out of "their" hotel, the tourists were pilloried without mercy by nearly every reporter and citizen in France. *La Vie au Grand Air* produced a multipage cover piece highlighting Taylor's career with nice photos of Daisy and Sydney. "Major Taylor," they wrote with an air of intoxication, "is with us once more."

But few newsmen were prepared for what they saw. Waddling into Le Havre at the mouth of the Seine River with his quaking belly stretching far over his belt stood Taylor, a few meals shy of a portly 200 pounds. Used to seeing him a svelte 160 to 165 pounds, the press was aghast. Some felt uncomfortable broaching the subject. Others proceeded gingerly. "You look as though you have put on a little weight, Major," remarked one reporter, trying not to make his understatement too obvious.

The fact was, Taylor had desperately wanted to train in the South before leaving, but the racial climate, including the frequent lynchings, hadn't changed much since he had been kicked off Southern tracks in 1898. He had to settle for trying to pound his excess weight off on the way over, beating a punching bag, while many of his rivals had been training under the swaying palms of the French or Italian Riviera. Unfortunately, clobbering a punching bag was nowhere near enough to overcome years of inactivity.

Taylor tried to shoo away the press and hunker down for six weeks of training—first a half hour, then forty-five minutes, an hour, and so on. Each day hundreds of puzzled Europeans looked on as he rode around the track, sauntering along at a turtle's gait. Little by little with each passing week the weight came off: five pounds, ten, fifteen, then twenty. On May 9, he had one final blowout before testing himself in a real race.

His contract called for a series of six races pitting him against weighty names like Poulain, Ellegaard, Dupre, Friol, Verri, Van der Borne, and none other than Edmond Jacquelin. On May 10, ready or not, he lined up at the Parc des Princes Track against Poulain. That race, and the series of five races to follow, proved to be the most humiliating of his career. Time and again he raced and lost, sometimes by ridiculous lengths. Coquelle and Daisy would sit in the grandstand each day and watch him go by, cringing at the sad sight of a racing legend getting trounced by a slew of younger riders or those he had previously handled. After his sixth straight loss, Daisy swept up the steps and out of the track.

Reporters, so used to interviewing Taylor, charged right past him to interview the young victors. Taylor watched them pass, feeling indifferent.

His stock had fallen through the floor. Had his stock traded on Wall Street, quipped one man years later, it would have been delisted. As expected, the crowds hissed and the press picked at him. Given his racing palmares, Taylor was angered that nearly everyone had all but given him up for dead. After he fell down during one race, some even claimed he had forgotten how to ride a bicycle. As though he was building a dossier on them, Taylor made a mental note of who was writing what, and rolled on.

Observers were even harder on Coquelle. They chastised him for lugging Taylor, who some viewed as all washed up, back to Europe. How could he sully Taylor's stellar reputation? Racing fans wanted to remember him as the invincible man he was earlier in the decade, not as an aged has-been. After all the hype, Coquelle read the reports with a tremor in his belly.

Taylor refused to give up. Hour after hour, day after day, he trained and trained, gradually increasing the length and speed of each session. He knew his body and the ins and outs of racing, and he hadn't come all the way over-seas for leisure rides. At his first race at the age of thirteen, he had learned how to ride and compete. Moving at high speed had become an integral part of him from that moment forward. Because fewer fans began showing up for his workouts, Taylor seemed to be the only one who noticed that he was gaining steam. What had begun as gentle canters around the track were now violent forward lunges at breathtaking speeds. Taylor was singeing the track like a bolt of lightning. His mind and body were in synch, begging to race again.

After his long period of convalescence followed by weeks of very intense training, Taylor glided back to the universe amazingly fit and lean. He now had an important decision to make. Upon completion of his first series of races, he had fulfilled his contract with Coquelle. With the lingering lawsuit finally settled, he could avoid any further embarrassment. Major Taylor was free to go home and retire in peace. He sat down and had a heart-to-heart talk with Daisy. He asked her if she wanted to go home. "Just say the word," he said. Before she could respond, he leaned across a café table and winked at her. "I'm just striking my winning form," he said assertively. "I did not want to leave Europe," he remembered later, "until I made a credible showing against the new field of riders over there." After years of careful and caring observa-tion, no one could read Major's idiosyncrasies better than Daisy. Seeing that familiar competitive gleam in his eyes, she shook her head. No, she did not want to go home.

Apparently Mrs. Daisy Taylor wanted to stick around and watch people eating their words. She would not regret her decision. One by one, the greatest cyclists in the world, new pros and veterans alike, fell by the wayside: Poulain, the previous year's French champion; Friol, current French cham-pion; Penyon, English champion; Verri, Italian champion; Van Der Borne, Belgian champion; Jacquelin; and then Thor Ellegaard, Danish champion. It was a remarkable comeback. Having seen Taylor on his first visit, Ellegaard, a two-time world champion, was stunned at the incredible turnaround. "In all our great match races," he told Taylor humbly, "I have never seen you display such form . . ."

The big crowds, which had subsided because of his weak early perfor-mances, returned. The reporters ate their words and newspapers flew off the stands again. *L'Auto's* daily circulation, which was twenty-five thousand before Taylor's 1901 visit, reached a quarter million. Daisy smiled. Coquelle rejoiced. And just in case anyone thought his series of wins were flukes, Taylor defeated them a second time.

In an important handicap event called the Race of Nations, Taylor passed Dupre, Friol, Schilling, Rutt, and others. Behind him, the world's fastest men were scattered all over the track. There was only one man left out in front of him, a ghost from the past riding hell-for-leather. Out of the corner of his eye, just as he had back in 1901, Edmond Jacquelin, his face twisted in pain, watched helplessly as Taylor ripped by him for a convincing win. Taylor had set a track record right in front of his old rival, the ultimate payback against his detractors. "We had the last laugh," he noted with an avenging tone, "and the papers were profuse in their apologies for rushing to their conclusions."

Before sailing home that fall, Taylor set two world records that would withstand decades and thousands of assaults—the half-mile standing start in :42 1/5, followed by the quarter mile in :25 2/5, both on the Buffalo Track in Paris. It took a while, wrote the *Worcester Telegram,* but "once he got going he cleaned them all up." All things considered—his age, inability to train in the South, and his long layoff—the latter half of 1907 may have been the most remarkable of his celebrated career. "Major Taylor," wrote Coquelle, "was the most extraordinary, the most versatile, the most colorful, the most popular, the champion around whom more legends have gathered than any other, and whose life story most resembles a fairytale."

B ut in the real world, all fairytales eventually end. The Taylors returned in 1908 with much of the same results—a sluggish start followed by a stronger finish. But for Daisy, every race that season took on a feeling of finality. Unlike previous seasons, she often stayed in Paris while Major's train whistled into one European town after another. Though he began winning again toward the end of the trip, she couldn't help but notice that it took longer each year for him to find his form. His age was showing. During one race his good friend and mentor Birdie Munger, who was in Paris on business, had the satisfaction of watching him win by a fraction. But the twenty-length routs of yore were now measured in inches.

In September, Daisy saw him race for the last time. He had a different way about him, heaviness in his stride. At times, he looked stale, tired, uninterested. Pictured wearing pants drifting halfway up his lower leg, even his meticulous attention to his attire began slipping. There was inevitability in the air, a strong sense that things would never be the same. "The advancing years," wrote one columnist upon his return, "have put on him the handicap which nothing can beat out."

Chapter 22

MY DARLING WIFE, I WANT TO COME HOME

The spring of 1909 emerged under rain clouds. So did much of the summer and fall. Taylor returned to his headquarters in Paris for one last season, struggling with the unusually wet weather, the waning interest in him, and the inevitable physical decline of aging. Perhaps not wanting to see him on his last racing legs and tired of lugging their daughter through myriad hotels, Daisy watched Sydney grow up in Worcester along with her maids and servants.

It would prove to be a wise decision. There was little to cheer about that season, especially the concession Taylor made to Breyer and Coquelle. Since breaking into professional racing in 1896, Taylor had almost certainly drawn more fans than any athlete in any sport anywhere in the world. But his position as the world's fastest man and greatest draw was fleeting. The enormous crowds that used to show up to watch him work out and annoyed him when they "looked him right in the eye," became a thing of the past. And everybody knew it, especially Coquelle, who had coldly given him the choice between racing Sundays or staying home.

As a deeply religious man, it had been an agonizing decision, a partial apostasy that weighed heavily on him. He had signed reluctantly. "I was obliged to break my rule never to ride on the Sabbath . . . when I thought of my wife and child I weakened, as better men have done, and signed the agreement that demanded my racing on Sunday." Birdie Munger thought he'd never see the day. "I did not expect that," he had told the *Boston Globe*, "for I believed Taylor would stick to his decision not to race on Sunday until he died." While working on Taylor's machine one Sunday in 1899, Munger told the *Globe* that Taylor even threatened to go home if he persisted. It would be only the first of many daggers to his pride. The next would come later—on the track.

In each town—Paris, Rome, Copenhagen, Milan, Bologna, Geneva, Roanne—he sat alone in his hotel room at all hours of the day and night, composing heartfelt letters to Daisy and Sydney, by then a lively five-year-old. In the letters his intense love for them flowed from each page, as did his strong feelings of separation. They reveal the heart, mind, and soul of a world-famous athlete on the decline, a man who had largely concealed his inner self from his fans and the press.

From his room at Berlin's Hotel Askanischer Hof in June 1909, Taylor watched the rain fall while penning a note on a postcard in the flowing Victorian script of that lost era. His mood, as it had throughout his career, mirrored the weather.

> *Daisy, my dear wife . . . everything is beautiful but the weather, and it is horrid. . . . Do not be surprised to see me at any old time now as I am riding very badly and things are not coming along my way too fast so I am liable to beat it for home soon. How is my darling little Sydney, how I long to see her, and as for you, dearie, I just cannot begin to tell you how very much I should like to hear from my granny more. . . . Don't forget to pray for me, you and little Sydney too. I need your prayers every minute in the day. Now good bye to both my dears, may God continue to keep you both for me, love and kisses from your loving husband. Marshall.*

His physical decline in previous years came gradually, like cotton falling through still air. But the regrettable season of 1909 saw a precipitous downward slide, more like a boulder tumbling down a cliff.

June 14, 1909

Daisy, my darling wife, only a few lines to say that I did not do as well as I expected to in the Grand prix of Neuilly. Rutt beat me in the semifinal, and he won the final also from Dupre. . . . Friol, Poulain and I were all shut out in our heats. I was awfully disappointed at not having made a better showing, because I was feeling fine, never felt better, but I was not there with the kick.

A few weeks later amid another rainstorm in Düsseldorf, Germany, Taylor watched out over the River Rhine, writing over the familiar din of trains whistling into town:

I failed again in the Grand prix of Buffalo last Thursday night, failed to even get into the final. And why? Try as hard as I may, I simply cannot ride as well as I did last year, and I have already had to make several sacrifices and concessions in my contract which means several hundred dollars, all because I cannot win often enough. But I am trying to use the best possible judgment in every way, to get all out of this seasons riding I can, because in all probability this is my windup, unless I can make good in the championship. So far I have only seven hundred dollars to show for all my hard work and tiresome sleepless nights, and this season is more than half gone.

Strangely, given his estimated net worth of around $75,000 to $100,000 in 1909 dollars, many of his letters revolved around money and expectations of greater material possessions—expectations he either placed on himself or was placed on him by others.

I am so pleased that you are a home loving girl, and that you appreciate your little home and keep it up so well, it makes me long to see you in a still nicer one, or in a beautiful little farm. You know how pleased I would be to give you all those nice things if I could, don't you dearie. But what I have given you was the best I could afford, and if the time ever comes that I can afford better, you will have still a nicer house. Now dearie, about coming home; It is true I am not winning as I expected to, but I am still getting paid for getting up, and as badly and

as anxious as I am to see you and dear little Sydney and to be home
with you once more, don't you think I had better stay a while longer
and get as much money as I can before leaving, because dearie, this will
surely be my finish this season owing to the poor showing I have been
making so far, so for that reason I rather thought I had better make as
much as possible while the sun shines.

Taylor's spirits temporarily lifted when he saw his friend, Hugh McIntosh, stirring in the grandstand one afternoon. After meeting with William Brady in New York, McIntosh romped through Paris with a gorgeous actress with whom he was having an affair, trying to track down Brady's old heavyweight champion Jim Jeffries. America had been searching the four corners of the earth for a "great white hope" to dethrone Jack Johnson, the new black heavyweight champion of the world. McIntosh, who had promoted the racially charged Johnson-Burns fight in Australia in 1908, thought he could dust off the thirty-five-year-old former champion and throw him in the ring with the younger Johnson. Being an avid and knowledgeable boxing fan, Taylor must have chuckled before wishing him good luck with such a crazy endeavor.

McIntosh had come into Taylor's good graces for his role in booting Floyd MacFarland and Iver Lawson out of Australia following their callous treatment of him. Deep into the reminiscing stage of his career, Taylor probably stayed up into the wee hours of the night with his friend, reliving that memorable royal honeymoon year of 1903. Underneath his magisterial and tough-guy persona, McIntosh had a soft spot for the downtrodden, including African Americans. One day, he noticed that a black man whom he had befriended at a Turkish bath in Australia was very ill. He asked him what had happened. When he was told that he had been beaten mercilessly by a racist white man, McIntosh agreed to replace the man's wages so that he no longer had to work in pain. It was a pledge he honored for the rest of the man's life.

McIntosh certainly enjoyed the fortune he made during Taylor's visits to Australia. "Gates of 50,000 to 60,000 were commonplace," he told the *Sporting Globe*. But he also appreciated what Taylor stood for and the message he had so eloquently spread. "He was almost as good a preacher as he was a cyclist," he often boasted.

McIntosh wished Taylor well, then slipped into the night, never to be seen again by Taylor.

Taylor then tried putting on a brave face as he composed another letter to Daisy:

My darling wife: I am getting down to weight slowly; I haven't got it on your friend Jim Jeffries very much now. Ha. Ha. Ha. After putting in a good solid weeks work when I come back next Monday I ought to be coming along nicely. I am sprinting as fast as ever even now but I am not strong enough just yet, it takes a long time for that part of my training, but it will come in time, you know . . . dearie how I wish you were here . . .

He soldiered on, riding and living in his own personal purgatory.

I rode yesterday against Poulain, Meyers and Arend, and what do you think, I actually finished last in every heat. . . . Well, I cannot possibly do any better, I have tried and tried, and have done everything possible to get going faster, but nothing I have tried seems to be of any use, so there. I am really discouraged for once in my life, and I am starting for Copenhagen at eight o'clock. It is now six a.m., and I would much rather be starting for home, dearie. However, I am going to be brave and try to make the best of it, but it surely makes me feel bad to think that I am well and strong but cannot beat these fellows. Well, I hope it will be over soon. It came near being over with yesterday, as I had another fine of a hundred francs to pay and it was most unjust at that. But say, sweetheart, when a man is married and has a good wife as I have, and a nice little baby girl, he will take a good deal, and stand for many things that he would not, were he not married. So . . . I just paid my fine like a little soldier, but it did hurt me so. I stand for many things now that I never thought I could put up with, and for which I never would stand up before I married.

When Daisy did not reciprocate promptly, Taylor's loneliness and anguish deepened, revealing vulnerabilities few knew he had.

Why don't you write any more dearie, almost in for over two weeks since I had a letter from you . . . I have received three post cards . . . but no letters, why have you stopped writing me? How is my dear baby?

Tell her that dad will be home soon and he is going to bring home something nice from Berlin, and also you too if you are a good girl dearie. Now I must close, will write to you again from Hanover. From your loving husband Marshall.

His intense love for Daisy was equaled only by his love for Sydney, who was frittering away time with their poodle and pet kangaroo in their backyard.

My darling little Sydney, here is a letter and some post cards for you from Berlin; I know you will be pleased to get them. Granny told me in one of her letters that you are now big enough to go to Sunday school, and that you are such a good little girl, I was very pleased when I read that and I hope that you will not miss a Sunday now that you have started, and if you go every Sunday "dad" will bring you something nice when I come home. I have tried to send you postcards every day, but I think I have sent you all of the different kinds; it is hard to find new ones. . . . you must take care of all the cards that dad sends to you and show them all to me when I come home. Now good bye, be a good little girl every day . . . your dear daddy. You must not forget to pray for daddy every night.

Now nearly thirty-two years old, Taylor's body couldn't recover from all the tiresome train travel like it had in his younger days. On the backstretch, wheelmen murmured that he was through. He had strayed into the great slipstream in which all athletes eventually find themselves. He was near wit's end as he bedded down for the night at the Palace Hotel S. Marco in the Etruscan city of Bologna, the steady susurration of the river Po in the distance.

August 28 1909.
Daisy my dear wife: . . . I am going to make one more desperate attempt to beat these boys before I leave, but I cannot do it while traveling so much . . . I did not get to ride my match with Poulain as I expected last Thursday night owing to my very poor showing in the big race in Copenhagen, but if I can get to riding like my old self I can easily get a match with him later. I would also like a match with Dupre if I get going better. Now cheer up both of my dear girls, it won't be very long

before you will have your own dear boy back with you once more, and dearie how pleased we shall be after almost five long months now, but it seems more like years than months doesn't it dearie; so keep up your courage and try and make out for a few weeks more.

October rolled in with thick dark clouds and strong autumn winds. Because he was not of the right mind to sit through a spate of emotional farewell parties, Taylor did not announce his true intentions to the press. In fact, he cut off their scent by expressing his desire to return in 1910. It seems to have worked. Comparatively few showed up on October 10, as he emerged on a European track for the last time amid the Roman-era ruins in Roanne, France.

What he had asked for in his letter to Daisy he received; Coquelle had saved Charles Dupre, the best rider for last. In match races, the young Frenchman had ridden away from every top rider that year. He had also won the prestigious Grand Prix of Paris before topping off his remarkable season by becoming world champion.

A pistol was raised at the line. The startman squeezed his fingers around the trigger. Dupre, always a fast breaker, tore from the gate at a blistering pace. Taylor, his famous early speed from the turn-of-the-century now a thing of the past, chugged in behind, trailing him by several lengths. The hometown crowd, sensing another French rout, roared as the two men careened around the backstretch into the homestretch, both preparing to unleash their greatest efforts to the finish line . . .

Meanwhile, back in Worcester, Daisy read another letter confirming the end was near:

Well dearie I had a talk with Coquelle about next season, and it is all off. He did not tell me outright that he could not engage me, but told me openly that he could not give me what I asked for and of course, I could not come over for what he offered me . . .

. . .Now after the terrible experience of this season, I am not at all grieved because I am not coming over again next year, but quite to the contrary, I am indeed pleased. As I told you several times before, dearie, I am full up with this business, and have been for a long time, and this season's work just put the finishing touches on it. I regret very much now that I ever came back again, because if I had finished last

year, you see how nice it would have been for you and little Sydney to have been with me on my last successful racing season and we could have finished by trimming them all, and on top. One thing that I am pleased for dearie, and that is that you and Sydney were not here to see everybody trimming me this year, so perhaps it is just as well that you did not come . . .

Several hundred times on tracks all over the world, Major Taylor had sat behind a rival poised for one of his famous last-second surges. But this was no ordinary race, and Taylor's speed was no longer considered extraordinary. Late on that crisp autumn day, the final bell signaling the final turn in the storied international career of Major Taylor rang out over the grandstand.* A loud echo reverberated back, just as an awed crowd watched Taylor, in a last show of supreme power and utter defiance, rip forward with every amp of his old power, crossing the line ahead of the new champion of the world. Dupre's hometown fans sat cold and motionless in their seats as the curtain fell on the career of an American legend. "In my opinion," one racetracker wrote, "he's the greatest racing cyclist the world has ever seen . . ."

Taylor scanned the faces in the crowd as they quietly slipped out of the stands. A somber group of diehard fans, some of whom had followed him since his first visit to the continent, watched as he left the track—his legacy and his shadow growing larger as he walked off into the sunset. "It is not likely," one man uttered "that we shall look on his like again . . ."

On October 16, 1909, Taylor left Paris's Gare St. Lazare station for the last time. Gone were the crush of fans and reporters that had greeted him his first time to France. He gazed out his window as the train chattered west over the same terrain that first brought him to Paris during that memorable season of 1901. His mind rolled back to that carefree evening when he entertained Parisians with his remarkable singing voice and piano playing skills from the lobby of the Malesherbes Hotel. He remembered the grand match races against Jacquelin, a glaze of nostalgia coating his eyes. "In his prime," Taylor would reminisce to a lone reporter, "Jacquelin was a faster rider than any of the men on the wheel today."

---

* Taylor did compete in a few insignificant races in America in 1910.

As he and five hundred other passengers boarded the *La Provence* in Havre, thick black clouds furrowed overhead. A light rain fell. Lingering over the Atlantic, a perfect storm awaited them. Twenty-four hours later, it struck with tremendous force. Gigantic tidal waves buckled steel plates and a tubular ventilator, threatening to capsize the vessel. Violently seasick, Taylor and other passengers hung on to whatever they could for dear life. Suddenly, sections of the handrail broke off and were carried away by the storm. Everyone onboard was seized by fear.

Back in Worcester, Sydney by her side, Daisy was alarmed by the shuffling feet of the postman. She sat down to read the last of the letters from her homesick husband.

> *Say, dearie, how anxiously I am counting every minute of the time that remains, just as I imagine someone in jail or prison must feel after doing about five years hard labor. Each month that I have put in over here seems like a year to me, but thank God it will soon be over with, and then I can return to you, dearie, well and strong, just as I left you; please God.*

The ship shivered and shook and metal bended and creaked as the bow plunged headlong into the sea and the stern rose toward the dark sky. Each time the ship's bow pointed back down, claimed one passenger, "it seemed as if it would be its last." Somehow the ship's orchestra, trying to calm the passengers, played on into the dark of the night. "When the nose of the ship pointed down after climbing over an immense wave," Taylor later told a reporter as though he was describing what would become of his own life, "it seemed as if it would never point upward again."

Chapter 23

HUMILITY

Eight years later, on a September day in 1917, Birdie Munger raced down a lonely New England road on his way to New Jersey. Not wanting to be late for an important event being held at the Vailsburg Track, he ripped along in his car, challenging the outer reaches of the speed limit. As he sped into a blind turn, out of the corner of his eye he spotted something rushing toward him at the same speed. He tried veering out of the way, but it was too late. He never said exactly what type of vehicle he hit, but whatever it was, it didn't have a lot of cushioning to it. After colliding broadside, both cars came to unhappy halts in a ditch. Munger piled out onto the dust-covered road shaken, but in better condition than his car.

Nothing was going to stop him from getting to the Vailsburg Track on time. He vacated his battered car, waved his thumb in the eastbound lane, went home, borrowed a friend's car, and sped west again. His luck would be no better; his friend's car broke down on a quiet New England side street. But Munger, like many former cyclists, had moved into the automotive business and was thus prepared. He tinkered and toiled and then drove night and day, stopping only for food, finally arriving in Newark on a Sunday afternoon.

At the track, Taylor and eleven of his former competitors, including Howard Freeman, Nat Butler, and Mile-a-Minute Murphy, stood waiting.

Much of the old guard had been invited as well, men like Arthur Zimmerman and Eddie Bald. They were in for an outrageous event.

It seems someone had dreamed up the crazy idea of an old-timers race, and the press had a field day with it. "Some of the champions" quipped the *Newark Times,* had competed "during Lincoln's first administration" and as a result, few fans "had seen such highly developed beer muscles." "One of the articles of agreement," he continued," is that all wheels be shrouded in cobwebs."

Because the race was being held on a Sunday, track manager John Chapman didn't think Taylor would show up. But to Chapman's surprise, Taylor cabled him saying he had just returned from a hunting trip and that he would be in Newark for the race "with both feet."

With the race being a novel idea, no one knew what to expect. But with Taylor's name on the program, fans came from all over, occupying every grandstand seat, press box, and open aisle space. Once the grandstand was overflowing, fans were herded into the infield.

In a heartfelt moment, Taylor and Munger—close friends since those early Jim Crow days—embraced each other at the starting line as more than twelve thousand people looked on. Though they hadn't spent a lot of time together since the late '90s, their relationship had remained a special one. Reporters had composed touching articles describing Munger's role in Taylor's career, and how his belief in Taylor during those early years in Indianapolis had bound them together in history. Like he had back in the mid-'90s, the old high-wheelsman held Taylor up at the line waiting for the crack of the pistol.

Taylor's pride may not have allowed him to reveal, even to his one-time surrogate father, the hard truth of his life since he had retired from the track. Today, with an abundance of financial advisors and diversified investments like mutual funds and managed portfolios, it's easier for a successful athlete to live comfortably on his investment earnings in retirement. But during his era, mutual funds were in their infancy and advisors were few and far between. So Taylor did as many others did at the time, something he once told a reporter he'd never do. After being turned down at the Worcester Polytechnic Institute because he lacked a high school diploma, he had sunk $15,000, a sizable chunk of his liquid net worth, into a low-maintenance automobile wheel. His invention, which seemed like such a good idea at the time, attracted several wealthy investors, including his old bike sponsor Fred

Johnson. But the Major Taylor Manufacturing Company, and other like ventures in which he invested more money, failed.

While holding up his old protégé on his bike, Munger's eyes clouded over when Taylor turned and uttered some of his last words to him. "Well, Birdie," Taylor said, "you started me in my first race and you're starting me in my last race." It was a sentimental moment, a touching testament to the depths of their friendship.

Despite three layers of excess weight around his waistline, Taylor hadn't forgotten how to ride a bicycle. The minute Munger released him from his closed fist, he ripped out of the gate like a thoroughbred. He punched into the belly of the field, weaving in and out of traffic, emerging comfortably in the front pack of riders. An anonymous photographer sitting in a lower box seat snapped the last photo ever taken of him on the homestretch of a bike track. He was a picture of dogged determination as he poured over his bike, fingers grasping the handlebars, face pressed into the head tube, legs spinning out of time. Just as he had two decades before, he roared down the track in second place, poised for the kill, a big crowd cheering him as he swerved around the leader and on to another convincing victory. "No rider before or since his day," wrote a newsman "ever developed a stretch sprint the equal of Taylor's."

In the intervening years, his popularity with American racing fans had been left whole. Even local star Frank Kramer, who had just won his *sixteenth* straight American championship, was amazed at the affection shown Taylor that day. "He received a greater ovation than I or anyone else," Kramer told a reporter in a 1953 interview. "Major Taylor," he continued, "was one of the greatest athletes of all time."

Munger stood at the finish line with the same look of amazement he had on his face when he first saw a fifteen-year-old Taylor pass him in training sessions. An early fall breeze licked over the track. The two men who had meant so much to each other through the worst and the best of times shook hands and then parted ways.

Christmas Eve, 1926, descended on Worcester like others that decade: falling snow, trees adorned with decorations, broad smiles on children's faces, stores packed with last-minute shoppers buying the popular gifts of the day—electric trains, snowdomes, and radios. The Roaring Twenties had ushered in an exciting time of social change and economic prosperity as the recession at the end of World War I was replaced by an unprecedented period of financial growth. The stock market was soaring to unimaginable heights, buoyed by the second Industrial Revolution.

But if one peered inside the window of Magay & Barron's on 368 Main Street, life appeared grimmer. On display for all to see sat nine jeweled trophies and various medals that Taylor had won in cities across the world: Montreal, Canada; Adelaide, Australia; Hartford, Connecticut; Sydney, Australia; Paris, France. Local residents walked by the exhibition solemnly, dropping money in a hat to help him out, their minds wandering back to happier times in the life of their Worcester Whirlwind.

For eighteen months, Taylor had been ill with shingles. The debilitating sickness had racked his body, sapped his energy, and further drained his finances. Having no real actuarial statistics to work with, insurance companies stayed away from insuring health-related risks. So Taylor, like most Americans in 1926, had no meaningful coverage. With the population shifting from rural to urban settings, more and more Americans were treated in hospitals instead of at home. This, and recent advances in medicine, drove the cost of medical care up substantially. Consequently, most of Taylor's remaining assets had to be liquidated to meet the high cost of his medical care. Gone were three triple-decker rental properties he had owned, the plots of land he won as prizes, and numerous bank accounts. The beautiful seven-bedroom home on Hobson Avenue was sold, and the Taylors eventually settled into a tiny rental apartment on Blossom Street. Even some personal effects, like jewelry, had to be sold.

But Taylor was not alone or forgotten. In a remarkable display of affection, the people and the newsmen of Worcester rallied on his behalf that Christmas season. Taylor was, and still is, perhaps its most famous citizen, but it wasn't just his racing fame that had endeared him to the townsfolk. Since retiring from the track, he had proudly served as the unofficial city greeter for visiting dignitaries. Widely known as an all-around model citizen, he had become the quintessential poster child of everything the growing New England city wanted to be known for—diversity, friendliness, and tolerance. All this, and the sportsmanship he had shown around the world against the greatest of odds, were put forth in their pleas for help. VOICE PRAISE OF MAJOR TAYLOR headlined the *Worcester Telegram* on Christmas Eve, 1926, CONTRIBUTORS TO FUND FOR FORMER CHAMPION EXPRESS APPRECIATION OF HIS SPORTSMANSHIP.

The fund for Taylor had been set up by, of all groups, the horsemen. He had become good friends with famous steeplechase jockey Harry Worcester Smith. In better times, Taylor, Smith, and other jockey friends—possibly the great Earl Sande, whom he mentioned in his autobiography—shot pool at Taylor's former home while laughing and joking and jabbering gaily for hours. Somewhere along the dusty trail that was their lives, reinsmen dubbed Smith "the gentlemen jockey." At no time had he earned this title more than during that cold Christmas season of 1926. "I believe Major Taylor, the black man, needs an interested and friendly audience more than ever," Smith told a local reporter, "and let it not be a faint echo of the deafening chorus of years ago."

Smith continued to rally the local newspapers. In turn, they wrote touching pleas for help, which fired up the giving spirit of people from New England to Canada and as far away as Australia. "Enclosed find a donation for Major Taylor," wrote one local woman. "I wish it were more, but a five-year illness has left me where this is the best I can do at this moment. If good wishes could be turned into cash, the amount herewith would be a million."

Money trickled in. Sometimes it was just a few dollars with a letter saying that was all they had. Others sent in more than $100. Individuals often sent contributions anonymously, saying only "from a friend." Corporations like John Hancock Insurance contributed as well. "I think the response to my appeal through the pages of the *Telegram-Gazette* was wonderful," Smith told a reporter. "I knew that Major Taylor's friends would quickly rally to his aid, if asked. Christmas has been brightened for the man who one time was Worcester's champion bicycle rider . . . I thank all those whose kind and charitable hearts are helping Major Taylor through a critical period."

A reporter eloquently spelled out the turn of events:

> *The black man, racing against white for large purses, beating his rivals, fighting combinations of race against race all over the world, wrote his name in flaming letters high in the sky of sportsmanship. None ever shone brighter. . . . At 47 years of age, an insidious grippe laid hold of the fame that no human was able to conquer and today those bronze legs, which were sculptured in Paris and pictured all over the world, and which were always pushing to the front, are hardly able to carry their master.*

Caring locals responded. A steady stream of letters and checks arrived at Smith's home, addressed to Smith's wife who oversaw the fund, including one from George Baker, an avid fan of Taylor's:

> *Having arrived at that time of life when I find myself more and more inclined to reminisce, the letter from your distinguished husband which appeared in this morning's Telegram, relating to Maj. Taylor brought to mind the many times I had seen the Major perform so brilliantly along with Eddie Bald and Tom Cooper—all stars of the day. Eddie Bald was from my hometown and well do I remember the brilliancy of these two performers—unquestionably the best in the world. I am highly sorry that the Major finds himself in an unfortunate position, and I am pleased to add my bit to the total. Please be assured this goes forward with every good wish—plus.*

> *George W. Baker.*

Throughout his life, Taylor had given generously to his church, community, and friends. He had given tenants breaks on rent when they couldn't make ends meet. He had even donated money to those who had previously abused and persecuted him. In 1906 when the ground underneath San Francisco—the city where he had been denied meals and lodging—imploded in a colossal magnitude 7.8 earthquake, Taylor wired a sizable sum of cash to its suffering citizens.

His inclination to give emanated from decades spent poring over the Scriptures, no doubt pausing on the verses of Matthew that dealt with helping the needy: "For I was hungry, and you gave Me something to eat; I was thirsty, and you gave Me drink; I was a stranger, and you invited Me in; I was naked, and you clothed Me; I was sick, and you visited Me . . ."

Now the former giver was one of them, the needy. Taylor had always lived his life under the central teachings of Jesus, the ethic of reciprocity: "Do onto others as you would have done unto you" and "love your neighbor as you would love yourself." The people of Worcester knew this about him and responded in kind with their letters.

From black and white, young and old, financial and moral support arrived—probably even from those who, decades before, had tried barring him from buying a home in town. The fund grew from $250 to $1,000.

Tracking Taylor down for comment on the fund, a reporter snapped one of the last photos of him, skillfully capturing all the pathos of the moment. He stood up against a building wearing a thick overcoat, crisp tie, and a black bowler hat. His face looked stern and solemn, blending in with the dark sky. His eyes hung suspended in space, gazing past the camera, as if he were hoping to catch a glimpse of the past off in the distance. There, in the town that sheltered him from the racial storm that continued to tear the nation apart, Taylor was trapped in a metaphor for his new life.

At forty-seven years old, he was afraid and empty. Despite the good wishes of his community, much of his money was gone. And with his waning health, the prospects for earning it back were slim. For a proud man who once stood on the highest pedestal in sport, relying on others spawned feelings of hopelessness.

One British journalist stated that in Taylor's younger days, "his humiliation was his fuel." But now there was no going back. "Please thank all my friends who have worked so hard to aid me," Taylor humbly told a reporter. "I'm in need of rest; wish all my friends a Merry Christmas. I feel all right," he continued, his voice fading, weakening, then withering down to a whisper, "but I am badly in need of rest and must be quiet at all times. It is a wonderful thing to have friends come to your support in a time of need; I cannot say enough to thank them."

The reporter for the *Worcester Telegram*, a paper that had played an important role in propagating Taylor's spectacular career, closed his piece with harsh truisms. "The years have a trick of crowding a man . . . what does Christmas hold for Major Taylor but memories which serve but to make today seem an *empty* thing? The whirlwind has lost its force, illness has left its mark and the years are piling in on him."

Behind closed doors, his story got no brighter. The financial strain had taken a toll on his marriage and his relationship with his daughter Sydney who, by 1926, was a bright twenty-two-year-old. To help out, Daisy reluctantly took a job as a seamstress at a drapery store in town. But their problems were not entirely financial. Sometime after Sydney's birth, Daisy had a miscarriage. From then on, Sydney believed that her father wished he had a son to carry on his racing legacy. As Daisy and Sydney grew closer, Major felt isolated. He had always been pleasant to everyone in town; ninety-five-year-old Worcester resident Francis Jesse Owens remembered shaking hands with Taylor—"the neatest dresser you have ever seen"—when he was a seventeen-year-old janitor. He'd received a gentle pat on the back and heard him say, "Keep up the good work, you're a good kid." But at home, Taylor was occasionally aloof and bristling.

Early in his career, perhaps out of necessity, he had often ignored the differences between him and his white opponents. Outwardly at least, he had developed a thick skin to their insults. Even after he had been nearly choked to death by William Becker in 1897, Taylor remained virtually mute, hoping the racism and all the talk of racism in the press would just go away. "Major Taylor," a reporter wrote shortly after the incident, "does not appear a critic of anything."

But at the turn of the century, there was no way to ignore the harsh realities. Instead of addressing these issues head on—which would have brought on other problems—Taylor had internalized and suppressed them. When those feelings surfaced after his retirement, the results were occasionally dour. Major, Sydney believed, was disappointed that she was born with his dark skin instead of Daisy's lighter complexion. At times, he even pulled her hat down over her eyes as she walked through town, perhaps not wanting to expose her dark face to the same "monster prejudice" he had endured. "Even though he loved his country and his race, I don't think he was proud to be a negro," Sydney told author Andrew Ritchie. "I always resented the fact that he didn't want me to be dark."

The proud family had become further divided in the early twenties when Major began piecing together his self-published autobiography, *The Fastest Bicycle Rider in the World*. Taylor spent hour after hour arched over his typewriter, poring over reams of old newspaper clippings, reliving his glory days. Daisy preferred to focus on the present and the uncertain future. "I don't think her heart was really in it," Sydney told Ritchie. "Her whole regime was upset because the dining room was full of papers and the typist, a white woman, was there all day. Her whole house was in disarray and she would say, 'we'll never get through.'"

Nearly every day for six long years came the tapping of typewriter keys and the swishing sound of crumpled, error-filled papers hitting the wastebasket in Taylor's writing room. In her bedroom, Daisy, who was obsessed with her appearance and would not leave her room until she was meticulously clothed and groomed, had listened to the repetitive sounds as she brushed and braided her long black hair. With each tap, they grew further apart.

Taylor pressed on without full support of his family or a publishing firm to help with research, marketing, editing, translators, moral support, or money. Considering the monumental task he faced—gathering thousands of articles from dozens of countries in myriad languages spanning decades, then trying to put them all together chronologically—it's a miracle he ever finished. Even today with modern technology and private companies that help would-be authors, self-publishing is difficult. But in the 1920s, without a computer, writing software, or the Internet for research, cobbling together his life story was an arduous, marathon undertaking. "It is the biggest job I ever tackled," he told Robert Coquelle in a letter asking for his help.

But Taylor had been a maverick since early childhood—getting his first job among whites during the Jim Crow era, racing at the highest level against an all-white peloton, refusing to race on Sunday despite substantial monetary inducement, buying a home in an all-white neighborhood, and now writing a book without the backing of an established publishing firm.

For better or worse, he finally completed his work late in 1928. How many copies he sold is unknown. "I don't think he made out good," said Francis Jesse Owens, "because we really hit hard times when the Depression hit in 1929." Sydney recalled him traveling tirelessly around New England, New York, and Pittsburgh proudly pedaling his memoirs. One report had him sitting in the stands at a Madison Square Garden six-day race impeccably dressed with a white straw hat and a cane, discussing his book with a pack of awestruck riders. All this suggests that he must have enjoyed at least enough success to cover the cost of traveling, printing, and marketing, and perhaps some profit.

Some of those who paid $3.50 to buy his 431-page memoir would have been disappointed. The book is long, repetitious, and chronologically jumbled. Despite frequent racism, Taylor's career had been filled with moments of incredible excitement and levity. Yet his text, for the most part, lacks humor. As well, he had a hard time pacing himself, often announcing the results of a big race before allowing for any dramatic buildup. He also relied heavily on the quoted words of others and overwhelmed the pages with his racing conquests without revealing the true color and personality of those who surrounded him. This is unfortunate because the people who were part of his life, both good and bad, were some of the most colorful of the era. Even Daisy was rarely mentioned. When she was, perhaps because they were already having marital problems, he referred to her as "my wife."

But without his dauntless determination and fighting spirit, the dramatic life story of this pioneering black man—and the grip his sport had on the nation and the world—likely would have remained untold. And though he struggled for the right words that would appeal to the masses, the book is loaded with valuable messages about faith, kindness, sportsmanship, and belief in the importance of being a good neighbor. Perhaps the most important attribute Taylor held—and one that sprang forth from the book's many pages—was one of forgiveness. The book, wrote cycling historian Robert Smith, "is remarkable for the absence of bitterness against the men who treated him so unfairly."

The final weeks of the Roaring Twenties rolled in with heavy black clouds. An air of uneasiness hung over Worcester. The city and the nation had enjoyed unprecedented growth and prosperity, but like most extended parties, a biting hangover—this time in the form of the Great Depression—awaited. It's dark morning would soon rise.

Inside their modest rented apartment on Blossom Street, Daisy and Major slept in separate beds, foretelling the end. Their initial courtship, the "royal honeymoon" in Australia, the love letters from Paris and Rome, had become faint memories. In recent years, their marriage had been held together by the threads of their strict religious beliefs. But with nothing but fading memories, they each went their own ways. Dejected, Daisy pushed west to New York, never to be heard from again. Humbled, Major rushed headlong into the unknown, pausing in New York before journeying west to Chicago, taking his books and what few possessions he had with him. For the once-loving couple who had been feted, praised, and admired in countries all over the world, there would be no roads leading back to Worcester.

EPILOGUE

The men who had surrounded Taylor during his epic reign had dispersed. On a cool day in 1929, Taylor drove down a New York road, looking up at a canopy of sycamore trees arching overhead. From his room inside the Hotel Dauphin, Birdie Munger looked out his window like an expectant father. A successful inventor and automotive executive, the sixty-six-year-old former bike racer was winding down in his last days of life. Despite his achievements in the fastest-growing industry in history, in his waning days, Munger's mind often drifted back to another place and time. He had followed Taylor's career both here and abroad, and though the automobile had provided him a good living, it had also separated him from his good friend.

He and Taylor had grown up in those enterprising years wedged between the horse and the automobile, a time when the bicycle had become a quintessential part of the great American way of life. Through trial and tribulation, the machine had become a part of them, a bond even old age couldn't erase. As simple as they may seem today, there was something special about those early days of the bicycle. Nearly all writers spoke of this at length. "Cycle tracks," wrote H. G. Wells, "will abound in utopia." And Munger, during his racing and manufacturing days, and later as Taylor's mentor, manager, prophet, and confidant, had been at the forefront of it all. He had moved into the automotive age because profit dictated he do so, yet it was those days with his protégé and around the sport he loved most that had shaped him and produced his fondest memories. "It was in our blood," wrote auto executive Charles Sinsabaugh, one of Munger's friends and former race reporter for the *Chicago Daily News*. The precise details of their last meeting are unrecorded, but a likely scene can be produced.

With thinning hair and arching back, Munger cinched his front door open and stared out. Taylor hobbled inside. The two old racetrackers embraced, then retreated to Munger's study.

Taylor had come west seeking words of wisdom on his book from his former advisor. He laid a pile of old newspaper clippings on a large table. As they had atop Munger's Indianapolis bachelor pad in the early '90s, the two talked bike racing for hours. A good deal of laughter was followed by silence and obvious moments of reflection.

As night fell, shortly before departing, Taylor reached for a large bag and spilled its contents on the table. Munger's face glowed as he ran his eyes over a series of old photos of him and Taylor, and the shops, like Hay & Willits, that once rimmed "bicycle row" in Indianapolis. There were surely photos of the old Newby oval where each of them had won races, near the area now bristling with the cars of the Indianapolis 500. Taylor flipped open his book and handed it to Munger. Munger read Taylor's dedication page:

> *To My True Friend and Advisor, Louis D. Munger:*
>
> *Whose confidence in me made possible my youthful opportunities for riding. Mr. Munger prophesized that one day he would make me the fastest bicycle rider in the world and lived to see his prophecy come true.*

Knowing he had played a significant role in one of America's greatest sport stories, Munger had difficulty containing himself. All the reminiscing stoked emotions that had lain dormant in the aged auto executive. The benevolent white man who saw special qualities in Taylor, when others were calling him a useless little pickaninny, broke down. Taylor joined him. In the adjoining room, Munger's wife, Harriet, must have felt the heavy air of emotion. Taylor gathered his belongings.

Late that night, Munger escorted Taylor to his front door and uttered his last good-byes. From his window, he watched the stiff form of his good friend disappear into the night.

A few short months later, in the waning days of the Roaring Twenties, Louis D. Munger, a man with the heart of a lion and the soul of a saint, passed into history. At some unknown place and time, in the fog that was his last years of life, Taylor read the news with grief.

After a successful racing career, Floyd MacFarland, Taylor's chief antagonist, became manager of the Vailsburg's Track in Newark, New Jersey. Vailsburg became the epicenter of American track racing, continually drawing large crowds throughout the 1910s while many others shuttered down. During winters he ventured overseas, promoting six-day races in Paris, Brussels, Berlin, and Vienna.

But MacFarland, the man who had tried to knock Taylor out of the sport, remained a controversial and pugnacious figure to the end. On an April morning in 1915, he became agitated with a man named David Lantenberg, who was setting up billboards along the rail of the Vailsburg Track.

Separated by over a half foot in height, the two men went at it jaw to chest. Realizing he was outmatched physically and orally, Lantenberg turned around and resumed screwing his sign into the wood board. When he felt a long, clawlike hand grasping his arm, Lantenberg spun around rapidly— screwdriver still in hand.

For Floyd MacFarland, life ended with the sight of Vailsburg's wood track and the sharp tip of a screwdriver, the loud angry shriek of Lantenberg's voice, the smell of wood shavings, and the searing pain of metal piercing his neck, sliding through his skull and into his brain. As MacFarland collapsed senseless to the ground and the dreadful cacophony of his large body thumped on the wood surface, some witnesses looked away as blood and matter spewed forth. Others rushed to his aid, including a grief-stricken Lantenberg. At the hospital, MacFarland was pronounced dead and Lantenberg, who never meant to kill him, charged with murder.

Papers all over the country carried the shocking front-page news. Thousands of people came to say farewell to MacFarland at the home of Frank Kramer, by then a legendary figure at the Vailsburg Track. Eighty-five floral arrangements were received, requiring three horse-drawn wagons to carry them to the cemetery. "He was a villain," admitted Hugh McIntosh, the man who escorted him out of Australia, "but a likeable one." Nearly every rider past and present was there.

There were no reports of Taylor being one of them.

William Brady was lying supine in a hospital bed when someone handed him the phone. With his legs in plaster casts, the longtime "ticker-fiend" learned that the stock market had, as he put it, "laid an egg." In no time, the fortune he had earned managing boxing, Broadway plays, and bike racing was gone. But having lived through the 1890s depression, he was able to take it all in stride. "I've seen too many depressions," he reasoned, "both Class A and Class B, to get brash about them."

Brady had lost his investments but not his knack for spotting successful ventures. One day, a desperate man named Elmer Rice handed him a tired manuscript that had been rejected by every manager in New York. Brady loved it, then somehow scraped together $6,000 to buy the rights to the play and movie. That tragic story called *Street Scene* won a Pulitzer Prize, cementing his place as America's most successful Broadway producer. It also reminded Americans of his uncanny knack for uncovering hidden success in a story or a person that others couldn't see—a talent gleaned from his early sporting days.

At his wife's, actress Grace George, urging, Brady had reluctantly quit pugilism and race promoting around the time Taylor gave up the American racing circuit in the early 1900s. He now passed time with celebrities like Milton Berle, Helen Hays, and David Warfield. But Brady was an anachronism who often eschewed modernity. With his doctor's blessing, he disposed of his automobile, preferring instead to walk or ride down the avenue where Manhattan Beach Track once teemed with howling racing fans. He had been caught up in the turn-of-the-century bike racing era; "A champion streaking round the track hunkered over on his wheel in one of them old-time races," he wrote in his second autobiography, "was the epitome of human speed." The two-person version of the six-day race that he created—now universally called "Madison's"—was still going strong, attracting 150,000 fans in the late '20s, the largest crowds for any event in the Garden's long history.

But Brady preferred the days of old when men like Taylor rode for six days nearly nonstop in his first professional race. "Major Taylor," he liked to tell reporters, "is the greatest rider on earth." He even ripped on his own creation. "Nobody has a better right to run a thing down," he wrote of the tamer two-person race, "than the fellow who invented it."

Whenever he could sneak away from his latest play, Brady would slip into the new Madison Square Garden and bounce around with happy abandon, tossing primes at the new crop of riders. Alongside his friends and fellow bike-racing fans Bing Crosby, Mary Pickford, and Douglas

Fairbanks, Brady often reminisced as he sipped his rye. "I remember when cigarette packages carried pictures of bike racers right up along with my musical-comedy stars and baseball heroes." Though his life had become devoted to the theater, he was proud of his days in the sport. "We left our mark on the business," he recalled, as the smoke from his cigar ringed out his window and onto Broadway. On a January day in 1950, the old raconteur would see his last sunset at the age of eighty-six, having indeed left his mark on three of America's most popular pastimes—and on one of its greatest sports legends.

The press never allowed Arthur Zimmerman to live down his racing days. Nor did he want them to. A prosperous businessman in retirement, sinking his six-figure racing fortune into successful New Jersey hotels, Zimmerman had a hard time staying away from the racetrack. Though he had retired and then returned to racing many times, his official retirement after a mid-'90s race in Paris was met with universal remorse. "Zimmerman's retirement," wrote one East Coast reporter years later, "was regretted just as much as the Babe's departure from baseball."

Whenever Brady or other race promoters needed an attendance boost for an event, he'd gladly show up to fire off the pistol, fine-tailored suit draped over his shoulders. Fans and reporters would flock to the track and wax nostalgic with "King Arthur," reminiscing about the early days of bike racing. "Just as Babe Ruth was the idol of the baseball fans and Bobby Jones of the golf followers," one writer remembered, "Zimmie was the favorite of the racetrack patrons."

For young riders like Taylor, Zimmerman was the sun around which all things had revolved. Taylor constantly measured his performances and his sportsmanship to Zimmie's, as did the press. Zimmerman stood tall as an ideal role model from that moment they first met when Taylor proclaimed himself to be the proudest boy in the world. With each season, a new batch of riders, hoping to emulate him and his friend the Flying Negro, came up through the ranks. With or without an invitation from promoters, Zimmerman—suffering from rheumatism in his declining years—was known to hobble up to track aprons, gazing out at the young riders, and watching as the wheels of his sport rolled on without him. He was, Taylor cooed, "the hero of all boyhood, as well as my own, ever since I was able to read the newspaper."

Even the ground he raced on was immortalized. When a Miami, Florida, developer learned that his golf course was set to cut through the very ground where the Great Zimmerman once raced, he wouldn't allow his workers to destroy the track.

On a breezy October day in 1936 while visiting friends in Atlanta, Zimmerman died of a heart attack at the age of sixty-seven. In one of the roughs on that Miami golf course, portions of the track rose up, standing as a testament to the one-time popularity of America's first international superstar.

Around the time Taylor was writing his autobiography, a disheveled man slept on a dirt floor in a garage near a bicycle track in Neuilly-sur-Seine France, where he had become a trainer. He was clutching a "magnificent" stopwatch that had been presented to him by "popular subscription" of the people of France in honor of his cycling achievements. The stopwatch represented the last real possession of this once wealthy and immensely popular man.

One had to look close to recognize this man as Edmond Jaquelin, bankrupt and grieving over the realization that he had to sell his most prized possession, awarded to him in the days surrounding Taylor's first voyage to France. His pride kept him from openly disclosing his downfall, but racing fans eventually found out and staged a benefit for him, albeit too late. The sickly, fifty-three-year-old former Triple-Crown winner died in 1931, revered by all of France, and remembered most as the one man that once bested the Great Major Taylor.

Sometime around 1930, a former bike racer named Jim Levy stirred nervously in the sales office of his Chicago Buick dealership. Prophetically, auto sales had begun dropping eight months before the stock market crash, and Levy, like most car dealers at the time, sat wondering where his next sale was going to come from. Just then, a wizened old man wearing clergy-like clothes and thick-rimmed glasses limped up to him. It was Taylor, in one of his only known sightings in Chicago before his death. After small talk about the old days—there is no indication they knew each other well—Taylor pulled out a copy of his blue-bound autobiography with a drawing of him inside a globe on the book's jacket. He splayed it open on Levy's desk. As he had at auto dealerships from Worcester to Chicago, Taylor tried talking Levy and his salesmen into buying a stack of his books to be given as a gift to car-buying customers. Levy reached for $3.50 and bought a copy or two, probably rare signed copies that, if a person could find one, sell for as much as $2000 today.

Much of Taylor's final movements remain shrouded in mystery—the kind of riddle that frustrates yet intrigues. Someday the gaps may be filled, but then again, perhaps this is the only way his final days could be drawn up.

What is known is that he descended into the same life of poverty and obscurity from which he had initially risen. Having left Worcester for Chicago in the same state as he entered it in 1895—a few dollars short of flat broke amid a depression and facing an uncertain future—Taylor watched helplessly as history repeated itself.

Taylor could not have picked a tougher time or place to sell his book, or for that matter, to sell anything. The Great Depression loomed heavy over the city. Thousands slept in parks, at rail stations, and under cardboard boxes. "I do not know how it may have been in other places . . . but in Chicago the city seemed to have died," one woman recalled. "There was something awful—abnormal—in the very stillness of the streets." Being the largest manufacturing city in the nation, Chicago was especially hard hit. By 1932, the worst year, 750,000 Chicagoans, nearly half the workforce, were unemployed. One hundred sixty thousand Chicago families received relief from private and public agencies. Soup kitchens dotted the landscape.

When Taylor took up residence at the YMCA on South Wabash Avenue, which often subsidized rents for those who couldn't pay in full, he may have been one of those receiving relief. Known as the "colored" Y and standing in a neighborhood called Bronzeville, the five-story brick building trimmed with Bedford limestone became Taylor's home for two years. It was there a few years before his arrival that Carter G. Woodson, a historian who stayed at that Wabash Y during visits to the city, formed the idea that if whites learned more about blacks, race relations would improve. In 1926, he started black history month. He chose February because it contains the birthdays of Frederick Douglass and Abraham Lincoln, plus Valentine's Day, a day of love and affection. Though he has never been properly recognized for his pioneering role, few men personify the spirit and the original meaning of Woodson's black history month better than Major Taylor.

In that respect, the Wabash YMCA, funded by Sears co-founder, Julius Rosenwald, may have been a fitting stop for Taylor. It did offer a swimming pool, music clubs, picnics, lectures, social clubs, athletic teams, health campaigns, and bible studies, perhaps ministered by Taylor. In other ways, it had to have been unsettling. For one, it was a far cry from the comforts of the seven-bedroom home, beautiful wife, and admiring neighbors he had enjoyed in his adopted town of Worcester. But more importantly, for a black man so used to mingling with whites—and one who had always judged people by their character, not their color—the segregation had to be disconcerting, even unnatural. During the Great Migration of blacks from the South to the North early in the twentieth century, formal and informal segregation limited them to only certain areas of the city. Taylor must have felt suffocated by this. One can imagine him, as he had throughout his life, testing those rigid racial divides, on occasion drifting across the artificial borders, stepping bravely into the white world, copies of his memoir tucked into his side. "In closing," wrote Taylor in his last chapter, "I wish to say that while I was sorely beset by a number of white riders in my racing days, I have also enjoyed the friendship of countless thousands of white men whom I class as my closest friends."

With the six-day race still going strong—helping to keep viable the new Chicago Stadium that had already teetered on bankruptcy—Taylor likely mixed with the diverse crowd at the endurance test that had launched his professional career. There, with more than 125,000 racegoers twice a year, he would have found the largest base of fans interested in his book. Chicago also still had outdoor racetracks. Taylor probably introduced himself to the new crop of riders, doting on them, filling their eager ears with tales of his races against Jacquelin, Bald, and MacFarland—then gently coaxing $3.50 for a copy of his book, signed by his wavering hand. "All the kids talked about Major Taylor and loved him," remembered ninety-five-year-old Worcester resident Francis Jesse Owens. "I have a soft spot in my heart for him because when we were kids and we'd be racing bicycles and a guy would say, 'Who do you think you are, Major Taylor?'" He had used a common phrase that would later be parodied by speeding motorist; "Who do you think you are, Barney Oldfield," referring to Taylor's former rival who became a famous race car driver.

But except for a few dozen cities, the colorful outdoor racing world that saw Taylor rise to superstardom had sadly atrophied. Many historians point to the automobile to explain the once-grand sport's demise. But a quick glance at horse racing brings pause to such claims. The popularity of the two sports had run parallel: wildly popular in the 1890s and early

1900s, each boasting hundreds of robust tracks, followed by near extinction, leaving only a few dozen mostly rundown tracks by the late '20s. Because of aggressive lobbying for relegalized wagering by a handful of wealthy, enterprising men, horse racing experienced tremendous growth in the 1930s and beyond.

There was mild debate in a handful of cities, including Chicago during Taylor's stay, about whether the new laws allowing pari-mutuel betting applied to bike racing as well as horse racing. With the same concerted effort, some believe, bike track racing could have remained on par with other sports in the American conscience like it has in much of Europe. At that seminal moment, and each year since, the sport needed a William Brady, James Kennedy, or "Huge Deal" McIntosh to pursue legalized betting. No such figure materialized. Much like Taylor's own life, the sport therefore withered on the vine, its legacy surviving mainly in the memory of those who lived it, or in a few rider's postmortems found only in obscure books now collecting dust in libraries or at rare auctions.

The halcyon days were over. One by one, the vibrant velodromes that had roared with millions of voices became wind-whipped and deserted. Others met with the wrecking ball, to be replaced with the distant din of baseball bats cracking, horses galloping, or industry churning. Even Madison Square Garden, a magnificent creation of the Gilded Age where Taylor's career began and Brady courted his wife, fell into disrepair. Before it was torn down and replaced in 1924, the once-grand pleasure palace was nothing but a creaky old place.

Early in 1932, Taylor weakened. In what is believed to be the last photograph ever taken of him, he looked frail and old. But he maintained his honor. Sporting a well-fitting suit, smart tie, and a handkerchief pressed neatly into his coat pocket, Taylor looked hallow-eyed at what appears to be a Bible, like a man of the cloth preparing to read from the gospel. Taylor had preached in Worcester and Australia, and the photo suggests that when strong enough, he had continued spreading the word of God to the attentive ears of Chicago's many needy, perhaps at one of the Baptist churches near the YMCA.

But as the nation sunk to its lowest ebb in the spring of 1932, Taylor faded. The excess weight he carried after his racing career and the shingles he suffered during the '20s combined to further weaken his heart and kidneys. Eventually his life contracted further, confining him to the Provident

Hospital. James Bowler, a longtime Chicago alderman and former pro racer, became Taylor's white benefactor. Bowler had competed at the 1899 World Championships in Montreal and had raced Taylor to a draw in Chicago that same year. Feeling content to have tied a rider of Taylor's stature, Bowler then refused a rematch. More than three decades later, Bowler stepped up on Taylor's behalf, bringing in the city's best surgeons. But Bowler's benevolence came too late. For a month, the doctors worked on him, probably until all money and hope was gone.

Weak, shaky, and virtually alone, Taylor was forced to live out his last days in the sterile internment of the Cook County Charity Ward. Suffering from chronic myocarditis, the resulting fatigue, shortness of breath, and severe chest pains made him a hostage in his own body. But as Taylor lay in that liminal state between life and death, he felt prepared for the afterlife. "And I have always said," he had told a reporter at the height of his career, "I'm not living for one day or two. I am going to live on and on—I am living for the eternal, and to a man who knows he is living for the eternal, and will one day face the Supreme Being, a day or two now isn't of much consequence. God has always taken care of me, and I believe he always will."

At two-thirty on the afternoon of June 21, 1932, Major Taylor's fifty-three-year-old heart failed him. In an undignified scene, the body of the world's fastest man lay in the Cook County Morgue unclaimed. Nine hundred miles south in New Orleans, his daughter Sydney received a copy of the *Chicago Defender*—the only paper to report his death—from a mysterious source. As is often the case, with age comes understanding and yearning for family reconciliation, sometimes too late. "I feel terrible he died alone in a hospital," she later said. "I didn't realize it then, because I was always mad at him. But I sure do wish I would have called him back and said, 'Daddy, I didn't understand what it must have been like to be a black man in those days.'"

Initially, she couldn't bring herself to tell Daisy. But eventually she found the words and the courage to tell her of his passing. Daisy, who would live in anonymity for another thirty-two years, could peer out her window in wistful silence, her thoughts drifting back to those glory years.

More than a week passed from the day of Taylor's death and still no one came forward to claim his remains. The county eventually arranged for his burial in an unmarked pauper's grave in the welfare section of the

Mount Glenwood Cemetery. There, a handful of anonymous men buried the man who once was the world's most popular athlete, a man who had attracted record crowds in dozens of countries on three continents. Almost no one came. The few who did watched him go under in a plain wooden box clutching a Bible, his last earthly possession, then turned their backs to his grave and walked away. Behind them, deep beneath that hardened Chicago earth, laid the memory of a lost era, and the remains of the gentle man who led it.

ACKNOWLEDGMENTS

If you're ever near the Library of Congress and have a great deal of time, ask a librarian to escort you to the bicycle history section in the Adams building. After strolling down a vast corridor, passing by better known American history, you will be ushered into a cavernous room. On its many shelves, weighed down by a century of gathering dust, rests one of the most remarkable and undertold collections of Americana. There, thick cycling periodicals like *Bearings, Cycle Age*, and *Bicycle World* line shelf after shelf. When you open their oversized pages, you will be transported back to a fascinating era, now largely lost to the world. Amid its countless photos and articles of one-time famous figures, one man's story stands out above all others. Yet as voluminous as those magazines are, only a portion of the decades-long story of Major Taylor can be found in their pages.

The rest of his epic saga was strewn in a dozen countries on four continents. It was buried in musty old books written in many languages. It has lingered in the fading memory of those few living people who'd met him or heard of him. Few life stories, in fact, require cobbling together more information from as many places as Major Taylor's. For four and a half years, we sifted through a rubric's cube of data. It was like a three-dimensional puzzle that seemed at times to have no end, a perpetual time warp of information, sometimes lacking exact dates, times, or places. Other times, it came to us in microscopic fonts needing magnifying glasses to decipher.

We scrawled our narrative's general outline from Taylor's autobiography. In line with the usual Victorian reticence about private matters, however, Taylor hid things from the public in his memoir. Our narrative was enhanced by his extensive scrapbook that, evidenced by his letters to Daisy, revealed his inner sentiments, vulnerabilities, and secrets. But had we stopped there, viewing the world from one man's eyes and remembrances, the story would still lack the depth and richness provided by the characters surrounding him. It was from Zimmerman's scrapbook that we learned of Munger's booming voice and Zimmerman's propensity to walk off stages, leaving dignitaries scrambling. In a coffee-stained seventy-year-old book—and Brady's ninety-two scrapbooks—we were entertained by his brawl with Virgil Earp and details of his love for and contributions to the sport of track racing.

Hidden in a friable sixty-year-old book from Asia, we read of Floyd MacFarland's profanity-laced tirades in front of Australian newsmen. Frank Van Straten's entertaining biography on Hugh McIntosh helped us better understand this fascinating but complex sportsman. We were able to trace the seeds of anger bubbling inside William Becker from a source that appeared in our mailbox one day. An errant phone call to a former wheelman from that era transported us into the grandstand at an early century bike race as well as any article we ever read. Much to our surprise, he also willingly shared stories that he had heard about the titillating nightlife in France. Francis Jesse Owens, a Worcester resident nearing his centenary birthday, and one of the few living people who had met Taylor, shed light on Taylor's declining days. When he spoke about the time Taylor patted him on the back and told him that he (seventeen at the time) was "a fine young boy," and then tried selling him a copy of his book, we listened.

Like Dorothy in the *Wizard of Oz*, our research led us down some bizarre roads. We will not soon forget our phone call to Bob Lommel at the Stearns County (Minnesota) Historical Society, as part of our research into the strange death of Joseph Griebler. Since Griebler was a little known rider who had raced professionally for only a few months, we expected to be greeted with a puzzled, "Joseph who?" But much to our amazement, the minute the word Griebler sprang out of our mouths, there was a resounding "yes, we know his story well." It turns out the society had a file with forty-five pages of letters and articles, enlightening everything from his prerace shoe shopping for his kids to his last dying words, "I'm awfully sick." But the eeriest part came when he told us he had just gotten off the phone—Griebler died 111 years before our call—with city council members discussing a new bicycle trail named in honor of obscure Joseph Griebler.

It was as if the story was waiting to spring forth from people's lips, to be unburied from auctions, dusted off in libraries. To get a better sense of the texture of the era, we bought (or tried to buy) everything we could get our hands on: Major Taylor buttons from an odd auction, rare Taylor trading cards from France, accordion fans and Ogden cigarettes bearing his likeness, *Wheelmen* magazines that survived the ruinous Pope fire era. Some purchases were flat-out scams—we are still waiting for that "one of a kind" Taylor trading card from someone in Finland. From an aged wheelman, we acquired a hard-to-find copy of Arthur Zimmerman's book that, among other enlightenments, placed us inside Paris's famous Café l'Esperance. We eventually amassed so much information the greatest difficulty was deciding what *not* to use; on one website alone, the phrase Major Taylor produced over two thousands hits. But many newspapers have yet to be scanned in for online searches. So we burrowed our heads under microfilm at libraries at various locations. Some trips added invaluable dimensions to the story. Philadelphia papers detailing the 1897 annual convention that attracted 50,000 fans, reportedly the largest paying crowd in American sports history, come to mind. Other trips were less revealing; one visit to a Midwestern town revealed so little new information, we had no choice but to turn it into a cycling vacation.

Except for the two years spent mired in a depression and some of his final years, Taylor's movements could be traced almost daily from all the above sources—his first race in Indianapolis, his last amateur race where reporters spoke of other more "promising" riders, the investigation into his controversial first-class stateroom on the *Kaiser Wilhelm*, the old-timers' race. On several occasions, we had to read lengthy books just to find one important tidbit or interesting quip. Others produced next to nothing; a valiant attempt to learn more about Harry Worcester Smith, Taylor's jockey friend, by reading a 1930, 1200-page tome proved to be a spectacular waste of time.

The file of those who helped us unravel Taylor's story is thick and filled with the names of people who showed incredible patience. We still remember the first time we met Keisha Tandy, the lovely young woman at the Indianapolis Museum to whom we are greatly indebted. Flanked by security guards, she led us down a long museum passageway and into a high-ceilinged room. Once inside, she handed us blue plastic protective gloves, then spilled out a treasure trove of Taylor memorabilia—letters to Daisy and Sydney, photographs, medals, scribbled notes, newspaper clippings, postcards written in graceful calligraphy. We immediately sensed an awesome responsibility as we fingered through the stack. The stack has since invaded our basements, overwhelmed our thoughts, absorbed our free time. Taylor's desire to preserve his forgotten star, combined with Keisha's kind assistance, has added color and vigor to the story.

We contacted an untold number of other museum curators, librarians, and researchers in the United States, France, Italy, Belgium, Canada, Germany, and Australia. Ian Warden, one of our Australian researchers, didn't quit until he had searched much of Australasia. What he unearthed—and the organized manner in which he delivered it—helped us bring to life two divergent years in Taylor's career: the extreme highs of his "royal honeymoon" year (1903), to the darkness and depression that began the following year. Ian became so excited by the story, he later wrote a five-page article on Major Taylor that appeared in an Australian paper. In a story like Taylor's that played out in dozens of countries, readings came to us not only in varied national languages but also in regional and era-specific tongues. We wish to thank our translators Pat Choffrut and Christine Schoettler who together are fluent in many languages. They helped us translate those idiolects and patois that have long since faded from our vocabularies. With regularity, Bonnie Coles at the Library of Congress foraged through a pile of papers that aided us greatly. Though he never showed it, George Labonte, chief librarian at the Worcester Public Library, must have grown weary of our never-ending requests for additional newspaper clippings.

Our local librarians in Excelsior, Minnesota, a quaint village overlooking Lake Minnetonka, remained patient amid an assortment of strange requests. Carla Zimmerman (not related) at the Monmouth (New Jersey) Historical Society dusted off Arthur Zimmerman's scrapbook, allowing us to paint a portrait of his dawn-age racing exploits and his singular contribution to Taylor's career. While making us laugh, Richard Ruenhke, chief librarian in Ottumwa, Iowa, sent us gads of articles on races in and the history of Ottumwa in the 1890s. Somewhere in the middle of it all sat articles on the brothels that stretched from one end of town to the other, forever altering our belief in the sleepy history of our neighboring state. Bob Williams, track director at the National Sports Center Velodrome in Blaine, Minnesota, shared his technical knowledge of track racing. Special thanks to Florence Christenson and Harold Schroeder, our long time assistants who helped with every facet of the book.

Linda McShannock of the Minnesota Historical Society and Ericka Mason Osen, Historic Clothing Coordinator at the Conner Prairie Museum in Fisher, Indiana, helped us with the Victorian-era clothing: Daisy's velvet walking suits, Taylor's pleated gambler suits, Zimmerman's gabardine shirts. Vince Menci at the United States Bicycling Hall of Fame introduced us to Jack Visceo. Only 104 years young when we interviewed him, Jack was living proof that cyclists really are the fittest athletes in the world. Through many contacts he developed over his long life, this honorary hall-of-famer helped fill in some holes.

Some of the most valuable insight came from the efforts of people we never met. It's not possible to express enough thanks to those nameless people who scanned hundreds of millions of newspapers pages into websites like the *Brooklyn Daily Eagle* (1842–1902), *New York Times* (1789–present), *Boston Daily Globe, Washington Post, Atlanta Constitution, Chicago Times, Newspaper Archives* (1607–present)—a website with 7,402 different newspapers—and *Geneology.com* (1640–present). Because of them, the information a historian can find in a few days would have taken years of painstaking research a few decades ago. We also thank our parents, Cyril and Madonna Kerber, for introducing the pleasures of reading to us at an early age. Our love for the written word began there.

It takes a prescient individual with a unique ability to see significance in obscure biographies. Perhaps our greatest reverence is owed to two such individuals, our literary agent, John Willig, and our editor, Holly Rubino. Possessed with great tenacity, John expertly got us a book deal with one of the fastest growing publishers in the United States. Holly saw in the contours of this story what it could be, and helped us get it there. We cannot thank her enough for doing so while simultaneously preserving our voice.

Our final thanks goes to Arthur Zimmerman for treating Taylor as an equal in an era lacking egalitarianism; Victor Breyer and Hugh McIntosh, for their contributions to Taylor's career and our favorite sport; William Brady, for sticking up for Taylor and for making us laugh until no further sound came out; Birdie Munger, for his kind heart and color-blind eyes, seeing qualities in a young Taylor no one else could; and

Andrew Ritchie, Taylor's first biographer, who spent years researching and writing about Taylor in a professional and chronologically correct style. And of course we thank Major Taylor, not only for leaving a traceable imprint but for leading a life of unparalleled sportsmanship, resoluteness, and transcendence in a world without equality for all. You have not been forgotten.

NOTES

A word on sources: We made every attempt to keep this book as historically accurate as possible (the sourcing alone took nearly a year) while at the same time providing a desirable reading experience. To this end, we scoured through thousands of documents from hundreds of different sources. The majority of the scenes we described in this book came from multiple sources where complete publishing information—the names and dates of the newspaper, magazine, or book—was available to us. But a small percentage of our sources, mostly newspaper clippings in Taylor's scrapbook held at the Indianapolis State Museum, were undated and/or unnamed. Others were dated, but the writer did not specify the date for the scene he/she was referring to—a 1926 article describing the time Taylor was pulled over by French police sometime in 1901 comes to mind. In most cases, we were able to uncover these hidden dates through other corroborating newspaper articles. In those instances when we were unable to corroborate the dates of a given scene, we placed the event in the chronological order that we, having researched Major Taylor's life for nearly a half decade, believe them to have taken place. Also, it should be noted that since we had no videos to aid in our race descriptions, we relied on published reports from various reporters covering the races. Because it is very difficult to write a play-by-play description of a race in which men are traveling at forty-plus miles per hour, these reports occasionally conflicted. Our descriptions reflect these disparate reports. Portions of Taylor's scrapbook were obtained from microfilm held at the University of Pittsburgh Library. We have used the abbreviation

UASP (unidentified articles scrapbook Pittsburgh) to annotate those sources obtained there. Finally, there were periods during Taylor's life that were not heavily reported on, especially 1905 to 1906 and some of his final years. In piecing these periods together, we did our best with what we had to work with.

Preface

xi. "Major Taylor Carnival trains" *Cycle Age*: May, 1901; Unidentified Australian newspaper clipping, Major Taylor scrapbook: Indianapolis History Museum.

xi. Four continents: North America, Europe, Australia, and Asia.

xi. Major Taylor billboards: Major Taylor autobiography, 9. 142.

xi. crowd marching to Taylor's hotel: *Andrew Ritchie, Out of the Shadows, A Biographical History of African American Athletes*, edited by David Wiggins, p. 31.

xi. largest throng to witness a sporting event: *Brooklyn Daily Eagle* August 9, 1897; *Baltimore Sun*, August 10, 1897

xi. fifty thousand people watched him race: *Worcester Telegram* May 10, 1896; *Baltimore Sun*, August 10, 1897; The Flying Negro Major Taylor by Robert Coquille, *La Vie Grand Air*, March 19, 1901 pp. 130-131.

xi. *Sporting Globe*, August 12, 1939.

xi. thousands mobbed tracks just to watch his workouts: *The Fastest Bicycle Rider in the World: The Story of a Colored Boy's Indomitable Courage and Success Against Great Odd, An Autobiography* by Marshall W. "Major" Taylor p.86; *Chicago Daily Tribune*, May 16, 1901.

xi. Taylor denied access to meals, restaurants, hotels, and sleeping in horse stables: *The Columbus Enquirer*, May 9, 1907; *Syracuse Standard*, November 4, 1898; *The Daily Northwestern*, March 16, 1901; *Cycle Age*, October 6, 1898; *Brooklyn Daily Eagle*, August 2, 1901; *Worcester Telegram*, August 2, 1901; *Boston Daily Globe*, August 2, 1901; *The Lexington Herald*, April 24, 1907.

xii. New York Times called the most talked about in sport: *New York Times*: Gossip of the Cycler's; "The Negro in Racing" October 3, 1897

xii. Virgil Earp in cow town: William A Brady, The Showman (Curtis Publishing, 1936-37) p. 90, 91, 92, 93

xii. he traveled more than two hundred thousand grueling miles: The Extraordinary Career of a Bicycle Racer by Andrew Ritchie p. 217

xii. handicaps as far back as three-hundred fifty yards: The Fastest Bicycle Rider in the World; The Story of a Colored Boys Indomitable Courage and Success Against Great Odd; An Autobiography by Marshall W. "Major"Taylor p. 292

xii. Most heavily advertised man in Europe: *Worcester Telegram*, April 8, 1901; *Boston Globe*, April 7, 1901.

xii. Talked about in newspapers and cafes as often as presidents of countries: *Cycle Age* April 14, 1901; *La Vie Grand Air* March 10, 1901, pp. 130-131; Unidentified French article May 1901, *Cycler's News* June 4, 1901

xii. Captured more attention than one of the world's richest citizens: *Chicago Daily Tribune*, June 29, 1901.

Chapter 1

3. Later described as polished ebony: *Brooklyn Daily Eagle* August 7, 1897

3. Twelve of the first twenty-two Kentucky derbies: Joe Drape, Black Maestro (Harpers Collins 2006) p. 27.

4. Born November 26th, 1878: Major Taylor, The Fastest Bicycle rider in the World Autobiography (Wormly Publishing 1928) p. 1.

4. "All we had was just what we needed…" *Sydney Daily Telegraph*, January 7, 1903; quoting *New South Wales Baptist* article "Thirty-thousand Dollars for Conscience Sake"

4. Introduction to Daniel Southard: Major Taylor, Autobiography p.1.

4. Private tutor: Andrew Ritchie, The Extraordinary Career of a Champion Bicycle Racer Interview Sydney Taylor Brown (John Hopkins 1988) p. 15.

4. Siblings educated by Milton Lewis: *The Freeman*, July 30, 1904.

5. "boneshakers, hobby horses, velocipedes" *The Evening Bulletin*, February 7, 1896.

5. Original meaning of the term teamsters: www.answers.com DL December 6, 2006.

5. Ohio legislation: Robert Smith, Social History (American Heritage Press) p. 183.

5. Jersey City order: Ibid p. 183.

5. Illinois legislature: Ibid p. 184.

6. Boston and Hartford: Ibid p. 49.

6. "For some reason the equine mind has a distinct aversion to motion" *Brooklyn Daily Eagle* May 29, 1883.

6. "He is not a pedestrian and cannot be catalogued as a horse" Ibid.

6. "the most powerful athletic group in the world" What Bicyclist have Done: *New York Times* September 11, 1892.

7. "Death by Wheel" http//moonrider.journalspace.com DL September 29, 2006.

7. Get a bicycle, you will not regret it if you live" www.quotegarden.com DL April 27, 2007.

8. "I dropped from the happy life of a millionaire kid: Major Taylor autobiography p. 2.

8. "bicycle row": Flyman's Handbook of Indianapolis, Max R. Hyman, Editor, M. R. Hyman Co., 1897, p. 378.

9. "My eyes nearly popped out of my head: Major Taylor autobiography p. 2.

9. I spent more time fondling that medal: Ibid p. 2.

9. I know you can't go the full distance: Ibid p. 3.

10. It gave me a fresh start: Ibid p. 3.

10. H.T. Hearshey's: Ibid p. 5.

10. Michaux Club: www.victorianstation.com DL June 29, 2006.

11. John D Rockefeller thirty-eight bikes: *Newark Sunday Advocate* June 9, 1895.

11. Riding academies replaced by bicycles: Joseph B. Bishop, *New York Evening Post*, June 20, 1896.

11. "why I feel as if I had never known my mother until…" Ibid June 9, 1895.

11. 1893 first year more bikes than horses: *The Standard*, April 4, 1893.

12. One third of all patents: "Major Taylor, Colonel Pope, and the General Commotion over Bikes," *The Ledger*, Spring 2001.

12. "one of much larger importance than all the victories and defeats of Napoleon." *New York Tribune*: 1895, quoted in Fred C Kelly, article "The Great Bicycle Craze: American," *Heritage Magazine*: December 8, 1956.

12. "It is pleasant to read in our livery trade…" *New York Times* August 28, 1898.

Chapter 2

13. Birdie Munger born in Iowa 1863: *Boston Globe*: November 7, 1885.

13. Munger accident: *Boston Globe*: October 29, 1885.

14. "Western Flyer" *San Antonio Daily Light* August 24, 1893.

14. "he left after his voice" Unidentified clipping: Arthur Zimmerman scrapbook, Monmouth County Historical Society Freehold, NJ.

14. Munger Cycle Manufacturing Company: *Newark Daily Advocate* June 27, 1896.

14. "The Munger" *Bearings* Advertisement, date unknown.

14. "Munger lived, ate, talked, slept and breathed bicycles" Andrew Ritchie; The Extraordinary Career of a Champion Bicycle Racer (John Hopkins) p. 23.

16. "pickaninny" *Chicago Daily Tribune*: May 4, 1898.

16. No darkey had ever amounted to a pinch of snuff": *Bearings*, July 1, 1897.

17. "We will bleach you and make you white": UASP.

17. "Its effect was ludicrous": *The Daily Republican*, August 2, 1901.

18. "he was as faithful and conscientious about the servile…" *Newark Daily Advocate* August 14, 1900.

18. "Mr. Munger became closer and closer attached to me…" Major Taylor Autobiography p. 13.

18. "took to Taylor as a duck takes to water": *The Sunday Herald Syracuse*, August 22, 1897

18. Taylor first meeting Arthur Zimmerman: Major Taylor autobiography p. 11.

19. "We are in favor of Zimmerman for president" Unidentified clipping: Arthur Zimmerman scrapbook: Monmouth Historical Society Freehold NJ.

19. June 11, 1869 birthday August Zimmerman: Zimmerman Abroad and Points on Training, John M. Erwin and A.A. Zimmerman (Blakely Printing Company 1895) p. 7.

19. "I liked it so well that I jumped into the game" Peter Nye: Hearts of Lions p. 43.

20. Twenty-nine bicycles, horses, carriages, and half dozen pianos: *New York Times* June 30th, 1893.

20. Zimmerman Raleigh stock: *Outing: Illustrated Monthly Magazine of Recreation* (1885-1906) September 22, 1893 p. 6.

20. Earnings estimate $10,000: David v. Herlihy, Bicycle (Yale University Press 2004) p. 252, sourcing *Bicycle World*, April 20, 1894 using $40,000. Authors believe this to be exaggerated and believe conservative figures are more likely.

20. "It was as if the man was mounted on rails so complete is the absence of wobbling and the semblance of effort." Victor Breyer Journalist/ Founding member L'Union Cyclist Internationale quoting French

spectator: Peter Nye; Hearts of Lions (W. W. Norton and Company 1988) p. 43.

20. "He at present runs a chance of being pictured…" Unidentified clipping, Zimmerman scrapbook, Monmouth Historical Society Freehold, NJ Echoes From Europe Column.

20. "a light warm up spin with the boys" *Harpers Weekly*, April 11, 1896 p. 286.

20. Zimmerman's scientific workouts: *Stevens Point Daily*, May 12, 1897.

21. Perhaps I can stand a little more than my share of rest: Zimmerman Scrapbook; Monmouth County Historical Association

21. "I'll go down and clean out that office if they don't set me right in the matter," Unidentified clipping, Echoes from Europe column: Zimmerman scrapbook Monmouth Historical Society Freeborn NJ.

21. "What happened to our eccentric riders, why doesn't she ask Zimmerman" Ibid.

21. "you have not only won from our athletes their praises and honor": Ibid.

21. "he was simply the best peddler of all-time" Peter Nye, Hearts of Lions (W. W. Norton and Company 1988): p. 43, quoting Victor Breyer Journalist/Founding member L'Union Cyclist Internationale.

22. Riders from as far away as South Africa: *Indianapolis Sun* August 24, 1893.

22. "a trunk full of gold and silver": unidentified clipping Arthur Zimmerman scrapbook Monmouth Historical Society, Freehold, NJ.

22. "Z" Ibid.

22. Parade route lit up with Chinese lanterns: Ibid.

22. "the town is yours": Ibid.

22. "I was always the friend of the struggling amateur": Arthur Zimmerman scrapbook Monmouth County Historical Association.

23. "He was surprised when I told him of that feat." Major Taylor Autobiography p. 11.

23. "crowds greater than turned out to greet the king" Arthur Zimmerman scrapbook: Monmouth County Historical Society, Freehold, NJ. Editor Referee July 2, 1892.

23. "I am going to make a champion out of that boy." Major Taylor autobiography p. 51.

23. "I have told Major Taylor that if he refrains." Major Taylor autobiography p. 50.

23. "Mr. Munger is an excellent advisor": Ibid p. 51.
24. "looked at thou peopled with harlequins of some other time and place" *Indianapolis Sun* August 24, 1893.
24. "It was the most ridiculous exhibition of them all": *Indianapolis Sentinel*: August 25, 1893.
24. "While on my way out to the track on errand..." Major Taylor autobiography p. 11-12.
24. "I was especially impressed with the friendliness": Ibid: p. 12.
25. "he is closely watched by hundreds of critics as if he were a favorite candidate for the derby": unidentified clipping: Monmouth County Historical Association: Arthur Zimmerman scrapbook.
25. "I think I will set a world record today boys": *Indianapolis Sentinel*, August 25, 1893: Arthur Zimmerman clipping from scrapbook Monmouth Historical Society Freehold NJ.
25. "Zimmerman shot by the grandstands like a stone from a catapult." *Indianapolis Sentinel*, August 25, 1893.
25. "They might as well have chased a locomotive" Ibid.

Chapter 3
27. "Three States steamboat en route carrying 500 passengers to the scene": Philip Dray: At the Hands of Persons Unknown: (Modern Library 2003) p. 91.
28. "My name is C.J. Miller..." Ibid p. 92.
28. "Hell fiend" Ibid P. 90.
28. "This is the man who killed my daughters... Ibid Page 91.
29. "under the circumstance however, a hanging would be acceptable." Ibid-p. 92.
29. "They were all that remained of a notorious character..." Ibid-p. 93.
29. "In Kentucky, this Christmas the favorite decoration of trees is strangled Negroes" Joe Drape: Black Maestro (William Morrow & Co.) p. 21.
30. Ida Wells-Barnett Negroes killed by whites since 1865 @ 10,000": Phillip Dray: At The Hands of Persons Unknown, p. 49.
30. "20,000 killed by Klan over four-year period": Ibid p. 49.
30. "Reach a mile high if laid one upon the other" Ibid p. 49.
30. "It was there I was first introduced to that dreadful monster prejudice" Major Taylor Autobiography p. 1.

30. "The White Caps" Phillip Dray: At the Hands of Persons Unknown; p. 143; Major Taylor autobiography p. 23.

30. "Why kill out the race by lynching when subordinancy…" *Newnan Herald & Advertiser* May 12, 1899.

30. Supreme court Judge Simeon Baldwin humanitarian policy" Phillip Dray: At the hands of Persons Unknown, p. 144.

31. "how my poor little heart would ache.." Major Taylor Autobiography p. 1.

31. "no discrimination against wheelman" *Brooklyn Daily Eagle* May 26th, 1894.

32. "whites only" *Lima Daily News* April 21, 1898.

33. "This would be a good spot for my competitors to carry out their dire threats" Major Taylor Autobiography p. 9.

34. Meeting to discuss colored cyclists: *New York Times*, October 10, 1892; *The Newark Advocate*, July 28, 1896.

34. Games of ten cent poker: Charles Sinsabaugh, *Who Me*.

34. "She made me promise I would never ride a road race again": Ibid p. 9.

35. "St. Louis Flyer" Ibid p. 7.

35. "It was the first time in my life I experienced such a reaction" Ibid p. 7

35. "he looks as thou he going to need it" Ibid p. 7.

37. "Down in my heart I felt that if I could get a even break" Ibid p. 7.

38. Taylor had spun off an unpaced mile in 2:09 on old horse track: *The Sunday Herald Syracuse* August 22, 1897.

38. "I can ride a wheel almost as fast as some of the cracks" *Newark Daily Advocate* August 14, 1900.

39. "With that little darkey" Major Taylor autobiography p. 13.

39. "He will return to this city as champion bicycle rider of America" Ibid p. 13.

Chapter 4

41. Griebler buying baby shoes prior to race: *Bearings*: August 6, 1896.

41. "I'm going to win one of the races" Ibid.

41. "poor Joe Griebler": *St. Cloud Journal*, July 30, 1896.

41. "frightful speed" *Bearings*: August 6, 1896.

42. "soft pillow-shoes, I'm awful sick": Ibid.

42. "passed him with his face set and riding like a wild man." Ibid.

42. "bicycle heart, eye, walk, face, twitch": Ibid p. 67, 69, 70, 71.

43. Taylor knowing of a dozen deaths on tracks: Major Taylor autobiography p. 421.

43. "glassy eyes": *St. Cloud Journal*, August 1, 1896.

44. "How to be plump" Reinier Beeuwkes & Rhonda Poe (Routledge Publisher).

44. He must abstain from drugs and alcohol: Major Taylor autobiography p. 308.

44. "dope fiends paradise" www.a1b2c3.com/drugs/opi003.htm DL 11/20/06.

45. 1890's, sixteen thousand newspapers Advertisements for Halls: www.bottlebooks.com/medicinf.htm History of Patent Medicines: The story of Halls Catarrh Cure: DL December 8, 2006.

45. Tom Cooper face on National Ads: *Bearings*: January 7, 1897.

45. Use of cocaine and strychnine: *The Philadelphia Inquirer*, December 11, 1898.

45. "The prevalence of the drug habit is now startling the whole civilized and uncivilized world": www.druglibrary.org The Peril of the Drug Habit p. 9 DL December 8, 2006.

45. "You have to be a masochist to suffer so much": *VeloNews*: A Permanent Addiction; Mike Schatzman May 28, 2007.

46. "The drink that relieves exhaustion": Mark Pendergrast, For God, Country and Coca Cola, The Definitive History of the Great American Soft Drink p.60. www.firehorse.com.au/addict/cocaine.html DL12/09/2006.

46. "The public was very curious to learn what Choppy Warburton handed Linton in a cup" *New York Times* June 24, 1894.

46. Choppy Warburton suspension: *Bearings* July 4, 1898.

46. Reggie McNamara "Iron Man" Ted Harper: Six Days of Madness (Pacesetter Press 1993) p. 82.

46. "Chop it off" Ibid p. 82.

47. "Only the clumsy get themselves killed": Les Woodland; *Pro-Cycling Magazine*, November 2006 article titled, "Using Your Head."

48. "Disposing of 200 yards of adhesive tape, ten gallons of witch hazel..." Ted Harper, Six Days of Madness, p. 47.

48. Thomas Edison Day incident: Ibid-p. 44, 45.

48. "Sometime riders appeared on the track, done up in bandages from head to foot" *Washington Post*: September 10, 1901.

48. Dan Pisceone death: *Peter Nye: Hearts of Lions,* (W. W. Norton & Co.1988) p. 103.

49. "spills" Author interview with Jack Visceo Honorary member Cycling Hall of Fame, January 2006.

49. "get em back on the bikes as quick as you can" Ted Harper: Six Days of Madness p. 49

49. "If you didn't ride, you didn't eat" Author's interview with Jack Visceo Honorary member Cycling Hall of Fame January 2006

49. "If spills had done it, I'd been back riding in thirty minutes..." Ted Harper, *Six Days of Madness*, p. 49.

49. Bing Crosby picking up the hospital tabs for injured riders: Peter Nye: Hearts of Lions (Norton Publisher) p. 108.

49. "I'll never forget the time I sat up operations": Ted Harper; Six Days of Madness p. 72.

50. Charles Walthour twenty eight fractures of right collarbone..." Peter Nye: Hearts of Lions p. 72.

50. "is the most dangerous sport in the entire catalogue, by the side of it football appears a game fit for juveniles only": *The Washington Post*: September 10, 1901.

50. George Leander death: Les Woodland, *Pro-Cycling Magazine*, November 2006 article "Using Your Head."

51. The fate of Harry Elkes: Ibid: *Sunday Review*, Decatur Illinois May 31, 1903.

51. "I want to ride again tonight" *New York Times*: May 31, 1903.

51. "He will someday drop from his wheel a corpse": *Boston Daily Globe*, July 30, 1901.

51. "it is the danger in the sport that makes it thrilling" *The Washington Post*: September 10, 1901.

51. "flash": Robert Smith: A Social History of the Bicycle: p. 149.

51. Cost of personal trainer valet between eighteen and thirty dollars a week. Ibid.

52. "Let us be content to applaud these few cycle stars": *Bearings*, November 18, 1897.

52. Griebler treatment for eye problems: *St. Cloud Daily Times*.

52. "a few more dollars for the kids" *St. Cloud Journal*: July 30, 1896.

52. "he was doubtless thinking of the prize money would gladden the hearts of the children at home" Ibid.

52. "Well, I expect you will see me brought back dead before two weeks are gone" Ibid.

53. Joe Griebler's mother buries other son: *St. Cloud Times*, August 1, 1896.

53. Joe Griebler is dead, you notify his wife telegram: Ibid.

53. "If I don't get killed before the end of the season I am going to quit" Ibid.

53. Albert Einstein reference: "The Noblest Invention," *Bicycle Magazine*, 2003 p. 30.

54. "The machine appears uncomplicated but the theories governing its motion are nightmarish…" Ibid-p.28.

54. It can carry ten times its own weight and uses energy more efficiently than a soaring eagle: "The Noblest Invention," *Bicycle Magazine*, 2003, p. 32.

54. "hearing the bell on the last lap is like a powerful drug" *VeloNews*: A Permanent Addiction Mike Schatzman May 28, 2007.

54. "When the spirits are low, when the day appears dark…" Arthur Conan Doyle, *Scientific American Magazine* January 18, 1896.

55. Salvators record 1:35.50 *HarpersWeekly* April 11, 1896.

Chapter 5

57. Pope Manufacturing largest employer New England: Stephen B. Goddard, Colonel Albert Pope and His American Dream Machines; (McFarland & Co.1941) p. 5.

57. huge appetite for food, wine, and women: Ibid-p. 1.

57. Address as colonel: Ibid-p. 52.

57. Captain in civil war: Ibid-p. 51.

58. self-promoter: Ibid-p. 5.

58. "giving the air a rich equine flavor" Ibid-p.72.

58. Fifty-acre Cohasset estate, Hartford penthouse, and Boston office: Ibid-p. 6.

58. 3800 high powered sales agents: Ibid-p. 113.

58. Roosevelt riding in automobile with Pope cycle secret service: Ibid p-184.

58. high school drop out: Ibid-p. 102.

58. "good roads movement" Ibid-p 1.

58. made up of 800 parts, inspected 500 times, by 24 quality control inspectors: Ibid-p 87.

58. Henry Ford reported visits Pope manufacturing: Ibid: Biographer unclear as the exact dates or purpose.

58. "If the Carnegies and Rockefellers were captains of industry" Ibid-p. 68.

58. Worcester Cycle Company: 1896 *Bearings* Advertisement.

59. largest trust in the country: *New York Times* January 17, 1896.

59. The Boyd & Lady Worcester: *New York Times* April 12, 1896.

59. The mechanical wonders of the world" Ibid.

59. "general office 45 Wall Street" Ibid.

59. "These models bare out all that was promised of them" *New York Times* January 11, 1896.

59. "speed boy" Major Taylor autobiography p. 308.

59. Taylor residing with Munger & wife at Bay State house. *Worcester Telegram*: February 21, 1898.

60. stock rise $5.00-$75.00: p. 71.

60. "The Birdie special is the fastest wheel made" *New York Times;* May 31, 1896

60. Taylor joints Albion cycling club: Major Taylor Autobiography p 16.

61. "I was pleased beyond expression…" Ibid-p. 14.

62. Famous George Street Hill climb: www.majortaylorassociation.org/events

62. "Everyone who knew him, knew he was the only guy…" Author's interview with Worcester resident Francis Jesse Owens August 10, 2006

62. Telegram Trophy Race: *Worcester Telegram* May 10, 1896

64. "I was in Worcester a short time before" Major Taylor autobiography p. 14.

64. Taylor competes Irvington-Millburn race: *New York Times* May 31, 1896

64. Black rider Simmons banned from racing: *New York Times* May 24, 1894

64. Arthur Zimmerman presence: Irvington-Milburn race: Ibid May 31, 1896

65. Ice water thrown in Taylor's face: Major Taylor autobiography p. 17.

65. Taylor finishes twenty-third: *New York Times* May 31, 1896

65. "For some of the many kindnesses he extended to me" Major Taylor autobiography p. 16.

65. Capital city track record: Ibid-p 6

66. Taylor sets track record 2:11" Ibid-p. 6.

67. As thou he knew where he was headed: Author's citation: Over his career, Taylor kept enough newspaper clippings to fill seven scrapbooks.

Custody of Indianapolis History Museum. Taylor later used these to aid in writing his extensive 432 page Autobiography.

67. Boston: Great fire of 72: www.wikipedia.org Article DL 12/20/2006.

67. Details of Pope manufacturing fire: *Boston Daily Globe*: March 13, 1896; *The Wheelman*: Number 61 November 2002.

69. "colonel pope is tired of the small dealers and makers": Robert A. Smith, *A Social History of the Bicycle*, p. 36.

69. Pay cut notices Munger manufacturing: *Brooklyn Daily Eagle* June 14 & 15 1896.

69. Pope slashes prices: *New York Times*, May 31, 1896.

70. Plessy v. Ferguson case: www.historycentral.com DL 12/18/2006.

Chapter 6

71. "Pop" www.oldandsold.com Article: William Brady-The Gambler from the West (originally published 1930) DL November 1, 2004.

71. "Alice Brady" Ibid.

71. U.S. Presidents from Grover to Cleveland: Ibid.

72. Mother named O'Keefe and a father named Brady: Ibid-p 13.

72. "kidnapping" www.americanheritage.com Richard Snow, *American Heritage Magazine*; American Characters: May 1980 DL January 24, 2006.

72. "We fought all the time on the bowery..." William A Brady: Showman p. 98.

72. "plenty of times I sat hungry..." Ibid-p. 15.

72. "whatever cash was rusteable" Ibid-p. 14.

72. "I never met the late Horatio Alger..." Ibid.

73. "I felt the west owed me and I was destined to own it" Ibid-p. 25.

73. "Including some that never existed..." Ibid-p. 30.

73. "If you couldn't starve well on occasion..." Ibid-p.43.

73. "After Dark" Edward Van Every: Brady Made History with Corbett and Jeff, International Boxing Hall of Fame Canasta NY, May 1950.

73. "It gave me such a swelled head..." William A Brady, Showman p.35.

73. "It was the worst pup I was ever sold..." Ibid-p.70.

73. "I was a upstart pigmy..." Ibid-p. 71.

73. "Under the Gaslight" Ibid-p. 72.

74. "James J. Corbett Champion of the World" Ibid-p. 98-99.

75. "deadheads" Ibid-p. *92*.

75. "the kind of voice a rattlesnake would have if it could talk" Ibid.

75. " Feminine theatre goers…" Ibid.

75. Complaints from the hatter, booksellers, watchmakers etc: Joseph B. Bishop; Editor: *New York Evening Post*, Article; Social and Economic Influence of the Bicycle: June 20, 1896.

75. Brady attempts to buy St. Louis Browns: *The Marion Daily*, June 26, 1897.

76. "was not the tariffs, not the currency, not the uncertainty of the McKinley financial position, but the bicycle" *New York Evening Post*: June 2, 1896.

76. Formation of American Cycle Racing Association and tracks they control: *The Cycle Age*, May 5, 1898.

76. Brady controlled Rochester track": UASP.

76. "Neither of these men were known to purchase a dead horse": *Minneapolis Journal*, November 16, 1897.

77. "engage" Major Taylor autobiography p.308. Unclear who took this call, William Brady or James Kennedy?

77. "Royal Suite": Williams A. Brady, Showman, p. 77.

78. "It would stir the whole of New York…" Robert Coquille French Sports Journalist as quoted in Major Taylor autobiography p. 308-309.

78. "no Irish need apply, drug abusing monkeys, violent drunken apes, white Negroes": *Harpers Weekly* www.nde.state.ne.us/SS/irish/unit DL December 22, 2006.

78. "Black or not, he was as fine and intelligent a man as ever walked" William A Brady: Showman p. 82.

79. "one of the greatest innovators in entertainment" Peter Nye: The Six Day Bicycle Races p. 30.

79. "he has sworn vengeance against everybody in connection with those acts" *New York Journal:* August 27, 1897.

79. Taylor as member of South Brooklyn Wheelman and Calumet: *New York Times:* December 6, 1896.

79. Taylor assigned number thirteen: *New York American*, July 22, 1898; *The Philadelphia Enquirer*, September 23, 1898.

79. "The training was rather rough…" *The Sunday Herald Syracuse:* August 27, 1897.

80. "Those men who were supposedly in the fast bunch" *Brooklyn Daily Eagle:* November 27th, 1896.

80. "a fine race" *New York Times*: November 27, 1896.

80. "promising" Ibid.

Chapter 7

83. The Forgotten Depression: A Look at the Causes of the 1893 Depression; http://bbrown.info/writings/html/1893.cfm DL October 4, 2004.

83. "carnivals of revenge" http://www.pbs.org/wgbh/amex/carnegie/gilded-age.html DL December 10, 2004.

84. "full dinner pail" Patricia Daniels & Stephen G Hyslop, citing President William McKinley: National Geographic Almanac of World History p.274.

84. Average American earning $345 per year: www2.pfeiffer.edu Hill House Maps & Papers DL March 29, 2006 www.e-scoutcraft.com DL April 6, 2007.

84. Popularity of lantern parades: *Bearings* May 1896.

85. "separate but equal" Plessy-Ferguson Act www.historycentral.com DL December 18, 2006.

85. "but a state of mind" *Herald Tribune* Editorial 1925 Referenced Garden of Dreams: George Kalinsky, p. 18.

86. "to get gloriously fried" William A. Brady: Showman p.232-233.

86. "Little ink stained fellow": *The Kansas City Star*, December 6, 1896.

86. "Dark Horse": *Fort Wayne Gazette*, August 25, 1901.

86. Eddie "Cannon" Bald; *Cycle Age* and *Trade Review* April 28, 1898.

86. Belmonts at six day race: *New York Times*, December 10, 1896.

87. "a runaway African" *Brooklyn Daily Eagle*: December 6, 1896.

88. "screaming themselves hoarse" Ibid.

89. Taylor defeats Eddie Bald: *New York Times*: December 6, 1896.

89. "laughed and chaffed at him" *Worcester Telegram*: December 10, 1896.

89. "looked as though he had been up all night" *Brooklyn Daily Eagle*: December 11, 1896.

90. "The star of the race thus far is Major" *Worcester Telegram*: December 10, 1896.

90. Food intake six-day races: Ted Harper; Six Days of Madness p. 40.

91. "It's just too easy" *Brooklyn Daily Eagle*: December 12, 1896.

91. "The wonder of the race is Major Taylor" *New York Times*: December 9, 1896.

92. "peevish and fretful" Unidentified clipping Major Taylor scrapbook: Indianapolis History Museum.

92. "you fellows want me to stay here until my legs drop off so you can sell it to the doctor." Ibid.

92. "I cannot go on safely for there is a man chasing me..." *Bearings*: The Crackajacks Corner by F. Ed. Spooner December 24, 1896.

92. "thin and emancipated" Ibid.

92. "he didn't care about brick and stones..." *Brooklyn Daily Eagle* December13, 1896.

92. Teddy Roosevelt, New York Police Chief: Colonel Albert Pope and his American Dream Machine Stephan Goddard (MacFarland Press) p. 98.

92. "it was nonsense. he died prematurely burned out I suppose just a month shy of ninety one." William A. Brady; Showman p. 228-229.

93. "Six Days of Madness" Ted Harper: Six Days of Madness Pacesetter Press

93. $37,000 gate receipts six-day race: *Bearings*: December 17, 1896.

93. Hotel Bartholdi meeting: *Brooklyn Daily Eagle*; December 14, 1896.

93. Payment in shining double eagles: Ibid.

94. "I still feel half starved" Ibid.

94. "swelled knees" Ibid.

94. "worked hard" Ibid.

95. "the highlight of the event was flashed in the bicycle world in the form of a veritable black diamond" *The Referee*: December 10, 1896.

95. "I feel very well considering" *Brooklyn Daily Eagle*: December 14, 1896.

95. "Major Taylor was none the worse for his ride" *New York Times*; December 14, 1896.

95. "Men and women who normally did not care for blacks..." *Bearings*; December 17, 1896.

95. "Black cyclone", "Ebony Flyer" "Black Whirlwind" "Ebony Flyer" "The Black Zimmerman" Major Taylor Autobiography: p 143.

96. Photo Taylor alongside several elite white riders: Major Taylor scrapbook; Indianapolis History Museum.

97. Taylor riding Stearns and Munger bikes: *Bearings*; December 17, 1896

98. "He is fairly modest, and not overly proud nor stuck up" Major Taylor autobiography p. 146; quoting *Erie Dispatch* article date unknown.

98. Bald slipping on resin: *New York, Times*, December 6, 1896.

Chapter 8

100. "kill his sprint." Major Taylor Autobiography p. 19.
100. "The colored boy is already making a stir" *Bearings* July 1, 1897.
100. Providence R.I. race: *Boston Globe*: July 24, 1897.
100. Taylor's mother dies: *Daily News*, July 12, 1901.
100. "was cheered to the echo by the crowd in the grandstands" *Philadelphia Record*: May 27, 1897.
100. 6000 fans Reading Pennsylvania: *Bearings*: August 12, 1897.
100. "his coming out will cause a ripple of surprise" Ibid.
100. "Taylor is one of the pluckiest little fellows of his race" *Brooklyn Daily Eagle*: August 2, 1897.
101. Eight million spectators spent $3.6 million to watch 2,916 bicycle races: Lou Dzierzak, *The Evolution of American Bicycle Racing*, p. 20.
101. One million paying fans attend bike races: *Brooklyn Daily Eagle* July 14, 1897.
102. "around fifty-thousand fans Willow Grove: Ibid: *The Baltimore Sun* August 10, 1897; *Brooklyn Daily Eagle* August 8-9, 1897.
102. Special bicycle excursion trains: *Philadelphia Record*, August 7, 1897.
102. "century rides" Ibid.
102. adding extra railcars to house thousands of bicycles at no additional charge" *The North Adams Evening Transcript*: July 18, 1897.
102. Large delegations from Omaha, Indianapolis, and Saratoga: *Brooklyn Daily Eagle* July 30, 1897; *Nebraska State Journal* August 1, 1897.
102. Supreme court justices plead: *Bearings* August 12, 1897.
102. "filled to the roof" *Brooklyn Daily Eagle*: July 28, 1897.
102. Trainers sleeping on tables and desks: *Chicago Daily Tribune*: August 6, 1897.
102. Presses broke down: *The Philadelphia Inquirer*, August 8, 1897.
102. Largest crowd for any sporting event in American History: *Brooklyn Daily Eagle*; August 9, 1897.
103. "skin covered in perspiration and shining like polished ebony" *Brooklyn Daily Eagle*; August 7, 1897.
103. "The most startling feature of the meet" *The Baltimore Sun:* August 10, 1897.
104. 100,000 cigars lit: *Bearings* August 1897.
104. "The league of the American Wheelman owned the town" *New York Times*: August 1, 1897.

104. "little Taylor the colored boy is surprising the whole country with his game riding" *Brooklyn Daily Eagle* August 2, 1897.

104. "Wheelman's night" *Philadelphia Press*; August 6, 1897; *New York Times* August 2, 1897.

104. "yes the wheelman own the town and some of them seem to think they own the earth" *Philadelphia Press*; August 7, 1897; *The Trenton Evening Times* August 2, 1897.

105. Governor's of every New England State presence: *Daily Eastern Argus*: August 19, 1897.

105. Lee Richardson cycling trick rider: Ibid: August 20, 1897.

105. "Horses and bicycles don't jibe very well" *Portland Evening Press*: August 10, 1897.

105. "The graceful young rider has captured the hearts of the fairer sex" Ibid.

105. The horseman did not take kindly to the bicycle boys" Ibid.

105. Twenty thousand fans: *Brooklyn Daily Eagle*: August 21, 1897.

106. "Being owned by the horseman who have no love for the wheelman was left in a very rough state" *Bearings*: August 26, 1897.

106. "abashedly" *Daily Eastern Argus*: August 21, 1897.

106. "Roasted the boys pretty hard" *Portland Evening Press*: August 10, 1897.

106. "The position of the Negro is a trying one…" *Bearings*: September 16, 1897.

106. "easily the rider of the day" *Brooklyn Daily Eagle*: September 11, 1897.

107. "I have a dread of injury": *Worcester Telegram*, September 20, 1897.

107. "A little more exercise might cure you": UASP.

107. "I know of no reason the boys should be against me…" Ibid.

107. "considering the length of time he has been in the game…" *Brooklyn Daily Eagle:* August 2, 1897.

108. "It's a pity that the old fogies" *The Massillon Independent*: September 10, 1896.

108. "tough as a pine knot." *The Steubenville Herald*; September 7, 1896.

108. "play to the crowd" *Bearings*: January 1897.

109. "The black cloud led the way" *Bearings:* September 16, 1897.

108. Twenty-five thousand Springfield crowd attendance: *Bearings*, September 15, 1897. **Authors believe this estimate may have been exaggerated by *Bearings*.

109. "they have threatened to injure me…" *Worcester Telegram* September 20, 1897.

109. "Taylor, Taylor" *The Daily Eastern Argus:* September 11, 1897.

110. Becker choking incident: *Boston Globe*: September 24, 1897.

111. "nearly twenty minutes" *New York Times*; October 3, 1897.

111. "I was too badly injured to start" Major Taylor autobiography p. 20.

111. "Someone ought to give him a sound thrashing": *Cleveland Gazette*, October 2, 1897.

112. "The Negro in Racing." *New York Times*; October 3, 1897.

112. "Recover the manhood he seems to have lost": *The Philadelphia Inquirer*, October 3, 1897.

112. "Becker will undoubtedly be punished with a lengthy suspension..." *Bicycling World*: October 1, 1897.

113. "to rule over the riders with a rod of iron" *Brooklyn Daily Eagle*: May 20, 1897.

113. "a mere disqualification from a race was too small a punishment..." *Naugatuck Daily News*: September 7, 1897.

113. Taylor arriving late Cleveland race: *Boston Daily Globe*, September 26, 1897; *Washington Post*, September 26, 1897.

113. "When racing men begin to kill each other": *Washington Post*, September 6, 1897.

113. Becker no suspension: *The News: Frederick Maryland*; September 25, 1897.

113. Paltry $50 fine: *Brooklyn Daily Eagle*; September 28, 1897.

113. "They were willing to identify themselves": *Philadelphia Inquirer*, October 3, 1897.

114. "I found that the color prejudice was not confined to the south..." Major Taylor Autobiography p. 20.

114. "caused more animated discussion than any event this year" New *York Times*: October 3, 1897.

114. "the southern meets would never stand his entry" *Bearings*: September 9, 1897.

114. Reference to special bicycle excursion trains: Iolanthe and Pickwick" *Bearings*; September 30, 1897.

115. "little Pete" *Bearings*: November 18, 1897.

115. "The colored boy thought discretion the better part of valor" *Boston Globe*: October 13, 1897.

115. Blacks barred from Fountain Ferry track: *Boston Globe*: October 17, 1897.

115. *Bearings* drawing criticism for including Taylor on thermometer: *Bearings*: August 19, 1897.

115. "I shall go to France, for there I can hold my own and will be thought something of maybe." *Boston Globe*: October 13, 1897.

116. Worcester Cycle Manufacturer demise: *Brooklyn Daily Eagle*, August 4, 1897, November 2, 1900.

117. "beautiful Parisian women" Arthur A. Zimmerman: Zimmerman Abroad and Points on Training; The Bicycle Girl in Paris p.40-49.

117. "Taylor Yearns For France" *New York Times*; November 17, 1897.

Chapter 9

119. "was written up in more newspapers than Teddy Roosevelt" William A Brady, The Fighting Man: p. 152.

119. "always trying to find a champion" William A. Brady, Showman p. 207.

119. "Billy Brady has always had plenty of admiration for the colored boy" *New York Journal*: August 27, 1898.

120. "the homestead" *Brooklyn Daily Eagle* May 2, 1898.

120. "Taylor will not lack proper encouragement to race…" Unidentified clipping; Major Taylor scrapbook, Indianapolis History Museum.

120. Willis Troy, trainer extraordinaire; *Brooklyn Daily Eagle* June 28, 1895.

120. "I'm out to whip the champions this season…" *Worcester Telegram* undated clipping Major Taylor scrapbook: Indianapolis History Museum.

121. Best dressed man in the peloton: *Newark Daily Advocate* July 11, 1898: Clothing description: Linda McShannock Minneapolis Historical Society, December 1, 2006.

121. Eddie Bald as lavish dresser: *Brooklyn Daily Eagle*, August 9, 1899.

121. "Camp Thunderbolt" *Brooklyn Daily Eagle* April 21, 1897.

121. "I think the change to a warmer climate will improve my health": UASP.

121. John Street Baptist Church; Reverend Hiram Conway: *Melbourne Daily Telegraph*, January 7,1903.

121. Major Taylor adult baptism: *Philadelphia Inquirer*, January 1, 1898.

122. "place where there is no mud on streets because of the high temperature" Robert A. Smith A Social History of the Bicycle p. 72 referencing: J.B. Bishop (editor of *New York Evening Post*) Article: Social and Economic Influence of the Bicycle, Forum August 1896 pp 680-689 requested HCL 12/22/06.

122. "all members who have had their teeth filled with gold or who rode bicycles" Ibid-p. 75.

122. "watchful eye, full brotherhood" *Boston Globe*: January 2, 1899.
122. "a closer communion with God" Robert Smith: A Social History of the Bicycle; p. 73.
123. Reverend John Shaw canonizes the inventor if only he knew his name." Ibid-p 73.
123. "I have the satisfaction of believing": *Melbourne Daily Telegraph*, January 3, 1903 Interview with Major Taylor.
123. "I am glad to say I am a Christian" Ibid.
124. "we have no intention of pacing a nigger," *Savannah Press*: March 19, 1898.
125. "Alright then, if you won't pace me, I'll pace you." Ibid.
125. "Mister Taylor, if you don't leave here before 48 hours you will be sorry" Ibid.
125. "White Cappers, tarred and feathered" *The Philadelphia Record:* August 8, 1897: *New York Times:* March 13, 1898: Major Taylor autobiography p. 23.
126. "Cowardly writer": UASP.
126. "Major Taylor de coon rider from de north..." *Savannah Press:* March 19, 1898.
126. "It is useless for a colored person to attempt to get along in the south" New York Reporter: Unidentified clipping: Major Taylor scrapbook Indianapolis History Museum.
126. Brady sends telegraph to Taylor: UASP.
126. Luke 6:27 King James Bible www.mybiblescripture.com DL January 23, 2007
127. "He gave the circuit chasers to understand..." *New York Journal*: August 28, 1898.
127. "must suffer with the others." Unidentified clipping Major Taylor Scrapbook; Indianapolis History Museum.
127. "To step on Brady's toes intentionally..." *New York Times*: January 8, 1950
127. "unjust discrimination" Major Taylor autobiography p.24 quoting unknown newspaper.
128. "I beg to assure the gentleman that any time the Major enters a race" Unidentified clipping: Major Taylor scrapbook: Indianapolis History Museum.

128. "the promoter who could debar a good drawing card like Major Taylor" Ibid.

128. "I am not in favor of barring Taylor…" *Philadelphia Press;* April 12, 1898.

129. "He rides so low": UASP.

129. "They can't outride me anyway": *New York American*, July 22, 1898.

129. Seven thousand fans: Ibid. *Philadelphia Press;* July 17, 1898.

129. "the idol of the meet" Ibid.

129. "Taylor, Taylor" Ibid.

130. Chairman Mott double-barreled opera glasses: *Cycle Age* July 21, 1898.

130. "The nerve of the men in doing teamwork right under the eye of the chairman" Ibid.

130. "Leave the boy alone and he will land a winner every time." Unidentified clipping Major Taylor scrapbook Indianapolis History Museum.

131. "He can beat any of them in a match race" *Cycle Age* July 21, 1901.

131. "the hero of all boyhood" Major Taylor autobiography p. 51.

131. Zimmerman near deadly case of Mexican Fever: *Cycle Age:* June 9, 1901.

131. Lack of racial prejudice Arthur Zimmerman: Major Taylor autobiography p. 12.

132. "I am very anxious to see you win the event…" Arthur Zimmerman quote; Major Taylor autobiography p. 52.

132. Jim Corbett starter for race: *Cycle Age*: July 28, 1901.

132. Papa Zimmie at race: UASP.

132. "No group of racing horse ever faced." Major Taylor autobiography p.52.

132. "crossed the tape fully ten lengths ahead of Bald, three time winner of the Championship of America" *Philadelphia Press:* July 17, 1898.

133. "Our friend Birdie Munger was right about you" Major Taylor autobiography p.53.

133. "he shared the honors with Major Taylor": *Boston Globe*: July 28, 1898.

133. "I have never seen a more happy man in my life than Arthur A. Zimmerman" Ibid.

Chapter 10

135. Brady cabled lucrative offers-of $1000 or more-to the "big four", Bald, Gardiner, McFarland and Kiser." *Worcester Telegram* Sept 20, 1897.

135. "I will match Major Taylor with any man…" *Cycle Age*: July 28, 1898.

136. "I want to race these men but they chose to ignore me entirely": *Boston Globe:* July 31, 1898.

136. "would affect him socially" Major Taylor Autobiography p. 42.

136. "race of truth" Bicycle Racing Terminology: www.amgentourofcalifornia.com DL January 27, 2007.

136. Description Brady as fighting man: The Fighting Man; William A. Brady p.45.

136. "Midget" *Brooklyn Daily Eagle:* February 20, 1897.

136. "the athletic marvel of the century" *Brooklyn Daily Eagle:* September 28, 1898.

136. "minors" *Brooklyn Daily Eagle:* April 21, 1897: *The Trenton Evening Times:* August 2, 1897.

136. "Michaels opponents laughed out loud…" William Brady: Showman p. 225.

137. "invincible" *New York Times*: December 25, 1897.

137. "guaranteed minimum of $22,500" *Cycle Age*: April 28, 1898.

137. "Take a spill off a speeding bicycle on a hardwood track…" William A. Brady Showman p. 224

137. Taylor receives Brady's telegraph ordering him to New Jersey: UASP.

137. Jim Corbett training grounds: UASP; *New York Times*, September 1898.

138. President McKinley receives Jimmy Michaels at White House: *Cycle Age*: January 1897.

138. "I dare say, no bicycle race that was ever conducted in this country…" Major Taylor autobiography p. 43.

138. "was the cutest thing they ever saw" William A Brady: Showman p. 225.

138. "made so much money and received so much adoration from the ladies his head was badly turned" Ibid.

138. Brady makes side bet with Michaels manager Dave Shafer: *The Sun:* August 28, 1898; *Brooklyn Daily Eagle*: August 30, 1898.

138. Picture bicycle accordion fans: Major Taylor autobiography p.53.

139. "I have seen enthusiast gatherings at bike tracks" Major Taylor autobiography p. 47.

139. "bounding about like a rubber ball." *The Sun:* August 28th, 1898.

139. "Taylor cried out to his pace men for more speed; but the pace was too much-all five men completely spent." *Brooklyn Daily Eagle:* August 28, 1898.

140. Michaels was hissed by the crowd: *The Decatur Review:* August 28, 1898.

140. Jersey thirteen: *New York American*, July 22, 1898.

140. "I am announcing a sweeping challenge for another match race between these two men for a purse of $10,000..." *Brooklyn Daily Eagle*: August 28, 1898; *The Sun*: August 28, 1898.

140. "The wildly popular challenge: *The Philadelphia Inquirer*, August 28, 1898.

140. "just a little present from one good sport to another" Major Taylor autobiography p. 49.

140. "we were always having a bottle of Champagne." William A. Brady Showman p. 141.

140. "Those fine sportsman who paced me..." Major Taylor autobiography p 49.

140. "I want to thank your paper": *The New York Sun*, August 1898.

140. "Was like an electric shock to many who did not believe a colored man could win." *New York Sun*: August 30, 1898.

141. "I knew I had a world-beater." Major Taylor autobiography p. 43.

141. "Coming as it did just after the unsuccessful efforts of certain race managers to debar him..." Unidentified New York newspaper reference Major Taylor autobiography p. 49.

141. T. Laing manager St. Louis Circuit City track: *Brooklyn Daily Eagle:* October 8, 1898.

141. "rebels" *Brooklyn Daily Eagle:* September 19, 1898.

142. Secret ballot: *Syracuse Standard*, November 4, 1898.

142. Meeting Trenton NJ: Formation American Racing Cyclist Union: *New York Times*: September 27, 1898: *Worcester Telegram*: September 26, 1898, *Nebraska State Journal:* September 27, 1898.

142. "the most historic day in cycling history": *Boston Globe*; September 23, 1898.

142. "anxious" Hotel operator trying to ban Taylor; *Cycle Age:* October 6, 1898.

142. New organization: American Racing Cyclist Union: *Philadelphia Press*, September 26, 1898.

142. Refused lodging twice in Connecticut: *Worcester Telegram*, September 23, 1898.

143. "busy bees" *Philadelphia Press:* July 17, 1898.

143. "It's against my religious scruples" Major Taylor autobiography p. 29.

143. Taylor winning percentage .517: *Boston Globe:* October 9, 1898.

143. Taylor beats Eddie Bald ten out of twelve times: *Cycle Age*: September 1, 1898.

143. "There are a few followers of the colored boys." *Brooklyn Daily Eagle*: September 26, 1898.

144. "It is now a case of black and white" *Boston Globe*: October 9 1898.

144. Local citizens sign paper asking Taylor entry be permitted: *Boston Globe*: October 14, 1898.

144. Taylor eating in kitchen: *Syracuse Standard*, November 4, 1898.

145. Firing of black waiter: Major Taylor autobiography p. 29-30.

145. "Where local opinion permits, there shall be racing on any day of the week" *Philadelphia Press:* July 17, 1898.

145. "But we entered into a gentlemen's agreement" Major Taylor autobiography p. 20.

146. Description Cape Girardeau incident: *The Daily Northwestern:* March 16 1901.

146. Taylor loses $10,000 in endorsements: *The Washington Post*: October 2, 1898.

146. Riders laugh at Taylor: *Syracuse Standard*, November 4, 1898.

147. Bible quote: John verse 14:27 www.mybiblescripture.com DL January 27, /2007.

147. "payment of lofty $400 fine" *Worcester Telegram:* May 28, 1898.

147. Taylor considered unofficial champion: Taylor's autobiography, p. 27.

148. "I am in a good position to comment on the relative speed…. If it were possible to make him white all the boys would gladly assist in the job." Unidentified Philadelphia newspaper comment by cyclist Howard Freeman referenced in Major Taylor autobiography p. 59-60.

148. Brady's group wanting to cash in on Sunday racing: *The Philadelphia Press*, October 19, 1898.

148. Tom Cooper 1895& 1899 American Champion: *New York Times:* August 15, 1896; *Cycle Age*: June 20, 1901.

149. "Orient; offer to pay Taylor him $500 for each world record and $10,000 if he brought the mile record under one minute thirty seconds." *New York Times* August 5, 1899; *The Star* November 16, 1898; Major Taylor autobiography p. 67.

149. Taylor obliterating 1/4, ½, ¾, 1 mile world speed records: Ibid p.68.

149. "teeth were chattering from the cold" *Boston Globe*: November 13, 1898.

150. "It is a serious fact that last week, when the horse was monarch in New York…" *The Evening Democrat:* January 25, 1899.

150. "with it came the sublime thrill that was beyond the power of words to express." Major Taylor autobiography p 67.

150. "unhampered he is simply the fastest man on the track." Quote: William A Brady Unidentified New York paper referenced in Major Taylor autobiography p. 43.

Chapter 11

151. "married Grace George" Article: Richard F. Snow, *American Heritage Magazine*: April/May 1980.

151. "a real man should be known as a fighting man." William A Brady, The Fighting Man (Indianapolis: Bobbs-Merrill, 1916).

151. "had a soft spot for Brady, the man with irons in the fire." *Brooklyn Daily Eagle:* July 17, 1901.

152. Taylor on chainless bicycles: *Brooklyn Daily Eagle*: Nov 4, 16, 24, 1898: *Cycle Age & Trade review*, 1898.

152. "Every colored man and women is proud of Major Taylor, the champion bicyclist." *Pittsburgh Press:* December 11, 1899.

152. Taylor handing out pamphlet's cycle show Chicago: *Chicago Daily Tribune*: January 8, 1899.

152. "You cannot imagine how much good it has done me" *Cycle Age*: July 1900.

152. "He demonstrated he can talk a wheel": Philadelphia Inquirer, February 25, 1899.

153. Taylor tendency to ride dangerously close to pole: *Boston Globe*; January 18, 1901 & April 19, 1908.

153. "I do not get half enough sleep for I think all the time about those Montreal races" *Boston Globe*: August 3, 1899.

153. Taylor in Chicago with Birdie Munger: Major Taylor autobiography p. 78.

154. Blacks were barred from the NCA: *Brooklyn Daily Eagle*: May 19, 1899.

154. "The most unsportsmanlike move on record." Ibid.

154. signing with Stearns: UASP.

155. "restore the supremacy of the white race," Rick Knott: The Jack Johnson v. Barney Oldfield match race of 1910; What it says about race in America: January 2005 DL www.findarticles.com February 15, 2007.

155. Headquarters of sin between Chicago and Denver; Quote by Richard Ruhnke Ottumwa Iowa Public Librarian: Interview January 20, 2007.

155. "blind tigers" Steve Welker: Ottumwa recalls 'red light' days; *Ottumwa Courier*: July 1, 1976.

155. "303" Ibid.

155. "The road to hell" Ibid.

155. "Battle row" Ibid.

155. "The Klu Klux Klan was said to linger there": Richard Ruhnke: Ottumwa Iowa Librarian: Interview January 20, 2007.

155. Stormy Jordan pouring whiskey on sidewalk to attract customers: Wapello County History: Self published by Ruth Sterling 1986 Sutherland Printing Montezuma Iowa.

155. "Taylor is a queer specimen, he is supremely arrogant..." Major Taylor autobiography referencing unidentified Ottumwa newspapers report on him p. 81.

156. "marble hearted...crowd did not like him" Ibid p.78.

156. "something on the order of that lawn party and the skunk business." Ibid-p. 81.

156. "I guess I spoiled their little party" Ibid p. 81.

156. For that seedy job he sent Frank Gately: January 24, 1900.

156. "Little Chicago" *Ottumwa Courier:* July 1, 1976.

157. "Black Whirlwind" *Brooklyn Daily Eagle*: December 1, 1898.

157. "I have never received the benefit of a close decision." Major Taylor Autobiography p. 77.

157. "most of the outlaw men are has-beens..." *Montreal Daily Star:* August 7, 1899.

157. Bald, Todd Sloan, lover of flesh pots" *Brooklyn Daily Eagle*: December 24, 1898; August 9, 1899.

157. "white flyer" *Brooklyn Daily Eagle*: June 16, 1897.

157. Ashinger Velodrome Builder: *Brooklyn Daily Eagle*: August 8, 1899.

158. Bell Telephone Company; *Montreal Daily Star*: August 10, 1899.

158. Montreal Mayor deemed it a civic holiday: *Brooklyn Daily Eagle*: July 17, 1899.

158. Governor General gave patronage: *Ibid*: July 24, 1899.

158. Race Headquarter Windsor Hotel; *Ibid*: July 17th, 1899.

158. Goldsmiths creating special medals; Ibid. July 17, 1899

159. Henry Sturmeny a giant of a man; *Montreal Daily Star*: August 1899.

158. Waltham Massachusetts rail station one hundred riders waiting: *Montreal Gazette*: August 14, 1899.

159. ICA banning waiting NCA riders: *Brooklyn Daily Eagle:* August 9, 1899.

159. "give us Major Taylor and we can run the meet…" *Montreal Gazette*: August 7, 1899.

159. "He is a very pleasing looking boy with looks as soft as velvet" *Montreal Daily Star:* August 10, 1899.

160. "bicycle excursion trains." *New York Times*: August 12, 1897.

160. Five thousand people being turned away: Major Taylor autobiography p. 87 quoting unknown Montreal Daily.

160. Forty thousand fans attendance World Championships: 12,000 *The Herald*; August 9, 1899, 13,000 *Montreal Gazette;* August 10, 1899; 12,000 *Montreal Gazette;* August 14, 1899; 11,000 *The Montreal Herald* August 11, 1899; some estimates were over 50,000, *Le Velo*; March 12, 1901.

160. "like a row of prisoners before the bar of the recorders" *Montreal Daily Star:* August 10, 1899

160. "official press organizer" *Montreal Daily Star:* August 11, 1899.

161. Every single man, women and child rose in unison: *Montreal Daily Star:* August 10, 1899.

161. Referee William Inglis; Ibid.

162. W.C Petrie inventor of photo finish: *North Adams Transcript:* February 10, 1898.

163. Grose's Secret service present: *Montreal Daily Star:* August 10, 1899.

163. "well, alright, if that is your verdict gentleman I shall have to abide by it" *The Montreal Gazette:* August 10, 1899.

163. "There was only one mistake and it is extremely difficult to account for and that was why Major Taylor was deprived of a race that he won." Ibid August 10, 1899.

163. "I was very nervous because I knew full well…"Major Taylor Autobiography p 89,90.

163. "Blessed are the meek" Matthew 5:5 King James Version Bible.

165. "the crowd fearing that their dark skinned boy began to be a little demonstrative" *Montreal Star:* August 11, 1899.

165. "The hold Taylor has taken upon the sympathies of the people in the grandstand is something wonderful" Ibid.

166. "I shall never forget the thunderous applause…" Major Taylor autobiography p. 92.

166. Even though next to the article in a Montreal paper praising him for his world championship title there was a article about another lynching back home: *The Gazette Montreal:* August 14, 1899.

166. "My National anthem took on a new meaning" Ibid p.92.

166. "The Major hasn't found his master": UASP.

166. "Despite that joyous demonstration…. regret" Ibid: p 92.

167. "Eddie McDuffie dropping the world one mile record to 1 minute 21 seconds." Ibid: p. 78.

167. "Taylor 1 minute 1.9 seconds one mile world record" *Chicago Daily News* November 18, 1899.

169. McDuffee retires from cycling: *Chicago Daily Tribune:* November 19, 1899.

169. "The colored boy who has astonished the world" *Worcester Telegram*: February 21, 1900.

169. "Major Taylor the wonder is now back home." *Brooklyn Daily Eagle:* December 1, 1898.

169. Taylor and Bert Hazard stop at Sager's: *Worcester Telegram*, February 9, 1900.

Chapter 12

171. 'Shovelors' earning twenty cents per hour. *Brooklyn Daily Eagle:* March 2, 1900.

171. Massive snowfalls dump 60 inches on New York: www.islandnet.com DL February 8, 2007.

171. Horses getting electrocuted due to snowstorm: *Brooklyn Daily Eagle*: February 28, 1900.

171. Northeastern seaboard was virtually cut off: *Brooklyn Daily Eagle:* March 1, 1900.

172. Little Hope for Major Taylor: *Worcester Telegram*: February 21, 1900.

172. NCA's ban on blacks: *Brooklyn Daily Eagle:* May 19, 1899.

172. Taylor hires Attorney William Allen: *Worcester Telegram:* February 21, 1900.

172. "I fear my sentiments do not meet with favor in the minds of the majority of the officials of that body." Ibid.

172. Massachusetts flooding eight feet deep: *Brooklyn Daily Eagle*: March 2, 1900.

172. Horses drowned in their stables: *Ibid*.

173. "Major Taylor's chances of reinstatement into the NCA are just about one in a thousand" *Worcester Telegram*: February 21, 1900.

173. "Thus far they have resolutely refused to consider Taylor's case" Ibid.

173. "If favorable action is not secured Taylor's career as a racing man is ended" Ibid.

173. Continental Hotel in Newark New Jersey discussion of Taylor ban" *Worcester Telegram*: May 11 & 29th, 1900.

173. Advertisement Major Taylor sponsored bicycles: *Cycle Age* & *Trade Review* June 1898.

173. Advertisement Major Taylor fans: Major Taylor autobiography p. 53.

173. Advertisement Major Taylor name on cigarette package: Unidentified Australian newspaper clipping, Major Taylor scrapbook, Indianapolis History Museum.

173. "I and Stevie" *Boston Globe*: July 23, 1899; July 8, 1900.

174. "Almost certain defeat stares him in the face" *Worcester Telegram:* February 21, 1900.

174. Taylor billboards: Taylor's autobiography, p. 140.

174. "The riders have drawn the color line, it is unconstitutional, un-American, unsportsmanlike…" *Worcester Spy*: April 29, 1900.

174. "If the NCA wants the endorsement of every fair minded lover of sports of the country it had better strike out that word "white" in its rules and strike it out quick." Unidentified newspaper clipping Major Taylor scrapbook: Indianapolis History Museum.

175. NCA $500 fine and Taylor Payment: *Worcester Telegram*: May 29, 1900 p.6.

175. Purchasing home under assumed name: *The Daily Northwestern:* March 16, 1901.

176. "$2850 price paid for home" *Worcester Telegram*: January 24, 1900.

176. Cornelius Maher local realtor: Ibid.

176. "ideal residential locality" Unidentified clipping Major Taylor scrapbook; Indianapolis History Museum.

176. Is he a good Yankee? *Worcester Telegram*: January 24, 1900.

176. What's his name? Ibid.

176. "you'll see him soon enough" *Chicago Daily Tribune*: February 4, 1900.

176. "what do you mean by this outrage" Ibid.

177. "I consider it an injury to me to have him come in and squat down on my plot against my will." *Worchester Telegram:* January 24, 1900.

177. "I don't know why I haven't as much right to buy a little place as any man in town." Unidentified Worcester newspaper clipping: Indianapolis History Museum.

177. "There must be democrats out at Columbus Park" *Worcester Telegram*: January 24, 1900.

177. Taylor as registered republican: *Worcester Telegram*: November 28, 1899.

178. "How about it Major" *Worcester Telegram*: November 30, 1899.

178. "If I was married I didn't know when it happened" *Worcester Telegram:* November 20, 1899.

178. "Just the work of some of those paragraphers" Ibid.

178. "they are always making me married" Ibid.

178. Description Daisy's clothing: Linda McShannock Minneapolis Historical Society: St. Paul MN.

178. Daisy Victoria Morris, graduate of Hudson Academy: *The Colored American Magazine*: September 1902 p. 344.

179. "new women" Robert Smith: A Social History of the Bicycle. American Heritage Press p.76.

179. "a bicycle was a better matchmaker than a mother" Ibid: *New York Herald: D*ate unknown: p. 79.

179. "bicycling by young women has helped more than any other media" *Chicago Tribune*: July 5th, 1896.

179. women weren't capable of controlling a bicycle: *Bucks County Gazette*: July 29, 1897.

179. "weaker sex" Robert Smith: Social History of the Bicycle, American Heritage Press p. 65.

179. "heating of blood" Ibid p. 65.

179. "it would be just as sweet and pleasant to make love to a women" *Minneapolis Tribune* August 17, 1895.

179. "cycling had come along just in time to rehabilitate the American women." *New York Herald*: June 13 & 27, 1897.

180. "nervous force was wearing out." Ibid.

Chapter 13

181. Iver Johnson contract: The *Cycle Age*: October 25, 1900; *The Bicycling World and Motorcycle Review*, May 23 & 30, 1901; *The Cycle Age* and *Trade Review* December 20, 1900; *Fitchburg Sentinel*: April 3, 1901.

181. "The colored whirlwind is almost elephantine": UASP.

182. Johnnie Fisher from Chicago: *Worcester Spy*: June 24, 1900.

182. Major Taylor Is Losing His Laurels: Ibid.

182. Frank Kramer: Born November 21, 1880: *Fort Wayne Daily News:* September 21, 1915.

182. Kramer retires for bed exactly nine o'clock each night: *Velo News*: January 15, 1996 by Peter Nye.

182. Kramer coming down with tuberculosis: *Fort Wayne Daily News:* September 21, 1915.

183. "He would earn as worldwide reputation as Arthur Zimmerman" *Boston Globe*; June 10, 1900; *New York Times* June 3, 1894

183. "Kramer is expected to clean up the whole bunch." Major Taylor autobiography p.115.

183. "Kramer was riding like the wind" *Brooklyn Daily Eagle*: July 1, 1900.

183. If I ever meet Kramer in a match race": *The Colored Magazine*, 1902, p. 342.

183. "Frank Kramer is the king-pin" *Ibid:* April 30, 1900.

184. Bookmakers: money chaser: Ibid. August 26, 1901.

184. "Experts pick Frank Kramer" Major Taylor autobiography p. 114.

184. "On the whole, Major Taylor is King Pin" *Brooklyn Daily Eagle:* July 1, 1900.

184. Frank Kramer legacy twenty-one years professional 1-year amateur: Peter Nye; Hearts of Lions, p.110.

184. Tom Cooper NCA champion 1899; *Brooklyn Daily Eagle:* December 1, 1899.

185. "July 13, 1900 Milwaukee $1000 purse" Ibid: July 14, 1900.

185. "interurban's" www.indianahistory.org DL February 21, 2007.

185. Taylor toasted at banquet: *Cycle Age*, August 11, 1898; *Chicago Tribune*, August 10, 1898.

186. Civil War Grand Army Uniform descriptions: Linda McShannock Minneapolis Historical Society; December 9, 2005.

187. Description Newby Oval: *Cycle Age* and *Trade Review* June 30, 1898.

187. "Well son, there is one thing I don't understand" Major Taylor autobiography p. 122.

187. "The innocence of old age." Ibid: p 122.

187. "You can't use my name sonny" Ibid: p. 141.

188. "You will go back to using your real name of Marshall and immediately refrain from using Major." Ibid: p. 141.

188. "But I can't stop all the kids in town from using my name." Ibid: p. 142.

188. "You have performed on the race tracks of this country" Ibid: p.142

188. "I will uphold the proud name of Major" Ibid: p. 142.

188. Vailsburg Frank Kramer 10,000 fans, 1900" Ibid: p. 129 referencing *Newark Dailies:* July 5, 1900 *New York Times*: July 1, 1900.

189. "greeted with a storm of applause" Major Taylor autobiography p. 118.

189. "astonished cycle fans" Ibid: p. 118.

189. "the neatest rider who sits in a saddle" Ibid p. 126 quoting unknown *New Bedford* newspaper.

189. "If America is to have a white champion this year" Ibid: p. 124 referencing unknown *Buffalo* Newspaper August 2-5, 1900.

189. "showed very plainly why the pro's of this country took such care not to permit him to mettle against them" *Brooklyn Daily Eagle*: July 5, 1900.

189. Agitating for a match race to settle the issue once and for all: Ibid.

190. "Brady, I've been mixed up in cycling, boxing and the stage..." *Mansfield News:* April 17, 1901.

190. "they are really just smelling machines" William A. Brady: Showman: p. 47.

190. "the politicians were simply not getting there's out of the big money in cycle races" Ibid: p. 228.

190. "I will never understand why Roosevelt signed that bill since he was both intelligent and a lover of sport." Ibid: p. 229: Fighting Man, William A. Brady p. 159.

190. "They were veritable mints for their promoters" *Brooklyn Daily Eagle:* April 15, 1899.

190. The Collins Bill: *Brooklyn Daily Eagle*: April 15, 1899.

190. "Madison's" www.cyclingnews.com DL February 21, 2007.

191. Taylor vs. Cooper: *New York Journal:* December 8, 1900.

191. Brady ACRA organization sponsoring Taylor/Cooper match race: *The Washington Post*: December 9, 1900.

191. "Bawb Tawm will now proceed to hand your little darkey..." Major Taylor autobiography p. 162.

191. Cooper financing Henry Ford: Henry's attic; Wayne State University Press.

191. "If ever a race was run for blood, this one was." Ibid: p. 165.

192. "standing on benches, tables, chairs and the railing to see the finish" *New York Times*: December 16, 1900.

192. "Taylor was simply toying with Cooper." Robert Coquelle Editor Le Velo January 21, 1901; Referred to Major Taylor autobiography p 166.

192. "I have never seen a more humiliated pair of Tom's in my life" Major Taylor autobiography p. 165.

192. 'It is a fearfully hot pace" *New York Times:* December 12, 1900.

192. "name your terms" Major Taylor autobiography p. 165.

192. Taylor breaks two world records: *New York Times*: December 15, 1900.

193. "60,000 fans showed up six day race 1900" Ibid Dec. 9-15, 1900.

193. "will beat you as he has beaten all cyclist" *Cycle Age*: December 1900.

Chapter 14

195. *Le Velo*: French Cycling 'daily' Publication started by Pierre Giffard in 1892; ceased publishing November 1904: Info from Hennepin County Librarian, Minneapolis MN February 27, 2007.

196. "the fastest sprinter in the world" *Brooklyn Daily Eagle:* March 26, 1901.

196. Taylor a skilled boxer: Major Taylor autobiography; p. 272.

196. French racing legend: Cassingnard; A bronze bust statue of Cassingnard surmounts a pillar of marble overlooking the City of Bordeaux France where all of France honors his memory: Zimmerman Abroad and Points on Training by J. M Erwin and A. A. Zimmerman The Blakely Printing Co. 1895 p. 116-117.

196. Bourrillon: Major Taylor, the King of the Cycle, his Affearance and Career by Paul Hamelle and Robert Coquelle. Major Taylor autobiography p. 304.

196. Constant Huret: www.wikipedia.org DL February 17, 2007.

196. "When I have beaten everyone in speed, I feel the need to take on the rest of them to see what they have in their guts" Unidentified French article (in file).

196. Jacquelin clobbering other riders: *Cycle Age*, May 1901.

196. "Surprises, demoralizes": *The Philadelphia Inquirer*, March 14, 1897.

196. "incorrectness of attitude" *Cycle Age*: May 19, 1901.

197. "unusual pleasures" of the Parisian night: *Bearings*: July 22, 1897.

197. "second rater" *Boston Globe*: January 13, 1901.

197. Jacquelin wins final of Grand Prix easily: *Cycle Age*: July 12, 1901.

197. As Jacquelyn's managers: *Worcester Telegram*: January 10, 1901.

197. "pickaninny" *Chicago Daily Tribune*: May 4, 1898.

198. "It is the big sport, they go wild over cycle races in Paris" *New York Times:* July 27, 1900.

198. Refuses $15,000, Major Taylor Won't Ride on Sunday: *Worcester Telegram*: Nov 29, 1899; The *Daily Gazette*: October 9, 1899.

198. Taylor's coming, Taylor's not coming: *The Daily Northwester:* March 16, 1901.

199. "Unless the champion is": *Cycle Age*, April 28, 1898.

199. Gertrude Taylor buried April 20th 1900: Sue Staten, Staff Genealogist Crown Hill Cemetery Indianapolis, Indiana.

199. "I stand today just where I stood a year ago, and hope to stand a year hence" *Worcester Telegram:* December 21, 1899.

199. "all we had was just what we needed" *New South Wales Baptist*, undated 1903 clipping in Taylor scrapbook. Reprinted in Sydney Telegraph, January 7, 1903 due to overwhelming public interest in the subject.

199. "Taylor's conscience still troubles him" *Bangor Daily Whig and Courier:* February 13, 1900.

199. "I have given up on France…" *Boston Globe*: February 5, 1900.

200. Thirty times the average Americans income for an entire years labor: http://www2.pfeiffer.edu Hill House Maps & Papers DL March 29, 2006.

200. "immortalized in Carerra marble": UASP.

200. "I am pleased indeed to know that there are still a few Christians left who possess the courage of their convictions " *North Conway Reporter:* April 5, 1900.

200. Everyday Taylor rolled into town to pick up another offer: Major Taylor autobiography p. 166.

200. "Mile-a-minute Murphy": *Scientific American*, July 15, 1899.

201. Eddie Bald; "Twig of Laurel"; *Brooklyn Daily Eagle:* October 25, 1898.

201. Bald receiving ten to twenty letters a day from women wanting to be heroine: *Cycle Age*: May 5, 1898.

201. "a solitary and silent figure loomed up in the gloom of the auditorium in the middle isle" *Brooklyn Daily Eagle* October 25, 1898.

201. "stage struck, I collapsed" Ibid.

201. Vaudeville home trainers Charlie Murphy: Major Taylor autobiography p. 157.

202. Taylor at Keith's theatre: *Worcester Telegram:* January 10, 1901.

202. "How do you like America?" La venue en France de Major Taylor, Cyclette-Reveue (Paris), March and April 1944.

203. "I believe in the saying that 'a mother's prayer will last forever,' and I honestly believe it's my mother's prayers that are standing by me now" *The Wheel:* June 10, 1900.

203. Edison's Vitascope: www.cinematreasures.org DL February 27, 2007.

203. All he could offer was $3000: *Worcester Telegram*: January 10, 1901.

203. Cutting off all negotiations with him and that he was going to devote all his energies towards managing his French legend: Ibid.

203. "All sorts of people have come to me—learned clever men—and tried to argue with me that Sunday racing is not wrong" *New South Wales Baptist*, undated 1903 clipping in Taylor scrapbook. Reprinted in *Sydney Telegraph*, January 7, 1903 due to public interest in the subject.

203. Brady stepped in negotiating $5000 European contract with no Sunday racing: Peter Nye: Hearts of Lions p.62.

204. European riders returned home mobbed by reporters asking questions about Taylor: *Worcester Telegram:* February 9, 1900: Major Taylor autobiography p. 166.

204. Contract to race Europe signed January 2, 1901: *Le Velo*, January 3, 1901.

204. Taylor on Contract. Great Sprinter Is to Ride All Europe: *Worcester Telegram:* January 10, 1901.

204. Jacquelin training at hippovelodrome: The Fort Worth Register, February 10, 1901.

204. "Let him come": UASP.

204. Jacquelin owning apartments with servants: *The Philadelphia Inquirer*, January 21, 1897.

204. Jacqueline to name his donkey-sized dog Major: UASP.

204. Taylor leaves on Kaiser Wilhelm der Gross: *New York Times:* March 6, 1901.

204. William Buckner trainer: *The Daily Northwester:* March 16, 1901.

204. Charlie Miller, friend of William Brady: William A. Brady, Showman; p.228.

204. Accommodations on Kaiser Wilhelm de Grosse: www.greatoceanliners. com DL December 2, 2005.

205. charming mulatto: *La Vie au Grand Air*.

205. Most universally admired passenger: UASP.

205. Kid McCoy on board: UASP.

206. Investigation: Taylor on ship using assumed name" *The Daily Northwestern:* March 16, 1901.

206. "France is cabling frantically" Ibid: March 16, 1901.

206. "the bronze statue": *Le Velo*, January 21, 1901.

Chapter 15

207. Major Taylor arrives Cherbourg France: Journal: *La Vie au Grand Air*, "Life Outdoors My Tour In Europe" by Major Taylor, May 4, 1901.

207. Taylor seasickness problems: Ibid.

207. Cluster European Journalist greeting Taylor in Cherbourg: Ibid.

207. Taylor wanting ship to turn back to New York: Ibid.

207. "Not since the great Zimmerman had a sports figure been so highly anticipated" "Le Negre a Paris": *Le Velo*, March 12, 1901.

207. Customs employees ignore other passengers: UASP.

208. "They say he's the best man in the world. Well, when I'm in form, we'll see how I measure up to him right enough." Ibid.

208. "Before I left home I swore to God that I would never race on the Sabbath, and I don't like the idea of going to hell." Ibid.

208. "La Belle Epogue..the beautiful period" www.clubmoulinrouge.com DL December 2 2005.

208. Pamphlet: Right to be lazy" http://debs.indstate.edu DL March 8, 2007.

208. Twenty-seven thousand cafes: www.clubmoulinrouge.com DL December 2, 2005.

209. Le Chabanais brothel" www.expatica.com DL October 5, 2004.

209. 'selection salon' Ibid.

209. Visiting wheelman", claimed one historian, "marched through the entrée as thou they were kicking tires on a shiny new bike" Author Interview: Jack Visceo Cycling hall of fame, January 2006.

209. Brothel Patrons: Ernest Hemingway, Humphrey Bogart, Marlene Dietrich, Cary Grant, Britain's King Edward Bertie" www.iafrica.com DL December 14, 2005.

209. French artist Henry de Toulouse-Lautrec Le Chabanais Address: www. metropoleparis.com DL March 12, 2007.

209. Japanese room wins award in Universal Exposition 1900: www.iafrica. com DL December 14, 2005.

209. Madame Kelly, high society Jockey Club; Ibid.

209. "pointy nose" "George the Cavalryman" Ibid.

209. Eroto-cycle: www.metropoleparis.com DL March 12, 2007.

210. "It has been three years": "The Flying Black Major Taylor" by Robert Coquille, *La Vie au Grand Air*, March 10, 1901, pp. 130-131.

210. "Major Taylor has a happy facility of keeping in the public eye about as prominently as any theatrical star ever did." *Brooklyn Daily Eagle*: August 2, 1901.

210. "Taylor's arrival in France the heroic guardian of the Sabbath..." *Worcester Telegram:* May 8, 1901.

210. Taylor arouses curiosity all the more, and is surrounded by mystery because of the color of his skin." Ibid: Major Taylor autobiography p.307, 317.

210. "No man had ever been presented to the public in a more flattering fashion" Unidentified French article.

211. "Major Taylor is one of the most beautiful athletes you will ever meet": "The Flying Black Major Taylor" by Robert Coquille, *La Vie au Grand Air*, March 10, 1901, pp. 130-131.

211. Reporters amassing at Hotel Scribe: UASP.

211. Newsroom overwhelmed: UASP.

211. "La Future Madame": *La Vie au Grand Air*, May 4, 1901.

211. "who came to see me and looked at me right in the eyes": *La Vie au Grand Air*, "My Tour in Europe" by Major Taylor, May 4, 1901.

211. "are blacks not seen in Paris he asked" Ibid.

211. everything from his birthday suit to a tuxedo: Unidentified French article.

211. Picture Major Taylor Henri Fournier: *La Vie au Grand Air*, May 4, 1901; Cycling and Outing; May 11, 1901.

211. Ominbuses wandering pitifully on the Champs Elysees" Ibid.

211. "The people of Worcester will be rather surprised to see me come back on a 16 Horsepower": Ibid.

212. "The Europeans were absolutely crazy over him" Interview with Taylor's trainer William Buckner: *The Daily Northwestern:* July 18, 1901.

212. Description Café Esperance: Zimmerman Abroad and Points of Training Interest by J. M. Erwin and A. A Zimmerman p. 33-37.

212. Presence of Famous French racers Huret, Bourillion & Morin at Café Esperence with Taylor and Jacquelin: Boston Globe: April 7, 1901.

213. Confetti tossed on the boulevard: UASP.

213. "You have splendid big legs" "Yes but yours are much prettier" " That may be so but yours are so much stronger than mine. But suppose yours are quicker than mine." *Cycle Age*: April 4, 1901. *Boston Globe*: April 7, 1901.

214. "A man comes to me and says, have a glass of beer, have a glass of wine" *Sydney Daily Telegraph:* January 7, 1903; quoting *New South Wales Baptist* article titled "Thirty-thousand Dollars for Conscience Sake".

214. "there was such a big crowd on hand I thought there was a race meet on": *La Vie au Grand Air*, May 4, 1901: *Le Velo*, March 16, 1901.

214. "On a bicycle his position is not disgraceful": "The Flying Black Major Taylor" by Robert Coquille, *La Vie au Grand Air*, March 10, 1901.

215. "I do whatever pleases me": *La Vie au Grand Air*, May 4, 1901.

215. "I am not superstitious" *The Daily Northwestern:* April 4, 1901.

215. "is said to attract the greatest delight…" Ibid.

215. "It strengthens the muscles and increases considerably the breathing" Journal: *La Vie au Grand Air*: Life Outdoors My Tour of Europe By Major Taylor: May 4, 1901.

216. Vive Taylor, Vive Taylor: Le Velo May 4, 1901.

216. Taylor takes in sites, Automobile Club, Palace de le Concorde: *La Vie au Grand Air*, May 4, 1901.

216. Reported claims Taylor one of them: UASP.

216. "They were throwing all kinds of money at him" Interview with Taylor's trainer William Buckner: *The Daily Northwestern:* July 18, 1901.

216. Sleeper number 13: *La Vie au Grand Air*, May 4, 1901.

216. "The earth under Germany shook": *Rad-Welt*, June 1, 1901.

217. Cold weather being a factor in Taylor decision to hesitate racing in France: Major Taylor autobiography p. 171.

217. fair weathered racer: *The Referee*, May 22, 1901.

217. Willie Arend preparations: *The Referee*, May 22, 1901.

217. Language barrier: *The Daily Republican*, August 2, 1901.

217. "If Americans are to go to France in numbers": Ibid.

217. "They are not of the same class as the top four or five French riders" Ibid.

218. "When the American aces go near Europe they vanished like smoke" Major Taylor autobiography; Reprint from booklet "Major Taylor, The King of the Cycle, his affearance and Career" By Paul Hamelle and Robert Coquille p.317.

218. "Watch on the Rhine" Major Taylor autobiography p. 171.

218. German chancellor and high military personnel attend race: *Rad-Welt*, June 1, 1901.

218. "that's one of the greatest demonstrations I have ever seen on a bicycle track." Ibid: p. 171.

219. "The sky seemed to be against our shivering son" Major Taylor autobiography; Reprint from booklet "Major Taylor, The King of the Cycle, his affearance and Career" By Paul Hamelle and Robert Coquille p.317.

219. Taylor beats Arend out by twenty lengths: *Brooklyn Daily Eagle:* April 12, 1901: *Cycle Age*: May 20, 1901.

219. "The French Champion Jacquelin is the only sprinter in Europe who can defeat the man" The Flying Black Major Taylor by Robert Coquille *La Vie au Grand Air*: March 10, 1901: *Cycle Age*: May 1901.

219. five hundred star struck fans escorted Taylor back to the train station: Andrew Ritchie: The Extraordinary Career of a Champion Bicyclist p. 171.

219. "Nothing was missing to make me happy, flowers thrown at his feet" *La Vie au Grand Air*: May 4, 1901.

219. Crowd marching to Taylor's hotel demanding he make appearance: Andrew Ritchie: Out of the Shadows, A Biographical History of African American Athletes; David K Wiggins Editor. P.31.

220. Buckner wearing cowboy hat: Picture *La Vie au Grand Air*: May 4, 1901.

220. "I have never before met such a gentleman in every respect of the word" *Cycle Age*: May 20, 1901.

220. "My friends" *Le Vie au Grand Air*: May 4, 1901.

220. "I have the greatest of confidence in him Taylor referring to Buckner" Ibid.

220. Taylor's left pedal hits concrete almost causing him to crash: Ibid.

220. "Room thirteen please" Ibid.

221. Taylor beats Grognia twice: *The Referee*, June 5, 1901.

221. Grognia Belgium National Champion undefeated on home track: *Cycle Age*: April 19, 1901.

221. "Alas, the new Zimmerman for whom we have waited" *Cycle Age*: May 1901.

221. "They gazed at the little Major and seemed not to understand whether he was an ordinary human being or a man having some kind of 4-5 horsepower motor in his body" *Cycle Age*: May 2, 1901.

221. "that part of the world hadn't seen such fanaticism since the tulip craze" Author Interview: Cycling Hall of Famer Jack Visceo January 2006.

221. "he didn't care to make his defeats too apparent" *Cycle Age*: May 1901.

221. "He's the most marvelous racing man I have ever seen…" *Cycle Age*: May 1901.

221. "Groggy": *The Referee*, June 5, 1901.

221. Major Taylor will have to ride faster than he ever did" *Boston Globe*: January 13, 1901.

222. "Taylor, was awaited like the messiah" *Le Velo*: January 27, 1901.

222. "civil" *La Vie au Grand Air*: May 4, 1901.

222. marble monument of the much-revered French hero Cassignard: Zimmerman Abroad and Points of Training Interest by J. M. Erwin and A. A Zimmerman p. 114.

222. "Neither the living or the dead could take exception to taking residence in Bordeaux" Ibid: p. 116.

222. Largest crowd ever seen in Bordeaux: *Cycle Age*: May 20, 1901.

222. "democratic" Zimmerman Abroad and Points of Training Interest by J. M. Erwin and A. A Zimmerman p. 115.

223. "flying Negro Volant" *La Vie au Grand Air*: November 1, 1898.

223. Riot in the stands Bordeaux France: *New York Times:* May 4, 1901: *Naugatuck Daily News:* May 4, 1901: *Boston Globe*: May 4, 1901.

223. "A French crowd is the most amiable thing extent, up to the point where it becomes convinced that an imposition is being practiced" Zimmerman Abroad and Points of Training Interest by J. M. Erwin and A. A Zimmerman p. 83.

223. "deplorable fiasco" *Cycle Age*: May 1901.

223. Ferrari and 333 meters in 20:1/5 second: *Cycle Age*: May 20, 1901.

224. "Besides five or six days that were passable, it rained constantly" *La Vie au Grand Air*: Life Outdoors My Tour in Europe" May 4, 1901 by Major Taylor

224. Strummed the mandolin: *La Vie au Grand Air*: May 4, 1901.

224. "I'm an African not a European" Andrew Ritchie: The Extraordinary Career of a Champion Bicycle Racer; No source listed.

224. "spectator trains" Unidentified French article, in file.

224. "He is as much talked about as the premier": *Cycle Age*, May 1901.

225. "What would I have to do to convince these half dozen stubborn journalist" Unidentified French article.

225. "Now they were going to unearth a Negro?" Ibid.

225. "He will have to undergo a miraculous change in form if he expects to defeat Major Taylor" *Cycle Age*: May 1901.

225. Major Taylor as spectator to Ellegaard race: *Cycle Age*: June 20, 1901.

225. Taylor 5-1 odds: *Cycle Age*: May 12, 1901.

225. Taylor wriggles into grandstand to watch Jacquelin Ellegaard match Nantes France: *Cycling News*: June 4, 1901.

225. Tire tape: *Fort Worth Register*, January 6, 1901.

225. "You will eat that American up next Thursday" Ibid.

225. Could not be had at even money" Ibid.

225. "If you think this darkey scares me": UASP.

225. Interminable calculations: Unidentified French clipping.

225. Muscles of Taylor and Jacquelin examined: UASP.

226. "The French populace had gone practically crazy over the coming meets" *Boston Globe:* April 28, 1901.

226. "Those who are familiar with Jacqueline and understand the pedestal pose" *The Sun:* May 16th, 1901.

226. Taylor keeping scrapbook of newspaper articles: Ibid.

226. Tickets selling at twenty times face value: *Cycle Age*; May 1901; *The Daily Northwestern:* April 25, 1901.

Chapter 16

227. Dull and threatening weather: *Cycler's News*, May 25, 1901.

227. Most anticipated sporting event in history: Unidentified French article: *Cycle Age*: May 1901.

228. "Major Taylor is having little trouble to trim the riders on the other side of the ocean" *Naugatuck Daily News:* May 14, 1901.

228. "all interest in cycling await the result with the keenest of interest..." *New York Sun*: May 16, 1901.

228. "Taylor is already more popular than Zimmerman was. Should he defeat Jacquelin I cannot venture to predict to what length people will go" *Cycle Age*: May 20, 1901: *The Daily Northwestern:* April 25, 1901.

228. People began gathering at the gates as early as six-o'clock in the morning: *Cycle Age*, May 1901.

228. Special trains: Ibid.

228. Sojourns over dusty roads: *Cycle Age*: May 27, 1901.

228. Ten access gates to Velodrome: Unidentified French Article.

228. Booth cost $16.00: *Cycle Age*: May 27, 1901.

228. infield seats $20: Ibid.

228. Vanderbilt's and other wealthy bettors: *Boston Globe*: May 19, 1901.

229. Twelve Paris dailies, six with money on Taylor six on Jacquelin: *Cycle Age* May 27, 1901.

229. Track manager Desgrange hollering "No more" Ibid.

229. "Twenty eight thousand people" *New York Times:* May 17, 1901; *Brooklyn Daily Eagle:* May 16-17, 1901; *The Portsmouth Herald:* May 20, 1901; Chicago Tribune May17, 1901.

229. Five thousand fans outside: UASP.

229. Race start time Three-thirty p.m.: *Chicago Tribune*, May 16, 1901.

229. Jacquelin superstition about entering track first: Unidentified French article.

229. Picture Jacquelin eyes glaring down, chin up: *La Vie Illustree*, May 24, 1901, Bibliotheque Nationale, Paris.

229. "I do remember getting a kick out of seeing my adversary..." Unidentified French article.

230. "The silence was sublime" *Cycle Age*: Sport and Pastime: May 1901.

230. Jacquelin fell flat on his side: Ibid.

231. metal from his monster machine began bending: Unidentified French article.

231. Jacquelin 104 inch gear; *Cycle Age*: April 4, 1901.

231. Taylor 92-inch gear; Major Taylor autobiography p. 78.

232. masses waving hats, handkerchiefs, canes and umbrella's: *Cycle Age*: May 1901.

232. Jacquelin defeats Taylor: *New York Times*, May 17, 1901; *The Town and Country*, July 6 and 13, 1901; *Table Talk*, June 27, 1901.

232. Jacquelin crossing the line a length in front: *Cycle Age*: May 1901.

232. "a scene which beggars description": *Cycler's News*, June 5, 1901.

232. tore after "prince of sprinters" with the force of a tidal wave: Unidentified French article.

232. Fans knocking over railings: UASP.

232. "acted as thou crazy" *Cycle Age*: May 1901.

232. fans could not utter a single word: Ibid.

232. "There is no way to describe it, it was as if some strong electric battery..." *Cycle Age*: Sport and Pastime, May 1901.

232. Band-playing Marseilles: Ibid.

233. "Villainous grimace" Ibid.

233. "Down with Taylor" Ibid.

233. Picture of Taylor leaving track in abject dejection: *Cycler's News*, June 4, 1901: Titled "The Nigger, Major Taylor after his defeat by Jacquelin".

233. Taylor sobbing: *Cycle Age*: May 1901.

233. "The turmoil had no precedence" *Cycle Age*: May 1901.

233. Picture Jacquelin after race: *Cycler's News*, June 4, 1901.

233. "The flying Negro beaten": *La Vie Illustree*, May 24, 1901.

233. "It was the most perfect speed event in the history of cycle racing" *Cycle Age*: Sport and Pastime May 1901.

233. "Jacquelin thumbed his nose at me": *Le Velo*, May 18, 1901 Major Taylor autobiography p 176.

233. "was a warm day" Major Taylor autobiography p. 175.

Chapter 17

235. "I thought I had beaten Taylor so convincingly there would be no question of a revenge match. But if he wants one I am at his disposal whenever and wherever he wishes." *Le Velo*, May 18, 1901.

236. "There was no more likable athlete than Major Taylor and he did not deserve that kind of treatment." Journalist Maurice Martin, *La Vie Illustree*, May 24, 1901.

236. "The French promoters calculate that if Jacquelin should defeat Taylor" *New York Sun:* May 16, 1901.

236. "pretty" French actresses present at race: *Cycle Age*: May 1901.

236. largest throng to attend single day sporting event: Ibid.

236. "If they had them at the time, the whole continent would have had their ears pressed against a noisy vacuum tube radio, listening" Author Interview, Jack Visceo Cycling Hall of Fame; January 2006.

236. Taylor having met President Teddy Roosevelt: "Major Taylor, The Forgotten Champion" by Ted Carol, *Our Sports Magazine*, August 1953; Autobiography p 422.

236. Brady preparing Grand Prix races modeled after events Paris: *Cycle Age*: May 15, 1901.

237. "It is believed on this side of the Atlantic, he can ride the legs off anyone who has ever sat on a bicycle saddle" *The Sun*: May 19, 1901.

237. "the cycling athletes of this country still have faith" Ibid.

237. Be strong and courageous: www.myscriptures.com Deuteronomy Chapter 31:6. Exact bible reading at the time unknown: It is general knowledge Taylor kept a bible with him at all times.

237. Picture Taylor a study of quiet confidence: Parc des Princes: May 27, 1901 Jules Beau collection, Bibliotheque Nationale, Paris.

238. Taylor snapping pictures of Jacquelin with brownie camera: *Le Velo*, May 29, 1901.

238. "The Frenchman had the same arrogant smile as he mounted his wheel." Major Taylor Autobiography p. 177.

238. "For the first time in his life someone had to wipe that big smirk of his Gallic face." Author Interview: Jack Visceo Cycling Hall of Famer, January 2006.

238. Euro riders loafing: *Fort Wayne Gazette*, August 25, 1901.

239. "There is something mysterious about his power, and that mystery is itself a potent force." Interview with Paul Hamelle by Robert Coquille, *Le Velo*, March 16, 1901.

240. First time Jacquelin cut to pieces: *The Referee*, July 24, 1901.

240. Daisy writing letters: scrapbook, Indiana Museum.

240. Taylor defeats Jacquelin: *Los Angeles Times*, May 28, 1901; *New York Times*, May 28, 1901; *The Referee*, July 1901; *Table Talk*, July 11, 1901.

240. Taylor being covered in bouquet of roses: Major Taylor autobiography p. 180.

240. "The redoubtable Jacquelin has been vanquished..." *Lincoln Evening News:* November 16, 1901.

241. Delancey Ward silver loving cup: *Cycle Age*: June 13, 1901.

241. 625,000 copies sold: *Le Velo*, June 13, 1901.

241. "*New York Times* circulation of just around 100,000 at the time." Madison Square Garden 100 Years of History: Joseph Durso p. 93; Hennepin County Library: April 5, 2007.

241. Paris gendarme waiving off Taylor speeding ticket Le Champione; *Worcester Telegram*: December 18, 1926.

241. Knights of the track: *Table Talk*, June 27, 1901.

242. "Do the honor of sharing a drink with me": *Le Velo*, May 29, 1901.

242. "Abstinence gives him spiritual pleasures": *La Vie au Grand Air*, March 10, 1901.
242. "Considering the thrashing he just received Jacquelin probably finished the bottle himself" Author Interview: Jack Visceo Cycling Hall of Famer, January 2006.
242. long tasteful poem dedicated to Taylor: *Cycle Age*: April 11, 1901.
243. Taylor nearly broke down as he discussed his past treatment in the south: *Cycle Age*: March 28, 1901.
243. "whetted knives" *Naugatuck Daily News*: May 14, 1901.
243. Brady leasing Manhattan Beach track, making offer to foreign riders: *Cycle Age*: May 15, 1901.
243. Taylor defeats Jacquelin in open race: *The Daily Northwester*, July 18, 1901; *The Referee*, July 1901; *Table Talk*, July 18, 1901.
243. Taylor wired home cable to Brady he would head home June 28, 1901. *Lincoln Evening News*: June 21, 1901: *Brooklyn Daily Eagle* June 15, 1901. *New York Times* June 22, 1901.
243. "I received enough flags to tapestry my bedroom": *Chicago Tribune*: June 29, 1901.
244. One of the world's richest men went unnoticed: Ibid.
244. "Hullo my Baby": *La Vie au Grand Air*, "My Tour in Europe" by Major Taylor, May 4, 1901.
244. "Remarkable singing voice" Ibid.
244. "messiah" Le Velo January 27, 1901.

Chapter 18
245. "Deutschland ship leaving France to New York" Le Velo: June 29, 1901.
245. Taylor arrives New York goes direct to Manhattan Beach track July 4, 1901: *Naugatuck Daily News:* July 4, 1901.
245. "Brady always does things on a big scale" *Trenton Times*: July 26, 1901.
245. "Wretched sailor": UASP.
246. Taylor rides exhibition spin: *New York Times:* July 5, 1901.
246. Band plays way down Dixie: Andrew Ritchie: The Extraordinary Career of a Bicycle Rider: p.187.
246. Taylor Dr. Comey vaccination: *Naugatuck Daily News:* July 12, 1901.
246. "Rest and hydrate or face the possibility of a more serious illness" *Worcester Telegram. August 2, 1901.*

246. "shake hands without a look of agony on his face" *Bearings*: June *24, 1897.*

246. "sick or not, tell him he must ride at once or he will be blacklisted" *Cycle Age*: July 18, 1901; *Trenton Times:* July 11, 1901; *The Portsmouth Herald:* July 11, 1901.

247. "when Zimmerman returned from overseas in similar condition a few years before no one dared to even question the returning superstar." *Cycle Age*: July 18, 1901.

247. "public sympathy seems to be with the rider and not the National Cycling Association" *Brooklyn Daily Eagle:* July 15, 1901.

247. Taylor threatens to quit racing on American tracks: *Naugutuk Daily News*: July 12, 1901.

247. "You can put this down": *Daily News*, July 12, 1901.

247. "Taylor was just being arrogant and pigheaded" *Brooklyn Daily Eagle*: July 15, 1901.

247. "A champion has got to put up with such things" Ibid: July 15, 1901.

247. Taylor so ill he can't leave his house: *Boston Globe*: July 11, 1901.

247. Taylor appearance Hotel Hueblein with Batchelder until 1:30 in the morning: *The Colored American Magazine*, September 1902, p. 337. *Boston Globe*: July 16, 1901.

248. "You have the alternative of being kicked out or walking out quietly, incident Vanderbilt Hotel" *Brooklyn Daily Eagle* August 2, 1901; *Worcester Telegram:* August 2, 1901.

248. "What are you doing at that desk, get out of here" Ibid.

248. "I guess you don't know who I am" Ibid.

248. Taylor switches to Yates Hotel, inflated price: Ibid.

248. "take his meals in his room" *Atlanta Constitution*: August 1, 1901.

249. "In all my travels over this country and Europe I have never been hurt more personally" *Worcester Telegram*: August 2, 1901.

249. Taylor threatens to sue hotel through his attorney Sam Packard: Ibid.

249. "Black whirlwind, white flyer" Major Taylor autobiography p. 34.

249. Buffalo Exposition crowd size, Taylor handicap win over Lawson: *The Anaconda Standard:* August 16, 1901. *The Washington Post*: August 16 & 18, 1901.

249. As Taylor train sped out of Buffalo, President McKinley last breath sighed into Buffalo. *New York Times:* September 15, 1901.

250. "Trim the nigger" Major Taylor autobiography p. 188.

250. "Many times the toss of a coin would decide which one would bring me down." Ibid: p. 187.

250. "None of the track owners were satisfied with the way Kramer had acted and did not believe the riders had given him a fair shake." *The Colored American Magazine*, September 1902, p. 339.

250. "perceptible limp" *Atlanta Constitution*: September 8, 1901.

250. "Whetted Knives" *Naugatuck Daily News:* May 14, 1901.

250. Taylor renting rooms away from track to avoid listening to bad language: *The Colored American Magazine*, September 1902, p. 338.

251. Taylor toe-clip broke: Ibid: p. 337.

251. "hard luck" *Naugatuk Daily News*: September 29, 1901.

251. "The track promoters do not believe that the man lives that can defeat Taylor in an honest match race" *Hartford Times*: Quoted in *The Colored American Magazine*, Sept. 1902, p. 341.

251. "there was ill will between Kramer and myself." Major Taylor autobiography p. 201.

251. Brady match race offers: *Brooklyn Eagle*, July 14, 1901; Taylor's autobiography, p. 201.

251. "Trial of the century causing 100,000 rise in circulation *New York Times*" Madison Square Garden 100 Years of History Simon and Schuster p. 93.

251. It's the one ambition of Kramer's life": *Trenton Times*, July 26, 1901.

252. "Taylor had blood in his eyes" Booklet: Major Taylor, the King of the Cycle, his Appearance and Career" By Paul Hamelle and Robert Coquelle, Major Taylor autobiography p. 314.

252. One thousand five hundred watts of power possibility: Bob Williams, Director of National Sports Center Velodrome: Blaine MN; April 11, 2007.

252. "Whenever his knees began to wobble I knew he was in trouble" Ibid: p. 222.

252. Taylor defeats Kramer: *Los Angeles Times*, September 27, 1901.

252. "The spectator were obliged to admit, the real champion was not the one to hold the title" Booklet: Major Taylor, the King of Cycle, his Appearance and Career" By Paul Hamelle and Robert Coquille Major Taylor autobiography p. 314.

253. "my good friend, William Brady the present theatrical producer in New York always stood ready to make good on his offers." Ibid: p. 201.

253. "demanded the presence of Major Taylor" Ibid: p. 204. Quoting Victor Breyer: Interview by sport writer of unidentified New York daily.

253. Announcement Taylor to leave for Europe racing: *Trenton Times:* December 20, 1901.

253. "I consider Major Taylor the greatest racer and drawing card of them all" Ibid: p. 204.

253. "I am delighted to sign him up again..." Ibid: p. 204.

253. Description Taylor marriage, Reverend Taylor: *The Colored American Magazine*, September 1902.

254. "The world's fastest man" Reference Iver Johnson promoting bikes: The *Cycle Age* and *Trade Review*: October 25th, 1900; *Fitchburg Sentinel*: April 5, 1901.

254. Iver Johnson informs agents: Taylor's autobiography, p. 155.

254. "I am absolutely convinced that his riding our wheel was a most profitable advertising investment" *Cycle Age*: July 22, 1901.

254. "Taylor literally annihilated", the world champion Ellegaard: *Le Auto-Velo*, date unknown.

255. Jacqueline declines match with Taylor: *The Colored American Magazine*, September 1902, p. 342.

255. "He was looked upon as an idol and when he took departure for his native shores it was with universal regret." Major Taylor autobiography p. 204; quoting Interview with Victor Breyer in unknown New York daily.

255. "The pastime took on a new lease on life." Ibid: p. 204.

255. Taylor turns down offer to race in South America: *Boston Globe*: September 1, 1901.

255. Tour de France first prize money $ 20,000: *Town & Country Journal:* March 18, 1903.

255. Batchelder sends rep to Grand Central Station: *The Colored American Magazine*, September 1902, p. 342.

255. "Taylor rule" Major Taylor autobiography p. 210.

256. "Is there no way to prevent detestable tricks" *New York Sun*: July 30, 1902 Reprinted in *The Colored American Magazine*, September 1902.

256. Victory on borrowed bike Ottawa: *The Ottawa Journal:* August 4, 1902; *The Citizen Ottawa Canada:* August 4, 1902.

256. "Whether the skin color should be white or black he is entitled to what he is worth..." Major Taylor autobiography p. 224.

256. "Throughout this season Major Taylor has been harassed to a point of desperation by these cheap fellows…" Ibid: p. 225.

256. "With anything like a fair show or an equal chance" Ibid: p. 225.

257. Taylor defending himself from McFarland with 2x4: Major Taylor autobiography p. 228.

257. "When it is considered that he divides his winnings with no man, nor teams up with anyone, as others do, the reason for his unpopularity by circuit riders is quickly detected." *Naugatuck Daily News:* September 28, 1901.

257. "That was the first time in my career I ever lost my head…" Major Taylor autobiography p. 228.

258. Taylor Daisy denied meals at three different restaurants on way to Newark's Vailsburg track: Major Taylor autobiography p. 225-226.

258. Lithographic displays in windows throughout the city: *Cycle Age*: September 1902.

259. "Whetted knives" *Naugatuck Daily News*: May 14, 1901.

259. "I was satisfied I could never again regain my American championship title with the entire field of riders…" Major Taylor autobiography p. 232.

259. "his will be the last black face probably ever seen in the professional cycling ranks in America" *Atlanta Constitution*: December 28, 1902.

Chapter 19

261. "Huge Deal" Frank Van Straten: Huge Deal: The Fortunes and Follies of Hugh McIntosh (Lothian Books 2004).

261. Never before and never since, anywhere in the world had one man poked his prodigy fingers into so many pies" Ibid; Introduction

261. "a distinctive blend of charlatan, genius, dreamer and bandit." Australians-Nine Profiles and Norman Lindsay, the Embattled Olympians; Writer: John Hetherington; Reference on McIntosh titled; The Unrepentant Buccaneer pp. 43-48.

261. Bellevue Hill mansion: Frank Van Straten; Huge Deal: The Fortunes and Follies of Hugh McIntosh; p. 113.

262. It was the nearest approach to hell on earth I've ever known" *Sporting Globe:* July 22, 1939.

262. "But if there was a case of misapplied strength, it was me on a bicycle" *Sporting Globe*: August 12, 1939.

262. McIntosh representing Summer Nights Amusements: I REMEMBER; J.T. Lang McNamara's Books Katoomba 1956 p. 284.

262. Numbers were bandied about: *The Referee*, November 19, 1902.

262. "McIntosh was not adverse to a good stoush, and he positively bristled with energy" *Melbourne Punch:* September 12, 1912.

263. "Offer of $7500 plus share of gate receipts and purses as high as $5000" *The Sportsman:* January 27 & March 24, 1903: Major Taylor Autobiography p. 240 & 300.

263. October 1, 1902 cable from Taylor to McIntosh, number of races too many: *The Referee*: October 28, 1903.

263. Referee, a newspaper McIntosh would one day own: Frank Van Straten: Huge Deal The Fortunes and Follies of Hugh McIntosh, p. 114.

263. "All doubts as to the comings of Major Taylor, the wonderful black rider, are now at rest" *The Referee:* November 19, 1902.

263 "I somehow figured that race prejudice only flourished in this country." Major Taylor autobiography p. 233.

263 "My first thought upon getting this information was to cancel my Australian tour." Ibid-p. 233.

264. Reference to seventeen pieces of luggage: *Worcester Telegram:* September 24, 1903.

264. "I am assuming the two of you are aware of the rigid color line in Australia." Major Taylor autobiography p. 232.

264. "White Australian Policy" www.wikipedia.org/White_Australia_policy

264. Racism San Francisco city policy: www.city-date.com DL June 4, 2007.

264. Taylor's being denied food and hotel accommodations: Major Taylor autobiography p.233.

264. Boarded R.M.S. Ventura: Ibid-p. 235.

264. Conversation with Ship's purser: Ibid-p. 233.

264. "What church or denomination do you belong to": *New South Wales* article titled Thirty Thousand Dollars For Conscience Sake; reprinted in *Sydney Daily Telegraph:* January 3, 1903.

265. "It certainly was a distressing outlook" Major Taylor autobiography p. 233.

265. "Taylor Taylor" Ibid-p. 234.

265. "The most beautiful in the world" Ibid-p. 234.

265. McIntosh yacht capsizing: *Smith's Weekly*; August 27, 1938.

265. "There in his yacht Mabel, that famously capsized due to too much champagne on board" *Smith's Weekly:* August 27, 1938.

266. "look, look do you see all those American flags, do you hear those whistles and horns" Major Taylor autobiography p. 234.

266. "now do you think you will be allowed to land in Australia?" Ibid-p. 234.

266. "defeated everyone in America and Europe." Major Taylor autobiography p. 235; quoting speech made by Lord Mayor of Sydney printed in unknown Sydney Daily

267. "Majah Taylor" *The Bulletin*: December 27, 1902.

267. "No one may smoke in the presence of a cycling chieftain." *Australian Cyclist*, February 3, 1904.

267. "The sole topic of conversation yesterday was the visit of the world champion Major Taylor" Major Taylor Autobiography p. 240.

267. "THIRTY THOUSAND DOLLARS FOR CONSCIENCE SAKE"; New South Wales Baptist article reprinted in *Sydney Daily Telegraph*: January 7, 1903.

268. "The Major Taylor Carnival" *The Referee*: Jan 14, 1903.

268. Sydney Cricket Grounds illuminated by cluster of electric arc lamps: *Sports by Keith Dunstan*, The Pedaling Passion (Casell, Melbourne 1973) p. 268.

269. Taylor sets ¼ mile Australian record in .26 seconds: *The Bulletin:* January 10, 1903.

269. Women in pinks and greens and heliotropes: *The Bulletin:* January 24, 1903.

269. "The scene was almost like fairyland" *The Town & Country Journal:* January 14, 1903.

269. "Never before has enthusiasm been so prolonged." Major Taylor autobiography p. 268; quoting unknown Sydney Daily.

269. More than one hundred thousand fans: *The Sportsman:* February 10, 1903.

269. Quarter million people attending twelve races: *The Bulletin:* February 7, 1903.

269. "one of the most fascinating of a fascinating sex": UASP.

269. "representatives of the world of fashion" *The Town & Country Journal:* January 13, 1903; *The Bulletin:* January 24, 1903.

269. "Put away the brooms boys here comes Mac, he's go after anything with hair on it" Frank Van Straten: Huge Deal; The Fortunes and Follies of Hugh McIntosh; Author Interview with Roy Purvers, 1977.
269. "Sometimes so many women surrounded him that H.D. himself could not be seen" Ibid: Author Interview with Charles Covell, 2004.
269. "He would have been cheap at half the price." *The Sportsman*: January 27, 1903.
270. "I cannot emphasize too strongly the pressure off my mind upon learning I would have no worry from the color line" Major Taylor autobiography p. 237.
270. "surging crowd. monster welcome reception..." No one present had heard anything of his ability as a speaker..." Major Taylor autobiography p. 272.
271. "McIntosh gave away enough champagne to christen every battleship in Europe" *Smiths Weekly*: August 27th 1938.
271. "no one present, he felt sure, had heard anything of his ability as a speaker" Major Taylor autobiography p. 272.
271. Taylor gets fever 104 temperature: *The Sportsman*: January 27, 1903.
271. "the newspapers treated me with the utmost respect" Major Taylor autobiography p. 271.
271. "What Major Taylor is as a record breaker": *The Sportsman*: January 27, 1903.
271. Our cigarettes do not injure one in training." Clipping Major Taylor scrapbook Indianapolis History Museum.
271. "It's no use he's just to good." *The Sportsman:* March 3, 1903.
272. "Major Taylor is a very cleanly built neatly packed parcel of humanity..." Major Taylor autobiography p. 273; quoting unknown Melbourne newspaper.
272. Taylor presence at Benefit Race: *The Sportsman:* January 27, 1903.
272. eight-thousand fans in attendance: Ibid: February 7, 1903.
272. Profit on race $1250: Ibid: March 17, 1903.
272. "It being nothing short of heroism to venture out at all" Ibid: February 17, 1903.
272. "Just the fortunes of war." Ibid.
272. "I didn't congratulate and shake Morgan's hand for show, I meant it." Ibid.
272. "Morgan could not suppress his feeling" Ibid.

272. "It was the proudest moment of my life." Ibid.

272. "Although I was a sick man when I reached Melbourne I left that city in a blaze of glory." Major Taylor autobiography p. 280.

272. One hundred fifteen riders entered in Sydney Thousand Handicap: *The Town & Country Journal:* March 7, 1903.

273. Railroad commissioners emergency meetings: Ibid.

273. 'Besieged" Unidentified Australian newspaper clipping Major Taylor scrapbook Indianapolis History Museum.

273. "I could have bought a place in the final of the Sydney Thousand but I'm here to win races not buy them." *The Sportsman*: March 24, 1903.

273. Fifty-five thousand fans showed up: *The Town & Country Journal:* January 21-28, 1903.

273. Taylor leaves Sydney enroute to Adelaide: *The Referee*: March 25, 1903.

273. "McIntosh turned on the parties as thou there was no future" Frank Van Straten: Huge Deal: The Fortunes and Follies of Hugh D. McIntosh p. 105, quoting *Sporting Globe*, February 3, 1940.

274. "Experts here are now satisfied, that he is really the marvel that the continental and American press proclaimed him to be." Major Taylor autobiography p. 287 quoting unknown Sydney Daily.

274. "He simply won as he liked." *The Sportsman*: March 17, 1903.

274. "puts the league on velvet." Ibid: March 31, 1903.

274. Incapacitation of rider named Wayne: *The Referee*: January 14, 1904.

274. Major and Daisy pay sympathy visit to injured rider: *The Bulletin*: May 2, 1903.

275. April 16, 1903 Taylor departure from Australia to Europe: *The Sportsman:* April 15, 1903.

275. Taylor wins twenty-three first places out of twenty-seven races: Major Taylor autobiography p. 300.

275. "The events aroused a pitch of enthusiasm that has never been witnessed here before" Major Taylor autobiography p. 241: quoting unknown Sydney Daily.

275. "Major Taylor who combines cycling with preaching in the Methodist chapels on Sundays is far on his way to making a fortune far more than the best paid editors, university professors, or nine-tenths of the legal profession. *New York Times:* February 16th, 1903.

275. "It will be many long years before the Americans phenomenal rides are forgotten." Major Taylor autobiography p. 279.

275. 1903 Europe record: Twenty-eight first, twenty-one seconds and nine thirds; Ibid p. 301.
275. 85,000 attendance multi-day meet Paris: *The Daily Northwestern*: February 13, 1901.
275. People of India present cane: *Boston Daily Globe*, September 28, 1903.
275. "Taylor defeats Ellegaard" *The Bulletin:* Jan 17, 1903.
275. Taylor sleeping upright: *The Colored American Magazine*, September 1902.
276. "up-to-date" raiment Daisy: *The Referee:* November 4, 1903.
276. "gentlemanly bow with cap in hand" Ibid.
276. Babe Ruth earning $20,000: *Velo News*, January 15, 1996.
276. "How many today are able to show the bank account": *The Daily Republican*, August 2, 1901.
276. $40,000-$50,000 richer: Major Taylor in Australia, Jim Fitzpatrick, Star Hill Studio.
276. William Rockefeller and Cardinal James Gibbons on return Ship to America: *Worcester Telegram:* September 24, 1903.
276. "I am satisfied I have done enough." Ibid.

** More than 100,000 fans Sydney races: *The Sportsman:* February 10, 1903.
** Taylor visit talked about this day: www.cyclingnews.com March 2005

Chapter 20
279. McIntosh never being taught meaning of no" *Punch:* September 12, 1912.
279. Reference to McIntosh: "pedaling pies at racetracks" National Library of Australia DL September 11, 2006 www.adb.online.anu.edu.au/biogs/A100280b.htm
279. Barrage of cablegrams: *The Referee:* October 28, 1903.
279. "retirement" Ibid.
279. "Renault car. poodle car ride" *Worcester Telegram*: November 13, 1904.
279. "if I ever ride again it will be right here in Australia." *The Sportsman:* April 20 & 23, 1903.
279. Taylor renovating his home: *The Sun*, November 13, 1902.
279. "a school of sharks" Frank Van Straten: Huge Deal: The Fortunes and Follies of Hugh D McIntosh, p. 12.

279. "Cannot leave before Aerangi; will not guarantee to race more than three times weekly for L2000 exclusive of prizes" *The Referee*: October 28, 1904.

280. "Taylor had a change of heart." *Worcester Telegram:* November 13, 1904.

280. "To note accept such an offer was like passing up too good a thing." Ibid.

280. Leaving Worcester November 13, 1903 for San Francisco: Ibid.

280. Taylor stop in New Zealand: *The Referee:* December 23, 1904.

280. Taylor arrives Australia for second tour: *The Bulletin:* December 27, 1904.

280. Floyd McFarland from San Jose: Peter Nye, Hearts of Lions p. 63.

281. "rioting" reference to Floyd McFarland: *New York Times*: November 11, 1900, January 8 & February 5, 1902.

281. Henry Desgrange banned McFarland from Parc des Princes track: *Cycle Age* and *Trade Review*: October 25, 1900: December 20, 1900.

281. "trim the nigger" Major Taylor autobiography p. 188.

281. "exception rule" *Atlanta Constitution*: December 8, 1902.

281. MacFarland as an autocrat: UASP.

281. "What do you take me for a …..Kangaroo." Curley H. Grivel: Australian Cycling in the Golden Days, p. 52 Unknown word not exact, author's assumed meaning of word.

282. "Bull Williams" "His word was law." Ibid: pg. 282.

282. "human motor" "warhorse" "handicap king" *Australian Cyclist and Motor-Car World* February 11, 1904; *The Referee:* January 27th, 1904.

282. "Floyd McFarland, my arch enemy of many years standing was the king-pin of all the schemes against me." Major Taylor autobiography p. 337.

282. "oh that damm nigger" *The Referee:* March 9, 1904.

282. "He made hacks out of Australia's best" *The Sportsman:* April 17, 1903.

282. Lawson second place 1902 American Championship: *New York Times*: July 21, 1902.

282. "the melancholy dane sober sided-athlete" *The Referee:* January 6, 1904.

282. "he carries the brand of the track yet" *The Referee:* March 9, 1904.

282. Lawson McFarland teaming: *The Referee:* March 30, 1904.

283. Taylor was the only rider to receive a large down payment: *Australian Cyclist*: December 31, 1904: Major Taylor scrapbook Indianapolis History Museum.

283. "His legs and riding capabilities have been sold to a syndicate that negotiates for him." Ibid: *Australian Cyclist*: December 31, 1904 Unidentified newspaper clipping Major Taylor scrapbook.

283. Iver Lawson on Columbia bicycle, MacFarland on Cleveland: Advertisement; *The Australian Cyclist:* February 11, 1904.

283. "The visiting Americans have brought their prejudice with them and want to atone for past defeats by Taylor" *The Referee:* January 20, 1904.

284. Taylor on Massey – Harris Ibid.

284. "No man in the world can have a chance against Iver Lawson when he has McFarland working in his interest." Major Taylor autobiography; quoting unknown Melbourne paper p. 344.

284. "It was as plain as a pike staff even to the palest faced laymen." Ibid: -p. 343.

284. McFarland out one month suspension, $125 fine for abusive language: *The Referee:* January 20, 24, 1904 & February 24, 1904; March 2, 1904.

284. Taylor went on grass on his own accord: Ibid.

284. MacFarland given option of paying reduced fine: *The Referee*: February 3, 1904.

284. "There is no love loss between the two factions here just now and every time Taylor meets his compatriots the curry is very hot" *Australian Cyclist and Motorcar World*: February 2, 1904.

284. "dead heat" *Punch:* February 4, 1904.

284. Prime minister in attendance: UASP.

285. "How would a jockey get on if he thought he had won and abused the judge and stewards that way" Major Taylor autobiography p. 353.

285. "McFarland donning clothes and leaving track" *Punch:* February 4, 1904.

285. battalion of police converges on track: *The Referee*: Feb 17, 1904.

286. "It was a big event in my life to beat Major Taylor" Ibid.

286. "Instead of watching the struggles of the worlds champions": *Australian Cyclist & Motor Car World:* February 11, 1904.

286. "If this is your summer": *The Sportsman:* April 15 & 21, 1903; Major Taylor scrapbook Indianapolis History Museum.

286. "He is as fit as a fiddle" Sid Melville trainer: *The Referee*: February 23, 1904 *Sydney Sportsman:* February 5, 1904.

286. On trams and trains impassioned debates: *Australian Cyclist*, February 11, 1904.

286. To-Night-To Night cycling championship of the world, Meeting of the worlds cycling giants!!" Advertisement: Major Taylor scrapbook March 4, 1904 Indianapolis History Museum.

286. "Major Taylor is not invincible" 200 wins-only 12 losses" *Australian Cyclist and Motor Car World:* February 11, 1904.

287. "Major Taylor Carnival" *Australian Cyclist:* February 18, 1904; Major Taylor scrapbook Indianapolis History Museum.

287. Extra turnstiles: UASP.

287. seventy-five bookmakers: *Mansfield News*, May 5, 1904.

287. Most influential people: *The Lowell Sun*, February 12, 1904.

287. "with McFarland out of it Lawson's feeding bottle was dry" Major Taylor autobiography p. 344; *The Referee:* January 27, 1904.

287. "He seems to be useless without him. Major Taylor autobiography: p. 344.

287. "I felt doubly sure I could defeat Lawson on even terms every time we started." Ibid-p. 402.

287. "Whatever you do, do not let Taylor win." Ibid-p. 403.

287. "he's a fine game nigger, but he won't come out in this race" *The Referee:* March 1904.

288. Lawson in pink gown: UASP.

288. Collision, Taylor goes unconscious from accident: *The Town & Country Journal:* February 18, 1904.

289. "that's the most treacherous thing I have ever seen" Major Taylor autobiography p. 403.

289. "Lawson will go out for life for this." Ibid-p. 403.

289. "It looked like murder" Ibid-p. 403.

289. Lawson claiming it was Taylor's fault: Mansfield, News, May 5, 1904.

289. "yells, hoots, groans and threats of dismemberment." *Australian Cyclist:* February 18, 1904.

289. "no race" *Australian Cyclist and Motor Car World*: February 18, 1904.

290. "Major Taylor's injury in Australia is likely to deprive the track": *The Mansfield News:* March 14, 1904.

290. Lawson, McFarland leave for Adelaide, MacFarland wins six consecutive races: *The Town & Country Journal:* February 1904, *Punch:* February 25, 1904.

290. track officials examine scar marks over fifteen feet of track: Major Taylor autobiography p. 403.

290. Emergency meeting Port Phillip Hotel, twenty witnesses: Ibid p. 358.

290. What rubbish the public is asked to follow" Ibid-p. 360 quoting unknown Melbourne paper.

290. Lawson boards Melbourne express: *The Referee:* March 2, 1904.

291. "Chairman Callaghan decision; your hereby suspended from racing anywhere in the world for one year." Major Taylor autobiography p. 358.

291. "All things considered Lawson may consider himself lucky he is not wanted in Australia…" Ibid-p. 358.

291. McIntosh escorts Lawson to ship to see him off: *The Referee:* March 16, 1904.

291. "And this is what they call justice" *The Referee*: March 2, 1904.

291. "He was taking meals off the mantelpiece" *The Referee:* March 9, 1904.

291. "Taylor's injuries are even more serious" *The Mansfield News:* March 14, 1904 Major Taylor autobiography p. 360.

291. "He will carry the sears in his buttock and arms the rest of his life" *The Referee*: March 2, 1904.

292. "Some of your officials have all along entertained a disgusting prejudice against me" *The Town and Country Journal:* April 27, 1904: *The Referee:* April 27, 1904.

292. "I am not a petrol machine, I am flesh and blood like the rest of you." *The Sportsman*: April 17, 1903.

292. "dealt with" *The Referee:* April 27, 1904.

292. "keep your eyes open" *The Town & Country Journal:* April 13, 1904.

292. "the entire field was going after me with a vengeance. I am frightened to race. *The Referee:* April 20, 1904.

292. "After what happened…the combinations and tricks employed in order to prevent him from winning has been heartbreaking." Ibid.

292. "We can't have the same man winning all the time" Keith Dunstan Sports: The Pedaling Passion, 1973 p. 269.

293. Thirty two thousand fans at Sydney Thousand: *The Referee:* March 3, 1904.

293. "Rather than submit to a licking by Major Taylor he has taken the rather undignified course of backing out of the match altogether." *The Referee:* March 30, 1904; Major Taylor autobiography p. 375.

293. "While the giants were still winded after their ride, he would lay them out one at a time" Frank Van Straten: Huge Deal: The Fortunes and Follies of Hugh D. McIntosh, p. 16, sourcing *Smith's Weekly*: August 27, 1938.

293. "you bastard" Ibid-p. 14.

293. Keep your fist to yourself MacFarland" Ibid-p. 14.

293. "you can't fight any better than you can ride" Ibid.

293. MacFarland three year suspension: *The Referee:* April 13, 1904.

293. "I was robbed" *New York Times:* June 2, 1904.

293. Lawson suspension one year: *Punch* March 18, 1904; Clipping Major Taylor scrapbook Indianapolis History Museum.

293. "It was injustice": UASP.

294. "If these are carried out much further nearly all riders will be disbarred" Major Taylor autobiography p. 383 quoting unknown Australian paper.

294. "It was a strange revelation for me to note how McFarland's victorious campaign": Ibid: -p. 337.

294. "It is said that other riders with whom McFarland and Lawson were intimate, have taken up their quarrel." Ibid-p. 399.

294. "I will never race in South Australia again." *The Referee:* April 27, 1904.

294. Sydney birth announcement: *The Referee*: May 18, 1904.

294. "Had been awaiting certain interesting developments" Major Taylor autobiography p. 406.

294. "start him on his fast career to championship fame and glory." Ibid-p. 406.

294. "of course he was going to be a champion bicycle rider." Ibid.

295. "Would make me the proud recipient of the greatest prize of them all." *Worcester Telegram:* July 6, 1904.

295. Sydney Taylor lives 102 years old: obituary, *Pittsburgh Post-Gazette*, May 13, 2005.

295. June 6th Taylor's Don Walker departure Australia on Samoa: *The Referee:* June 8, 1904.

295. Hugh McIntosh and dignitaries present for sendoff: Ibid.

295. 1904 was the single most amazing season of cycle racing in the history of Australia: Jim Fitzpatrick: Major Taylor Down Under on Tracks of Glory, p. 4.

295. Taylor brings home cockatoos, parrots and wallaby: *The Referee:* June 6, 1904.

295. "It's all such a disgrace" Major Taylor autobiography p. 396; quoting unknown Melbourne newspaper.

296. Being turned away in San Francisco hotels & restaurants: Major Taylor autobiography p. 408

296. "Not my kind of hotels." *The San Francisco Call,* June 28, 1904.

296. "So this is the America about which you have been boasting in Australia": Ibid-p. 408.

296. Taylor expert boxer flattens man insulting Daisy: Andrew Ritchie: The Extraordinary Career of a Champion Bicycle Racer: Author Interview with Sydney Taylor Brown p. 202-203.

297. "Took the heart out of him." *Worcester Telegram:* July 31, 1904.

297. "I suffered a collapse" "This was caused by my recent strenuous campaign in Australia augmented by the incidental worries of life." Major Taylor autobiography p. 410; *The Chicago Defender:* May 29, 1948.

297. Death of Taylor's father: *The Freeman*, July 30, 1904. It's unclear exactly when Taylor first learned of his father's death.

** One year suspension for Lawson reduced to three months: *The Referee:* April 6, 1905.

** Iver Lawson wins 1904 World Championship: *New York Times:* September 11, 1904.

Chapter 21

299. Coquille sues for $10,000: Major Taylor autobiography p. 410.

300. "Little did they realize the great physical strain..." Ibid-p. 420.

300. April 1905 $35 speeding fine: Andrew Ritchie: The Extraordinary Career of a Champion Bicycle Racer, p. 205.

300. Taylor in auto accident $1000 damages: *Boston Daily Globe*: July 12, 1905.

300. "auto hospital" Ibid: May 19, 1906.

301. Poem: Taylor's autobiography, p. 426.

302. "You may take a break but you'll always come back" *VeloNews*: Mike Schatzman; May 28, 2007.

302. Coquille personal meeting: Major Taylor autobiography p. 410.

302. "I wanted the suit ended..." Ibid.

302. "free from the chance of losing such a sum of money" Ibid.

303. 1907 Average Life expectancy black male 32.5 years: www.cdc.gove/nchs/date/dvs/nvsr52_14t12.pdf DL April 19, 2007.

303. "I advised him to do it" L' Auto: April 2, 1907.

303. La Touraine French Liner warned titanic www.greatoceanliners.com DL April 19, 2007.

303. "THE RESURECTION OF THE NEGRO" L'Auto: March 7, 1907.

303. Peugeot bicycle sponsor: *The Evening Telegram:* July 29, 1907.

303. "Le Negre Volant" L'Auto: April 20, 1907: "Major Taylor est arrive!"

303. "Major Taylor is with us once more" La Vie au Grand Air: May 11, 1907.

304. "You look as if you have put on weight" Robert Coquille: L' Auto: April 2, 1907.

304. May 9, 1907 loss to Poulain: *The Washington Post*: May 10, 1907.

304. "Had his stock traded on Wall Street…" Author interview: Jack Visceo Cycling Hall of Famer, January 2006

305. "just say the word, I'm just striking my winning form" Major Taylor autobiography p. 412.

305. "I did not want to leave Europe" Ibid-p. 412.

305. Taylor beats 6 Champions from five countries: *New York Times:* September 2, 1907.

305. "In all our great match races…" Major Taylor autobiography p. 414.

306. "We had the last laugh and the papers were profuse in their apologies for rushing to conclusions" Ibid-p. 415.

306. : 25 2/5 and: 42 1/5 records at Buffalo track: Ibid-p. 413.

306. "Once he got going he cleaned them all up" *Worcester Telegraph*: October 25 1909.

306. "the most extraordinary, the most versatile, the most colorful…" Robert Coquille and Paul Hamelle. Major Taylor, Ses Debuts, Sa Carriere, Sa Vie, Ses Aventures. Paris, 1904.

306. "Birdie Munger in Paris on business" Andrew Ritchie: The Extraordinary Career of a Champion Bicycle Racer, p. 208.

307. "The advancing years have put on him the handicap which nothing can beat out" *Worcester Telegram:* October 25, 1909.

Chapter 22

309. Daisy raising Sydney at home with maids and servants: Steve Levin, *Pittsburgh Post-Gazette*; Obituary: Sydney Taylor Brown, May 18, 2005.

310. "I was obliged to break my rule…" Major Taylor autobiography p. 410.

310. "I did not expect that, for I believed Taylor would stick to his decision not to race on Sunday's until he died" *Boston Globe*: June 21, 1900.

310. Daisy my dear wife…everything is beautiful but the weather: Letter date unknown Major Taylor scrapbook Indianapolis State Museum.

311. "only a few lines to say that I did not do as well" Ibid, letter June 14, 1909.

311. "I failed again in the Grand Prix of Buffalo" Ibid, letter August 1, 1909.
311. Net worth approximately $75,000; Andrew Ritchie: The Extraordinary Career of a Champion Bicycle Racer, p. 220.
311. "I am so pleased that you are a home loving girl" Major Taylor scrapbook Indianapolis State Museum, letter date unknown.
311. "now dearie, about coming home" Ibid, letter August 15, 1909.
312. Taylor meets with McIntosh in Paris: *Worcester Telegram*: October 25, 1909.
312. "gates of 50,000-60,000 were commonplace": *Sporting Globe:* August 12, 1939.
312. "he was almost as good a preacher as he was a cyclist" Ibid.
313. "I am getting down to weight slowly" Major Taylor scrapbook, Indianapolis State Museum, letter date unknown.
313. "I rode yesterday against Poulain, Meyers and Arend" Ibid: letter date unknown.
313. "Why don't you write any more dearie..its been almost two weeks" Ibid, letter August 9, 1909.
314. "My darling little Sydney, here is a letter and some post cards" Ibid, letter August 5, 1909.
314. "I am going to make one more desperate attempt" Ibid, letter August 28, 1909.
315. "Well dearie, I had a talk with Coquille about next season" Ibid, letter October 1, 1909.
316. Taylor double victory over Charles Dupre: *Worcester Telegram*: October 25, 1909. **This was Taylor's last European race, he did take part in insignificant races in United States in 1910**
316. "in my opinion, he's the greatest racing cyclist in the world" Sporting editor of unknown Sydney Australia newspaper; Major Taylor autobiography p. 423-424.
316. "It is not likely that we shall look on his like again" Ibid.
316. "In his prime, Jacquelin was a faster rider than any of the men on the wheel today" *Worcester Telegram:* October 25, 1909.
317. Taylor boards La Provence in Harve for stormy ride home: Ibid.
317. "say dearie, how anxiously I am counting every minute" Major Taylor scrapbook Indianapolis State Museum, letter October 1, 1909.
317. "It seemed as if it would be its last" *Worcester Telegram:* October 25, 1909.

317. "Orchestra playing music" Ibid.

317. "When the nose of the ship pointed down after climbing over an immense wave it seemed as if it would never point upward again" Ibid.

Chapter 23

319. Munger's exploits, car problems, driving day and night with stops only for meals and repairs getting to the old timers race: *Newark Evening News*: September 17, 1917 p. 14.

319. "The rheumatic stakes for aged bikers" Ibid; September 15, 1917 p. 16.

320. "some of the champions competed during Lincoln's first administration" Ibid.

320. "Few had seen such highly developed beer muscles" Ibid.

320. "One of the articles of agreement is that all wheels be shrouded in cob webs" Ibid

320. "with both feet" Ibid.

320. Stands filled to capacity 12, 500 spectators day of old timers race: Peter Nye: Hearts of Lions, p. 99.

320. Taylor telling a reporter he would never invest in risky investments: *New York Sun*.

320. Being turned down at the Worcester Polytechnic Institute: Peter Nye: Hearts of Lions, p. 81.

320. Taylor loses $15,000 in automobile tire business: *Worcester Telegram*: December 17, 1926.

320. Other wealthy investors including old bike sponsor Iver Johnson: Ibid.

320. Picture Taylor old-timer race: Ibid.

320. Taylor wins old-timer race: Oneonta Star.

321. "Well Birdie, you started me in my first race and you're starting me in my last race." *Newark Evening News*; September 17, 1917.

321. "No rider before or since his day ever developed a stretch the equal of Taylor's": *Newark Evening News:* September 15, 1917.

321. "He received a greater ovation then I or anyone else, he was one of the greatest athletes of all time" Ted Carrol: *Our Sport Magazine*, August 1953 p. 17. DL www.majortaylor.com January 17, 2007.

322. Peered inside the window of Magay and Barrons 368 Main Street: *Worcester Daily Telegram*: December 17, 1926.

322. Taylor's resettle into apartment 14 Blossom Street: Ibid.

322. "VOICE OF PRAISE FOR MAJOR TAYLOR" *Worcester Telegram*: December 24, 1926.

323. Fund set up by Harry Worcester Smith: Ibid.

323. Famous horse jockey Earl Sande: Major Taylor autobiography: p. 429.

323. "I believe Major Taylor, the black man needs an interested and friendly audience more than ever..." *Worcester Telegram*: December 17, 1926.

323. "I wish it were more, but a five year illness has left me..." *Worcester Evening Gazette:* December 24, 1926.

323. "a friend" Ibid.

323. John Hancock Insurance Company contribution to fund: Ibid.

323. "I think the response to my appeal.." *Worcester Sunday Telegram*: December 26, 1926 p. 12.

323. "The black man racing against whites..." *Worcester Telegram:* December 17, 1926.

324. Having arrived at that time of life when I find myself more inclined to reminisce: *Worcester Telegram*: December 24, 1926.

324. Taylor contribution to San Francisco earthquake victims: Major Taylor autobiography p. 409.

324. Verse of Matthew: Matthew 25:36, New International Version.

324. Mrs. Harry Worcester Smith: please tell the Major: *Worcester Telegram*: December 24, 1926.

324. Fund grew to $1000: *Worcester Telegram:* December 24, 1926.

324. Apart from a good cocktail: Ibid.

325. Picture Taylor thick overcoat, bowler hat: Ibid: December 18, 1926.

325. "his humiliation was his fuel" www.findarticles.com Article; Lance Armstrong & Major Taylor: A century and a World Apart, Cycling's two legends show courage in motion- Sports Trailblazers DL April 10, 2007.

325. "I'm in need of rest, wish all my friends a Merry Christmas" *Worcester Telegram*: December 26, 1926.

325. "The years have a trick of crowding a man" Ibid: December 18, 1926.

325. Daisy miscarriage: Andrew Ritchie: The Extraordinary Career of a Champion Bicycle Racer; Author interview with Sydney Taylor Brown p. 229.

326. "the neatest dresser you have ever seen..." Author Interview: Worcester resident Francis Jesse Owens August 10, 2006.

326. "Major Taylor does not appear as a critic of anything" *Cycle Age*: July 28, 1898.

326. "Even though he loved his country and his race…" Andrew Ritchie: The Extraordinary Career of a Champion Bicycle Racer; Author Interview with Sydney Taylor Brown p. 229.

326. I don't think her heart was in it" Ibid-p. 235.

327. "It's the biggest job I ever tackled" Ibid-p. 234. Copy of letter to Robert Coquille, March 1923, Taylor paper's Pittsburgh.

327. "I don't think he made out good" Author Interview: Francis Jesse Owens: August 10, 2006.

328. "my wife" mentioned fifteen times in Taylor's autobiography.

328. "is remarkable for the absence of bitterness against the men who treated him so unfairly" Robert Smith: A Social History of the Bicycle: (American Heritage Press) p. 164.

328. Report of Taylor in stands December 1927 Six Day Race Madison Square Garden: Peter Nye: Hearts of Lions, p. 121-122.

Epilogue

329. Munger successful inventor, automotive executive: *The Daily Northwestern:* December 19, 1899.

330. Major Taylor autobiography dedication: To my true friend and Advisor, Louis D. Munger" Marshall W. Taylor Autobiography Copyright 1932 Printed in the U.S.A. by The Commonwealth Press Worcester, Massachusetts Wormly Publishing Company 14 Blossom Street Worcester Massachusetts.

331. Circumstances of Floyd MacFarland death: *New York Times*: April 18th & 22nd, 1915; *Nevada State Journal:* April 18, 1915; *The Syracuse Herald:* April 18, 1915.

331. "He was a villain, but a likable one" Frank Van Staten: Huge Deal: The Fortunes and Follies of Hugh D McIntosh, p. 14.

332. "ticker-fiend" William A. Brady: Showman p. 276.

332. "laid an egg" Ibid.

332. "Depression A, Depression B" Ibid-p. 77.

332. Brady acquires "Street Scene": Richard F. Snow; *American Heritage* article, April/May 1980; William A. Brady; Showman, p. 277.

332. "a champion streaking around the track…was the epitome of human speed" Ibid- p. 229.

332. "Madison" reference to two man six-day races: Ibid-p. 227.

332. "Major Taylor is the greatest rider on earth" *The Syracuse Herald:* September 4, 1898.

332. "nobody has a better right to run a thing down than the fellow who invented it" William A Brady: Showman p. 230.

332. Brady tossing preemies to riders: Author interview with Jack Visceo January 2006.

333. "I remember when cigarette packages…." Ibid-p. 224.

333. "We left our mark on the business" Ibid-p. 225.

333. "Zimmerman's retirement was regretted just as much as Babes departure from baseball" *Newark Daily News:* October 22, 1936.

333. "Just as Babe Ruth was the idol of baseball fans and Bobby Jones of golf followers, Zimmie was the favorite of the racetrack patrons." Ibid.

333. "I was the proudest boy in the world…" Major Taylor autobiography p. 12.

333. "There was no race prejudice in his make-up.." Ibid-p. 12.

333. "Flying Yankee" *Newark News:* October 22, 1936.

333. "Flying Negro" *Brooklyn Daily Eagle:* August 17th, 1898.

333. "The hero of all boyhood, as well as my own" Major Taylor autobiography p. 51.

334. Portions of the track still rise up standing as a testament to the one time popularity of Zimmerman" *Newark Daily News:* October 22, 1936.

334. Taylor meeting Levy: Christopher Sinsabaugh, *Who Me? Forty Years of Auto History*, p. 33.

334. Taylor traveling Worcester to Chicago selling book: Francis Jesse Owens, telephone interview, August 10, 2006.

334. Four hundred times $3.50: Taylor 1st edition on Abe books $1,400.

334. "I do not know how it may have been in other places but in Chicago, the city seemed to have died" www.roosevelt.edu/chicago history/mod3-chap2.htm DL May 12, 2006.

335. 750,000 Chicagoans nearly half the work force unemployed: Ibid.

335. 160,000 Chicago families received relief: Ibid.

335. Colored Y Bronzeville www.ci.chi.il.us/landmark/W/WabashYMCA. html DL May 12, 2006.

335. Carter G. Woodson, P.H.D. historian starting black history month: www.naperymca.org/history.htm DL May 12, 2006.

335. Chicago stadium teetering on bankruptcy: *Appleton Post-Crescent:* August 30, 1930.

336. 125,000 race-goers twice a year: Ibid.

336. "All the kids talked about Major Taylor" Author Interview with Francis Jesse Owens: August 10, 2006.

337. Last photograph taken of Taylor: *Chicago Defender:* July 2, 1932.

337. James Bowler becoming Taylor's benefactor: Ibid.

337. "And as I have always said, I'm not living for one day or two..." *Sydney Daily Telegraph:* January 7,1903; quoting *New South Wales Baptist* article, Thirty-thousand Dollars for Conscience Sake.

338. Major Taylor obituary: *Chicago Defender:* June 25, 1932, Ibid July 2, 1932.

338. "I didn't realize it then..." William C. Rhoden: Forty Million Dollar Slaves, (Crown publishing 2006), Author interview with Sydney Taylor Brown, p. 91.

338. Daisy Taylor deceased: April 21, 1965 Major Taylor Association (confirmation obituary never printed local Pittsburgh paper).

INDEX